about the (authors)

CHARLES E. BAMFORD is the managing partner at Bamford Associates, LLC, a firm focused on the development of implementable strategic plans and an entrepreneurial orientation to growth (www.bamfordassociates.com).

He is an adjunct professor of strategy and entrepreneurship at the University of Notre Dame (Mendoza) and Duke University (Fuqua). Dr. Bamford worked in M&A/Business Analysis for 12 years prior to pursuing his PhD.

A regular speaker at conferences, trade shows, and conventions, he is the author of five textbooks used by businesses and universities throughout the globe. His writings include regular contributions to news organizations, a popular press book on strategy design *The Strategy Mindset*, and a fiction novel *Some Things Are Never Forgiven*.

Chuck's research has been published in the *Strategic Management Journal, Journal of Business Venturing, Entrepreneurship Theory & Practice, Journal of Business Research, Journal of Business Strategies, Journal of Managerial Issues, Journal of Technology Transfer, and Journal of Small Business Management*, among others.

Chuck has taught courses in strategy and entrepreneurship at the undergraduate, graduate, and executive levels. His teaching experience includes courses taught at universities in Scotland, Hungary, and the Czech Republic. He has been a professor at the Duke University, University of Notre Dame, Queens University of Charlotte, University of Richmond, Texas Christian University, and Tulane University. He has won 21 teaching excellence awards including 12 Executive MBA Professor of the Year awards. He is a Noble Foundation Fellow in Teaching Excellence.

Chuck earned his BS degree at the University of Virginia (McIntire School of Commerce), MBA at Virginia Tech, and PhD in strategy and entrepreneurship at the University of Tennessee.

GARRY D. BRUTON is a professor of entrepreneurship and strategy at the M. J. Neeley School of Business at Texas Christian University in Fort Worth, Texas. He received his BA with Honors from the University of Oklahoma, MBA from George Washington University, and PhD from Oklahoma State University. Garry worked as a bank economist for one of the leading commercial banks in the southwest United States prior to pursuing his doctorate.

Dr. Bruton has published or has forthcoming over 100 academic articles in some of the leading academic publications, including the *Academy of Management Journal, Strategic Management Journal, Journal of International Business, Journal of Business Venturing, Entrepreneurship Theory & Practice*, and *Strategic Entrepreneurship Journal*. Garry currently is an associate editor of

entrepreneurship

THE ART, SCIENCE, AND PROCESS FOR SUCCESS

third edition

Charles E. Bamford
University of Notre Dame & Duke University

Garry D. Bruton
Texas Christian University

ENTREPRENEURSHIP: THE ART, SCIENCE, AND PROCESS FOR SUCCESS, THIRD EDITION

Published by McGraw-Hill Education, 2 Penn Plaza, New York, NY 10121.

This book is printed on acid-free paper.

1 2 3 4 5 6 7 8 9 LMN 21 20 19 18

ISBN 978-1-259-91219-1
MHID 1-259-91219-1

Portfolio Managers: Laura Hurst Spell & Anke Weekes
Marketing Manager: Debbie Clare
Content Project Managers: Melissa M. Leick, Bruce Gin, Karen Jozefowicz
Buyer: Laura Fuller
Design: Jessica Cuevas
Content Licensing Specialists: Lori Slattery
Cover Image: ©ra2studio/Shutterstock.com
Compositor: Lumina Datamatics, Inc.

Library of Congress Cataloging-in-Publication Data

Names: Bamford, Charles E., author. | Bruton, Garry D., author.
Title: Entrepreneurship : the art, science, and process for success / Charles E. Bamford, University of Notre Dame Duke University, Garry D. Bruton, Texas Christian University.
Description: Third edition. | New York, NY : McGraw-Hill Education, [2019] | Includes index.
Identifiers: LCCN 2017038007 | ISBN 9781259912191 (pbk.)
Subjects: LCSH: New business enterprises. | Small business. | Success in business.
Classification: LCC HD62.5 .B36 2019 | DDC 658.1/1—dc23 LC record available at https://lccn.loc.gov/2017038007

dedication

To my family for all the support and fun we have together: my amazing wife, Yvonne; sons, Rob and Sean; daughter, Ada; daughter-in-law, Jane; son-in-law, Andrew; my grandsons, Silas and Isaac, and my granddaughter, Clara.

Charles E. Bamford

To my parents, John C. and Ruth W. Bruton, who empowered me with their love, encouragement, and support throughout their lives.

Garry D. B

the *Strategic Entrepreneurship Journal*. He is also the past president of the Asia Academy of Management. His research interests focus on entrepreneurship and strategy in emerging economies.

Garry's publications have been used in some of the leading MBA programs around the world, and his writings have appeared in the *Wall Street Journal*. He was selected as the first holder of the Kathryn and Craig Hall Distinguished Chair in Entrepreneurship in 2005, sponsored by the Fulbright Program. He is one of the scholars in the world selected to hold a Fulbright Chair twice and will in 2018 hold the Craig Hall Distinguished Chair in Entrepreneurship again.

Garry has taught around the world, including courses in Russia, Austria, multiple locations in China and Hong Kong, Korea, France, and Poland. The courses he has taught at the graduate and undergraduate levels have included small business management, entrepreneurship, venture capital, international strategy, strategy, and international management. Currently, he is an honorary professor at Sun Yat-sen University and Jilin University in China.

Garry has won a variety of teaching and research awards at each of the schools with which he has been associated. In addition, he has advised a number of MBA teams that have participated and placed in regional and national competitions for business plans and case analysis.

brief table of contents

preface

Crafting the third edition of this book was both a pleasure and a challenge. The overwhelming goal of the book is to emphasize three core tenets to starting an entrepreneurial venture:

1. *Science* of practice as the heart of starting and running a successful entrepreneurial venture.
2. *Art* of turning an entrepreneurial venture into a success.
3. *Processes* that tie these two areas together into a coherent and organized business.

The first tenet is that the *science* of practice is central to your success as an entrepreneur. There is an inherent belief by many potential entrepreneurs that they know what needs to be done. However, extensive research suggests that one of the biggest causes of entrepreneurial failure is a lack of knowledge about how to design and build a business. The business that seems so clear to the entrepreneur at founding turns out quite differently. The result is that a lack of knowledge leads to the entrepreneurial venture running out of cash and time.

This book presents a systematic and thorough means for students and potential entrepreneurs to think through their venture and the rich range of concerns around it. Extensive research has been going on in this area for decades, and we know a lot more about what works and what does not work. One of the significant goals of this text is to provide you with information about what really works. Without trying to overwhelm the reader with research citations, but also ensuring that the student has well-researched information, this text is grounded in the academic research with a practitioner view to everything that is done.

The second tenet is that there is a lot of *art* to the concept, design, and implementation effort required to start a new business. To teach the art we present what other entrepreneurs have done in the past, so students can consider what they would like to have as their own approach. In this text we provide a great variety of real-world examples.

To fulfill this real worldview of entrepreneurship as an art, you will find that each chapter starts with a story about a successful entrepreneur and how he or she grew their business. Additionally, you will find throughout the text two running cases that provide direct, applicable context to the chapter contents. The first running case is Kosher Home, which was created by two friends to provide an Internet food service based on kosher food. The second running case is a business called YrFurn: An App for Furniture. This running case follows the development, design, troubles, and start-up of a business that is a Software as a Service (SaaS) firm, a firm that has no physical product. Finally, we have included fourteen MiniCases at the end of the book where we personally interviewed entrepreneurs about their story. Each MiniCase finishes with advice from the entrepreneur and questions to consider about applying the MiniCase learning to the development of your own business.

The third tenet of our approach involves the *processes* of conceptualizing, designing, starting, and running a new business. Hundreds of things must be considered, analyzed, and completed to take an idea to a successful business. We firmly believe that these processes are crucial steps along the way and have built this book in a manner that allows the reader to build upon each concept by developing a process that results in a fully crafted plan by the time you finish the book.

The ability to apply the science, art, and process of entrepreneurship developed here, we argue, will lay the foundation for succeeding in entrepreneurship. We say proudly that the overarching desire of this book, *Entrepreneurship: The Art, Science, and Process for Success,* is that students establish highly successful and very profitable businesses. We believe that following and acting on the issues we lay out here will establish the foundation for that success.

Entrepreneurship Is Not a Scary Word

If you are taking this course, you have at least some level of desire to be your own boss one day by establishing an entrepreneurial venture. You have a plan to start (and succeed) at your own business venture, and you see this course as groundwork for that plan. Beyond a personal desire to be an entrepreneur, there are real, applicable reasons to take this course. Today, 50 percent of all U.S. employees work for entrepreneurial businesses. Even if you do not ultimately start an entrepreneurial venture, the odds are at some point in your career you will work for one. Entrepreneurial businesses are everywhere. They include a wide range of visible firms on the Internet. These firms are the makers and sellers of a myriad of other goods plus providers of services that impact our daily lives. Understanding the components of success and failure for your future employer makes you a better employee.

Book Outline

To develop the understanding necessary to design, start, and manage an entrepreneurial business, we have organized the book into fourteen chapters that are, in turn, organized into five major sections. The first section lays the groundwork needed prior to developing a new business idea. Many individuals have considered starting a new business when an opportunity was presented to them or when they were frustrated by their current positions. However, prior to this step there are several areas that demand examination. Chapter 1 introduces the students to the text with a fun and engaging look at the twenty-first-century entrepreneur. Chapter 2 examines the potential entrepreneur's personal propensities or willingness to take on risk, a core aspect of entrepreneurship. Chapter 3 focuses on how to generate ideas and perform an initial evaluation for a new business.

The second section of the text is entitled "Due Diligence on the Business Idea." In the last chapter of section one, the potential entrepreneur has generated a business idea. In this section there is due diligence on that idea. Due diligence is a process of examining the environment around the new business to establish the opportunity for the new business and then using that knowledge to craft the approach. Chapter 4 launches the first step in the due diligence process by developing a set of methods for examining the external environment in which the new business might operate to understand if there is an opportunity for such a business. Chapter 5 develops the crucial steps necessary for the development of a strategy, including the firm's mission.

A key element in the success of the entrepreneurial venture is the financial foundation of the venture; no matter how good the idea, without a solid financial foundation the business will likely fail. Accordingly, Section 3 is titled "Establishing a Financial Foundation." The chapters in this section include Chapter 6, which establishes how to analyze the cash flow of the firm. Chapter 7 discusses methods that the entrepreneur can use to analyze the financial health of the new business.

The fourth section of the text is titled "Building the Business" and focuses on putting the new venture in operation. Chapter 9 discusses marketing the business. Chapter 10 reviews the legal frameworks for a new business, including the many approaches that are available to protect the business. Chapter 11 details human resource management. Chapter 12 rounds out this important section of the book by discussing the business operations design.

The last section of the book is titled "Important Issues for Entrepreneurs" and examines two other issues critical for an entrepreneur to consider as the entrepreneur starts a business. Chapter 13 examines both exiting the business and the need to turn the firm around if performance is not as great as desired. Chapter 14 examines two means to buy into a business rather than starting it from scratch. They are buying an existing business and franchising.

Features New to This Third Edition

- The opening vignettes to each chapter have been changed from the prior edition to include cutting-edge entrepreneurial companies including Bull and Beard, Tatcha, Scholly, TerraCycle, Hello Alfred, and Rad Power Bikes, among others.
- Two new running cases are in each chapter in the revised text. Each chapter follows Kosher Home and YrFurn: An APP for Furniture as they moved from idea to successful businesses. Each running case is tied to the chapter material.
- In addition to Review Questions in the end-of-chapter material, every chapter also includes a section called Business Plan Development Questions. The goal of these questions is to turn the material in the chapter into actions for the business plans being developed by the students. Also, both Individual and Group Exercise sections have been added to help students develop their entrepreneurial skills individually as well as within a group.
- Fourteen MiniCases are now included at the end of the text. Each case is based on interviews by the authors and provides context and entrepreneurial advice simply not available in any other text. These include: Cuba Educational Travel, Great Clips, JITA Printing, Value Connect, GaGa Ball Pits, and American Meltdown.
- A Business Plan (The Fraudian Slip) has been carried forward from the previous edition and annotated by the authors as an example of how this is all pulled together by students in a course.

Additional Changes by Chapter

Chapter 1 The Twenty-First-Century Entrepreneur

- New Opening Vignette: Bull & Beard.
- Updated to provide a more engaging and fun introduction to the text.
- Every statistic brought forward to 2016.
- Redesigned how the Business Plan is developed.
- New one-page pitch sheet example titled The ToolGym.

Chapter 2 Individual Leadership and Entrepreneurial Start-Ups

- New Opening Vignette: Home Instead and Ray Corkran.
- Kosher Home running case is introduced. This case develops in each chapter through the rest of the text. It follows the design, start-up, and running of a business with friends as business partners.
- YrFurn: An APP for Furniture running case is introduced. This case develops in each chapter through the rest of the text. It follows the design, start-up, and running of a business that is strictly a Software as a Service (SaaS) firm, a firm that has no physical product.

Chapter 3 Business Idea Generation and Initial Evaluation

- Updated Vignette: Uber Changes the Business (the wildly fast-growing ride-sharing business)

Chapter 4 External Analysis

- New Opening Vignette on Mo's Bows and Moziah Bridges, our youngest entrepreneur.
- Introduced the concept of applications and its definition and nature in the industry.

Chapter 5 Business Mission and Strategy

- New Opening Vignette: Tatcha (luxury skincare).

Chapter 6 Analyzing Cash Flow and Other Financial Information

- New Opening Vignette: Partpic (a visual recognition technology company).

Chapter 7 Financing and Accounting

- New Opening Vignette: Scholly.
- Section on crowd funding, a popular entrepreneurial finance mechanism.

Chapter 8 Business & Financial Analysis

- New Opening Vignette: TerraCycle (a recycling company).
- Added a section on the use of Hypothesis-Driven Analysis.

Chapter 9 Legal Issues with a New Business

- New Opening Vignette: Hello Alfred (your own personal butler).
- Everything was updated to reflect changes in the law.

Chapter 10 Human Resource Management

- New Opening Vignette: Moosh Walks (a sock company).
- The chapter includes the dramatic changes in recruiting methods that have occurred in the past few years.

Chapter 11 Marketing

- New Opening Vignette: Rad Power Bikes.
- New key terms Software as a Service (SaaS) and Search Engine Optimization (SEO) are introduced and explained.

Chapter 12 Establishing Operations

- New Opening Vignette: Weedmaps: The Yelp of Marijuana Buying. This formerly appeared in Chapter 9 and has been updated.

Chapter 13 Exit/Harvest/Turnaround

- New Opening Vignette: Evernote (a note-taking app).

Chapter 14 Franchising and Purchasing an Existing Business

- New Opening Vignette: Chocolate Works.

Outcomes

Our ultimate goal is that students will leave this class not only with a much greater appreciation for what it takes to start a business but with the foundations necessary to actually start that business. The entrepreneurial businesses that surround you every day did not come into operation or stay in operation by chance. Instead, it took tremendous effort and work for these businesses to exist and succeed.

We expect that students will be able to take what we present here as a foundation for your own business. Entrepreneurs are the economic backbone of this nation and the central hope for its future.

acknowledgments

We would like to acknowledge the dedicated instructors who have graciously provided their insights for this third edition. Their input has been extremely helpful in pointing out corrections to be made, suggesting areas that needed further development, or topics that needed to be included or covered earlier in the text.

George Bernard
Seminole State College of Florida

Nancy Brown
Lakeland Community College

Carlene Cassidy
Anne Arundel Community College

Raven Davenport
Houston Community College

Bethany A. Davidson
Western Carolina University

Kimberly Ann Goudy
Central Ohio Technical College

Kurt Heppard
United States Air Force Academy

R. Michael Holmes
Florida State University

Andreea N. Kiss
Iowa State University

Jonathan Krabill
Columbus State Community College

Ted W. Legatski
Texas Christian University

David Lucero
Greenville Technical College

Tim McCabe
Tompkins Cortland Community College

Jeffrey E. McGee
The University of Texas at Arlington

Michelle Neujahr
Southern Maine Community College

Diane R. Sabato
Springfield Technical Community College

Kristin Trask
Butler Community College

Leo Trudel
University of Maine at Fort Kent

Cassmer Ward
Queens University of Charlotte

Mark Zarycki
Hillsborough Community College

Key Text Features

Each chapter includes key features that help illuminate important ideas in interesting and applied ways.

Chapter-Opening Vignettes

Every chapter begins with a profile of a real entrepreneurial business. These portraits provide an overview of both the everyday successes and the failures associated with business ownership. Each of these vignettes end with thought-provoking questions for discussion.

part 1 chapter 1

The Twenty-First-Century Entrepreneur

©Hero Images Inc./Alamy RF

learning objectives

After studying this chapter, you will be able to:

LO1-1 Explain the rationale behind starting an entrepreneurial business.

LO1-2 Discuss the history of entrepreneurship in the United States.

LO1-3 Identify the type of people who are entrepreneurs.

LO1-4 Describe the impact of entrepreneurial businesses on society.

LO1-5 Discuss the worldwide impact of entrepreneurial businesses.

LO1-6 Define an entrepreneurial business.

BULL & BEARD

Source: Bull & Beard

While it is often assumed that the key motivator for entrepreneurs is money, often there is an even stronger motivator—freedom. This is not to say money does not matter—but the ability to control their lives is even more important. A prime example of this is Robby Berthume. When he first started his business, his sole focus was money. Over time that motivation did not prove to be the one that ultimately carried him forward in his successful entrepreneurial efforts. At the age of 14, Robby started his first business conducting training, constructing websites, and marketing businesses. After relocating the business to California when he was 21 years old, the business grew to the point that he was recognized at the age of 23 in the Los Angeles Business Journal's "Twenty in Their Twenties." But health issues from stress lead to bad decisions and business failure. Which ultimately led him to lose that business. After the failure of the business, he moved on to head other people's marketing firms for a few years and took some time to diversify his experiences. But ultimately he established his own business again with the desire for an entrepreneurial venture strong, but this time with a different focus other than just a financial goal. The ability to manage his own business and build the life he desired with stronger confidence was the ultimate goal. Today Robby heads a very successful firm in North Carolina—Bull & Beard—that connects advertising agencies with brands and entrepreneurial ventures. Bull & Beard supports ad agencies and brands by helping them position, price, pitch, and perform in a digital world. Now Bull & Beard's clients include Intel, eBay, PayPal, and hundreds of other companies.

Questions

1. What is your principal motivation for starting a business?
2. What are the secondary motivations for starting the business?
3. How do you plan to balance these motivations?

Sources: YEC, "Networking Advice from Robby Berthume, CEO at Bull & Beard," *Businesscollective*, https://businesscollective.com/networkingadvice-robby-berthume-bull-beard/; D. Brustein, "1 Entrepreneur's Journey Striking Gold, Striking Out, Then Striking the Right Balance," *Entrepreneur*, October 14, 2016, https://www.entrepreneur.com/article/283488; Forbes Agency Council, "Forbes Agency Council Member Spotlight: Robby Berthume, CEO of Bull & Beard," *Forbes*, May 2, 2016, https://forbesagencycouncil.com/blog/2016/05/02/forbes-agency-councilmember-spotlight-robby-berthume-ceoof-bull-beard/http://www.bullandbeard.com/

KOSHER HOME

Jack Cohen was not particularly religious. Since he was Jewish, he would abstain from pork, which was no small accommodation growing up in an isolated community in Oklahoma, but beyond that his commitment to observing kosher traditions was relatively low. Growing up in an isolated Jewish community, there was one synagogue where people from a variety of towns would come to mostly for various holidays. Even holding services each Friday at the synagogue would not occur consistently as the rabbi travelled in from several hours away. The issue was not that Jack was not proud to be Jewish, but it was just that to keep kosher and many other aspects of being Jewish were quite hard so far from anyone else doing anything similar.

When Jack went to college on the West Coast of the United States, he found a large and active Jewish community. Through the campus Hillel, he was able to find a part of his life that he had really never known. In this learning process, he began to keep the kosher traditions of the Jewish diet much closer. There are a variety of rules associated with observing kosher such as avoiding not only pork but also shell fish. In addition, pots and pans cannot mix the cooking of milk and meat products or drinking milk with meat products.

For prepared foods there are special rules that apply. These rules have resulted in the development of specialty lines of food products to serve this market. The difficulty for most retailers is that if you have only a few Jewish families that live in your area, you will not stock the kosher food products. This means that even if someone is seeking these types of products they cannot easily keep kosher if they live isolated from a larger Jewish community.

Jack realized there was a need to serve the isolated Jewish communities as increasingly such communities are being hollowed out. The elderly stay, but the young either drop away from observing the Jewish traditions as the dominant culture takes over their lives or as the younger generation moves away, like Jack did, to areas where there is a critical mass of people who can share their practices. While Jack moved he also came to realize he hoped not everyone else would move. Many of these isolated communities have strong historical roots in the regions they are located. He felt that the Jewish community provided a critical element of tolerance and concern in the broader areas where they were located. The country overall being poorer if these isolated Jewish communities were not there.

Discussing this concern with two friends, Ellen and Toby, who were also active at Hillel, they decided they would like to determine a means to serve these isolated communities. They knew there were Internet-based services to help isolated communities that included helping singles meet and providing support. However, they did not know of any Internet services that would help individuals keep kosher through the delivery of specialized food. They had seen a rapid growth in Internet services that provided meals that are shipped for gourmet or health-based cooking. However, it did not appear that any competitor was doing this for kosher eating. After several months of general discussion, they decided to reach out to others to get advice.

The three potential entreprenours had a conversation with Ellen's uncle who had started several successful businesses. The uncle advised them to spend a little more time investigating their motivations and personal risk orientation before they actually considered going into business together. He related the story of his first business, which he had started, with his best friend. The two had been lifelong friends and thought they knew all there was to know about each other. Not only had they been friends since childhood, but also each had been the best man in the other's wedding. Although they thought they knew each other well, when it came to money and the level of risk they were capable of handling, they were substantially different people. Whereas the uncle was very frugal, his partner believed that money needed to be enjoyed today. Ultimately their business partnership fell apart. Although the financial loss was significant, even more devastating was the loss of the friendship between the two men and their families. He has always felt the experience was a significant failure and not one he wanted to repeat.

Ellen's uncle has had other businesses and partnerships since that initial failure. He now believes that although he needs to like a person in order to work closely with him or her, it is much more important that they agree on such key issues as money and risk. Therefore, the uncle suggested the three friends prepare four simple issues to discuss among themselves:

Issues to Discuss Among Themselves

1. Compare how each of them prepared his or her monthly family budget.
2. Discuss how much debt each was willing to take on credit cards.

(continued)

Chapter Two Individual Leadership and Entrepreneurial Start-Ups 23

Running Cases

Kosher Home

Beginning with Chapter 2 and running throughout the rest of the book, this case looks at chapter topics within the context of a new entrepreneurial business in the Internet food-delivery service. Each chapter provides a new aspect of this business to consider, ultimately giving you a fully realized look at how a business must work through a series of issues as it moves from idea to reality. Each chapter's case concludes with questions designed to help the students think through issues related to the business they wish to start.

YrFurn: An App for Furniture

A second running case throughout the book focuses on one of the more popular types of business. A SaaS (Software as a Service) business operates primarily in the cloud and requires no physical delivery to the customer. More and more businesses are moving to this model, and it is a very popular start-up type of business. The case also ends with questions designed to help the students to think through issues related to the business.

> **YRFURN—AN APP FOR FURNITURE***
>
> Kyle Moon, Brad Rossy, and Brandy Jeffer spent two years working together in teams in various classes during their MBA program. Over that time the three continued to talk about starting a new business rather than going to work for someone else when they graduated. Kyle and Brandy had over three years of experience each in technology firms in the Silicon Valley prior to starting their MBA. The two were well versed in the agile methodology known as Scrum and felt that it along with what they knew about developing a lean start-up positioned them well. Agile approaches have become the go-to means for programming. It involves short sprints of work designed to produce rapid, small changes for customers rather than big annual releases of new software that incorporate thousands of changes. Brad brought a different set of skills with his five years of experience working at a firm on Wall Street.
>
> As a part of their entrepreneurship class, the three students explored creating a business that was strictly a software as a service (SaaS) firm. That is a firm that has no physical product. Consumers purchase and use the software via the cloud. They liked the ability that approach provided them to scale the business quickly, and keep fixed expenses low and did not require a customer-friendly physical location. They were all three particularly fascinated by the camera capability of the newer smart phones and they looked for an opportunity to solve a "pain" for customers using that capability.
>
> As they bounced around ideas they rapidly focused on the furniture industry and more specifically the U.S. retail furniture industry. What they found was an arcane industry that had not changed very much in 200+ years. There were new businesses starting to impact the industry by providing customers the ability to customize their furniture and have it delivered. This threat had finally started to move the established industry into considering changes to their established model.
>
> To this day most furniture in the United States is purchased by consumers who travel to a showroom usually armed with the dimensions of the room that they are trying to furnish. They try to imagine how the furniture will look in their place, buy the furniture, and then wait for it to be delivered. Only then do they really know how it looks and whether it works. There had to be a better way.
>
> The three came up with a concept for a two-way app that would solve the problem, they thought the app would be welcomed by the retailers as it would help serve customers better and also be welcomed by consumers since it would make buying furniture easier. The customer would take pictures of their room from two to three angles (like they were selling their house). The app would allow the customer to remove any furniture in the room that was being replaced. Once at the store, the customer could take a picture of any furniture, and it would be superimposed in exact dimensions on the picture of the customer's room. Customers and salespeople could evaluate how it would look and make changes while in the showroom.
>
> The group decided that the idea was so good and had so much potential that they did not pitch it in their entrepreneurship class. They used the class to learn how to develop a business with another average idea. During their last semester, they went to work developing the business model.
>
> After the class the students decided they would like to pursue the venture. Each of the partners had saved up quite a bit of money and was willing to invest $100,000 each to the venture. The three friends realized that this would not be sufficient and were open to bringing in investors when the time was right. There were a lot of things to do over the next few months if this was going to be a reality, but the team was truly excited about the business. They all agreed and decided to take the plunge and YrFurn was born.
>
> QUESTION
>
> 1. What are the risks and benefits to the team of focusing on an app versus a traditional business like a restaurant?
>
> *The names and some details have been changed in this running case. We will use this case throughout the text to illustrate concepts raised in each chapter and how this particular firm addressed them as they built the business.

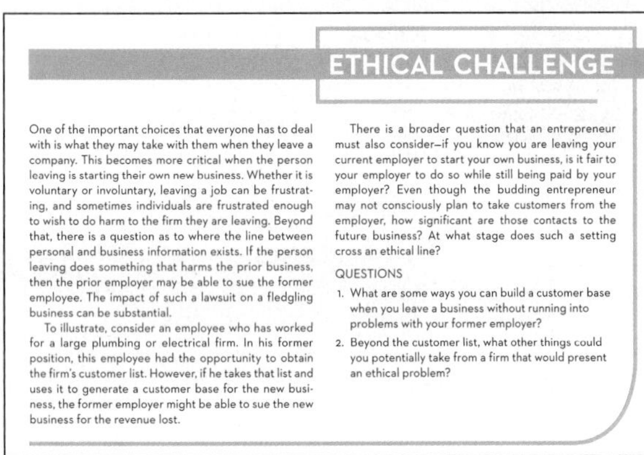

ETHICAL CHALLENGE

One of the important choices that everyone has to deal with is what they may take with them when they leave a company. This becomes more critical when the person leaving is starting their own new business. Whether it is voluntary or involuntary, leaving a job can be frustrating, and sometimes individuals are frustrated enough to wish to do harm to the firm they are leaving. Beyond that, there is a question as to where the line between personal and business information exists. If the person leaving does something that harms the prior business, then the prior employer may be able to sue the former employee. The impact of such a lawsuit on a fledgling business can be substantial.

To illustrate, consider an employee who has worked for a large plumbing or electrical firm. In his former position, this employee had the opportunity to obtain the firm's customer list. However, if he takes that list and uses it to generate a customer base for the new business, the former employer might be able to sue the new business for the revenue lost.

There is a broader question that an entrepreneur must also consider—if you know you are leaving your current employer to start your own business, is it fair to your employer to do so while still being paid by your employer? Even though the budding entrepreneur may not consciously plan to take customers from the employer, how significant are those contacts to the future business? At what stage does such a setting cross an ethical line?

QUESTIONS

1. What are some ways you can build a customer base when you leave a business without running into problems with your former employer?
2. Beyond the customer list, what other things could you potentially take from a firm that would present an ethical problem?

Ethical Challenge Boxes

These dilemma-based scenarios and questions look at ethical realities within the successful creation of a business, and challenge students to examine the moral complexities of starting a business. Each challenge ends with questions designed to encourage the students to think how such ethical challenges will apply to their potential business.

Exercises

Extensive exercises in every chapter include open-ended questions for students to ask themselves as potential entrepreneurs. These exercises not only provide general exercises for discussion in class but also help guide the student so that by the last chapter the students will have developed a full business plan that can be used to launch a new business.

> **EXERCISE 1**
>
> 1. Evaluate your own views on the issues raised in Kosher Home. Discuss your results with others in your class. What is the range of answers that were given?
> 2. Have you ever lent money to a relative? Or have you heard stories from others who have? Would it be different if it were a close friend with whom you went into business?

End-of-Chapter Material

Each chapter concludes with the following:

- Summary
- Key Terms
- Review Questions
- Business Plan Development Questions
- Individual Exercises
- Group Exercises

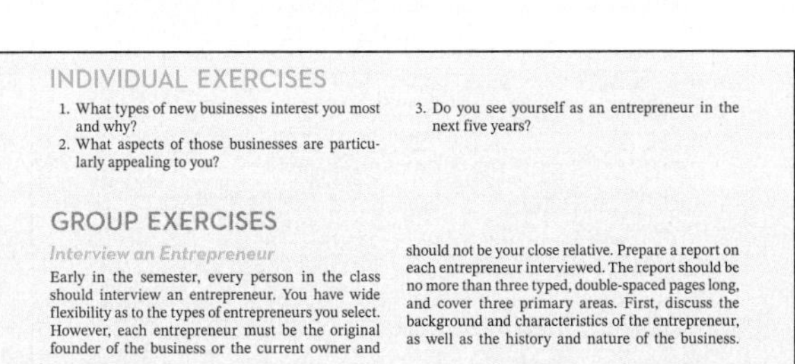

INDIVIDUAL EXERCISES

1. What types of new businesses interest you most and why?
2. What aspects of those businesses are particularly appealing to you?
3. Do you see yourself as an entrepreneur in the next five years?

GROUP EXERCISES

Interview an Entrepreneur

Early in the semester, every person in the class should interview an entrepreneur. You have wide flexibility as to the types of entrepreneurs you select. However, each entrepreneur must be the original founder of the business or the current owner and should not be your close relative. Prepare a report on each entrepreneur interviewed. The report should be no more than three typed, double-spaced pages long, and cover three primary areas. First, discuss the background and characteristics of the entrepreneur, as well as the history and nature of the business.

MiniCases

MiniCases are now included at the end of the text. These longer cases look at real businesses. They examine a real entrepreneur and how that owner approached the business and the struggles associated with success. They offer practical, real-world examples of core concepts within the entrepreneurial framework discussed in the book.

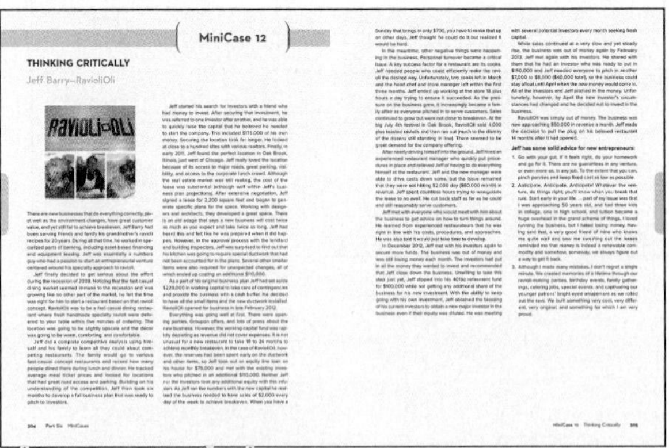

MiniCase 12

THINKING CRITICALLY

Jeff Barry—RavioliOli

Results-Driven Technology

McGraw-Hill Connect

McGraw-Hill Connect® is a highly reliable, easy-to-use homework and learning management solution that utilizes learning science and award-winning adaptive tools to improve student results.

Homework and Adaptive Learning

- Connect's assignments help students contextualize what they've learned through application, so they can better understand the material and think critically.
- Connect will create a personalized study path customized to individual student needs through SmartBook®.
- SmartBook helps students study more efficiently by delivering an interactive reading experience through adaptive highlighting and review.

Connect's Impact on Retention Rates, Pass Rates, and Average Exam Scores

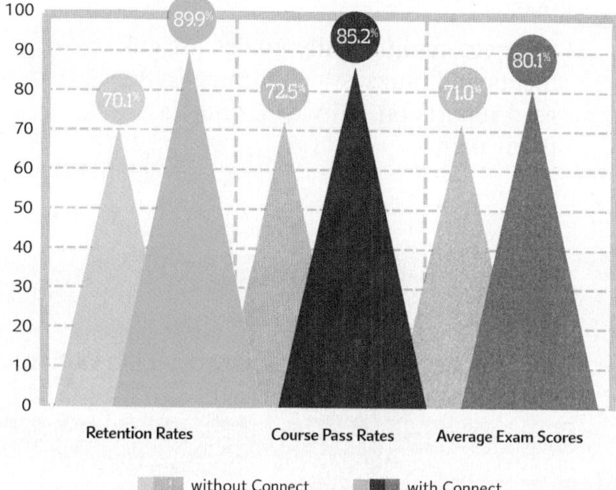

Using **Connect** improves retention rates by **19.8%**, passing rates by **12.7%**, and exam scores by **9.1%**.

Over 7 **billion questions** have been answered, making McGraw-Hill Education products more intelligent, reliable, and precise.

Quality Content and Learning Resources

- Connect content is authored by the world's best subject matter experts, and is available to your class through a simple and intuitive interface.
- The Connect eBook makes it easy for students to access their reading material on smartphones and tablets. They can study on the go and don't need internet access to use the eBook as a reference, with full functionality.
- Multimedia content such as videos, simulations, and games drive student engagement and critical thinking skills.

73% of instructors who use **Connect** require it; instructor satisfaction **increases** by 28% when **Connect** is required.

©McGraw-Hill Education

Robust Analytics and Reporting

- Connect Insight® generates easy-to-read reports on individual students, the class as a whole, and on specific assignments.
- The Connect Insight dashboard delivers data on performance, study behavior, and effort. Instructors can quickly identify students who struggle and focus on material that the class has yet to master.
- Connect automatically grades assignments and quizzes, providing easy-to-read reports on individual and class performance.

©Hero Images/Getty Images

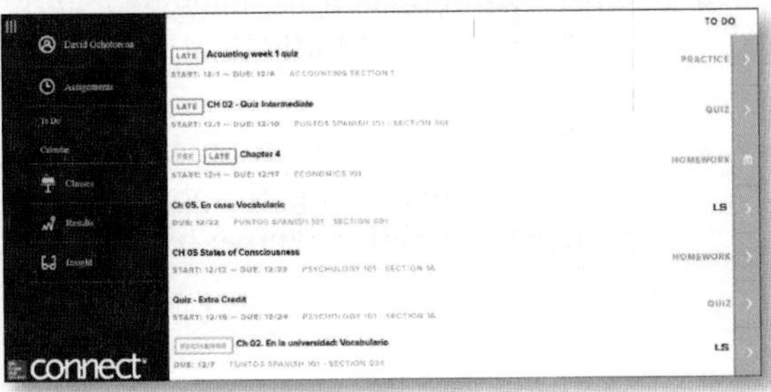

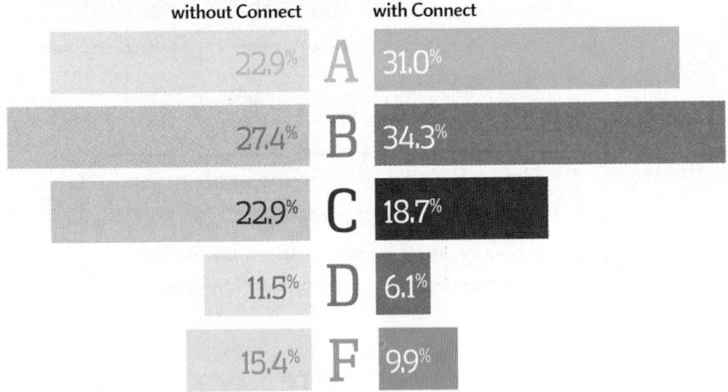

More students earn **As** and **Bs** when they use McGraw-Hill Education **Connect.**

Trusted Service and Support

- Connect integrates with your LMS to provide single sign-on and automatic syncing of grades. Integration with Blackboard®, D2L®, and Canvas also provides automatic syncing of the course calendar and assignment-level linking.
- Connect offers comprehensive service, support, and training throughout every phase of your implementation.
- If you're looking for some guidance on how to use Connect, or want to learn tips and tricks from super users, you can find tutorials as you work. Our Digital Faculty Consultants and Student Ambassadors offer insight into how to achieve the results you want with Connect.

Connect Instructor Library

Connect's instructor library serves as a one-stop, secure site for essential course materials, allowing you to save prep time before class. The instructor resources found in the library include:

Test Bank: Every chapter provides a series of true/false, multiple choice, and short answer test questions, available in our Test Bank. Questions can be organized by Learning Objective, topic, level of difficulty, Bloom's Taxonomy, and AACSB.

Instructor's Manual: The IM outlines course materials, additional in-class activities, and support for classroom use of the text. It has been organized by Learning Objective to both give instructors a basic outline of the chapter and assist in all facets of instruction. For every question posed in the text, the IM provides a viable answer. Ultimately, this will be to an instructor's greatest advantage in using all materials to reach all learners.

PowerPoint Slides: PowerPoint slides include important chapter content and teaching notes tied directly to Learning Objectives. They are designed to engage students in classroom discussions about the text.

Videos: The video collection illustrates various key concepts from the book and explores current trends in business and entrepreneurship.

www.mheducation.com/connect

Create

Instructors can now tailor their teaching resources to match the way they teach! With McGraw-Hill Create, **www.mcgrawhillcreate.com**, instructors can easily rearrange chapters, combine material from other content sources, and quickly upload and integrate their own content, like course syllabi or teaching notes. Find the right content in Create by searching through thousands of leading McGraw-Hill textbooks. Arrange the material to fit your teaching style. Order a Create book and receive a complimentary print review copy in three to five business days or a complimentary electronic review copy via e-mail within one hour. Go to **www.mcgrawhillcreate.com** today and register.

table of contents

chapter 5

BUSINESS MISSION AND STRATEGY 80

PART 3 Establishing a Financial Foundation

chapter 6

ANALYZING CASH FLOW AND OTHER FINANCIAL INFORMATION 100

chapter 7

FINANCING AND ACCOUNTING 122

chapter 8

BUSINESS & FINANCIAL ANALYSIS 140

PART 4 Building the Business

chapter 9

LEGAL ISSUES WITH A NEW BUSINESS 162

entrepreneurship

THE ART, SCIENCE, AND PROCESS FOR SUCCESS

third edition

part 1

chapter 1

©Hero Images Inc./Alamy RF

learning objectives

After studying this chapter, you will be able to:

LO1-1 Explain the rationale behind starting an entrepreneurial business.

LO1-2 Discuss the history of entrepreneurship in the United States.

LO1-3 Identify the type of people who are entrepreneurs.

LO1-4 Describe the impact of entrepreneurial businesses on society.

LO1-5 Discuss the worldwide impact of entrepreneurial businesses.

LO1-6 Define an entrepreneurial business.

The Twenty-First-Century Entrepreneur

BULL & BEARD

BULL & BEARD

Source: Bull & Beard

While it is often assumed that the key motivator for entrepreneurs is money, often there is an even stronger motivator—freedom. This is not to say money does not matter—but the ability to control their lives is even more important. A prime example of this is Robby Berthume. When he first started his business, his sole focus was money. Over time that motivation did not prove to be the one that ultimately carried him forward in his successful entrepreneurial efforts. At the age of 14, Robby started his first business conducting training, constructing websites, and marketing businesses. After relocating the business to California when he was 21 years old, the business grew to the point that he was recognized at the age of 23 in the Los Angeles Business Journal's "Twenty in Their Twenties." But health issues from stress lead to bad decisions and business failure. Which ultimately led him to lose that business. After the failure of the business, he moved on to head other people's marketing firms for a few years and took some time to diversify his experiences. But ultimately he established his own business again with the desire for an entrepreneurial venture strong, but this time with a different focus other than just a financial goal. The ability to manage his own business and build the life he desired with stronger confidence was the ultimate goal. Today Robby heads a very successful firm in North Carolina—Bull & Beard—that connects advertising agencies with brands and entrepreneurial ventures. Bull & Beard supports ad agencies and brands by helping them position, price, pitch, and perform in a digital world. Now Bull & Beard's clients include Intel, eBay, PayPal, and hundreds of other companies.

Questions

1. What is your principal motivation for starting a business?
2. What are the secondary motivations for starting the business?
3. How do you plan to balance these motivations?

Sources: YEC, "Networking Advice from Robby Berthume, CEO at Bull & Beard," *Businesscollective.* https://businesscollective.com/networkingadvice-robby-berthume-bull-beard/; D. Brustein, "1 Entrepreneur's Journey Striking Gold, Striking Out, Then Striking the Right Balance," *Entrepreneur,* October 14, 2016. https://www.entrepreneur.com/article/283488; Forbes Agency Council, "Forbes Agency Council Member Spotlight: Robby Berthume, CEO of Bull & Beard," *Forbes,* May 2, 2016. https://forbesagencycouncil.com/blog/2016/05/02/forbes-agency-councilmember-spotlight-robby-berthume-ceoof-bull-beard/http://www.bullandbeard.com/.

LO1-1

Explain the rationale behind starting an entrepreneurial business.

Why Start a Business?

There are many reasons that individuals decide to start a new business. A lifelong dream, a desire to make a difference in the lives of other people, a realization that you can solve a nagging problem for yourself and others, your sudden unemployment, a desire to be your own boss, a response to an opportunity brought to you, and many more. These reasons have been shared with us by many people who are part of the tremendous pent-up desire by many people to be an entrepreneur. Although people are regularly bombarded with stories about the new businesses that explode into massive companies (Amazon, Facebook, Five Guys, Starbucks, Apple, etc.), most new companies stay well under the press radar. Yet many of these firms you never hear of are very successful and are an essential element in any economy.

The evidence of entrepreneurial businesses' importance to the economy can be seen in the following 2016 statistics from the **United States Small Business Administration (SBA)**[1]:

- 99.9 percent of all businesses in the United States are small.
- 48 percent of private sector employees (57 million out of 118 million employees in the United States).
- 33.6 percent of known export value ($471 billion out of $930 billion).

Furthermore, these entrepreneurial businesses are growing rapidly. Whereas corporate America has been downsizing, the rate of start-ups has grown, and the rate for small-business failures has declined.

Small businesses accounted for 63.3 percent of net new jobs from the third quarter of 1992 until the third quarter of 2013.

Beyond the statistics, there are also countless stories of successful entrepreneurial new ventures in every community around the world. Every business in the **Fortune 500** started out as a new venture. Each one was the brainchild of a single individual or a small group of people. Recall from history that entrepreneurs such as Henry Ford (Ford Motor Company), Ron Brilland and Pat Farrah (Home Depot), Thomas Edison and Charles Coffin (General Electric), Barney Kroger (Kroger), Ralph Lauren (fashion), Sam Walton (Walmart), Estee Lauder (cosmetics), Oprah Winfrey (media), and Richard Branson (Virgin) all started out as small-business owners.

To illustrate how entrepreneurial businesses can grow to be on the Fortune 500 list consider how in 1976, Steve Jobs worked with Steve Wozniak to design and sell the first Apple personal computer from Jobs parents' garage. To raise the approximately $1,600 in capital to start the business, Jobs sold his microbus and Wozniak sold his calculator. Their second Apple computer design had earned over $200 million by 1979. In 1985 Jobs was pushed out of the company. He went on to found NeXT and funded the spinout of the computer graphics division of Lucasfilm, which he renamed Pixar. In 1997 as Apple floundered, Apple bought NeXT and brought Jobs back to Apple to lead the turnaround at the firm. Jobs would go on to pioneer entire categories of products that individuals did not even know they needed, including the iPad, iPhone, and iTunes.[2]

We do not mean to suggest that every new venture will ultimately grow to dominate some aspect of world business. What it does mean is that new ventures are the foundation for all businesses. Some grow large; some do not. Regardless, they all initially go through a process much like the one you will study in this book, and that process of business development from scratch is quite different from the processes followed by established businesses. The process of developing, initiating, and running a new business is so unique that it has developed into one of the most sought-out areas of study at colleges and universities around the globe.

United States Small Business Administration (SBA)

The SBA is the agency officially organized in 1953 as a part of the Small Business Act of July 30, 1953, to "aid, counsel, assist and protect, insofar as is possible, the interests of small business concerns." The agency provides a wealth of information and assistance at all levels of organizational development and management for new entrepreneurial businesses. See www.sba.gov.

Fortune 500

The Fortune 500 is published annually by *Fortune* magazine and documents the 500 largest corporations (by sales) in the United States.

The success of entrepreneurial businesses occurs partially because they are simply more focused than their large corporate counterparts. Without the burden of policies, procedures, corporate layers of management, and public stockholders, new businesses are free to put all their energy into satisfying the needs of their customers. A customer calling on a big jewelry chain to get a battery changed in his or her watch will find that the chain either does not perform those services or treats the effort to change the battery as a burden. The same customer calling on a locally owned jewelry store, however, will most likely get immediate assistance and gratitude for the business. The local business has the advantage of an owner whose fortunes are directly tied to the success of the firm. The average manager of a large firm, although interested in the success of the company, does not have any personal capital at risk. If the firm does not do well, the manager moves to another firm, whereas an owner may lose everything.

Frank Perdue, of Perdue Farms, is an excellent example of a small-business owner with a vision that exceeded expectations. In his case, he took a commodity and turned it into a unique, sought-after product.

©Pixtal/Age fotostock RF

Large firms can obtain **economies of scale** in some industries. In other words, large firms can sometimes do things more efficiently because of their ability to operate on a larger scale than can a small firm.[3] For example, advertising is typically much cheaper per unit if purchased in large volume. Thus, a large firm such as Walmart can buy its advertising much cheaper on a per-unit basis than can a small retailer. Similarly, in manufacturing it is often much cheaper on a per-unit basis to produce large volumes of a product than to produce small volumes. This is the reason that small car manufacturers must charge an extraordinarily high price to cover their costs. Tesla Motors, which produces an all-electric car, has taken the battery car concept and crafted it into a high-performance car. By 2016 the firm had sold close to 200,000 cars. Today most major cities in the world have a Tesla dealership. An individual can charge his or her car at home or at one of the approximately 5,000 charging stations around the world.[4] While it still takes considerably longer time than filling with gas, the effort to grow charging stations will at some point allow an individual to charge his or her car essentially in the same manner a person fills up with gas in a combustion engine. Many cities provide prime parking for such charging stations as the cities seek to limit pollution and encourage more electric cars. The infrastructure may allow a critical mass of charging options at some point. The expectation is that the sales of electric cars will expand even faster and the economies of scale may allow Tesla to lower the cost for the vehicle.

economies of scale
A condition that allows the long-run average cost to continue downward as production increases. It leads (in its most extreme case) to a condition where a single firm making 100 percent of the product is the most efficient. In reality, this condition is moderated by the ability of management to control the size.

Many years ago the apparent efficiencies of very large businesses led some economists to predict that small entrepreneurial businesses would be largely replaced by a much smaller number of large businesses. The exact opposite has happened. The ability of entrepreneurs to respond more quickly and to operate more effectively (more focused on the specific needs of customers) has led to a growth in the raw number of entrepreneurial businesses rather than a decline.

This text develops the methods, applications, and processes that lead to the idea generation, investigation, start-up, and successful management of a new entrepreneurial business. How you grow your new business is a function of how you start your business. We firmly believe that the development and implementation of a new business is part art and part science. This field has been studied for a long time and there is a well-developed body of knowledge that should be the foundation of all your efforts. This text lays out a process for the "science" of forming and managing a new entrepreneurial business in a clear, sequential manner that is rich in its practical application as well as well-grounded in research. The "art" is a matter of practice, example, and the skill of the founder or founders of the new business. The text encourages you as you go through the process of developing your ideas and work to develop your own business plan. Although we will not be with you as you actually found your business, the goal of this text is to provide you with the fundamentals of starting the business and help you to develop your business into a functioning entity. Beyond all the statistics about how many new businesses fail (and many of them do fail), research (including our own studies) has found that there are three critical elements that an entrepreneur must solve for success:

1. An effective sales generation model. You are only as good as your pipeline. You must develop the ability to generate consistent and growing sales.
2. Sustainable operating profit margins. Profit margins are key to successful businesses.
3. Being properly financed. It is crucial that you have sufficient resources (either yourself or by raising funds) to get the business to the point where it is self-funding.[5]

We believe that the principal way to be a part of the group that survives and thrives is to thoroughly plan and lay a solid basis for the business.

LO1-2

Discuss the history of entrepreneurship in the United States.

A Brief History of Entrepreneurial Businesses in the United States

Before we start looking at entrepreneurial businesses today, it is important to note that entrepreneurs have always been a critical part of the country's success. Alexis de Tocqueville was a Frenchman who toured the United States in the early 1830s and wrote a famous analysis of the country. One of his observations was that the United States was not so much a nation with ventures that were marvelous in their grandeur, but instead a nation of innumerable small ventures. The history of the United States has always been intimately tied to entrepreneurial businesses. In fact, until the mid-1880s, almost all U.S. businesses were still relatively small.

The 1880s saw the initial development of the nation's large industrial base. It was from these beginnings that the robber barons developed. We associate their names today not only with great success but also with great abuses in business. They took advantage of the economies of scale that were suddenly possible with the industrial age and quickly came to dominate new sectors of the economy (e.g., Andrew Carnegie's domination of the steel industry). However, the robber barons were coming to dominate industrial sectors that had not existed historically, so they generally did not put smaller operations out of business. In fact, smaller entrepreneurial businesses continued to thrive during these times as new businesses grew up to serve the needs of these new industrial sectors.[6]

The Great Depression of the 1930s was harder on entrepreneurial businesses than on larger more mature businesses, and as a result it encouraged industrial concentration. The outcome was that following World War II, entrepreneurial business as a percentage of the U.S. economic output began to decline. It was during this time that Charles Wilson, secretary of defense for President Eisenhower, made the famous statement that "what is good for General Motors is good for the nation." The implication was that what was good for big business would be good for all of the people in the country.

In the late 1970s and early 1980s, the nation was in economic turmoil as many of the large firms that had grown to dominate the U.S. economy were having difficulty, owing to global competition. Entire industries, such as steel and automobile manufacturing, were in decline. It was during this time that President Jimmy Carter described the country as in a "malaise." The Japanese were in the dominant economic position in the world, and the widely discussed fear was that the United States was in decline much as Britain had been 100 years earlier. However, the decline of the large multinational firms in the United States opened new opportunities that entrepreneurial businesses rose to fill. The economic growth and success that the nation experiences today is due primarily to the entrepreneurial firms that found an economic footing and grew very rapidly. Today many of the multinational firms in the United States are technology firms that began in the late 1970s and early 1980s. The vast number of businesses that start up each year are responsible for much of the innovation that pushes established companies to new levels.

Therefore, as you begin your study of entrepreneurial businesses, you should recognize that you are examining a domain that has historically been the backbone of the economic success of the nation. Entrepreneurial businesses today continue to play a dominant role in the ability of the nation to adapt quickly and to make economic progress. The time line of business in the United States (Figure 1.1) highlights the central role of new business development.

Figure 1.1
Business Time Line
The time line of business provides both constants and natural evolution.

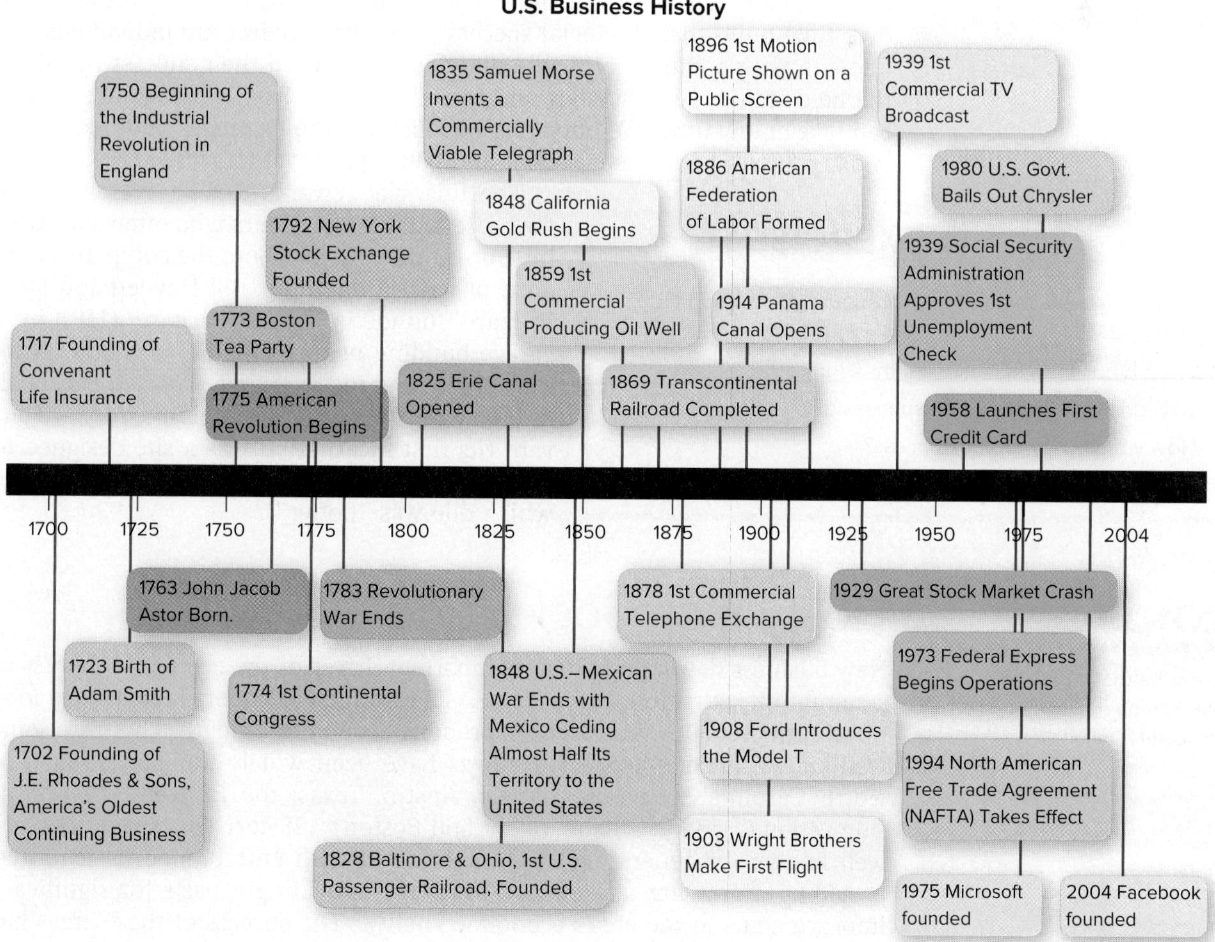

LO1-3

Identify the type of people who are entrepreneurs.

Who Are Entrepreneurial Business Owners Today?

One of the huge advantages of starting one's own business is that it provides the setting where the business owner can be the boss. As we will discuss in Chapter 2, the owners of a new business are the most important single factor in the business's success. The new business owners have both the opportunity and the responsibility to lead. However, although many new business owners want this independence, they also need to recognize they are not alone in the business; there are other important **stakeholders** of their entrepreneurial business. These are individuals or other organizations that may impact the success of the business and depend on the success of the business for their own livelihood. Stakeholders include key suppliers, customers, and employees—all of whom are critical to the success of the new business.

stakeholders
Individuals or other organizations that impact the success of a business.

It is true that the rewards of owning a business extend far beyond the financial. That said, the financial rewards to entrepreneurs can be stunning. In their book entitled *The Millionaire Next Door,* Thomas Stanley and William Danko highlight statistics that demonstrate the potential for financial rewards from starting a business.[7] For example, they point out that almost two-thirds of U.S. millionaires are self-employed, despite the fact that self-employed people make up fewer than 20 percent of the workers in America. They go on to state that 75 percent of these self-employed millionaires are entrepreneurs; the other 25 percent are self-employed professionals, such as doctors and accountants. So, close to 50 percent of the millionaires in this country are entrepreneurs. These are the individuals who start a business, run it well, and over time build their financial success. Most millionaires are individuals you know in your community. These individuals achieved their success by taking the bold step to actually start and run a business. This is the same step you can take at any time. We hope that by following the processes outlined in this book, you will be more confident and better prepared to succeed.

The financial rewards can be overwhelming for successful entrepreneurs who often start with little or no thought of where the company could grow or what it might be. Bill Hewlett and Dave Packard founded Hewlett-Packard (HP) in a garage building using an audio oscillator. Mark Zuckerberg and his roommates started Facebook as a way to connect with other students at Harvard (its first incarnation was a site designed to compare two people at the same time and decide which one was "hotter").

EXERCISE 1

1. Name some successful entrepreneurs you personally know.
2. What types of businesses do they run?
3. Why do you think they are successful?
4. How would they define success?
5. How did these individuals start their business?

LO1-4

Describe the impact of entrepreneurial businesses on society.

How Does Society Benefit?

New business development is an important driver of the economic success of a community, a region, and a state. As a result, civic leaders increasingly look up to entrepreneurs as a means to promote economic strength. There are some well-known areas where such efforts have been widely publicized, such as North Carolina's research triangle, Austin, Texas; the Denver–Fort Collins Innovation Corridor; Silicon Valley, and Boston's 128 corridor. These areas are well known for generating new employment with entrepreneurial ventures, providing a growing tax revenue base, and providing a basis for significant improvements to the area's economic vitality.[8] The success of these areas has encouraged others to seek to promote entrepreneurship to a much greater degree. A program called Economic Gardening is growing across the

United States to help start new entrepreneurial businesses in an area. The support provided includes financing for the venture, tax incentives, support classes, and more. Memphis, Tennessee, has used the program as a way to revitalize key elements in the city's economy.[9]

Entrepreneurial businesses act as a catalyst for societal change in other ways as well. They have the ability to garner profits in markets that have been ignored by large corporations. Large organizations will regularly ignore business opportunities if they do not believe the results will generate high profits, whereas entrepreneurial businesses are more flexible and willing to pursue a wider range of opportunities. The owners and employees of the entrepreneurial businesses have an understanding of the local community not easily obtained by a large conglomerate. For example, after a large military base or factory closes, there is obvious economic damage to that region, as the businesses that catered to the base or factory must either reset their target market or close their doors. Examinations of these areas suggest that a crisis such as a military base closing can lead to the formation of a much higher level of new business formations. Those individuals who have lost their jobs generally do not wish to leave the area (or cannot afford to leave the area). These individuals may have been satisfied with their location, and while they dreamed of starting a business, it was only when faced with the challenge of unemployment that they took the risk to start their dream. Studies have found that people facing a crisis from closure of an existing business often form new businesses, which, in many cases, can turn the economic fortunes of the area around.

The federal General Accounting Office did an analysis of the impact of the closure of military bases. It found that in cities with base closings including Salt Lake City, Kansas City, and San Jose, the areas around the bases had unemployment rates lower than the national average and income growth higher than the national average. There had been large initial job losses in these communities; however, the state and community leaders had responded to the closing of the bases with tax breaks and programs to support the development of new businesses. The result was that numerous new businesses rose up to fill the economic gap that had resulted from the closing of the bases.[10]

In Aurora, Colorado, the Fitzsimons Life Science District was developed on the site of the former Fitzsimons Army Medical Center. Within two years of its opening, the area had 17 start-up or early-stage bioscience businesses housed there.[11] Today it is a thriving center of research, employment, and new business growth. Pittsburgh Pennsylvania was once severely depressed economically as the U.S. steel industry faltered. However, by 2016 the downtown area was a center of renaissance as technology companies like Google, Facebook, and Uber established offices in the area to tap local talent from the University of Pittsburgh and Carnegie Mellon University.[12]

Entrepreneurial businesses provide more than just jobs; they also provide a means to meet the varied demands that individuals face in a society. Individuals can become frustrated with large corporations over the lack of promotion opportunities or the inflexibility of the corporations in dealing with the needs of family and children. Starting a new business may allow individuals to meet these demands in their lives in a way that large corporations are simply unwilling to do.

A view of downtown Pittsburgh Pennsylvania's skyline showing the Duquesne Incline.

ETHICAL CHALLENGE

What motivates you to start a business? Just as the opening case notes, there can be multiple motivations. Finance is clearly a strong motivation. Individuals desire money, and clearly the rewards for entrepreneurship can be substantial. As the opening case shows, a key motivation can also be other things such as control over your life and doing those things you enjoy. It is simply not true that success in an entrepreneurial business can only be achieved with brutally hard and long hours. Many entrepreneurs make a very good living working limited numbers of hours each week. These entrepreneurs could clearly make more money in their life, but they structure their business as a means to live rather than why they live.

The opening case illustrates that ultimately an entrepreneur must think through what their motivations are for the business and structure the business accordingly. The opening case in this chapter highlights that ultimately if the person does not do this, the business and their own health can suffer. The entrepreneur must be honest with themselves and their potential partners and investors. We place this consideration here in an ethics box to start because we think the absence of honesty about an entrepreneur's motivations with themselves and others is a critical ethical decision that should be made at the very foundation of the firm.

QUESTIONS

1. What do you see as your key motivations for starting a business?
2. If you had to allocate percentages to lifestyle, money, freedom, and family for motivators, what would they be?

The number of women starting new businesses has increased to the point where they are now the largest single group of new business founders. In part, this growth has come from the fact that women are often frustrated by what is referred to as the "glass ceiling." This refers to the fact that women, like minorities, may be hired by large firms but experience limits placed on their advancement. As a result, these women leave the large firms and start their own businesses. Women entrepreneurs also start businesses to allow them to have greater control over their lives, so they can better balance their family's and children's needs. A new business provides a valuable safety valve so that the citizens of a society can address the demands and needs in their lives.

Courtesy of Heather Schuck

Heather Schuck (left) worked in investments and then in a psychiatric treatment home before her frustration with work–life balance helped push her to start her own business, Glamajama, which makes trendy baby clothes. Founded in 2003, the firm's products today can be found at national retailers such as Bed Bath & Beyond, Nordstrom, Target, and J.C. Penney. Using her experience, Schuck wanted to encourage women to achieve business success while also being allowed to stay focused on family, so she later started the very popular GlamaLIFE.com online community, which connects women interested in business. This community is built around the ideas in Schuck's 2013 book entitled *The Working Mom Manifesto: How to Stop Hoping for Happiness and Start Creating It.* The central argument is that women can create successful businesses around family rather than forcing the family to be centered around the business. Schuck has appeared on every significant talk show and is a classic example of how one can achieve in many facets of life.[13]

Entrepreneurship Around the World

LO1-5

Discuss the worldwide impact of entrepreneurial businesses.

New and growing businesses are critically important around the world. The World Bank estimates that one of the strongest factors in the growth in any nation's GNP is the presence of entrepreneurial small- and medium-sized enterprises (SMEs). Today there are widespread efforts in almost all nations to encourage the development of small and medium enterprises. These governmental efforts range from tiny contributions of capital or time to large, multidimensional programs that cross the boundaries of multiple nations.

Some of the efforts to encourage SMEs around the world are quite small, but still have a big impact. For example, microloan programs have been in existence for years to encourage self-development. These loans are often for only a few dollars each and are made directly to entrepreneurs, often women. The businesses founded through such loans can be as simple as delivering lunches, weaving baskets, or washing clothes. However, the success of such loans has been substantial, with great strides being made in many desperately poor nations. It is interesting that the repayment rate on such loans is typically 99 to 100 percent, a much higher repayment rate than on most types of loans. The success of these loans has resulted in an increasing dedication of the U.S. aid budget to microloans for developing nations.[14]

At the other extreme are nations that have prepared a full range of programs to encourage new venture start-ups. A program in Singapore is aimed at encouraging high-technology ventures among highly educated individuals. The government is providing a range of services and facilities to assist in the development of these ventures and encourage the founding of firms that might result. Although these two examples are at different extremes, they both demonstrate a high level of interest and investment by governments in small-business initiation. The result of these efforts is that the pace of small-business start-ups is increasing around the world.

EXERCISE 2

1. What motivates your interest in entrepreneurship?
2. What opportunities do you see in your community?
3. Have these opportunities attracted other businesses, large or small? Why or why not?

What Is an Entrepreneurial Business?

LO1-6

Define an entrepreneurial business.

It is clear from the previous discussion that new businesses have benefits for individuals and society within the United States and around the world. Individuals typically associate small and entrepreneurial businesses together. For classification purposes, the U.S. government considers any business with fewer than 500 employees to be a small business while the European Union caps that number at 50. We would suggest that a business with almost 500 employees is actually a large firm requiring formal personnel policies, specialized groups, and an administrative structure that is in no way close to the reality of most small businesses. For the vast majority of people, the businesses formed will have far fewer than 500 employees.

We suggest that there is a further level of definition that is needed for clarity. Multiple terms can be used to refer to the same types of businesses including *entrepreneurial businesses*, *small businesses*, sometimes as *small-to-medium-sized businesses or enterprises* (SMBs or SMEs), and *family businesses*. These terms are roughly equivalent and do not specify the differences between the two main types of new business. We see two main categories of start-up businesses.

The first category of start-up businesses are those formed as high-growth, often high-tech, ventures that have several unique characteristics and are generally venture capital–backed firms. Venture capital start-ups can be characterized by the following descriptions:

1. The businesses are well-funded by venture capital or angel investment. In fact, without such capital it is virtually impossible to begin this particular type of venture.* Venture capitalists are a specialized type of investor; they typically do not invest less than $2 million and in return they expect extraordinary returns.
2. These businesses are formed with a **harvest plan** in place; this is a plan to exit the business that allows the investors to take advantage of growth. A harvest plan may include selling the business to another firm, selling it to a group of investors, or even participating in an IPO (a public offering of stock). Size is the deciding metric in a potential public offering or sale to a larger organization.

harvest plan

A plan to exit a business. Typically, the owners have the intention to sell the business to another firm or take it to an IPO.

3. As a result of the harvest plan, these firms are organized to grow as quickly as possible and are generally heavily laden with debt. Many are harvested before they can achieve positive net cash flow.
4. They have a developed organizational structure.
5. They often hire an experienced president to grow the company.
6. They tend to develop operations in multiple locations very shortly after the initial investment.
7. They are inherently risky operations whose growth is dependent on the exploitation of unknowns in the market (a new invention, unique patents, etc.).
8. These businesses either start or grow quickly to employ a relatively large number of employees.

The second category of business is a more common type of business and is the focus of this book. These firms are most often referred to as entrepreneurial firms and are defined by these characteristics:

1. The start-up is self-funded or closely funded.
2. The development plan is oriented around positive cash flow.
3. The management structure is designed to take advantage of the skills of the founder or founders.
4. The operation is designed in the image of the founder(s).
5. The business is oriented toward the personal goals of the founder(s).
6. The number of employees may be zero or as few as one, and typically would not be expected to grow to more than 50 to 100.

When we discuss *entrepreneurial businesses* throughout this text, it is this second category of firms to which we refer. Such entrepreneurial businesses are the type you are much more likely to found than are venture capital–backed firms. This is not to suggest that a business founded as an entrepreneurial business does not sometimes become a capital-backed business. Although Facebook or even LinkedIn was founded as an entrepreneurial business, we would more accurately describe either of them as a venture capital–backed business, since both quickly required millions of dollars of investment from venture capitalists to grow. In contrast, the businesses of the majority of millionaires discussed in the book *The Millionaire Next Door* almost always started as entrepreneurial businesses. These individuals made their fortunes in areas such as lawn care, plumbing, and electrical work, and

*The concepts of venture capital and angel investors will be dealt with in greater detail in later chapters. For reference here, both are investors who provide capital to the start-up firm in exchange for ownership in the new firm. This ownership level can be and often is at over 50 percent of the firm.

their businesses were almost all founded in a manner consistent with the second category of business. This second category of business is also what typically will be found outside of the United States. The presence of venture capital for start-ups is limited outside of the United States. Often even funds that say they are venture capitalists are in fact only providing funding for mezzanine or mature, existing firms that are looking to expand. In the text we will discuss some of the differences that can be expected outside of the United States, but we argue that most of what we present here is relevant outside for firms starting up in a wide variety of markets.

Mark Zuckerberg is a great example of massive entrepreneurial business success. His story is more the exception than the rule. What lessons can we learn from Zuckerberg's success that might apply to businesses on a smaller scale?

Although some of the concepts discussed in this text are applicable to venture capital–backed firms, the focus in this text is on the systematic designing of a successful entrepreneurial business start-up. The U.S. Census tracks employment by number of employees (among many other statistics) and the latest census reports indicate that firms with fewer than 99 employees represent the majority of all firms in the United States, and also represent approximately 35 percent of all full-time employees in the United States.[15]

Business Plans—Another Difference in Types of Firms

Another critical difference between an entrepreneurial business and a venture capital–backed firm is in the size and detail required in their initial business plans. An entrepreneurial business's resources are significantly more constrained than those of venture capital–backed business. Whereas the entrepreneurial firm generally develops a business plan as a promotional tool to be sent to venture capitalists and other potential investors, the entrepreneurial business develops a business plan as a guide for the running of the business. Many entrepreneurial ventures hire professional consultants to assist them in the development of their business plans; in contrast, we strongly advise all entrepreneurial business owners to develop their own plans as a part of their process.

EXERCISE 3

1. Do you have any initial ideas for a new business? Write these ideas down. As we go through the course you will be asked to evaluate your business idea in light of the concepts presented in that chapter. Most ideas will undergo significant evolution as you begin to study the topic more.
2. How many employees would your initial business require?

A venture capital–backed business plan runs from 25 to 45 pages long, though we have seen many that are more than 100 pages (ugh). The business plan for a small business should be relatively short (15 to 25 pages) and should be developed in a manner that helps the small-business person understand the industry, the firm that he or she wishes to develop, and what will be needed to create success in that business. Thus, the business plan for a new entrepreneurial business is developed with three goals in mind:

1. To be a guide to managing the business in its early development.
2. To provide a self-evaluation: Putting the information down in writing allows for evaluation and honest analysis.
3. To provide potential closely held investors with the critical information necessary to evaluate the key criteria of the business: its cash flow, management team, and competitive advantage.

The business planning process that we develop in this text is a very practical and logical guide for the establishment and initial management of a new business. We do not discuss the long, intricate business plans that are sometimes written to attract venture capital. Instead, you will develop a working document that is grounded in the needs of the new entrepreneurial business. A well-thought-out business plan has heightened importance for the new business as a tool for you to think through a wide range of issues, as most new businesses will not actually obtain financing from big-money investors. This type of business will either be self-funded or obtain financing from friends and family. These types of investors are not looking for a slick five-year formal plan; instead, they are looking for a document that explains the value of the business and how it will succeed.

Therefore, you should note the following:

1. *No cookie-cutter business plan programs.* We will not use any of the cookie-cutter business plan programs that are available. If you google the term *business plan,* you will find any number of programs on the Internet that encourage you to plug in information and allow the program to "generate" a plan. We believe such programs really inhibit the process of designing a business. Each business plan, much like each business, should have its own voice, feel, and presentation. We suggest to you that a good business plan is best developed by the individual(s) contemplating the business, not by paid consultants who will have none of the enthusiasm of the founder(s). The fact that potential investors to an entrepreneurial business will be those closest to the founder makes it critical that the entrepreneur(s) seek to ensure the chances of success by doing thorough planning and thinking. It is one thing to lose money and close a business if the investment comes from investors you know casually. However, if the investors are your parents, in-laws, grandparents, or siblings and the business closes, it can be truly painful and may, in fact, cause ruptures in the relationships you hold most dear. A well-designed business plan has already helped the founder(s) consider every aspect of the new business and allows everyone else involved to have a true "feel" for where this opportunity is heading.
2. *You should plan to develop the elements of your plan as you finish each chapter.* This text is designed for you to have a full business plan crafted by the time you reach the end of the book. Crafting that section of your plan along the lines developed in the chapter leads to a more comprehensive and well-designed plan that is fresh in your mind as you write. The final section of the book has a fully developed entrepreneurial business plan and a full discussion about each section of that plan. The plan in the appendix is one developed by students as a class project. Our hope is that you will be able to produce an equally detailed plan in this class. The business plan you produce should ultimately be a good solid start on a plan you could use to begin your own business. You will want to refine the plan more after you leave the class, but the class will provide you with the tools to begin the process of forming your own business.
3. *Do not be intimidated by the effort needed to bring forth a business.* It is a daunting task to think about all the aspects of crafting a new business. It should be done in pieces with each piece fitting into a whole picture. At the end of every chapter, you should ask yourself whether the business you are designing still makes business sense. There is as much value in deciding not to pursue a particular business idea as there is in actually starting a business. It is a process; take it step-by-step.
4. *Craft a one-page pitch for your business.* We will discuss this several times in this text, but it is crucial that you develop an attractive, one-page pitch about your business as you go through the process of developing your business plan. It clearly lays out the crucial information about the new business idea and provides an effective starting point for every potential supplier, employee, or investor. Although each one will be somewhat unique, a one-page pitch generally should look like the one in Figure 1.2.

Figure 1.2
One-Page Pitch Sheet
An example one-page pitch sheet provides a snapshot of the business at a point in time.

The ToolGym

The ToolGym A gym-like facility and atmosphere provides access to the tools and expertise necessary to allow anyone to pursue their interest in woodworking.

We solve the problem of niche woodworking tool availability and variety and eliminate the common barriers to entry in pursuit of these interests such as personal time, space, and money.

Business Summary Operating under a similar guise as a gym membership or cloud computing model, the user wants access to assets without acquiring, setting up, and maintaining the equipment.

Initial Product Offering: We will provide all access to the tools, workspace, storage, and expertise for woodworking hobbyists and professionals under one roof. Our pilot will consist of one location, strategically positioned, whose benefits offer high density of target demographic as well as ease of materials access.

Customer Problem/Target Market: The ToolGym solves the problem that exists with any expensive hobby: The resource utilization typically does not commiserate with cost. Much like SaaS models in technology, ToolGym solves this issue with a consumption-based model that commoditizes time, money, and accessibility for the woodworking hobbyist.

Our target market is the trade craftsman and fine woodworking segments where the cost-to-utilization ratio unbalance exists.

Management Team: Our executive team has an extensive experience in developing companies from incubation to exit or sale with a deep domain knowledge of the trade craftsman and woodworking industries.

Our finance expertise is based on years of financial strategy consulting deeply rooted in emerging markets and hypergrowth opportunities.

Our sales and marketing team is highly skilled in direct and indirect (channel) sales strategies and leverages a wealth of market analytics expertise to execute market entry and sales growth initiatives.

Our Customers:

- The woodworking hobbyist who is constrained by the time, space, and money required to own and maintain a workspace to tackle significant woodworking projects.
- The woodworking beginners—those with entry level skills but the desire and resources to pursue.
- The trade unions in need of a training facility or apprentice program as well as schools that have carved out shop classes but have an interested audience of students.

Sales Strategy: Full immersion into the woodworking hobbyist culture using positioning (location) and partnerships (with fine/rare woods and finishes suppliers) that will add instant credibility to the services resources we deliver.

Marketing Strategy:

- Classes for beginners
- Partnerships with suppliers, storage facilities, and industry trade shows
- Storage for projects in progress

Competitors:

- Every hobbyist garage and/or home woodworking space within our target demographic.

Competitive Advantages:

- **Exclusivity:**
    - The ToolGym will offer a line of unique tools and tool accessories that can only be used and/or purchased at The ToolGym (i.e., Miter boxes, jigs, decorative molding templates). ***The Craftsman Tool model.***
    - Partnerships with fine woods and craftsman stores, given their limited supply, adds immediate credibility and exaggerates the importance of being first to market.

Risks:

- Inability to grow membership
- Liability; Insurance requirements necessary
- Highly skilled labor
- Target audience messaging
- Space and tool use optimization

What we need:

- **Phase 1:** $225,000 for 20 percent equity in the ToolGym
    - Equals 12 months of operating expenses
    - Cash flow positive at 13 months

Lean Startup

The approach we have in this text is consistent with a concept you may hear often—lean startup. The term *lean startup* indicates that a start-up business will need to rapidly change. Rather than pursuing a fixed business idea you should visualize the startup as an experiment. The focus is on building a business that generates something that the customer actually desires. The lean approach means seeking a model that is scalable—or able to build into something bigger. The approach we have detailed here fits with this approach. The lean startup seeks to shorten the product/service cycles by quickly testing and experimentation of a product. The goal of this book and of the lean approach to business startup seeks to iteratively build products or services with a particular focus on early customers. This process requires constantly testing the business's products/services with real customers and incorporating their feedback into the entrepreneurial effort. The result is that your ultimate business may look very different than what you initially start. One key to this model that we stress later in the text is measuring your outcomes. Your measures of success—financial and otherwise—must be exacting as you build a quick understanding of your actions and their outcomes. One key to the lean entrepreneurial process and where the term originates is the startup must be lean. To make changes an entrepreneur must be flexible. If you have invested heavily in a piece of equipment, for example, you may be unwilling to abandon it when it is clear that this is not what the business needs. Thus, the entrepreneur must recognize that change will be the nature of the business, and so whether such an investment is helpful or confining must be evaluated by the entrepreneur. The key for the entrepreneur is the adaptation. Keeping any production or action simple can quickly be eliminated if it does not generate the success the entrepreneurial team is seeking. We stress throughout the book that a plan is useful as a discipline to think through concepts and ideas. However, the goal is not to generate a long, involved document that does not change. From day one, the entrepreneurial team must be flexible.

SUMMARY

This chapter began by discussing the impact that new businesses have on the economy. A brief history of new ventures was discussed, with the observation that every business you can think of, regardless of size, was started by one person or a small group of people. Given that, there are still two very distinct types of businesses: (1) those that are funded by large amounts of outside venture capital with the intent of growing them as fast as possible and (2) those that are primarily in business for the benefit of the founders and their families. The second group is far more prevalent around the globe and is the focus of this text. The remainder of the chapter set up three main principles we want you to remember: (1) No cookie-cutter business plan programs should be used, (2) build your own business plan along with the chapters in this book, and (3) this is a process, so take it in bite-sized pieces. The concepts of a Lean Startup were discussed and will be incorporated throughout the book.

KEY TERMS

economies of scale 5
Fortune 500 4
harvest plan 12
stakeholders 8
United States Small Business Administration (SBA) 4

REVIEW QUESTIONS

1. How do entrepreneurial businesses impact the economy?
2. Name several entrepreneurs who have grown their businesses into major organizations.
3. Explain what is meant by the science and the art of starting and managing a business.
4. How have entrepreneurial businesses impacted the growth of the United States?
5. Why does "profit as a goal" present an ethical challenge to new business owners?
6. What differentiates an entrepreneurial business from one that is a venture capital-backed business?

INDIVIDUAL EXERCISES

1. What types of new businesses interest you most and why?
2. What aspects of those businesses are particularly appealing to you?
3. Do you see yourself as an entrepreneur in the next five years?

GROUP EXERCISES

Interview an Entrepreneur

Early in the semester, every person in the class should interview an entrepreneur. You have wide flexibility as to the types of entrepreneurs you select. However, each entrepreneur must be the original founder of the business or the current owner and should not be your close relative. Prepare a report on each entrepreneur interviewed. The report should be no more than three typed, double-spaced pages long, and cover three primary areas. First, discuss the background and characteristics of the entrepreneur, as well as the history and nature of the business.

Second, discuss lessons learned by the entrepreneur as related to you by the entrepreneur. Third, include your evaluation of the entrepreneur, and state what you can personally take away from the experience. You should plan to make a short (5- to 7-minute) presentation on this individual to the rest of the class by midsemester.

ENDNOTES

1. "Frequently Asked Questions," *U.S. Small Business Administration*. https://www.sba.gov/sites/default/files/advocacy/SB-FAQ-2016_WEB.pdf.
2. J. Markoff, "Apple's Visionary Redefined Digital Age," *The New York Times*, October 5, 2011. http://www.nytimes.com/2011/10/06/business/steve-jobs-of-apple-dies-at-56.html.
3. R. Makaodok, "Interfirm Differences in Scale Economies and the Evolution of Market Share," *Strategic Management Journal* 20 (1999), pp. 935–52.
4. B. Vlasic. "Tesla's New Model 3 Jump-Starts Demand for Electric Cars," *The New York Times*, April 1, 2016. https://www.nytimes.com/2016/04/02/business/teslas-new-model-3-jump-starts-demand-for-electric-cars.html?_r=0.
5. K. H. Vesper, *New Venture Strategies* (Englewood Cliffs, NJ: Prentice Hall, 1990); C. E. Bamford and E. B. Douthett, "Venture Capital and Risk Management: Evidence from Initial Public Offerings," *Journal of Managerial Issues* 25, no. 3 (2013), pp. 220–40.
6. M. G. Blackford, *A History of Small Business in America* (New York: Twayne Publishers, 1991).
7. T. J. Stanley and W. D. Danko, *The Millionaire Next Door* (New York: Simon & Schuster, 1998).
8. Z. J. Acs, "Small Firms and Economic Growth," in *Small Business in the Modern Economy*, ed. P. H. Admiral (New York: Blackwell, 1996); A. Zacharakis, P. D. Reynolds, and W. D. Bygrave, "National Entrepreneurship Assessment: United States of America." Paper presented at Kauffman Center for Entrepreneurial Leadership, Kansas City, MO, 1999.
9. http://growth-engine.org/.
10. General Accounting Office, "Military Base Closures: Overview of Economic Recovery, Property Transfer, and Environmental Cleanup." Statement by Barry H. Homan, Director of Defense Capabilities and Management, 2001. www.gao.gov/new.items/d011054t.pdf.
11. http://fitzscience.com/; J. McCurry, "A Fighting Chance: Former U.S. Military Bases Are Now Home to Thriving Industry," *Site Selection Magazine,* November 2002. www.siteselection.com/issues/2002/nov/p803/.
12. M. Vitner and J. Feik, "Pennsylvania Economic Outlook: July 2016," *Wells Fargo Securities*, July 5, 2016. https://www08.wellsfargomedia.com/assets/pdf/commercial/insights/economics/regional-reports/pa-outlook-20160705.pdf.
13. N. Fallon, "10 Female Entrepreneurs Who Inspired Us in 2013," *Business News Daily*, December 23, 2013. www.businessnewsdaily.com/5668-female-entrepreneurs-2013.html.
14. "How Can Microfinance Better Serve the Poor? Readers Weigh In," *The Wall Street Journal*, April 1, 2015. https://www.wsj.com/articles/do-microloans-lift-people-out-of-poverty-readers-weigh-in-1427258714.
15. A. Caruso, "Statistics of U.S. Businesses Employment and Payroll Summary: 2012," *US Census Bureau Report*, February 12, 2015.

chapter

2

Individual Leadership and Entrepreneurial Start-Ups

learning objectives

After studying this chapter, you will be able to:

LO2-1 Explain how entrepreneurial founders impact the business world as a whole.

LO2-2 Discuss the importance of an entrepreneurial orientation.

LO2-3 List the triggers that encourage new business formations.

LO2-4 Compare and contrast various types of new business supports.

LO2-5 Explain how you can evaluate those things that you enjoy the most and discover how they may lead to business opportunities.

RAY CORKRAN—ENTREPRENEURSHIP LATER IN LIFE

The decision to become an entrepreneur can come at any time in a person's life. Often people look at the Silicon Valley and assume that only those less than 35 years old can start a firm. However, many entrepreneurs start their first business later in life whether it be when they retire from an established firm, loose a job, or simply see an opportunity that only becomes clear at that point and time.

Ray Corkran was 60 when he bought a Home Instead Senior Care franchise. The franchise provides part-time, full-time and live-in non-medical service for the elderly who can manage their physical needs but require assistance, supervision, light housework, and companionship to remain in their homes. The franchise requires between $110,000 and $125,000 to start. Corkran recognized that there was uncertainty over Medicare and Medicaid in the United States, and these are the major funders of elderly care. These providers increasingly want to find cheaper means to provide the necessary services to the elderly that allow them to remain in their homes. The aging baby boomers will increasingly push the need for such services.

Corkran realized there was a need for such an operation in his home-town of Houston from his firsthand experience with family and friends, especially his mother who died at home. At worst he has joked that in 20 years he can be his own customer. The Home Instead franchise now covers southeast Houston, including Clear Lake, Friendswood, Pearland, and League City. As the owner, Ray Corkran already had made a big impression on other entrepreneurs and staff. One of the staff, Jessica said, "I love working with seniors, and I am so blessed to be working for Home Instead. They are unlike any other employer I've had—there's no comparison."

Questions

1. How old are you?
2. How does your age impact the entrepreneurial venture you are planning?
3. Do you think the ventures you do over your lifetime will change as you age?

Sources: OnlineMBA, "Elderly Entrepreneurship: 10 Seniors to Look to for Inspiration," Alley Watch, October 24, 2013. http://www.alleywatch.com/2013/10/elderly-entrepreneurship-10-seniors-to-look-to-for-inspiration-2/; O. Linderholm, "Older Entrepreneurs: The Startup Mentality Is Not Bound by Age," Yahoo Aabaco Small Business. https://smallbusiness.yahoo.com/advisor/older-entrepreneurs-the-startup-mentality-is-not-bound-by-age-000959494.html; D. Omholt, "Senior Care Franchises Grow to Serve Boomers," The FRANtastic Blog, November 26, 2012. http://eauth.com/the-frantastic-blog/senior-care-franchises-grow-to-serve-boomers. https://www.homeinstead.com/435/blog/caregiver-of-the-month-jessica-r.

In large, well-established organizations, no one person is crucial to the survival of the business, even the president of the company. The lack of dependence of large organizations on any one individual is due to the strong structures in the large firm such as extensive written procedures, clear lines of responsibility, and the presence of other individuals or units to step in when some failure occurs. Large organizations also have wide dispersion of knowledge throughout the business; in other words, there are multiple people who know about any given aspect of the business. As a result, if any single person leaves the organization, it has the ability to continue with minimal interruption. Finally, large organizations have greater excess resources, including financial resources, which allow them to hire outside experts to fill any critical need that arises. These excess resources are referred to as **organizational slack**; they allow large organizations flexibility that is not available to the typical entrepreneurial venture.

organizational slack
Excess resources in an organization that allow for redundancy and the quick deployment of personnel in crisis.

In contrast an entrepreneurial business is generally dependent on a single individual or a few individuals for the business to survive. A new entrepreneurial business starts as the brainchild of a single person or a small group of people, each of whom has an ownership stake in the business. The new business has few formal procedures, a concentration of knowledge in those individuals who start the business, and limited slack resources.[1] The absence of slack financial resources means the new firm has limited flexibility in responding to emergency issues such as the need to hire replacements if the company loses key individuals. As a result, the founders of an entrepreneurial business and the leadership they provide play a far more critical role in the business's success than does the senior leadership of the typical large organization. The importance of the individual in the founding and managing of a new business leads to the focus in this chapter on the individual who starts a business and his or her leadership. The prior discussion of lean start-up in Chapter 1 stresses this fact—the new entrepreneurial venture must be lean to survive as it changes and evolves.

Understanding and collaborating in small groups can be an essential part of new business success. What are some of the key characteristics you would look for in a partner?
©Monashee Frantz/Getty Images RF

This chapter includes a discussion of why individuals are so important to the success of a new business. It also provides ways for you to understand your own predisposition to start a business. The examination of your orientation includes an examination of your risk tolerance and the boundaries that may exist in your perception of events in the environment. It also includes an exercise to test your own entrepreneurial orientation.

Every individual brings a unique set of supports that can be used to help in the founding process; these supports are critical in the success of a new business. Therefore, we will examine those supports, the most important of which is the family. In some businesses the family is a more valuable support than in others as the family may all work in the firm. These businesses are referred to as **family businesses**. Family businesses have unique issues that extend beyond those of the normal new entrepreneurial business. We will address family businesses more at the end of this chapter.

family business
A business in which ownership and employment are centered around the family.

The authors of the text have had extensive experience working with entrepreneurs as they start and run their businesses. Throughout this text you will find that many of these firms are used as examples. In particular, we will follow two specific start-up businesses throughout the text. The first one we will see in this chapter is Kosher Home. This venture was the outcome of three friends' discussions after work and the effort to find new opportunities for themselves.

KOSHER HOME

Jack Cohen was not particularly religious. Since he was Jewish, he would abstain from pork, which was no small accommodation growing up in an isolated community in Oklahoma, but beyond that his commitment to observing kosher traditions was relatively low. Growing up in an isolated Jewish community, there was one synagogue where people from a variety of towns would come to mostly for various holidays. Even holding services each Friday at the synagogue would not occur consistently as the rabbi travelled in from several hours away. The issue was not that Jack was not proud to be Jewish, but it was just that to keep kosher and many other aspects of being Jewish were quite hard so far from anyone else doing anything similar.

When Jack went to college on the West Coast of the United States, he found a large and active Jewish community. Through the campus Hillel, he was able to find a part of his life that he had really never known. In this learning process, he began to keep the kosher traditions of the Jewish diet much closer. There are a variety of rules associated with observing kosher such as avoiding not only pork but also shell fish. In addition, pots and pans cannot mix the cooking of milk and meat products or drinking milk with meat products.

For prepared foods there are special rules that apply. These rules have resulted in the development of specialty lines of food products to serve this market. The difficulty for most retailers is that if you have only a few Jewish families that live in your area, you will not stock the kosher food products. This means that even if someone is seeking these types of products they cannot easily keep kosher if they live isolated from a larger Jewish community.

Jack realized there was a need to serve the isolated Jewish communities as increasingly such communities are being hollowed out. The elderly stay, but the young either drop away from observing the Jewish traditions as the dominant culture takes over their lives or as the younger generation moves away, like Jack did, to areas where there is a critical mass of people who can share their practices. While Jack moved he also came to realize he hoped not everyone else would move. Many of these isolated communities have strong historical roots in the regions they are located. He felt that the Jewish community provided a critical element of tolerance and concern in the broader areas where they were located. The country overall being poorer if these isolated Jewish communities were not there.

Discussing this concern with two friends, Ellen and Toby, who were also active at Hillel, they decided they would like to determine a means to serve these isolated communities. They knew there were Internet-based services to help isolated communities that included helping singles meet and providing support. However, they did not know of any Internet services that would help individuals keep kosher through the delivery of specialized food. They had seen a rapid growth in Internet services that provided meals that are shipped for gourmet or health-based cooking. However, it did not appear that any competitor was doing this for kosher eating. After several months of general discussion, they decided to reach out to others to get advice.

The three potential entrepreneurs had a conversation with Ellen's uncle who had started several successful businesses. The uncle advised them to spend a little more time investigating their motivations and personal risk orientation before they actually considered going into business together. He related the story of his first business, which he had started, with his best friend. The two had been lifelong friends and thought they knew all there was to know about each other. Not only had they been friends since childhood, but also each had been the best man in the other's wedding. Although they thought they knew each other well, when it came to money and the level of risk they were capable of handling, they were substantially different people. Whereas the uncle was very frugal, his partner believed that money needed to be enjoyed today. Ultimately their business partnership fell apart. Although the financial loss was significant, even more devastating was the loss of the friendship between the two men and their families. He has always felt the experience was a significant failure and not one he wanted to repeat.

Ellen's uncle has had other businesses and partnerships since that initial failure. He now believes that although he needs to like a person in order to work closely with him or her, it is much more important that they agree on such key issues as money and risk. Therefore, the uncle suggested the three friends prepare four simple issues to discuss among themselves:

Issues to Discuss Among Themselves

1. Compare how each of them prepared his or her monthly family budget.
2. Discuss how much debt each was willing to take on credit cards.

(continued)

(Continued from previous page)

3. Discuss whether each was willing to lend family members money and the reasons for their answer.
4. Have each person answer this question: If you inherited $250,000, what would you do with it?

The outcome of this exercise for our three potential business owners will be discussed after Exercise 1 in text.

QUESTION

1. What other questions would you add to what Ellen's uncle suggested?

The three potential entrepreneurs completed the exercise. Jack and Toby realized from the exercise they were far more frugal in their lives than Ellen. From this insight Jack and Toby realized that they were more compatible as partners than either was with Ellen. They realized that if they went into business with Ellen they would soon have significant conflicts regarding both the approach to and the actual finances of the new business. The result would most likely be a loss of their friendship with him, and also the potential failure of the business. The discussions among the three friends also brought these issues home more clearly to Ellen, who ultimately decided that a business was not for her. She realized that because of her current debt, if the business needed more money, she would not be able to put any more money into it; also, if the business failed, she had so few resources to fall back upon that she might have to file for bankruptcy.

EXERCISE 1

1. Evaluate your own views on the issues raised in Kosher Home. Discuss your results with others in your class. What is the range of answers that were given?
2. Have you ever lent money to a relative? Or have you heard stories from others who have? Would it be different if it were a close friend with whom you went into business?

LO2-1

Explain how entrepreneurial founders impact the business world as a whole.

Founders Are the Reason Why Entrepreneurial Businesses Work So Well

New businesses have some significant advantages over large businesses. For example, the very fact that entrepreneurial businesses start out small means that these firms have greater flexibility. Smaller firms can also respond quickly to changes around them, whereas a large firm tends to use many committees or project teams to approve the work of other committees or project teams. This feature alone allows the smaller firm led by the aware entrepreneur to respond quickly to opportunities or threats as they arise. Entrepreneurial firms also fill niches that large firms simply cannot afford to fill. Large firms do have an advantage in those situations where there are economies of scale; that is, the large firms have the ability to produce a service or product more cheaply because it is done on a large scale.[2] However, in small niches, the large firms' systems are not able to do small volumes of a particular activity profitably because of their large fixed costs and overhead. These niches are ideal for new businesses.

Even though these advantages can be substantial, the greatest advantage for an entrepreneurial business is that it is owned and run by the same person(s). Contrast this to most large corporations, where there is a division between owners and managers. The individuals who manage the operations of a large, established corporation do not typically have substantial ownership in the company. The managers (agents of the owners) may own some stock, but in a large business such as General Motors they own a very small percentage of the total stock.

Agency theory suggests that individuals act to maximize their own individual benefit.[3] The result in a large corporation is that the manager of a business will tend to act to maximize his own benefit, not necessarily that of those who own the firm (typically the shareholders). This does not mean that the manager seeks to steal from the firm; instead, in subtle but pervasive ways, the manager will act for his or her own benefit. In contrast, the individual who owns the business will always act to maximize the value of the business, since the interest of the owner and that of the business itself are aligned: If the business makes money, the owner makes money.

agency theory
A managerial theory that believes individuals act to maximize their own benefit. Thus, in settings where there is a split between ownership and control (as in most publicly traded corporations), the agents (managers) must be monitored or they will act to maximize their own benefit, not necessarily the benefit of those who own the firm (the shareholders).

To illustrate, the manager of a large firm can easily justify why it is important to fly nonstop, first class across the country for a meeting in New York City or Los Angeles. That manager might argue the need to arrive fresh, with room to work, and rest on the flight. This trip may easily cost $6,000 if the ticket is bought on short notice. This comes out of the corporation's income, money that really belongs to the shareholders (the owners).

Compare this with the typical behavior of an entrepreneur. Just as it is for a corporation, the airline ticket is an expense; however, in this case, every dollar spent comes directly out of the pocket of the entrepreneur. The entrepreneur is more likely to go on the Internet and find the cheapest ticket possible. Although the entrepreneur would also like to arrive fresh and be able to work during the flight, he or she is more likely to fly economy class and fly through a hub airport to save the $4,500 or more. If the large, established business is doing poorly, the manager still collects a salary and benefits, although the shareholders (owners) are getting few rewards. The manager will move on to another firm if the business collapses, having no significant stake in the financial failure of the previous company. In contrast, if an entrepreneurial business is doing poorly, the owner may ultimately have to close the business and be responsible for any debts that have accumulated. As a result, the entrepreneur will treat the costs of the business very differently than will the manager of a firm. (When we deal with the legal structure of entrepreneurial business in Chapter 7, we specify in greater detail if and when an entrepreneur is responsible for the debts of the business.) If the managers of a large business had to spend their own money or were responsible for the debt of the organization, agency theory would argue that the manager would behave in a thriftier manner.

The cost of luxuries such as first-class airfare is an extravagance few entrepreneurial businesses can afford. How would you, as an entrepreneur, decide what constitutes a luxury and what is a necessity?

Thus, one of the greatest assets of the new business is the owner of the business due to their personal involvement in, and dedication to, the business. It is because of the owner's importance to the business that students need to consider their own abilities and resources early as they begin to look at building an entrepreneurial business.

EXERCISE 2

1. What will you do if the business fails?
2. How much time are you willing to dedicate to the success of the venture?
3. How much of your personal assets are you willing to put into the venture?

LO2-2

Discuss the importance of an entrepreneurial orientation.

Evaluating Your Entrepreneurial Orientation

There are a number of issues that potential entrepreneurs need to consider about themselves as they look at starting a new business. Examined with some depth, these issues will shape the entrepreneur's analysis of the potential of any business idea. These include (1) risk tolerance, (2) prior experience, and (3) personality orientation of the individual.

Risk Tolerance

Potential entrepreneurs must determine their own individual level of tolerance to risk. You are probably familiar with the concept from dealing with your own financial expenditures. The typical advice provided to most individuals is to spend no more than your personal risk tolerance.[4] Thus, if you have a low risk tolerance, you need to spend less and save more for that proverbial rainy day. If you have a high risk tolerance, you will spend more, assuming there will not be a rainy day. We use a similar concept here, but we use it more broadly, asking you to consider your tolerance to a wide range of potential risks that extend far beyond just financial considerations. Initially, you need to evaluate whether you have the risk tolerance to actually start a new business. The next step is to evaluate what level of risk you will accept in a given business situation.

break-even point
The time when a new business has reached a level where revenue coming into the firm is sufficient to cover expenses.

To illustrate, if you work for a large corporation, there is relatively low individual financial risk. In a normal economic environment, even if a large corporation has a poor year and loses money, it will still meet payroll, pay the workers' benefits, and not close its doors on short notice. On the other hand, the entrepreneur is faced with a substantially different situation. When starting a business, it takes time for the business to reach a level where the revenue coming into the firm is sufficient to cover expenses. (We examine this in significant detail in Chapter 6; the point where the revenue coming into the firm is sufficient to cover expenses is referred to as a **break-even point**.) However, the new business may quickly reach a point where the funds have run out and the business needs to close its doors quickly. If the business does close, then the entrepreneurs may find that they have to pay the debts of the firm that are left, as they had to sign personal guarantees for the loans of the business. Thus, the financial risk for the entrepreneur can be quite high. As a potential entrepreneur, you will need to consider how much debt you are willing to take on. In general, the greater the debt you are willing to take on to start your business, the higher your risk tolerance.

Evel Knievel has become a cultural reference point for risk taking. An interesting counterpoint to this image was Knievel's very vocal stand against the risks associated with taking drugs. This dichotomy illustrates that risk levels can vary, even within the same person.
©Ralph Crane/The Life Picture Collection/Getty Images

Potential new business owners need to determine their personal willingness to accept risk in a new business and let that information help decide which business to pursue.[5] There is not one correct answer as to what level of risk tolerance new business owners should be willing to take on. Instead, the key is that individual entrepreneurs must be aware of their tolerance of risk and establish their business in a manner that is consistent with that tolerance. New business owners need to be sure that the level of risk is consistent with their background, values, and family situation. Evaluation of the risk profile for a particular type of business is more art than science.

One well-known entrepreneur provides valuable advice on risk tolerance. He suggests that entrepreneurs never do anything that does not allow them to sleep at night. This rule of thumb can help businesspeople determine the risks with which they will be most comfortable. In future chapters we will return to the evaluation of risk as we look at specific risks, such as financial risks, strategic risks, and market retaliation risks.

EXERCISE 3

To help you determine your own tolerance for risk, answer the following questions.

1. How much debt would you be willing to undertake to provide a foundation for your business idea?
2. How much of your personal savings would you be willing to risk on your business idea?
3. If you were the recipient of a $100,000 inheritance, what portion would you be willing to invest in your business?

Given your answers to the above questions, how would you rate your financial risk tolerance?

Prior Experience

The second element of entrepreneurial orientation is prior experience. Every individual brings to a new business his or her own view of the world. This view of the world places boundaries on what a decision maker will consider as he or she makes decisions. These boundaries are set by experiences, history, culture, and family values, among other things. Boundaries help each of us make sense of the world. For example, in the United States, when you see a red octagonal sign at a corner, you typically assume it is a stop sign. You assume that it is a stop sign because of your history and experience.

However, if you were in another country, such an octagonal sign may not be a stop sign; it might be another highway warning. Our experiences, history, culture, and values not only help us interpret the world, but they also place boundaries on how we see that world. Thus, our experiences, history, culture, and values also establish what we consider to be both possible and practical. This is referred to as the individual's **bounded rationality**. It is the presence of bounded rationality that often leads young people to be pioneers in an area, as they are not limited by the restrictions of the past.

bounded rationality
Rational decision making that is constrained by the background and history of the person making the decision.

Bounded rationality is the reason individuals from outside an industry are able to establish a new business in a manner not previously considered. To illustrate, cattle processing historically was done by large, established firms in meat processing centers such as Chicago, Fort Worth, and Kansas City. The cattle were shipped there and processed by well-trained butchers from the moment of slaughter until they were ready for packaging. An entrepreneur had an idea for viewing the entire process differently. Rather than shipping cattle to a central location, why not process the cattle where they are raised? In addition, instead of hiring well-trained butchers, why not use individuals who make the same cut repeatedly, in an assembly-line manner? This new approach grew quickly, others copied the model, and today virtually all beef is processed this way. Those individuals who had grown up in the beef industry believed that cattle processing had to be done in a specific way. Others came from outside the industry and saw new ways to do things. Their analysis was not bounded by history in the industry.

In a similar vein we could consider the airline and industry maverick Southwest Airlines. Today it is a major employer, but it started as a new business with a few rented planes. At the time everyone in the airline industry believed that air travel was most efficiently handled with a hub and spoke system. That is, the planes would fly into a very large airport such as Chicago, Los Angeles, or Dallas Fort Worth (DFW) from all the airports in that region.

There are varying aspects to everyone's personalities. How might knowing your strengths and weaknesses impact business decisions?

©Ned Frisk/Blend Images LLC RF

Then, people from all of the feeder airports would be placed on the same flight to a given location. Southwest used a model that focused on many short-haul flights of less than an hour between airports. Herb Kelleher (one of the founders of Southwest) was trained as a lawyer and brought fresh insight on how to compete in the industry.

It is important for individuals to understand how their decision making is bounded by their own version of rationality. It is important to know your potential partners' backgrounds and how their decision making is impacted by their history. These issues will impact how you and your partners act both as you run the firm, and as you analyze problems that arise in the development of the business.

Personality Orientation of the Individual

The third element of entrepreneurial orientation is an examination of your own personality. There is a wide variety of personality tests available to assist individuals in analyzing their traits and tendencies. These tests should not be used, however, to determine whether you are capable of starting a new business. There are successful businesspeople in all personality categories. In general, you as an individual will probably score differently on the same test if you take it on different occasions.

Therefore, use these tests to help better understand yourself and your strengths, not as a guide for your career. In general, if you are very outgoing and extroverted, you may wish to focus on a business in which you have extensive interpersonal interactions. In contrast, if you are more introverted, you may wish to focus on a business, such as an Internet-based business, in which interpersonal interactions are more limited. In this section, we review some of the major personality tests that are available. If you enter the names of these tests into a search engine, you will find that there are numerous versions of the tests available online, often for free. We want to stress here again that a start-up demands frequent change and adaptation. Below we will highlight some of the more established and validated personality tests all of which you can take online.

Myers-Briggs. This is one of the most widely used tests for personality evaluations. It was developed by Katherine Briggs and her daughter Isabel Myers. The rationale for the test is drawn from Carl Jung, a Swiss psychoanalyst who sought to incorporate broader issues into his analysis than had Freud. The test focuses on four pairs of variables: extroversion-introversion (focus on outward world or internal); sensing-intuiting (how people gather information); thinking-feeling (how they make decisions); and judgment-perception (order vs. flexibility). The different potential arrangements of variables are believed to indicate the different ways that individuals deal with other people and their environments.

Enneagram. The underlying philosophy of this test is that a person is the result of all the experiences in his or her life. Thus, the factors in childhood are central in developing who we are today. A bias in this test is that adults will not change their personality over time as the assumption is that we form that personality as a child.

The test suggests that there are nine different types of personalities. Through a series of questions, the test assigns you to one of these primary types. These nine types and a few of the characteristics of each type of individual are as follows: reformer (idealist/perfectionist); helper (caring/good interpersonal skills); achiever (competent/driven); individualist (sensitive/dramatic); investigator (cerebral/focused); loyalist (committed/pessimistic); enthusiast (fun-loving/impatient); challenger (action oriented/cynical); and peacemaker (easygoing/passive aggressive).

Big Five Test. The Big Five is a popular personality test in universities. It is composed of five factors: open-mindedness, conscientiousness, agreeableness, emotional stability, and extroversion (the factor names vary a little among authors). These are considered by many researchers to be the five key components of an individual's personality.

The Big Five test was developed by two independent research teams. These researchers asked thousands of people hundreds of questions and then analyzed the data statistically. The researchers did not set out to identify the five factors; instead, the factors emerged from their analyses of the data.

ETHICAL CHALLENGE

One of the important choices that everyone has to deal with is what they may take with them when they leave a company. This becomes more critical when the person leaving is starting their own new business. Whether it is voluntary or involuntary, leaving a job can be frustrating, and sometimes individuals are frustrated enough to wish to do harm to the firm they are leaving. Beyond that, there is a question as to where the line between personal and business information exists. If the person leaving does something that harms the prior business, then the prior employer may be able to sue the former employee. The impact of such a lawsuit on a fledgling business can be substantial.

To illustrate, consider an employee who has worked for a large plumbing or electrical firm. In his former position, this employee had the opportunity to obtain the firm's customer list. However, if he takes that list and uses it to generate a customer base for the new business, the former employer might be able to sue the new business for the revenue lost.

There is a broader question that an entrepreneur must also consider—if you know you are leaving your current employer to start your own business, is it fair to your employer to do so while still being paid by your employer? Even though the budding entrepreneur may not consciously plan to take customers from the employer, how significant are those contacts to the future business? At what stage does such a setting cross an ethical line?

QUESTIONS

1. What are some ways you can build a customer base when you leave a business without running into problems with your former employer?
2. Beyond the customer list, what other things could you potentially take from a firm that would present an ethical problem?

LO2-3

List the triggers that encourage new business formations.

Triggers for Starting a Business

Starting a new business is often the result of some particular event or condition within an individual's environment. These triggers encourage the forming of new businesses, as they encourage individuals to think creatively. Individuals get comfortable with their lives, and it takes a trigger to force them to think in new ways. You may not be faced with such triggers as motivations, and still decide to start a new business. However, many people do start their businesses when one of these triggers is present, and therefore, it is useful for you to understand them. The triggers in the formation of a new business can come from either positive or negative stimulus that occurs in an individual's life. Some typical triggers include the following:

1. Being laid off from established employment.
2. Being approached by one or more people with a new business idea.
3. Reaching a point financially where the risk–return level of a proposed new business is tolerable.
4. Having very little to lose financially by a failure.
5. Receiving evidence that an idea is not only doable, but there is a concrete way to address a given problem.
6. Being spurred to action by attending a seminar, reading a book, or talking with successful entrepreneurs.
7. Experiencing a midlife (or early-life, or even late-life) crisis.
8. Observing the establishment of an incubator, accelerator, or business development effort within the community.
9. Experiencing the inability to climb the corporate ladder due to circumstances beyond one's control. These might include not having graduated from the "correct" school, being female in a male-dominated business, and having a marketing background in a manufacturing business.
10. Graduaing from college you may also see new opportunities that others have not seen. Today more so than any time in the history of the United States starting a business from college is seen as highly possible.

Often, more than one of these triggers may be present at the same time. For discussion purposes, we segment these triggers into two categories: personal motivations and circumstance motivations. Although the exact dividing line between these two categories is somewhat fuzzy, this categorization will allow for the examination of the various issues involved in starting a business.

Personal motivations come from the individuals themselves and as such are the strongest motivations available. Personal motivations drive people to make career and life-altering moves irrespective of "practical" advice. Entrepreneurs driven by personal motivators will tend to be more proactive and drive relentlessly toward their goals.

Circumstance motivators tend to result in more of a defensive positioning. The environment and environmental changes make opportunities available to potential business owners, but the motivation is substantially different. This is an opportunistic start-up whose staying power is more determined by other competing opportunities.

To illustrate personal triggers, consider that today one of the fastest-growing groups of entrepreneurs are women. In large part, women are starting new businesses when their career opportunities are blocked at larger corporations. As noted in Chapter 1, this barrier is generally referred to as the "glass ceiling." It involves not formal rules, but the practical reality that in some organizations there are limits to the level in the corporate hierarchy to which women are allowed to progress. If you question the presence of such ceilings, simply note how many women are in senior management positions at most major corporations. The result is that women-led businesses are formed at a rate 50 percent greater than that of men-led businesses. A particularly fast-growing segment of entrepreneurs are minority women owners; today more than one-third of all female businesses are headed by women of color.[6]

Human nature is such that most people get comfortable with their current status and financial position. When they are laid off, are demoted, are forced to take reduced pay, or even survive a layoff, they are forced to think about new opportunities that they never would have considered previously. As we pointed out in Chapter 1, research has found that when a factory or military base closes, there is a blossoming of new businesses in that area.[7]

Our opening story of Kosher Home Health illustrates how personal and circumstance motivations merge to encourage an entrepreneur. For Kosher Home one of the entrepreneurs wanted to aid individuals following the same religion. But in every new business, each entrepreneur will have their motivation that drives them. These motivations can include more flexibility with their families, living in a region they want, better control of their lives, or improving their standard of living. The key is that entrepreneurship empowers a person to change their life in the way they desire.

Supports

LO2-4

Compare and contrast various types of new business supports.

This chapter focuses on the individual who starts the business. It has been stressed in the chapter that this individual, and his or her leadership, is central to the entrepreneurial firm's success. Generally, the founder is far more important than a single individual in a large firm.

This does not mean that an individual, or team of individuals, creates a successful business without help. There are supports and resources available to the entrepreneur. No one of these supports or resources assures success, but the new businessperson should evaluate which resources and supports he or she has access to in an effort to increase the chances of success.

The supports and resources available are typically unique to the entrepreneur and where he or she lives. Not all individuals come to the process of founding the business with equal endowments or supports. The entrepreneur should seek to understand all the supports possible to make the entrepreneurial effort successful. The support and resource areas the entrepreneur might examine include (1) family, (2) social networks, (3) community, and (4) financial resources.

Family

Few people know you—including both your abilities and shortcomings—like your family. These individuals are a resource for support, guidance, suggestions, and potential funding for a new business. A spouse who is willing to handle the financial burden while you begin a new venture, a parent who will contribute time and money, an uncle who has been in the industry and is willing to review your plan and advise you so that you might avoid basic pitfalls are all immensely valuable to the new entrepreneur. We advise potential new entrepreneurs to work with their family members not only for their advice and potential funding but also

Like a classic architecture, a solid business is built upon a variety of support systems.

©Carson Ganci/Design Pics RF

as a reality check and support structure. Family members are in a unique position to provide you with key insights when you may be pursuing the wrong approach to an issue. Too many other individuals will not be willing to tell you when you may be wrong. Most individuals will tell you only positive things. In addition, you will need your family's support to push you forward to success, as there will be times that you will have to deal with significant discouragements.

To fully utilize your family resources, we suggest you list those family members with whom you have regular contact, and also list the capabilities those individuals possess that might provide support to the new business. The benefit of such an activity is that it will allow you as a new business founder to think systematically through the items that need to be discussed with various family members. You need to make sure you obtain the resources desired from family members without wasting the time and effort of these individuals.

The role of family is so critical to the success of a new business that many new ventures end up being what are referred to as family businesses. In such firms, the principal staff members of the business are family members. There may be other employees in the firm, but typically, family members hold the key managerial decision-making positions.

The long-term management of family businesses is unique when compared to that of nonfamily-owned businesses. In the initial stages of formation, the support of the family can help the entrepreneur overcome many difficulties that might cause the failure of nonfamily-supported new businesses. For example, when family members are the principal staff, a month in which payroll cannot fully be met by the company is more acceptable. These individuals' level of commitment to the founder may be high enough that they are willing to take only a partial or no salary that month. These individuals also are often willing to work at times and in conditions that other employees would not accept. For example, Christmas season is critical to all retailers, but paid staff may not be willing to work the extra hours needed at this time, whereas family will. It is this level of commitment that has produced success for many immigrant families. In these settings, the reliance on family is a key reason the firms are able to survive and prosper.

However, there are also potential negative long-term issues that accompany a family business. While family members have a greater commitment to you as an entrepreneur because of your close relationships, those close relationships make issues such as firing family members difficult. If a family member is not a good employee, how will you fire that person, or even reprimand them, without rupturing the close relationships in the family? One business founder who did fire a relative described Thanksgiving that year as horrible and silent. Similarly, since family members know each other so well, they are willing to say negative things to an entrepreneur that a regular employee would never say. These negative statements may have no connection to work but might be issues that are simmering in the family. The negative comments can be particularly caustic in the firm because the owner may be hesitant to fire the family member, and the situation can eventually rupture all relationships with the individual and other extended family members. Finally, the presence of family in the firm can cause difficulties with other employees who are not family members. As will be discussed in Chapter 10, human resource management is one of the most important and contentious issues in a firm. Unfortunately, if it appears there are different expectations and rewards for workers depending on whether they are related to you, it can cause turmoil among employees and make holding onto key nonfamily employees all the more difficult.

Family is usually an important resource for a new business. The new entrepreneur needs to consider the balance of benefits and drawbacks to building a family-based business.

Networks

Beyond your family, another key support is the network of individuals in your life. These networks may be formed from former employers, individuals you know from a fraternal organization such as the Rotary Club, friends at school, or individuals you know from another organization including a church or synagogue. Individuals in your network can be particularly helpful in providing some legitimacy to your business, in addition to providing feedback and advice to you.

There is a rich pool of resources for networking online. For example, many communities have formed blogs and chat rooms aimed at individuals interested in forming local businesses. These online communities can be a rich source of advice on forming a business and potential sources of funding. There are also numerous crowd sourcing sites including Kickstarter.com and Crowdfunder.com. These websites allow a firm to reach out to a wide community online to get funding and often advice in the process of raising those funds.[8]

To illustrate, a start-up manufacturing business would be considered high risk until it developed a steady flow of customers and revenue. Established businesses are often hesitant to buy from a start-up business, because it is not clear if the new business will be able to fulfill an order or service the product in the future. Thus, many firms will initially buy only small amounts from a new business in an effort to observe the quality and reliability of the new firm. Similar effects are also experienced with suppliers, such that the new firm may not be able to obtain credit from a supplier for some time. Only after a history of prompt payment is built up might the supplier allow the new business to carry credit. A network can help overcome some of these debilitating issues early in the life of the business by providing a level of legitimacy. Support from companies in your network cannot only provide revenue but can also help to indicate to others your seriousness and staying power.

As noted previously we will follow two small firms throughout the text to illustrate the concepts in the text. The first one we have looked at is Kosher Home. The second firm we will follow in each chapter is YrFurn app.

Community

There are also more formal community supports that can lower the overall risk for a new business in the community.[9] For example, many communities have business **incubators**[10] that house new businesses and provide many critical services for the entrepreneurial businesses. An incubator will typically provide all of the office machines, basic furniture, Internet connections, telephones, fax, copying equipment, and maintenance necessary for a business to begin operations. As we have noted, one of the difficulties for a new business is the establishment of some level of legitimacy. Those businesses that look as if they are ongoing businesses may have more opportunities. Most new businesses cannot afford a receptionist, whereas in a business incubator there is a common receptionist. This individual is typically trained to answer phone calls from a central location, using the firm's own name. The impression made by such simple things can be significant. In contrast to an answering machine, the ability to have a message taken by a receptionist can help build credibility.

incubator
A facility that houses new businesses and provides many critical services for the new ventures. New businesses are expected to develop and typically leave the facility often within 18 months of founding.

A business incubator also offers its space to tenant firms at subsidized rates in order to stabilize cash flow. There are professionals such as accountants and lawyers available to help the new businesses. Local community leaders hope that all this aid will lead to businesses that are more likely to succeed than unsupported new business start-ups. Thus, if an entrepreneur can locate the business in an incubator, then the firm's risk of failure drops. Business incubators work best with office-based service firms, scientific-based firms requiring lab space, or small, clean manufacturing firms. Clearly, a business incubator cannot effectively house a restaurant: A restaurant needs to be located somewhere near a flow of people. However, even for such a firm there

YRFURN—AN APP FOR FURNITURE*

Kyle Moon, Brad Rossy, and Brandy Jeffer spent two years working together in teams in various classes during their MBA program. Over that time the three continued to talk about starting a new business rather than going to work for someone else when they graduated. Kyle and Brandy had over three years of experience each in technology firms in the Silicon Valley prior to starting their MBA. The two were well versed in the agile methodology known as Scrum and felt that it along with what they knew about developing a lean start-up positioned them well. Agile approaches have become the go-to means for programming. It involves short sprints of work designed to produce rapid, small changes for customers rather than big annual releases of new software that incorporate thousands of changes. Brad brought a different set of skills with his five years of experience working at a firm on Wall Street.

As a part of their entrepreneurship class, the three students explored creating a business that was strictly a software as a service (SaaS) firm. That is a firm that has no physical product. Consumers purchase and use the software via the cloud. They liked the ability that approach provided them to scale the business quickly, and keep fixed expenses low and did not require a customer-friendly physical location. They were all three particularly fascinated by the camera capability of the newer smart phones and they looked for an opportunity to solve a "pain" for customers using that capability.

As they bounced around ideas they rapidly focused on the furniture industry and more specifically the U.S. retail furniture industry. What they found was an arcane industry that had not changed very much in 200+ years. There were new businesses starting to impact the industry by providing customers the ability to customize their furniture and have it delivered. This threat had finally started to move the established industry into considering changes to their established model.

To this day most furniture in the United States is purchased by consumers who travel to a showroom usually armed with the dimensions of the room that they are trying to furnish. They try to imagine how the furniture will look in their place, buy the furniture, and then wait for it to be delivered. Only then do they really know how it looks and whether it works. There had to be a better way.

The three came up with a concept for a two-way app that would solve the problem, they thought the app would be welcomed by the retailers as it would help serve customers better and also be welcomed by consumers since it would make buying furniture easier. The customer would take pictures of their room from two to three angles (like they were selling their house). The app would allow the customer to remove any furniture in the room that was being replaced. Once at the store, the customer could take a picture of any furniture, and it would be superimposed in exact dimensions on the picture of the customer's room. Customers and salespeople could evaluate how it would look and make changes while in the showroom.

The group decided that the idea was so good and had so much potential that they did not pitch it in their entrepreneurship class. They used the class to learn how to develop a business with another average idea. During their last semester, they went to work developing the business model.

After the class the students decided they would like to pursue the venture. Each of the partners had saved up quite a bit of money and was willing to invest $100,000 each to the venture. The three friends realized that this would not be sufficient and were open to bringing in investors when the time was right. There were a lot of things to do over the next few months if this was going to be a reality, but the team was truly excited about the business. They all agreed and decided to take the plunge and YrFurn was born.

QUESTION

1. What are the risks and benefits to the team of focusing on an app versus a traditional business like a restaurant?

*The names and some details have been changed in this running case. We will use this case throughout the text to illustrate concepts raised in each chapter and how this particular firm addressed them as they built the business.

are still supports available. In most communities there are **Small Business Assistance Centers**. These centers are funded by the Small Business Administration and advise individuals who intend to start new businesses. The supports vary widely but usually include research aids such as information on funding sources in the area for new businesses. There are other services available, such as counseling provided by SCORE. SCORE, previously known as the Service Corps of Retired Executives is now recognized as SCORE, Counselors to America's Small Business. Both working and retired business professionals voluntarily work with new businesses as advisors on a wide range of issues. Still other supports are available at centers tailored to aid women or minority entrepreneurs. One specialized program is the Minority Enterprise Development Program. There are also programs targeted to veterans or those firms that are geared to export.

Small Business Assistance Centers
Centers funded by the Small Business Administration that provide free advice to individuals wishing to start new businesses.

Each community has its own unique set of resources. The federal government provides some of the funds, but it encourages the local administrators and government entities to tailor the services to what is needed locally. Therefore, each potential entrepreneur needs to survey what services are available. A quick look online for local economic development will provide a strong list of these services. The potential entrepreneur would be well served to take an hour or two to visit the offices identified and obtain information about their services. The potential entrepreneur should also ask these entities for leads on other agencies that have services for the start-up business. Almost all such agencies work with each other and want entrepreneurs to take advantage of all resources available, whether from them or from other agencies.

Financial Support

Another key element for a new business is the financial support it develops. The detailed evaluation of financial resources will be covered in Chapter 7 where we will examine the financing issues related to starting a firm. However, a few points need to be made briefly here. Potential entrepreneurs need to have a full understanding of the cost–benefit of the business.[11] In particular, the entrepreneur needs to account for the financial resources that may be required in starting and running a new business. It is simply good business practice to ensure that sufficient financial resources are available prior to the start of that business. It may be a waste of effort to go forward if the goals of an individual are widely divergent from the financial resources that are available. The development of the new business is not "blue sky" thinking. The processes detailed in this book are a practical and applied effort to make this a reality.

From an individual evaluation of capability, nothing more is required at this point other than a realistic vision of what resources are needed and available. If, for instance, a potential entrepreneur is considering starting a restaurant, there needs to be recognition that the equipment and setup for even a very small, modest carry-out restaurant may exceed $150,000. This cost goes up dramatically if the potential entrepreneur buys new equipment. If used equipment is purchased, that cost can be cut by over half depending on the

EXERCISE 4

Using the chart below, begin to fill in the supports and resources you might be able to call on. Describe briefly the support and resource that you list. Fill in the chart as much as you can now.

CATEGORY	SOURCE	DESCRIPTION
Family		
Network		
Community		
Financial		

quality of what is obtained. Regardless of the type of business contemplated, it is critical that the entrepreneur be able to fund that business or obtain the necessary funding. Therefore, the potential entrepreneur needs to have a broad understanding of what financial resources are available and a realistic idea of what will be needed to expend. Chapter 6, entitled "Analyzing Cash Flow and Other Financial Information," devotes an entire section to this exact issue.

LO2-5

Explain how you can evaluate those things that you enjoy the most and discover how they may lead to business opportunities.

Form a Business Doing What You Like

This chapter has emphasized that new businesses are so often successful because the entrepreneur both owns and runs the business. You bring to the business a focus that simply does not exist in large businesses. You also bring unique supports that can help make the venture successful. Ultimately, the greatest contributor to your success is that you are doing something you enjoy.

An entrepreneur will need to spend considerable time at the business for it to be successful.[12] In fact, the entrepreneur will likely spend more time starting and running the business than doing anything else in life. Consider that in a typical day you have 24 hours, out of which you might typically sleep 7 hours. If you work 8 to 10 hours at a minimum in a business for five days, plus half a day each weekend, you will be spending the greatest amount of your time either sleeping or working. You need to enjoy what you do. If you do not enjoy weather extremes, do not seek to establish a heating and air-conditioning business that requires you to work on broken air conditioners and heaters (which always seem to need repair in the extremes of weather). If you do not enjoy working with people, do not establish a retail shop where you must work with the wide variety of individuals who walk in the door. On the other hand, if you like people and find conversation easy, a retail business would make much more sense than an Internet business where you see very few people and primarily work alone. It is quite possible for someone to see great potential in a new business idea; however, if the new business is not something that the entrepreneur has a passion for, history suggests that the business is not likely to be successful.

Positions in the retail industry are very social. The more workers can make conversation with potential customers often times more sales opportunities can result.

©Digital Vision/Getty Images RF

If you are considering starting a business you also need to clearly recognize the trade-off between the time commitment and the return you expect. While clearly part of the equation, the time–reward relationship in a new business involves more than simply financial reward. We will deal more with profitability as we consider the finances of the firm in Chapters 6 to 8. However, your time is your most valuable asset and should be treated as such. This text is designed to help you think through the start-up business process in a formal manner and provide you with the tools necessary to be successful.

EXERCISE 5

1. List up to five businesses you potentially could happily work at every day.
2. List up to five businesses you potentially would not enjoy running every day.

SUMMARY

The most critical resource in a new venture is the entrepreneur or entrepreneurial team. The founder(s) are the reason that a new business is so successful. In forming a start-up, the entrepreneur's choice of business needs to be consistent with his or her own individual risk tolerances. The entrepreneur also needs to be aware that one's own biases and bounded rationality will shape the interpretation of opportunities.

The thought process associated with developing the new business needs to be consistent with the actual resources that are present. The process of developing the business is both time consuming and rewarding. There are many supports available to anyone wishing to pursue this course of action in business. The potential entrepreneur should look to family, networks, and communities for assistance and honest feedback.

KEY TERMS

agency theory 25
bounded rationality 27
break-even point 26
family business 22
incubator 33
organizational slack 22
Small Business Assistance Centers 35

REVIEW QUESTIONS

1. How does the lack of "slack" resources impact new ventures?
2. Why is founder involvement in a new venture so critical to its success?
3. Is there some minimum level of risk tolerance required to start a business? Explain.
4. How does bounded rationality affect the way an entrepreneur determines what type of business to start?
5. How do you think personality differences matter in the starting of a business?
6. List some triggers that push people into starting a new business.
7. Have you experienced any of these triggers? Did it cause you to consider starting your own business?
8. Which supports do you believe you might rely on the most if you started your own business?

BUSINESS PLAN DEVELOPMENT QUESTIONS

1. How would you evaluate risk tolerance?
2. What is your risk tolerance? Why?
3. Have you formed a team before in a class or other setting? What criteria did you use?
4. If you have not formed a team, what are the criteria you think you should rely on? Are the criteria for the class teams in questions 3 and 4 the same you would use for your business teams?
5. What are your supports that you can call on for your business plan?
6. If you have a team for your business, are there gaps in the support you can call on?
7. Does your community have a business incubator? If so, what are the admission criteria?
8. How would the personality tests results you get online affect your choice of a partner or employee?

INDIVIDUAL EXERCISES

1. Individually list up to five businesses at which you could happily work every day.
2. Do the same thing for five businesses for which you would not enjoy working every day.
3. How do your personal interests impact these choices?
4. Do you think the criteria you used to decide to work for a particular business would be the same for starting a business?
5. How would these commonalities and differences affect your decision to start a business?

GROUP EXERCISES

We discuss family businesses extensively in the chapter in terms of entrepreneurial businesses. It is estimated that up to 25 percent of the Fortune 500 are family businesses. These are organizations in which a single family owns a high enough percentage of the firm's stock to have control of the business: Control can be maintained with ownership of as little as 5 percent of the shares. How do you think family-owned corporations differ from more typical corporations? Do you think these same differences apply in entrepreneurial firms?

ENDNOTES

1. C. B. Schoonhoven and K. M. Eisenhardt, "Speeding Products to Market: Waiting Time to First Product Introduction in New Firms," *Administrative Science Quarterly* 35 (1990), pp. 177–208.
2. F. K. Pil and M. Holweg, "Exploring Scale: The Advantages of Thinking Small," *MIT Sloan Management Review* 44, no. 2 (2003), pp. 33–40.
3. J. J. Chrisman, J. H. Chua, and R. A. Litz, "Comparing the Agency Costs of Family and Non-Family Firms: Conceptual Issues and Exploratory Evidence," *Entrepreneurship Theory & Practice* 28 (2004), pp. 335–55.
4. J. E. Grable and R. H. Lytton, "The Development of a Risk-Assessment Instrument: A Follow-Up Study," *Financial Services Review* 12 (2003), pp. 257–75.
5. C. Penttila, "Risky Business," *Entrepreneur* 36, no. 11 (2008), pp. 17–18.
6. American Express report, "The 2016 State of Women-Owned Businesses Report."
7. R. D. Atkinson, "The Impact of the Defense Build-Down on State and Local Economies," *Economic Development Review* 10, no. 4 (Fall 1992), pp. 55–59.
8. N. F. Taylor, "Crowdfunding for Startups: 10 Kickstarter Alternatives," *Business News Daily*, August 19, 2015. http://www.businessnewsdaily.com/4847-crowdfunding-small-business.html#sthash.u6iX9IzE.dpuf.
9. H. M. Neck, G. D. Meyer, B. Cohen, and A. C. Corbett, "An Entrepreneurial System View of New Venture Creation," *Journal of Small Business Management* 42 (2004), pp. 190–209.
10. P. D. Hannon and P. Chaplin, "Are Incubators Good for Business? Understanding Incubator Practice—The Challenge for Policy," *Environment & Planning: Government & Policy* 21 (2003), pp. 861–82.
11. K. Jones and R. Tullous, "Behaviors of Pre-Venture Entrepreneurs and Perceptions of Their Financial Needs," *Journal of Small Business Management* 40 (2002), pp. 233–49.
12. H. H. Beam and T. A. Carey, "Could You Succeed in Small Business?" *Business Horizons* 32, no. 5 (1989), pp. 65–70.

chapter

3

Business Idea Generation and Initial Evaluation

learning objectives

After studying this chapter, you will be able to:

LO3-1 Describe a systematic means for examining skills in order to generate new business ideas.

LO3-2 Discuss the elements of opportunity analysis.

LO3-3 Analyze how to choose a business.

UBER CHANGES THE BUSINESS

UberCab was founded in San Francisco in 2009 as a means of connecting for-hire drivers with potential passengers. Using a mobile platform, the company connects people needing a ride with those offering rides. The system is more efficient than calling a single cab company and more on-demand-oriented than hiring a traditional limo. The application was an instant success and the name was quickly changed to *Uber* when the company purchased the website Uber.com. Uber takes 20 percent of the charge for the ride and handles the financial transaction via their mobile platform.

The founders of the business are Travis Kalanick and Garret Camp. The company started with no employees and a shoestring budget. The first prototype was developed, and the app was launched in San Francisco in 2010.

Since its inception, the business has quickly grown to more than 66 countries around the world. Uber allows drivers who are not employed or even certified by the company to use their own vehicles to pick up passengers. This business model has generated some problems for the company. For example, a class-action lawsuit was filed against the companies by taxi drivers who claim that Uber is stealing their tips. Cities have also tried to shut down the service by claiming that Uber is skirting their taxicab laws. In Paris, cabbies who were on strike slashed tires and smashed windows of cars working with Uber. In 2014, an Uber-arranged ride resulted in an accident in which a 6-year-old girl was killed. The company was sued for wrongful death.

The company started as an entrepreneurial venture but has now grown into a venture-backed company with reported revenues in 2013 of over $125 million. Uber was born from an idea to better address the needs of both drivers (who want to maximize the number of rides for hire per day) and passengers (who don't want to wait for a taxi to pull over or arrange a ride ahead of time) using technology that is now in the hands of virtually everyone. Today the firm remains private.

Questions

1. Uber entered an entrenched industry using mobile technology. What other applications for this technology do you see in the personal transportation industry?
2. Why haven't the established cab and limo companies adopted these approaches?

Sources: E. Griffith, "The Uber Effect: The Hot Startup's Early Investors Are In-Demand," *CNN Money*, February 4, 2014, http://fortune.com/2014/02/04/the-uber-effect-the-hot-startups-early-investors-are-in-demand/; J. Brustein, "Uber Explains Why $35 a Mile Is the Right Price," *Bloomberg Businessweek*, December 17, 2013, https://www.bloomberg.com/news/articles/2013-12-17/ubers-travis-kalanick-explains-the-car-services-surge-pricing; J. Brustein, "Uber's Workforce Is Built to Do More Than Chauffeur," *Bloomberg Businessweek*, December 11, 2013, https://www.bloomberg.com/news/articles/2013-12-11/ubers-workforce-is-built-to-do-more-than-chauffeur; D. Streitfeld, "As It Shakes Up the Taxi Business, Uber's a Target," *The Boston Globe*, January 27, 2014; C. Matlack, "Paris Cabbies Slash Tires, Smash Windshields in Protest Against Uber," *Bloomberg Businessweek*, January 13, 2014, https://www.bloomberg.com/news/articles/2014-01-13/paris-cabbies-slash-tires-smash-windshields-in-protest-against-uber; N. Scheiber, "How Uber Drivers Decide How Long to Work," *The New York Times*, September 4, 2016, https://www.nytimes.com/2016/09/05/business/economy/how-uber-drivers-decide-how-long-to-work.html?_r=0

KOSHER HOME

Toby and Jack had previously determined that they wanted to start a business and that they had a similar propensity for risk taking, as discussed in Chapter 2. It was clear to Ellen, Jack, and Toby that Ellen was not as good of a fit, so she decided to pursue graduate school instead and wished the two entrepreneurs good luck.

Even though the two entrepreneurs wanted to start an Internet food business focused on kosher food, they were not sure of the dimensions of the potential business. Kosher food must conform to the regulations of *kashrut* of the Jewish dietary law. The partners would discuss the specifics of such food preparation later as they examine operations. But as they started, they knew to keep Kosher at home was challenging. For the business, they would need separate kitchens with separate refrigerators, prep stations, etc., for meat and dairy. It would be preferable, in fact, that these two kitchens had a wall in between them. They would also need a mashgiach, or a person (often a rabbi) who would certify that everything they did was kosher. Often such a person would make occasional inspections like the FDA, but they realized that they may need one on staff. They would also need kosher delivery trucks. Basically, every step of the production and distribution process had to be overseen for compliance with kashrut. Their goal was to generate a product that could be certified as kosher by the Orthodox Union (the biggest kashrut certifying agency) standards.

Beyond the cost, the potential partners knew there was a very high failure rate among entrepreneurial businesses, so they wanted to be sure to examine their business ideas carefully so that this would not be one of the failures. Therefore, they visited a successful entrepreneur in their area. This successful entrepreneur gave Toby and Jack some general ideas about the key issues in starting a new business and suggested that the two of them needed to conduct an audit of them to better understand what type of focus the business might need. This audit would help them to determine their views on a number of topics. The successful entrepreneur suggested that the audit include questions such as:

1. What skills did they have that would fit with the new business?
2. What was their expertise that related specifically to the business they wanted to start—either food or Internet?
3. What things about the Internet food industry did the two really like?
4. What did they want to achieve with a new business?

The two budding entrepreneurs initially answered these questions separately and then summarized their answers as follows:

	JACK	TOBY
Skills	Marketing major	Computer science major
Experience	• Keep Kosher at home. • Understood isolated Jewish community and challenges faced. • Worked for start-up that had just graduated from an incubator. The company provided hospital supplies to veteran-related health care facilities.	• Web design (it was a small venture Toby ran out of his dorm room but never registered it formally.) • Working more recently as a technical employee of an Internet B2B firm that was relatively young and provided industrial inputs in a chemical-related business. • While Jewish it should be noted that Toby was not observant.
Industry Preference	Helped others in faith to be more observant. The food-related Internet business was a route to a social value that he believed in very much.	Internet business that he felt was the future for business.

(continued)

	JACK	TOBY
Achieve	Personal happiness most important with financial achievement a distant second.	Financial achievement first and only.

This exercise was valuable for Jack and Toby. They shared many values and had similar backgrounds. They both wanted to make money in their venture, but their priorities were different. They both had some experience with start-ups, so they both understood to some degree the challenge they were undertaking.

However, there were also many differences between the two, including one of them being relatively observant, while the other was not in any real sense. Perhaps more important to them was that while it was clear that the two had differences, they also complemented each other very well. Jack was more into marketing and external aspects, while Toby was more interested in the internal and technical aspects of the business. The religious component of the business appealed to both men. Through this exercise, they had a clearer vision of each other and their roles in the potential business.

QUESTION

1. Would you have added other audit questions for Jack and Toby? What would be those questions?

Individuals come to the decision to begin a new business from many different perspectives and backgrounds. From this widely diverse group of individuals come many successful business ideas. Research shows that successful new business ideas are not determined by who your parents are, your race, your gender, or your religion. Instead, quality ideas are a function of the creativity and thoughtfulness of the person or persons creating the business.

So how does someone come up with an idea for a new business? Among the most popular resources is the individual's professional background or hobbies. These are domains that the individual knows very well and where it is easier to see shortcomings in the current business offerings and needs that are not being meet. Great insight can also be gained from individuals that the entrepreneur respects or those who have been successful in founding a business. There are a wide variety of sources that can be called upon for ideas about potential businesses. In this chapter we identify a systematic way in which to generate a list of potential businesses. The initial steps in evaluating the viability of these ideas will also be presented as a key element in this process.

EXERCISE 1

1. Do you think the similarities and complimentary differences are enough for a successful business?
2. What fault lines do you think they should be aware as they go forward to prevent future problems?
3. Do you think there are other options they should pursue other than the one they identified?

Generating Business Ideas

LO3-1

Describe a systematic means for examining skills in order to generate new business ideas.

Even when individuals may determine that they want to open a new business, the exact type of business to open is much more difficult to determine. We encourage everyone, even individuals who feel that they firmly know which type of business they wish to open, to examine all options through the processes detailed in this chapter. We have found that potential new business owners often feel strongly about the type of business they wish to open and yet, upon a more systematic examination, move to an alternative idea. Frequently, they do find an opportunity in the market, but it may not be the exact business concept they initially conceived. Alternatively, they may conclude after their analysis that the business they conceptualized would not be successful. Therefore, rather than reacting in a knee-jerk manner to what appears to be an opportunity, or even worse, quickly dismissing a promising idea, an individual needs to make a rational evaluation of a business opportunity and its potential.[1]

As discussed in Chapter 2, the desire to own and operate a business is a first step in entrepreneurship—but what business might that be? The generation of business ideas is not something that occurs automatically. Rather, it is a process of identifying the skills of the potential founders, identifying opportunities in the market, matching the initial financial funding available, and then marrying these together into a business idea that interests the potential founders. As noted in Chapter 1, the establishment of a successful new business is challenging. The high demands placed upon everyone involved in the process necessitate that the founders truly enjoy what they are doing. The process presented below is intended to be an open one that considers passion and enjoyment as important elements to success.

While not a sequential formula, we would suggest the following approach to the development of a quality business idea.

- First, the potential founders should list and evaluate their own personal skill sets. These skills may arise from hobbies, current work, past work experience, personal values that are very important to the entrepreneur, and/or family history.
- Second, the potential founders should carefully analyze the market and look for a gap, or some need that is not being met effectively.
- Finally, the potential founders need to compare their ability to fill those gaps with the opportunity that seems to be available. We suggest that the best means to do this is the development of a chart (see Table 3.1) that allows for an open, systematic examination. We will look at each of these steps in more detail.

Skills Analysis

You might be asking yourself why we suggest starting with the skill set of the potential founders rather than an "opportunity" in the market? The fact is that there are literally millions of "opportunities" in a wide variety of fields, but without the requisite skill set, pursuing (or even considering) these opportunities is simply a frustrating exercise of wasted money and time.

There may be tremendous opportunities in the spa services or health food advising business. However, if a potential business owner had no skills in this area, then those supposed opportunities are of little use to the potential founders. Without the needed skills, the founders would be faced with not holding any advantage over competitors who have the necessary depth in the area. A founder or founding team must have not only the necessary skills but also a depth of understanding so that they can build a long-term advantage in the market; they need a **synergy** that connects skills, understanding, and a competitive advantage such that the sum of the parts is greater than the individual parts by themselves. Perhaps as important as the business owner's skills in a particular area is the need for the potential owner(s) to have interest in or passion for starting a business in that domain. We have found that founders without a passion for the business are not willing to devote the time and energy necessary for the business to be successful.

synergy
The connection between the entrepreneur's skills, understanding of an industry, and the ability to create a competitive advantage such that the sum of the parts of the new business is greater than the individual parts alone.

As we mentioned previously, skills come from a variety of areas and are relatively idiosyncratic to the individual. In general, skills are derived from our history, experience, and interests. Several specific areas that potential business owners might examine include hobbies, education, work experience, and family history.

Hobbies and Activities

We all pursue hobbies and activities because we love them. In these hobbies or activities, we develop skills specific to the hobbies or skills. The avid skier who opens up a ski shop, the distance runner who opens up a running store, the ham radio operator who becomes a radio equipment dealer are all examples of hobbies leading to a business. If there is a great passion associated with hobbies or activities, that passion can help the success of the new business. A rule of thumb in the founding of businesses has always been that the owner whose business is both a vocation and an avocation is difficult to beat. That person is willing to stick with the business through lean times and develop a following of fellow enthusiasts. A problem that can arise is that the "business" of running the business takes over at some point and time, and the entrepreneur does not enjoy the business like he or she once did. That problem is something we will address in later chapters.

Your hobbies can impact how you approach business ventures. Do you have any hobbies that might lend themselves to a solid business idea?

At this point the questions the potential business owner should probably ask include:

- What hobbies or activities do you pursue on an active, perhaps daily basis?
- What hobbies or activities have you pursued in any manner over your lifetime (whether or not you were serious about them)?
- What is it about your hobbies or activities that excites you?
- What were the specific skills that these hobbies or activities required?
- What have your experiences in the hobbies or activities taught you that could help others?
- What products and services did you use in these hobbies or activities?

Education

From the time we are very young, we are in learning mode. From primary school to whatever level of education we pursue, the knowledge gained provides a skill set that can be the basis of a new business. An opportunity that uses your education (formal or informal) is another source of a business. The technological skills developed during the entrepreneur's education can be particularly valuable.[2]

- What courses did you take that were particularly enjoyable?
- What courses did you take where the material came to you very easily?
- Have you attended any unusual education programs that gave you unique skills?
- Have you taken specialized training in any specific area?
- If you had to do it all over again, what areas of education would you pursue now?

Work Experience

Another source of skills for a new business comes from your work experience. Your work experience builds skills that can have direct applicability to the pursuit of a new business. In each job, individuals build up skills that they take with them when they start a new business.

- In what businesses have you worked?
- What skills were critical to the jobs you performed?

Your family can be a great help in developing a business. What are some of the risks and rewards that you associate with the idea of working with your family?

©Blend Images/Getty Images RF

- What positions have you held in business?
- In what areas would you be considered a type of expert?
- What did you *really* enjoy about the positions you have held?
- What frustrated you about the positions that you have held?
- When were you the most excited about your work?

Family

Family experiences are an often overlooked source of skills for a new business. As we are well aware, every family is unique. There are often things that you do with your family in which you develop expertise. Many times potential entrepreneurs overlook these family experiences as a source of knowledge and skills. Cooking with family members, tracing family history, working on the house or around your family property are all sources of knowledge that can grow into a new business opportunity. One of the authors regularly hires a guide when vacationing in Sedona, Arizona. This particular guide grew up hiking and exploring the Sedona area with his family. After working for the park service for many years, he decided to open his own tour operation. He takes individuals or very small groups on customized adventures in the area that cater to the desires of the customer. He turned his family passion into a business that has grown to include other guides and is a year-round operation. Your pursuits can similarly be the source of a unique skill set for a business.

- What is your family history with new business ventures?
- What types of travel and vacations does your family enjoy?
- What skill sets exist within your nuclear family?
- What are the financial resources of your extended family?
- Are there unique things your family does that others seem very interested in?
- What skills do you develop in your family activities?

Additional Skills

Beyond these categories, we suggest that you also ask yourself the following questions:

1. What are your top three personal skills?
2. What things do you like doing best each day, each week?
3. When you look back over the past year, what one or two things did you enjoy more than any others?
4. What are the magazines and books you read?
5. What are your three greatest accomplishments in life? What skills were involved in these accomplishments?
6. Do you enjoy working with people? Or would you prefer to be left alone to concentrate your efforts in a particular area?
7. In what industry (retail/wholesale/manufacturing/service) would you prefer to work?

YRFURN—AN APP FOR FURNITURE

Kyle, Brandy, and Brad were very excited about the potential for the new furniture app business but still didn't know if they could really make it work or whether it was really even a good idea. The three had researched the furniture industry originally for a class, but they realized they needed to go deeper. Therefore, they began to examine what furniture companies were doing technologically. What they found was that technology in the retail furniture industry was focused on (1) improving customer service after the sale, (2) making check-out easier at the store, (3) improving the websites for the firms, and (4) providing information to smartphones as a customer walked around a store. Only IKEA had the ability to show electronically a full room of furniture to a customer; however, it was a generic room where only the size of the room could be changed and was only shown with all Ikea furniture in the room.

Looking honestly at the team, the three recognized that while they had extensive knowledge of the technical side of the business, they did not know the furniture business at all. In fact, while all three had bought some furniture, it had been very ad hoc purchases. Brandy and Kyle had bought desk chairs at an office supply store, Brandy had purchased a filing cabinet at an IKEA store, and only Brad had purchased anything at a traditional furniture store (it was a bed). Therefore, they decided to examine some aspects of the industry before they committed to the idea. From their coursework, they knew this would require them to have a detailed knowledge of the customer who would use their app as well as the retail store that would need to be supportive of the app. The three also realized that stores themselves might end up being competitors if the team did not execute this business idea precisely or have buy in from the retailers.

Financially, the team's experience told them that the $300,000 that they could raise among themselves would not be sufficient to get the business up and running. In order to fully develop the app, craft together the promotional materials, implement a visibility strategy, and grow the business to the point that it was self-funding might take another $2 million. They were confident that they could each make enough money with part-time work to support themselves while the business developed, but the need for equity investors was going to come quickly since there would be a need for staff to develop the technology and promote it.

After weighing all the factors, the three decided that they would commit to starting the business.

QUESTIONS

1. Do you think the expertise of the entrepreneurial team gives them the background they need for the business?
2. How could they have had a better rounded team?

Clearly, the goal from all these questions is to explore the range of potential skills and abilities that each of us possesses. A few more questions can help you tailor your business to your unique skills and personality:

1. Do you prefer to work extensively with people or not? If not, you need to focus on a business that has minimal interpersonal demands (an Internet-based business or a business that performs tasks for other businesses by handling back-office operations, such as bookkeeping, billing, order fulfillment, etc.). If you thrive on people and have the corresponding skills, then a retail or service-oriented business may be ideal.
2. Do you have an intense detail orientation? If you are very detail oriented, then a business that is procedurally complex and involves managing a wide variety of details may be appropriate. Remember that there are many people and companies out there that will pay handsomely for someone to manage the details of life. For example, a supply company to large manufacturers that customizes a product on a wide variety of details might be appropriate. Another area might be project management. Alternatively, an individual who finds this level

of detail frustrating should pursue a business with a simpler or more forgiving business model.

3. Are you trained in the area in which you want to work? Your experience and educational skills will have a critical impact on the direction of the business. Someone may believe that there is a need for a computer repair shop in your part of the city. However, if the individual does not have the skills from either educational training or experience to do such repairs, it does little good to consider such a business. As a general rule, focus on what you know best.
4. How quickly and easily can you change? As noted earlier the quick adjustments needed using lean startup and evolution is often key in successfully starting a business. One opportunity may look promising, but as you investigate more it is not the opportunity for you. You have to ensure that you have the ability to pivot as you develop more insight into an industry and an opportunity.

What is clear from the questions above is that in this text we believe that the founder(s) of a business need to be intimately involved in the design, funding, and running of the new business. Although we sometimes read about individuals who like to claim they are "idea" people and plan simply to hire everyone needed to run the business, we would suggest that these individuals are not founders—they are bankers with vision. They are simply providing funding and the concept. Such a model might work for people with large amounts of money; however, this model is difficult to pursue successfully for most people. Therefore, in this text in general, and in this chapter in particular, we use the basic assumption that the founder will be intimately involved in the new business.

LO3-2

Discuss the elements of opportunity analysis.

Opportunity Identification

Once you have developed a list of your skills, abilities, and interests, the next step is to examine the marketplace for opportunities to use these in a business. The method that we use and recommend is a form of **gap analysis**. In such an analysis, individuals identify a gap or opportunity that exists between the demand for a product or service and the supply provided by firms in the market. It is then up to you to determine if you have the skills and abilities to fill that gap.

gap analysis
A relatively simple process of systematically examining the difference, or gap, between what is expected and what occurs. One type of gap analysis, called opportunity analysis, examines opportunities in the marketplace side-by-side with the individual's ability to address those gaps.

Potential Businesses

There are a variety of ways to identify gaps, or business opportunities, in the marketplace. These include the following:

1. Examining trends around the region, nation, or world that may not have reached your particular geographic location. Trends do not start uniformly. Notice that a number of regional coffee chains have developed significant businesses in specific cities throughout the United States. Some of these chains (especially those in the Midwest) were developed by their founders examining how firms such as Starbucks were achieving success in major cities on the coast. These businesses achieved a strong local position before the national firms could make significant investments in their local markets.
2. Interview and talk about opportunities with key successful entrepreneurs in the area. Most successful entrepreneurs have great ideas that have the potential to be successful given the right set of circumstances and people. From their own experiences, these individuals have a keen eye for what businesses are needed in an area. However, these individuals often have too much to do with their own businesses to pursue

new ventures themselves, so they are willing to share their insights. The result is that they are willing to advise new entrepreneurs, as well as to identify and perhaps fund such opportunities. In effect, they become mentors to new entrepreneurs.

3. Discuss potential businesses with family members. Your family members know your abilities and disposition. Furthermore, they are uniquely positioned to provide a much-needed honest perspective on your efforts. Particularly if any of these individuals have a small business of their own, they might be useful in the process of helping you decide which businesses are best suited to your particular set of skills.
4. Look for environmental changes that create opportunities that did not exist before. Significant regulatory changes create new openings in an industry that did not exist before that regulatory change. Consider all the changes associated with health care reform, for example. Regardless of what you think of the law, it has clearly changed the industrial setting in health care and created new opportunities that entrepreneurs can take advantage of.
5. **Brainstorming** with key entrepreneurs and family members can also be useful to the potential entrepreneur. Brainstorming is a creative process in which a group of individuals are brought together and asked to generate ideas related to a specific topic or problem, with little effort given to evaluating the true potential for those ideas. In this case, the scenario might be one where a group is provided information on the skill set of the founder and asked to generate a list of businesses that might be appropriate. The interaction within the group leads to a dynamic that can lead to new, innovative ideas. Such brainstorming sessions work well in informal groups. Think of friends or family gathering over a meal and talking in depth about the options that are available; this is brainstorming. Family or friends discussing a potential business together as they decide on a path to pursue is one such form of brainstorming.[3]

brainstorming
A creative process whereby a group of individuals are brought together and asked to generate ideas with little or no effort made to evaluate the potential for each idea rather the focus is to generate numerous ideas.

6. Take a look at the things that frustrate you and your family. Daily frustrations are an incredible source of ideas. How would you solve the frustration? What is it about the frustration that needs to be solved? You will find that you might have as many as a dozen daily frustrations that could be solved, but only a few that truly fit with your capabilities and interests. Most (if not all) needs in a developed society are currently being met. However, the degree, level, detail, efficiency, effectiveness, politeness, or access all provide means for improving the satisfaction of a particular need being met.
7. If the potential entrepreneur has an interest and skill set based in technology, one of our personal favorites for the generation of business ideas is the examination of patent files. Millions of patents exist and are maintained by the original inventors and have never been the subject of a commercial attempt. We recommend an examination of patent files (available at www.uspto.gov) to find several that interest the potential entrepreneur. We suggest that you contact the inventor (all of the contact information is included with the patent) to see if that individual would be willing to work exclusively with you in the development of a commercial business. We have worked with entrepreneurs who started with their interest area, found a set of patents that had not been developed into businesses, successfully contacted the inventors, and then based their business on those patents.

EXERCISE 2

1. Create a list of ideas.
2. Do any of these ideas strike you as particularly intriguing for your future business? Why?

LO3-3

Analyze how to choose a business.

Choosing a Business

The process of generating ideas is not something that is done in a single sitting. Instead, it is a process that takes time, interaction, consideration, evaluation, and iteration. These steps do not occur in a linear fashion but should occur in an interactive manner. For example, if a successful entrepreneur suggests a new business that seems to fit well with your skills, then an investigation into the opportunity may be warranted. In discussions with trusted friends and family, the idea will morph and be refined. As the business idea evolves you may realize that you need new skill sets to be successful. This might require including others on the founding team. As a result, the generation of ideas is truly a process that takes time and interaction. However, done well, this effort should lead to a list of three to five business ideas where the founders have the appropriate skills and there appears (at least on the surface level) to be an opportunity.

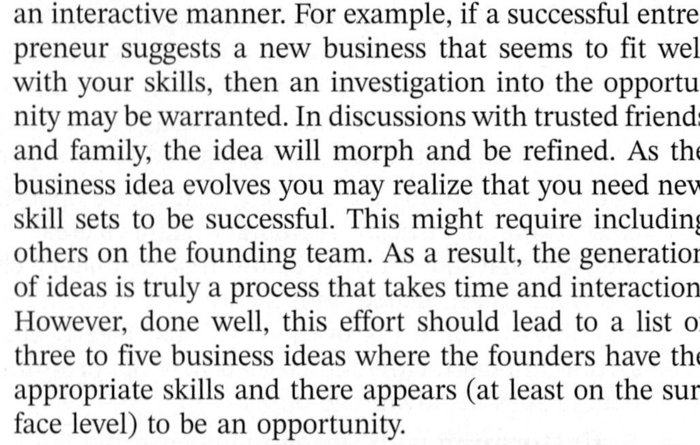

The generation of ideas along the way to selecting a business is a process that takes time and frequent interaction.

To illustrate, we worked with an entrepreneur who had strong retail experience. This individual enjoyed working with people and had great orientation to detail. Three opportunities were initially identified by the individual. First, several family members who operated a flower shop in another city were encouraging him to pursue a similar business in his city. These family members thought the potential entrepreneur had the skills for that business, and they could coach him in the business. Second, some experienced businesspeople that he knew identified a gap in the printing services offerings that were available in their area. There was a chain copy shop in the small downtown area of town, but that shop did not provide any really high-quality business printing, despite the relatively large number of small businesses in the area. The focus of the chain store was on individuals, self-service, and low-volume printing jobs. Finally, this individual had noted a trend on the West Coast of the United States (not his area of the country): the growth of restaurants that were in-between fast-food restaurants and full-service restaurants. These restaurants typically focused on regional food offerings. This type of restaurant had an upscale decor, but individuals ordered at the cash register and had their food delivered to them at the table. Thus, it was a different format for a restaurant than he had noticed in his area.

Each of these businesses had a relatively high level of detail involved in the operation of the business, and yet the processes to operate the businesses were relatively well known. Additionally, each of the businesses required high levels of interaction with customers, and customer service seemed to be a critical element of the business model. The background and skills of the potential entrepreneur appeared to fit with all of these businesses. Now he would have to pick one business idea.

Initial Analysis

The potential entrepreneur, just as in the example above, will likely have several ideas but will need to identify one business on which to perform a due diligence analysis. Chapters 4, 5, and 6 identify the process for performing an in-depth analysis on that single business idea. It is possible that after doing the in-depth analysis, the potential entrepreneur will decide not to pursue that particular business and will begin the analysis of business ideas all over again. However, the nature of the effort required to perform an effective due diligence study necessitates a focus on a single business concept. The analysis and thought processes require focus, time, and usually some financial investment. If the potential entrepreneur is to be successful, then the process is to move from the three to five ideas initially generated to a single idea on which to focus. Our would-be entrepreneur in the prior example had to determine whether to focus further analysis on the flower shop, the printing business, or the restaurant. One means to identify which business to pursue is through a gap analysis.

Gap Analysis

How do you decide that a sufficient business opportunity exists and that you have the resources necessary to take advantage of that opportunity? While there is more art to this process than science, starting with the list of three to five ideas that you have generated, you can now develop a chart that examines the issues that might impact the success of the new business. The business ideas are listed down in the first column, with a brief explanation of what each idea entails. (Later, each of these descriptions will be put into a short paragraph explaining the business and its opportunity for economic success.) You should be able to tell anyone succinctly—in less than two minutes—what your idea is and how it will bring substantial success. (You will see student business plan competitions called "elevator pitches" that are essentially the same concept—pitch your business in two minutes, or the time to ride the elevator to the top of a building.) Taking more time simply indicates that you have not clearly identified the opportunity or how it will work. We refer to this as gap analysis, and it should look roughly like the one in Table 3.1. We have filled in the three business ideas generated by the small business founder discussed in the previous section (flower shop, printing shop, and restaurant). However, you would use this form for your own business ideas.

In the second column, next to a given idea (and this may take several spreadsheet pages), list each category you will use to analyze the idea. We urge you to consider, one at a time, at least these five categories, which are crucial to the founding and successful running of a business: finances, time, nonfinancial resources, risk, and competitors. Each of these categories will be discussed in greater detail once we illustrate why this is a gap analysis.

In the third column, you should provide a realistic estimation of personal resources. In the fourth column, you should list your estimates of what resources are required for success. For the last column, you should qualitatively compare your skills and resources with the perceived requirements of that particular business, and record the perceived deficit or gap. Then you can answer an important question: Is that deficit surmountable, or is it one that kills the idea?

This qualitative chart can be completed with minimal or no research. What we are suggesting at this stage of investigation is a gut-level, reasonably quick analysis to see if the business passes an initial test. The gap analysis is intended to be completed by the entrepreneur or entrepreneurial team in a very short time period.

As we mentioned before, the second column lists "categories." These are categories that should be used for analysis. There are a number of categories that the entrepreneur needs to consider for a gap analysis. Following are the five important categories we have listed briefly. We will examine all of these in greater detail in later chapters. The list below is not meant to be exhaustive, as every type of new business will have its own unique categories.

1. *Finances.* You must examine the amount of money required to start and operate a business. A principal cause of new business failure is insufficient financial resources at founding. An entrepreneur may have a good idea but then run out of funds long before a sufficient client base can be built. This will be discussed further when we examine

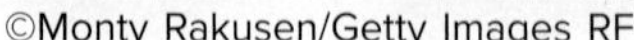
©Monty Rakusen/Getty Images RF

©Zoonar GmbH/Alamy RF

©Ariel Skelley/Blend Images LLC RF

BUSINESS IDEA	CATEGORY	OUR RESOURCES	RESOURCES REQUIRED	DEFICIT
Printing Shop	Finances			
High-quality; commercial	Time			
	Nonfinancial			
	Risk			
	Competitors			
Flower Shop	Finances			
Family history and support	Time			
	Nonfinancial			
	Risk			
	Competitors			
Restaurant	Finances			
Fast-food cross with service	Time			
	Nonfinancial			
	Risk			
	Competitors			

Table 3.1
Form to Compare Three Different Business Ideas

cash flow in Chapter 6. However, we feel that at this stage of analysis, the entrepreneur needs to have a basic understanding of the financial demands of the business.

a. Your resources—What financial resources do you have that you can realistically commit to the new venture? This should include estimates of savings, retirement accounts that may be used, your spouse's salary, and other. Do you have family resources that could be committed to the effort? How much money could you realistically raise on short notice?

b. Business need—Estimating how much money do you expect to need to start and to stay in business for one year? Without a lot of investigation, consider the following: rent, furniture, utilities, advertising, renovation, equipment, supplies, cost of an employee or two, taxes, and fees. Take whatever number you develop and add 50 percent to it. A standing rule-of-thumb is that start-ups take twice the money that was initially forecasted to achieve a sustainable level of operation. Is this number within the range that you would be willing to commit?

2. *Time.* It takes time to start a business. You will hear many successful entrepreneurs say that they estimate the time it will take to do something from scratch and then triple it. Again, you need to assure that you have the time necessary to start the business. Each type of business started will require different time frames. This is an area that many entrepreneurs grossly underestimate.
   a. Your resources—If you are currently employed, how much time can you dedicate to starting this new venture? Will you quit your current job to work in the new business? How much time on a weekly basis are you willing to commit to the business once it is up and running? What other time commitments have you made? Does your family support your efforts?
   b. Business need—What will the hours of operation require? How many additional hours will be required to manage the operation? Do you need staff early in the life of the business? When do you eat, sleep, and so on? What can be done concurrently versus sequentially?
3. *Nonfinancial Resources.* There are many other resources the new business will need beyond financing and the time commitment. This list can be long and should include such things as special contacts with suppliers or customer groups as well as the physical location of the business. This is a category where the entrepreneur should exercise some creativity in the analysis of the situation and the needs of the business.
   a. Your resources—What do you bring to the business beyond the financial? What unique capabilities/experiences/knowledge provide you with a competitive advantage? Are these visible to the rest of the world? Are there others, such as family members, who can provide critical needs of the new firm?
   b. Business needs—What unique skills will be required to run the business? Can you contract with individuals for the areas that you are missing? Can you obtain the resource in short order? (For example, to open a printing business, it would be very helpful to have wide experience on various types of printing presses. This could be gained by going to work for someone else for a period of time or by taking classes offered by contractors or the printing press company.) What unique resources are necessary to develop a competitive advantage in this business?
4. *Risk.* All new businesses have an inherent amount of risk associated with the starting and operation of the business. Whereas what constitutes that risk is determined by the entrepreneur, the level of risk needs to be commensurate with the rewards and within the tolerance level of the individual involved in the business founding. To determine your own risk tolerance, you should look at your own life over the past few years. When the economy is not in a recession, do you invest primarily in high-risk stocks or in safer places such as savings accounts? If you invest in savings accounts, then you are probably somewhat risk adverse. There are two types of specific risk you should consider: personal and business.
   a. Personal risk—Risk at a personal level has many definitions and potential means of examination. It is certainly well beyond just the financial. What level of risk to personal reputation are you willing to live with? If the business fails, what will you do? There is a strategic risk to starting a business when you are not ready, not

committed, not sufficiently funded, and the like. A failed business idea may lead to others imitating your idea and doing it better, or may affect your ability to pursue that or a similar type of business in the future.

b. Business risk—How aggressively does the business need to grow to be successful? Is there a competitive advantage that is fleeting? What level of product or geographic breadth is necessary to not only be a player but be a success in the industry? What are the limiting factors in the growth of this business? What are the factors that could disrupt your supply chain?[4]

You can also characterize and examine business risk by considering three threats to business success: (1) threats to the profit margin, (2) threats to sales generation schemes, and (3) threats to operational financing.[5] Each of these areas represents a systematic examination of business risk.

threats to profit margin
The threat of not being able to achieve a profit margin sufficient to allow the business to attain substantial returns.

1. **Threats to Profit Margin.** A significant threat to the success of a new venture is its ability to establish and maintain a high-margin product or service. That is, the firm is unable to make a high level of profit on each unit of product or service sold. What might inhibit your pricing or cost structure? Who are your significant competitors? Why do people shop with your competitor? How does pricing impact your ability to attract customers from your competitors?

threats to sales generation schemes
The threat of not being able to generate sufficient sales required to make the firm profitable.

2. **Threats to Sales Generation Schemes.** A new venture must have the opportunity to sell to many customers and to obtain repeat business. The ability to develop a sales scheme that is broad enough to appeal to a wide variety of customers is critical to the development of a successful business.[6] Can your competitors meet or exceed your quality? Undercut your price? Position themselves better physically? Lock you out of suppliers?

threats to operational financing
The threat of not obtaining sufficient financing to operate a firm.

3. **Threats to Operational Financing.** There are a number of specific threats to the new venture in obtaining the necessary financing for its growth. Some such threats are high development costs, rapid expansion plans, high inventory needs, and/or an entrepreneurial team with a low asset base. As will be discussed in Chapter 6, one of the greatest risks to a new business is fast growth. Typically, you will be selling products or services effectively on credit (delayed billing) but having to pay cash for your inputs as a new firm. Thus, rapid expansion can quickly overextend your financial resources. Research has shown that firms with higher initial capitalization have the opportunity to grow faster.[7] How much additional capital might you need if sales grow twice as fast as you predicted? What might impact your assessment of "enough" money to start and grow your business?

4. **Competitors.** The new business also must be realistic about its competitors. There are competitors for every business contemplated. If the potential entrepreneur cannot think of any company doing exactly the same thing as the new potential business, then what are customers doing now to satisfy that need/want? That current solution to the customer's problem is a competitor and will have to be dealt with by the new business. Most of the time, there are obvious competitors trying to lure the same set of customers as the potential new business. List who exists in this competitive set and why you believe they are competitors for your new business.

To illustrate how critical the accurate evaluation of these issues is to the success of the new firm, consider a business we worked with at the onset of the first Internet boom (late 1990s). This firm proposed to use the Internet to automate (and make remarkably more efficient) a process that previously had been done only through extensive use of the telephone—one call at a time. The former process involved making 30 or more phone calls to various individuals and then trying to coordinate their activities in a stepwise fashion while waiting for each to return the call (which usually came in while the initial caller was on the phone with another individual). The product developed by the founding entrepreneurial team was a Web page–based product that would perform this function on one screen at the same time (something we take for granted today). The initial response by the customers was immediate and positive. The software behind the product was modestly complex; nonetheless, once the Web page was available and visible, it would not be overly difficult for a well-heeled competitor to imitate it in just a couple of months. Some of the founders believed that the Web page itself and the software code that supported it was the key to success, and that the rollout could be incremental. They wanted to limit their risk and use cash flow to fund their expansion with a systematic plan to expand the business slowly. Another group of the founders believed that the critical limiting factor was obtaining exclusive commitments from as many of the 300 core customers as soon as possible, before the competition realized what was happening to the industry. Once the key customers were secured they were less likely to change to another provider of the service.

This focus on the importance of the customers as the source of competitive advantage changed the whole approach for the new business. The owners decided that rather than rolling the business out incrementally, they would seek to sign up the core customers as quickly as possible. The solution chosen by the team was to hire a sales company that put 35 contract salespeople on the project for 90 days. The cost and risk of this approach was significantly

ETHICAL CHALLENGE

There are a wide variety of choices that must be made as someone starts a business. One of the key choices that a firm must make is the source of the funds to start the firm. Different sources of funds represent different risks and responsibilities. For example, your family is one of the key potential sources of funds. But, before you accept money from your family or close friends, consider how you will handle that money in your business and how you will reward their confidence in you. All new ventures are inherently risky. As part of your risk analysis, you have to consider how much financial risk you are willing to commit to personally and with funds provided from those close to you. There are a rich set of questions that an entrepreneur should ask themselves as they move forward.

QUESTIONS

1. How would having your grandmother's retirement funds invested in the firm affect your judgment of the risk of a venture?
2. What if the business investment from your parents involves a choice—either the business funding or the funds for your coll?
3. What if those funds had been left to you by a relative?
4. How does the risk equation change if you had children that were young as opposed to -approaching college?

higher for the founders. However, the result was that before competitors even realized that there was a new company in the field, the founders had locked up over 210 of the 300 customers. The first competitor showed up 70 days after they started their operation and was able to sign up only 14 customers after a year in operation.

For this new business, there was a significant strategic risk of misreading the critical factor(s) in the business, and a great idea could have simply limped along because of a poor implementation decision. If the business founders had not recognized the risk of their business idea being copied, they might have implemented the wrong approach and would likely have been replaced in the market by a larger, richer firm. As the entrepreneur learns more about how the business might exist in the industry, the entrepreneur must be able to shift to new ideas if a greater opportunity appears.

Now let's go back and take a look at our entrepreneur who is debating between a printing shop, a flower shop, and a restaurant. The entrepreneur contemplated the situation and developed the following insights about location and the associated cost. The printing shop would not have to be in prime retail space, because it was not going to focus on retail customers as did the large chain near campus, but instead was to focus on business customers. The flower shop needed to be in prime retail space to obtain the impulse purchases that are a high percentage of the flower business. The size of the space needed and the need for excellent access to customers would make the restaurant's location the most expensive of all three.

The entrepreneur in thinking through the competition and profits realized that the flower shop's competition would be the strongest, and the profit margins in that industry were lower than in the other two industries. The printing shop had good profit margins, but the investment in the equipment necessary was relatively high. The restaurant seemed to have the highest competition risk. The nature of eating out is both eclectic and faddish. Individuals might desire one type of food for a while and then switch to another type of food. Additionally, returns in the restaurant industry are historically low, although individual restaurants can be quite profitable.

Considering time, the entrepreneur realized that the time needed to start up the flower shop and the printing shop would be shortest. The time it takes to set up and start a restaurant can be quite high, due to the nature of the finish to the interior that is required in the restaurant itself. The restaurant will have to develop a character and must be decorated, whereas the print shop might just have white walls. Finally, in terms of staffing, a far bigger staff is required in the restaurant, so the need for extensive hiring and training is an inherent and integral part of the business.

The entrepreneur had financial support from his family as well as some personal savings; had been laid off from his job, so he had lots of time to dedicate to the business; was single; and was dedicated to starting a business. His personal take on the deficit analysis for these three factors is provided in Table 3.2.

As a result of this analysis, the entrepreneur decided to focus his due diligence on the printing business. The due diligence proved that there was a need for the business (this concept will be discussed more in Chapter 4); that a successful and sustainable strategy had the potential to be developed (this concept will be discussed more in Chapter 5); and that the potential business had the opportunity for positive cash flows (this concept will be discussed more in Chapter 6). As a result of that due diligence process, the small-business person established the business and has made it a success.

BUSINESS IDEA	CATEGORY	OUR RESOURCES	RESOURCES REQUIRED	DEFICIT
Printing Shop	Finances	Savings and some ability to get loans	Need additional funds for equipment	*Medium*
High quality; commercial	Time	Full time	Full day—high volume work with deadlines	*Low*
	Nonfinancial	Little knowledge	Need printing expertise	*High*
	Risk	Moderate—cheaper space, expensive equipment	Rapid acquisition of used equipment and cheap space	*Medium*
	Competitors	Moderate	Advertising and sales to counter	*High*
Flower Shop	Finances	Savings, loans, family money	Cooler, basic equipment, Display cases	*Low*
Family history and support	Time	Full time + family time	Full day in house; delivery	*Medium*
	Nonfinancial	Significant family knowledge	Arrangement, design, stocking knowledge	*Low*
	Risk	Smaller footprint; expensive interior	Knowledge of market, high availability	*Low*
	Competitors	Strong and many	Positioning, leverage family; differentiation	*High*
Restaurant	Finances	Savings, loans	Significant resources needed for equipment; customer face	*High*
Fast food crossed with service	Time	Full time	10-9 daily; lots of staff needed for cooking, serving, etc.	*High*
	Nonfinancial	Little knowledge	Food prep, licensing, ordering, serving	*High*
	Risk	Heavy investment and employees; could be easily copied	Attract based on concept unproven. Fickle customers; holding onto concept	*High*
	Competitors	Numerous in general; few specifically	Pricing, positioning, newness issue	*High*

Table 3.2
Example of Entrepreneur's Personal Deficit Analysis

SUMMARY

In this chapter we presented a method for the potential new entrepreneur to develop and perform an initial evaluation of various business ideas. This process starts with an evaluation of the skills that the individual brings to the new business. What education, experience, hobbies, and other interests do you already have in your pocket before the new business gets founded? The next step is to look at the world around you and systematically evaluate the potential opportunities. There are literally millions of ideas out there. The real question is: Do you have the ability to successfully take advantage of those ideas to create a successful business? Finally, we presented a gap analysis methodology that has been used successfully for some time to determine potential fit with a business idea.

KEY TERMS

brainstorming 49
gap analysis 48
synergy 44
threats to operational financing 54
threats to profit margin 54
threats to sales generation schemes 54

REVIEW QUESTIONS

1. Based on your *education*, what are the skills you have that could be the basis for a business?
2. Based on your *work experience,* what are the skills you have that could be the basis for a business?
3. Based on your *hobbies,* what are the skills you have that could be the basis for a business?
4. What are your top three personal skills?
5. What things do you like doing best?
6. What magazines and books do you read?
7. What are your three greatest accomplishments in life? What skills were involved in these accomplishments?
8. Do you enjoy working with people?
9. In what general industry (retail/wholesale/manufacturing/service) would you prefer to work?

BUSINESS PLAN DEVELOPMENT QUESTIONS

Conduct the following for yourself to determine which businesses would be an appropriate match for the skills and traits as you work on your business plan.

1. Think about what trends around the region/nation/world you know about that have not reached your area.
2. Interview and talk about opportunities with key successful entrepreneurs in the area. Where do they find a match between opportunity and your skills?
3. Discuss with family members what potential businesses they believe might be best for you.
4. Take the business ideas that have met your criteria thus far and perform a deficit analysis of those ideas. Which idea has the most potential for success, given your resources, time, risk position, and so on?

INDIVIDUAL EXERCISES

1. Pick a successful business in your area that is not a franchise. What was the opportunity this business identified? Does that opportunity still exist for another business in either another location or if addressed in a different manner?
2. For this business, what key skills would the entrepreneur need to be successful?
3. If you can visit with this entrepreneur, then see if you can determine if your analysis was correct.

GROUP EXERCISES

1. Break into teams of three to four. Present each of your personal deficit analyses. Help each other think through their accuracy and the means by which you could overcome any shortcomings in skills or resources.
2. The team has a combination of experiences and resources. If the team, instead of just one person, were putting together a business, how would the analysis change?

ENDNOTES

1. C. P. McAllister, B. P. Ellen, and G. R. Ferris, "Social Influence Opportunity Recognition, Evaluation, and Capitalization Increased Theoretical Specification through Political Skill's Dimensional Dynamics," *Journal of Management* (in press).
2. D. A. Gregorie and D. A. Shepherd, "Technology-Market Combinations and the Identification of Entrepreneurial Opportunities: An Investigation of the Opportunity-Individual Nexus," *Academy of Management Journal* 55 no. 4, (2012), pp. 753–85.

3. S. Levine and D. Stark, "Diversity Makes You Brighter," *The New York Times*, December 9, 2015. https://www.nytimes.com/2015/12/09/opinion/diversity-makes-you-brighter.html.
4. D. Simchi-Levi, W. Schmidt, and W. Yehua. *Harvard Business Review.* 92, no. 1/2 (2014), pp. 96–101.
5. K. H. Vesper, *New Venture Strategies* (Englewood Cliffs, NJ: Prentice Hall, 1990).
6. P. P. McDougall, J. G. Covin, R. B. Robinson, and L. Herron, "The Effects of Industry Growth and Strategic Breadth on New Venture Performance and Strategy Content," *Strategic Management Journal* 15 (1994), pp. 537–54; E. Romanelli, "Environments and Strategies of Organization Start-up: Effects on Early Survival," *Administrative Science Quarterly* 34 (1989), pp. 369–87.
7. A. C. Cooper and F. J. Gimeno-Gascon, "Entrepreneurs, Processes of Founding, and New Firm Performance," in *The State of the Art of Entrepreneurship,* ed. D. L. Sexton and J. D. Kasarda (Boston, MA: PWS Kent, 1992), pp. 301–40; K. M. Eisenhardt and C. B. Schoonhoven, "Organizational Growth: Linking Founding Team, Strategy, Environment, and Growth Among U.S. Semiconductor Ventures, 1978–1988," *Administrative Science Quarterly* 35(1990), pp. 504–29.

learning objectives

After studying this chapter, you will be able to:

LO4-1 Describe how to examine the industry that the new business plans to enter.

LO4-2 Discuss how to create a profile of the target customers for a new business.

LO4-3 Explain how to categorize competitors of the new business using external analysis.

LO4-4 Explain how to construct competitive maps.

LO4-5 Ensure that the entrepreneur has considered a full set of concerns in his or her external analysis.

LO4-6 Differentiate between those elements of the business that provide a competitive advantage and those that do not.

External Analysis

MOZIAH BRIDGES

HANDCRAFTED
MO'S BOWS
BOW TIES
EST. 2011

Moziah Bridges is only 13 years old but already runs a business with seven employees including his mother and grandmother. The firm (Mo's Bows) has annual sales of several hundred thousand dollars. Moziah comes from a single-parent household in a poor section of Memphis. His mother was a seamstress who ultimately set Moziah on the path for this business not only by teaching him to sew but also teaching him that a man should dress well and be able to tie his own tie. From this background Moziah started to make his own bow ties from old scraps of cloth. These ties became so popular in his neighborhood that Moziah began to sell the ties through Facebook and then ultimately opened his own Etsy location to sell online.

Moziah became one of the youngest people ever to appear on the TV show *Shark Tank* in 2013, when he and his mother appeared on the show and asked for $50,000 for the business. He received great advice on the show from investor Daymond John who is a regular on the show and a well-known clothing entrepreneur. John's advice was to not take any investment. Instead he suggested that Moziah continue to build his brand and his sales without outside aid. Mr. John saw in Moziah much of his own story of poverty and being raised by a single parent. Through entrepreneurship he was able to grow a business that allowed him to be worth several hundred million dollars. Mr. Johns continues today to bean informal advisor to Moziah.

Building on Mr. John's advice, Moziah has pursed extensive free publicity such as stories in *O* magazine and *Vogue*. He has also appeared on *Steve Harvey* show. His efforts have resulted in a branding relationship with Cole Hahn in addition to having his ties appear in the Neiman Marcus online store and in some brick and mortar stores. Today the future looks very bright for both Moziah Bridges and his family through his entrepreneurial efforts.

Questions

1. What special problems does Moziah Bridges face with his family in the business?
2. What other products could Moziah diversify into that would take advantage of his skills?

Sources: L. Kim, "This 12-Year-Old CEO Runs a $150,000 Business," *Inc.*, September 15, 2014. http://www.inc.com/larry-kim/this-12-year-old-ceo-runs-a-150k-business.html; S. Reporter, "Moziah Bridges Net Worth: 13-year-old CEO Making Millions with His Bow Tie Empire, Declined FUBU," *Realty Today*, November 16, 2015. http://www.realtytoday.com/articles/52310/20151116/moziahbridges-net-worth-13-year-old-ceo-making-millions.htm; R. Feloni, "Meet the 13-year-old CEO Who Built a $200,000 Business and Is Mentored by Daymond John," *Business Insider*, March 20, 2015. http://www.businessinsider.com/mos-bows-and-daymond-john-2015-3; M. Cummings, "13-Year-Old CEO Moziah Bridges Builds $200,000 Business," *BET*, April 18, 2015. http://www.bet.com/news/national/2015/04/18/13-year-old-ceo-moziah-bridges-builds-200-000business.html; https://www.mosbowsmemphis.com/meet-mo

Starting an entrepreneurial business should be based on the observance of an opportunity.[1] The recognition of an opportunity may come from a frustration with the way that existing businesses operate (poor service, lack of selection); a new technology that makes an idea that was previously impractical become available (i.e., an Internet-based service, computer animation); a hobby that provides you unique skills and insight; or a new vacancy at the perfect location for a business. However, even though there are many ways to identify an opportunity, the entrepreneur must ensure that what he or she is observing is truly an opportunity. What may appear to be a great opportunity to one person may in fact not be viable as a business. The key to effective opportunity recognition is a detailed understanding of the external environment.

There are a number of critical steps in examining the nature of the external environment. These include the following:

1. Define the industry in which you are competing.
2. Define your customers.
3. Research the industry yourself.
4. Identify competitors within that industry.
5. Research those competitors.
6. Draw a set of competitive maps.
7. Examine and develop insights about additional economic aspects of the industry, including substitutes, elasticity of demand, ease of entry and exit, benchmarking, and industry trends.
8. Start developing an understanding of your competitive advantage.

We will look at each of these steps in turn in analyzing the external environment.

LO4-1

Describe how to examine the industry that the new business plans to enter.

Defining Your Industry

The first part of an external analysis is to determine the industry within which the new business will compete, as well as the general makeup of the industry.[2] In doing so the entrepreneur should seek to be as specific as possible. For example, if you want to open a new ice cream store, you might ask, in what industry does a new ice cream store compete? Clearly, the industry will include other ice cream stores. However, if the ice cream store will make a significant part of its revenues from selling ice cream cakes, then the industry might be best viewed as including a broader group of dessert providers, such as bakeries and other businesses that sell competing products. If the ice cream store has both dipping operations where the ice cream is sold in cones and prepackaged gallons of ice cream, perhaps the industry includes competitors that sell ice cream in grocery stores. The industry may also vary if the ice cream is high end with a high milk-fat content (referred to as "frozen custard" in many states such as Wisconsin) versus more typical ice cream that has much lower milk-fat level. Defining the firm's industry is not something that should be taken lightly.

Nowadays, most information can be obtained on the Web or via a magazine or journal that covers a broad category of firms to which you believe your new business will belong. Industry associations are another prime source of this type of data. Industry associations for virtually any industry you can think of probably exist at the national level, and many have local or state organizations as well. These associations exist primarily to support and promote their industry. They have extensive data on their industry and are usually quite willing to share that with the public.

To obtain statistical data, the potential entrepreneur will want to obtain the industry categorization. Two relatively simple means are available. The first is to locate your industry's NAICS (North American Industry Classification System) code for the industry. An NAICS code is a code that can vary from two to seven digits in length (the more digits, the more specific the classification). The codes were generated by the U.S. government in an effort to gather, track, and publish data on specific industries. You can locate this code either on the Internet via a number of sources including the U.S. government websites (www.census.gov/epcd/www/naics.html). The second way to find nationwide information is to locate a public company that might be a direct competitor to the new business and simply use its NAICS code to look up overall industry data (via Dun & Bradstreet, LexisNexis, etc.).

Housing construction slowed in recent years due to the recession with the amount of decline varying from state to state.

At an aggregated national level, the data gathered on a firm's industry have some value; however, it is the rare new business that intends to draw customers from across the United States at its founding. Most of the data available will be on a national basis, which provides you some information on national trends but provides little understanding of the local competitive environment. The national industry may be doing very poorly, but your immediate area might contain virtually no competitors and have the potential to do very well. For example, in the recent recession, housing construction businesses in California, Florida, and Nevada were severely hurt, while at the same time the housing construction industry in Texas and Missouri experienced only limited economic slowdown.

Entrepreneurs should define the industry in which they will compete broadly enough to be inclusive of all potential competitors, but not so broadly as to be overwhelming. If you are starting a new jewelry store, it is most likely that not even all the jewelry stores in your area are direct competitors. If your store will be in a shopping mall, clearly, other stores in similar malls will be competitors. However, if there is a Tiffany's in the same city, it might or might not be a direct competitor, depending on the specific customer market you are seeking to serve. Someone who buys jewelry at Tiffany's is not likely to purchase items in a small, shopping-mall store, and vice versa.

Even more important, the entrepreneur must be clear about the practical level of actual competition. An entrepreneur should ask, what is a reasonable geographic customer draw for a new business? Opening up a sandwich shop in the downtown area of a city means that the shop most likely competes with other sandwich or fast-food shops within a 10-block radius—and perhaps less, if walking is the primary means of transportation for downtown lunching workers. There are limits to how far someone will travel for a sandwich. Drawing a practical radius around your potential new business location will also help target the customers who are most likely to patronize your business. This raises an interesting question for a potential restaurant or a bar someone may open. How far do you believe a potential customer would travel to get to such a restaurant or bar? What is your formula that may make the customers drive further than they may normally? As we think of other businesses such as Internet businesses, the draw may be national—people really don't care where they order things from. However, as we will discuss later in the book, the key to Internet business becomes more how to ensure a business gets through the clutter of the Internet to reach the customers they want, no matter where they live.

industry
Those direct competitors selling similar products or services within a specified geographic radius that is consistent with a customer's willingness to travel to purchase those products or services.

For a new entrepreneurial business, the **industry** is defined as those companies within a specified geographic radius (if the business has a physical presence) that will be in direct competition for the same customers and sales as that of the new business. Thinking further about the restaurant and bar we discussed in the prior paragraph, how will you define this business's industry? Many restaurants make most of their money from alcoholic drinks. Similarly, many bars sell food. So when do you define the industry as "restaurant" and when as a "bar." Depending on how you define things pushes the entrepreneur to design the business differently and also plan differently. For example, consider how your competitors are different depends on how you define things. To illustrate, a customer normally chooses from a wide variety of restaurants within categories such as price, class, ambiance, and location. Just as we highlighted with jewelry stores, a high-end steak house such as Ruth's Chris is not likely to compete against the local chicken-fried steak house. How to determine such choices will be examined next.

The definition of an app's geographic area can be hard. There is not per se a geographic domain for an app other than language. Thus, if you go to the outlets such as the Apple Store, there will be thousands of apps from many different lands. The greatest barrier to the spread of an app is the social media that promotes the app. While there will be written media on an app that is very helpful, the greatest factor that spreads its use is how customers and potential customers communicate with each other on the app. Thus, in defining the industry, the app should be conceptualized in its use and not as a physical item.

LO4-2

Discuss how to create a profile of the target customers for a new business.

Defining Your Customers

Once the industry is broadly defined, then the exact nature of the customer should be developed. It is important to define a narrower group of individuals whom you believe will constitute your most likely customers. Where are they located? Where do they currently obtain their product or service? A new burger place opening up near a university is not competing against all burger places in the country, so overall industry figures for the nation, state, or even city are of little assistance. Instead, the customers are going to be the students, faculty, and staff of the university, and the immediate residents of the university area.

In defining the customer, the entrepreneur should be diligent in the effort to be as accurate as possible. We will discuss promotional activities such as advertising in Chapter 11 ("Marketing"), but here we note that defining the customer to which your company caters is important for the effective use of your marketing dollars, as well as the satisfaction of core, repeat customers.

One potential restaurant owner told us that he viewed his target customer market as those individuals from ages 2 to 90, from all income ranges, anywhere within a 50-mile radius. Indeed, he became quite upset when we suggested that this was unreasonable. His view was, why not seek every potential customer he could?

What would this type of definition mean to the operation of the business? The entrepreneur would have to have food items that appealed to children, teenagers, adults, and senior citizens in all price ranges. The entrepreneur's original concept for the restaurant was that it was to be an upscale restaurant with some "flash" oriented around the extensive wine selection. However, if he defined his customers as everyone aged 2 to 90, his wine selection would have to run the gamut from alcohol-free wine to jugs of cheap wine to rare

KOSHER HOME

As we discussed in the previous two chapters, Jack and Toby want to start an Internet kosher food business. Their goal is to develop a business that provides them an opportunity to both contribute to their religious community and make a significant profit. To be successful they know that a clear understanding of some of the external elements of the business will be a crucial start to the design.

Industry

The two friends intend to be strictly in the Internet food business. There are some food businesses with only physical facilities, some that are strictly Internet-based, and others that are utilizing both approaches. Especially in food preparation, it is relatively easy for a restaurant with a famous cheese cake to ship it to anyone in the country and keep it cold. There are firms that ship steaks, fruit, dry goods or a box of fresh goods so that an individual can cook a single meal. Thus, before they can define their industry, the two entrepreneurs knew that they would have to define the industry more precisely. To do this they decided to refine their thinking about what business they were in.

- Create an Internet-based business.
    - The entrepreneurs wanted to offer their service exclusively on the Internet with no physical locations.
- Food business
    - The two entrepreneurs knew they wanted to do something with Kosher food, but the key decision would be whether to do either of the following:
        - Fresh food needing some level of temperature control.
        - Dry goods
            - While they wished to offer fresh food, they wanted to be flexible as they discovered more about what would be most desired by the customer.
    - Another decision would be how extensive their offerings of fresh food should be:
        - One model would be to offer a full variety of fresh goods.
        - Another model would be to offer food for a single meal that the person or family could make.
            - The entrepreneurs thought they would pursue the fresh meal approach but wanted to be sure that approach would be the most desired. They were clear that they would be willing to change if the market desired.

Competition

Looking online, Jack and Toby found there were several firms that sold kosher fresh food, and it appeared they were generally located in heavily Jewish areas such as South Florida. These firms were not looking to serve isolated communities. There were other firms that were selling nonfresh items such as mixes or things that could be shipped easily such as bread. They could not find any direct competitors that sold nationwide kosher fresh food. There were a number of larger companies that sold preboxed meals for one or more in a household. None of these competitors were offering kosher meals.

QUESTIONS

1. Would you focus on a broad range of products or shipping a prepared meal?
2. If you ordered a prepared meal, is being kosher a unique enough domain for the firm?

vintages, because the range of customers he was targeting would demand to be satisfied, and all of these customers would be equally valued. This egalitarian approach is probably appropriate for a political movement but is a poor approach to business success.[3] The offering of alcohol-free wines and cheap wines turns off the customer who likes high-end wines. Similarly, a large wine list with lots of expensive wines is frustrating and intimidating to the customer looking for a $3 glass of wine.

Once the entrepreneur realized the expansive—and expensive—scope of the plan he wanted to pursue, he decided to narrow his true target to adults aged 30 to 50 with a median income of $60,000 who lived within about 20 minutes' drive from the restaurant. This is not to suggest that he will, or would want to, turn away anyone who wishes to dine at his establishment. It does, however, suggest that the only patrons that he specifically caters to are those in his demographic target. An outcome of this approach is that if a college-aged couple comes in and complains about the wine selection being too expensive, the owner no longer has to feel the need to appeal to them and provide inexpensive wines. In fact, he specifically does not want to do that as it would affect the image and cost structure of the restaurant. The college couple is not his perfect customer.

This approach helps the entrepreneurial business clearly focus on its core customer. It also helps the business maintain a strategic distance between itself and its competitors, as the firm is not trying to do what everyone else may do. Finally, a clear understanding of the business's customers assists the owners in controlling expenses, as the business does not try to be everything to everybody. The inventory can, therefore, be much more focused than if the entrepreneur tries to be everything to everyone.

EXERCISE 1

1. What are the next questions that Jack and Toby should ask as they decide which path to choose for the new venture?
2. Do you believe there is an opportunity for this business?
3. There are many competitors in fresh boxed meals, although not kosher, what information does that provide Jack and Toby?

LO4-3

Explain how to categorize competitors of the new business using external analysis.

Developing the Information for the External Analysis of Competitors

The Kosher Home founders were able to develop some very good information for their external analysis. They accomplished this with a lot of legwork and by using publically available information. Next we discuss a number of ways to conduct such research.

Research Your Industry Yourself

At this point in your efforts to start a new business, you should have defined the industry that interests you, determined who your potential customers might be and why they might want to buy from your business, and gathered some information on these domains. The next issue is to identify the exact competitors within that industry. These competitors are those firms that directly compete for the same set of ideal customers as your proposed business. If the new business owners are very clear regarding their customers' needs, then the ability to identify direct competitors becomes significantly easier. For many new entrepreneurial ventures, these businesses will be geographically local. Thus, the most obvious and mundane places to look for these competitors are the local telephone book and the front seat of your car.

Although it is certainly possible to hire a consulting company to perform the type of customer research service discussed above, the entrepreneur will gain invaluable insight by handling this process personally. We assisted a small group of highly committed golfers who had the idea of developing an affordable, nonmember 18-hole golf course in the Dallas–Fort Worth (DFW) metroplex. Their idea was to offer a country club–level course without the membership commitment and expense involved with playing on some of the area's quality courses. The group had a tract of land that had been in the family of one of the potential founders and had been given to him upon the death of his father. Although this is substantially larger than the usual entrepreneurial business idea we present in the text, we believe the concepts point out the critical issues that any potential entrepreneur must address.

When planning new development like a golf course, knowing your market is crucial. What activities would you want to control personally when developing your business?

©ZoccoPhoto/Getty Images RF

At the first meeting, the golf professionals were clear that they knew the market and what the market needed. However, basic market questions kept coming up that they were unable to answer. Some of the questions raised for which they had no answers included these:

1. How many 18-hole courses are there in the DFW metroplex?
2. How many of these courses are not tied to a country club?
3. How many rounds of golf are played on a typical weekend at these courses?
4. How far does the average golfer drive to play a round?
5. Are there capacity problems at some of the more popular courses?

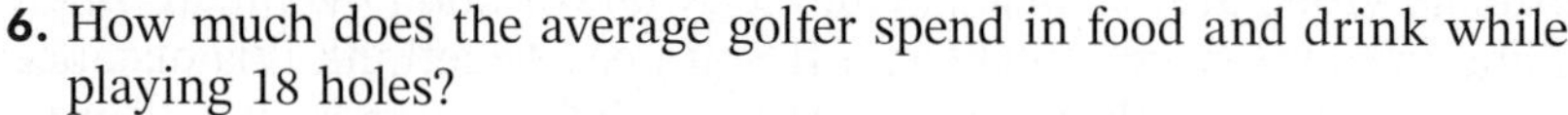

6. How much does the average golfer spend in food and drink while playing 18 holes?
7. What is charged to play at various times of the day or week at each of the open courses?
8. Where is the population growth area for golfers?
9. What is the profile of a typical golfer?

It was clear that these individuals who wanted to start the business loved golf and thought they had a great understanding of the local industry; however, the golfers had not done any in-depth study of the market. These individuals were frustrated when they realized that they did not have a detailed understanding of the potential customer. In response, they were ready to hire a company to collect this information, despite the high cost of pursuing that option. Instead, we encouraged them to collect this information themselves. Doing so would make them the experts in the area and enable them to develop a plan for a business that would give them a competitive advantage. The benefits of planning and analysis are the nuanced insights it provides the individuals performing the activities. Hiring a company to gather information is not only expensive but also limits the insights to more factual data.

Therefore, the founders prepared a list of questions about a golf course that would help differentiate their business. After doing some quick research to find every 18-hole course in the metroplex, they divided up the courses and individually visited each one. They played each course and tried to experience all the offerings at the course. The questionnaires that they developed were completed after each visit and an overall analysis was completed describing the entire market.

EXERCISE 2

Using the golf course initiative as an example, pair up with one other person and explain your business idea to him or her. Have the person role-play a friend who would be investing in your business. Have the person ask you questions about what the customer desires to get out of the product or service. Use the list as a starting point for your own competitor analysis.

Defining Actual Competitors

An effective industry analysis starts by identifying every potential competitor within that previously defined reasonable distance of your planned establishment location. What a reasonable distance consists of is a matter of interpretation, and the interpreter is the new businessperson. Although someone could argue with any individual's assessment of that distance, it must be established, and this is much more a matter of art than a matter of science. In any case, the first step is to define a radius from which you believe you will draw a majority of your customers. Make this distance reasonable, not just a wish.[4] If the business does not have a physical restriction to its operation, then it is important to create a list of competitors that can easily be found electronically by your customers.[5]

A woman in Knoxville, Tennessee, was planning a quick-serve, breakfast-oriented restaurant. She needed to define a reasonable radius from which she would draw her ideal customers. She originally said that she would draw customers from the entire metropolitan Knoxville area and (much like our previous restaurant owner) was adamant that she did not want to forego any business. Once again, we certainly do not suggest that you forego business unnecessarily, but an assessment that a business draws from an entire region is unreasonable for many reasons. Just one is that if you try to cater to everyone in a metro area, you will distort your advertising efforts, and you will dramatically increase your costs. Instead, this entrepreneur needed to focus on customers within a reasonable commuting distance from the restaurant. She eventually narrowed that distance to 20 minutes of driving in traffic. Although you may indeed draw customers from outside this area, they are not your primary group at the outset. (Think of yourself and how much time you are willing to travel to get breakfast?) If you need to rethink this distance as your operations mature, then you can. The core information is already in hand and will still be relevant if you expand or contract the market radius later.

Once our breakfast restaurant entrepreneur had identified the area she wanted to serve, she began driving around the area to see what competitors might be in operation. She also identified businesses through the phone book. The end result was that with relatively little expense, she was able to identify those restaurants that would be her direct and indirect competitors.

Once you have established a reasonable radius from which you will draw your primary customer, the next step is to examine each of your potential competitors. It is easy to discuss practices in the industry in general terms. For example, you might hear that all the area photocopying places have poor service, wait times are long, and the local shops have poor-quality equipment. These general feelings about the industry may help an entrepreneur believe he or she sees an opportunity, but actually running a business requires specific knowledge about the competitors. Even in a poor industry, there are probably some competitors who will be tough to beat. The entrepreneur must identify those competitors, what they do well, and where they are located.

fragmented markets
Markets in which no one competitor has a substantial share of the market and the means of competition vary widely within the same market space.

Most entrepreneurial businesses compete in what is referred to as **fragmented markets.**[6] These are markets that have no clear dominant competitor and are instead made up of a large number of similar-sized firms. If the entrepreneurial business is competing directly with well-established firms, this virtually guarantees that at a minimum the entrepreneurial business will be operating at a cost disadvantage and will have to compete on some other basis. The number and size of all competitors need to be detailed so that the entrepreneur has a rich and full understanding of their competition. Additionally, the differences in how the various businesses compete and their competitive advantages also need to be well understood.

This is the case for most Internet and phone applications. In some domains there are dominant players like Amazon. But in many other emerging domains, there are numerous small competitors. One of the key concerns facing entrepreneurs in such domains is to identify both those current competitors and those that are forthcoming.

EXERCISE 3

1. What other external research would you have recommended to the team developing the golf course?
2. Do you think they have a good understanding of their competitors? What other competitors do you see do other sports and activities compete?

YRFURN—AN APP FOR FURNITURE

The three founders knew from their coursework that the next step in their process was to determine who their customer was going to be and who they were really competing with in the business. The entrepreneurs saw two potential customers, the individual consumer who wanted a much better furniture shopping experience and the firms who sold the furniture.

Very unscientifically the three entrepreneurs talked with their friends and found that most thought the idea was very cool but didn't really see the problem being solved. You could measure your room and bring the tape measure with you to a furniture store. Their friends were young, and none had ever had to buy a room full of furniture before and saw it as a one-time type of purchase, and not something that they would let sit on their phone. The team thought that maybe they didn't have the right customer base for this and wondered about whether people would download something like this app on their phone.

The entrepreneurs decided to visit furniture stores and generated a set of questions that each should ask to gain greater insight into customer actions. The entrepreneurs split up the stores that they visited. Brandy visited one of the nation's largest chains and traveled to make sure she was visiting one of their flagship store locations away from their college location. The flagship store was a so-called Super Center with more than 1.5 million square feet under roof. By calling ahead and discussing the idea for the business, Brandy was able to convince the VP of store operations to meet with her. Kyle visited a well-known, family-run chain that had its headquarters store in a suburb near a major city. It was a solid six-hour drive for him, but he also called ahead and described the business idea to the owner of the store, and the owner agreed to meet with him. Brad picked a furniture store that had only one location and had been in business less than two years. It was pitched as a cutting edge store catering to millennials in the city. The founders graduated from the same undergraduate institution as Brad, so he was also able to secure a meeting easily.

The three entrepreneurs gathered again a week later to discuss their findings. There were consistencies and differences that surprised the team. All three found that a real frustration for the furniture salespeople was customers not knowing dimensions of rooms and exact colors and an inability to picture furniture in their homes. This lack of knowledge elongated the whole sales process and led to more than 15 percent of customers trying to return furniture that did not fit or look like they thought it should. All three also found that the companies were very interested in anything that might give them a competitive advantage, and the large chain that Brandy visited started talking to her about an exclusive deal with their chain. Surprisingly, the newest operation that Brad visited did not like the YrFurn solution to the problems they faced. They thought that their salespeople should visit the customer's house and use an app they were developing to map the room and then help customize the offering.

They had originally thought that the furniture stores might be their competitors, but now they started considering whether they might be their customer. The decision on the real customer of the business was significant. The two potential customers, individuals and firms, would take the business in very different directions. Thus, the firm had to choose whether they wanted to be more of a B2B (business to business) or a B2C (business to consumer) operation. If they operated as a B2B, the team did not want to be exclusive to one company and they saw the commissioned salespeople who worked the floor as the group with the most to gain from their approach. But the dynamics of the B2B would be hard for the start-up. Convincing large mature conservative firms to adapt their technology could be difficult. They felt the consumer would be much more likely to be willing to change. Thus, they decided to focus on individuals.

With the consumer as the target customer, the competitors in the market ranged from consultants who visited the home to individual businesses who were developing their own applications that may be attractive to individuals. There were also competitors that were online, customized furniture operations that sold individual pieces. However, these pieces were no more likely to fit into an established room than those picked out in a store. Other versions of the YrFurn app might be in the works, and it would be reasonable that there would be since there was an intense interest in the furniture stores they visited.

The team felt confident enough to move forward. However, they felt some time pressure to move forward quickly as they feared others may be in the market soon.

In the Knoxville restaurant example discussed, the ability to drive by and visit the various existing restaurants allowed the entrepreneur to understand each of those establishments in greater depth as well as which might be the strongest competitors. Straightforward observations made by an entrepreneur who understands the competitive issues of the industry can provide valuable insight. However, there is another tool available to the entrepreneur that can provide additional information. Specifically, an analytical tool that has the ability to digest information and display this information to others is a **competitive map.**

competitive map
An analytical tool used to organize information about direct competitors on all points of competition.

LO4-4

Explain how to construct competitive maps.

Developing a Competitive Map

At this point in the process, the amount of detail about competitors that needs to be organized raises the need for a systematic means to categorize that information. Thus, the next step in your external analysis is to develop a competitive map to better understand competitors and their capabilities.[7] Although there are many companies available that are in business to examine competitors, as we have stated previously, we recommend that the entrepreneur develop this map personally, for the following reasons:

1. It is less expensive.
2. Knowledge of what is right and wrong with each of the competitors allows the entrepreneur to better position the new business.
3. Insights will be developed regarding positioning, pricing, and even facility layout.

Developing a competitive map requires that the entrepreneur visit *all* of the potential competitors in whatever form they run their business. Further, we recommend that you be a customer of your competitors. Even if your desired entrepreneurial business sells business to business, you can still seek to interact with the competitors to try to understand their activities. There is nothing like obtaining the customer perspective from a series of such visits; the comparisons to your potential competitors become easier with this type of insight. With this in mind, the entrepreneur must develop a list of criteria that they wish to take away from each visit and record that information after each visit. Although this list might change depending on the type of establishment, we suggest a list of potential items to consider if the business is a retail business selling to customers in a brick-and-mortar location:

1. Parking availability (how many spots and what quality?)
2. Access from road
3. Nearby attractions for customers
4. Size of facility
5. Décor
6. Pricing
7. Product breadth
8. Product depth
9. Staffing (number and quality)
10. Capacity
11. Brochures/advertising material
12. Customer traffic at several different times of day
13. Average sale
14. Friendliness/helpfulness
15. Unique features
16. Suppliers (what company is delivering to their business?)

Although this list is most applicable to retail businesses that have a set location, you should recognize that many of the same concepts apply to any Internet business or other business types. The key in each case is to determine the key competitive factors that you wish to understand about your competitors.

An example of a competitive map is shown in Table 4.1. This competitive map (for the Dallas–Fort Worth golf course discussed earlier) encompasses a number of criteria that could be used in the evaluations of the business. The eight-mile radius employed in this map is based on the distance the partners determined from their research that someone would drive to play golf.

Some of these items (and there will be other ones for your venture) can be easily categorized and analyzed. Others are more descriptive and give you a rich sense of what is available to customers right now. We have included a description of some of the findings from the group seeking to establish the golf course.

At the time of this investigation, the DFW area had 74 golf courses. However, it was determined from surveys with potential customers that on average, individuals would drive no more than 30 minutes one way to the golf course. Therefore, rather than examine all 74 courses, the entrepreneurs chose to examine only those courses in Fort Worth because that is where their land was and those no farther than 30 minutes from downtown. This resulted in our entrepreneurial team visiting 24 golf courses, 25 percent of which were private. The private courses in this particular area are very difficult to join. The membership or initiation fees at these clubs are quite expensive, several

Table 4.1
Competitive Map: Golf Course (Eight-Mile Radius)

	COMPETITOR 1	COMPETITOR 2	COMPETITOR 3	COMPETITOR 4	COMPETITOR 5
Population in area					
No. of households in area					
Household income					
Average age in area					
No. of driving ranges					
No. of golf shops in area					
No. of customers per weekday					
No. of customers per weekend					
Average no. of customers per hour					
Peak flow of customers					
Average charge per transaction					
Tee charge: peak and off-peak					
Clubhouse feel					
Course feel					
Variety of menu offerings: clubhouse					
Variety of menu offerings: course					

are at capacity, the current members appear to be very particular about who is a member, and the benefits of belonging to the club are more about social/business connections than the golf. Therefore, the focus of the entrepreneurial team shifted to the remaining 18 nonclub courses.

Five of the 18 public courses appeared to be poorly maintained. However, the other 13 were in good shape, with at least 6 of those in excellent shape. In visiting with golfers at the courses and playing the courses themselves, the potential entrepreneurs discovered that there was no difficulty in getting on the courses. Both the access and the nature of the courses were generally excellent. The fact that they were public courses was a result of city government subsidies, which provided the operators with subsidized lease payments and some assistance with the maintenance expenses.

After completing their map, the potential golf entrepreneurs concluded that the competitive landscape was not at all what they had envisioned. They concluded that the DFW area was overbuilt and that the presence of public subsidies for many courses distorted competition. They decided that the market was not as attractive as they originally had thought.

EXERCISE 4

Develop the basis of a competitive map for your proposed venture. Outline in columns each of the items that you would like to observe while visiting your competitors. Present this to the class and ask for help in developing a complete map.

LO4-5

Ensure that the entrepreneur has considered a full set of concerns in his or her external analysis.

Additional Issues for External Analysis

There are a number of other economic issues that founders of a new business will want to consider as they develop their external analysis. These include substitutes, elasticity of demand, ease of entry and exit, benchmarking, and industry trends. Each will be discussed briefly.

Substitutes

substitute

A product that performs a similar function or achieves the same result, but is not a precise imitation.

The potential new businessperson should keep in mind potential substitutes for the activities of the business. A **substitute** exists if the service or product performs a similar function or achieves the same result as the planned business, but is not a precise imitation.[8] In the case of golf, a substitute might be tennis or boating. Any other sport that the customer can pursue in place of golf could be a substitute.

In developing a competitive map, the entrepreneur needs to be aware of such substitutes and the potential impact they can have. However, it is also important that the new businessperson not get overwhelmed with so many potential substitutes that it appears there is no way to compete in the industry. Each new businessperson must judge the potential impact of a substitute, but the important issue is the recognition that at some price trade-off point, customers will switch to substitutes. For example, if you charge $500 for a single round of golf, individuals will eventually seek out other means of entertainment (unless you are Pebble Beach). Thus, substitutes can help form a ceiling on the price that can be charged for the product or service.

Elasticity of Demand

elasticity of demand

Consumers' respond to price changes. For example, as the prices of luxury items increase, the demand usually declines as these goods are not essential and their purchase can be delayed. This would be called *elastic demand*. Conversely, items such as gas for your car typically have relatively inelastic demand as you will not stop using it as the price increases.

Elasticity of demand refers to customers switching to substitutes or not using a product as the price of the product rises.[9] A product or service for which customers are willing to pay virtually any price is said to have a very inelastic demand. In other words, for your cancer medicine, the price is irrelevant; you will still seek out the medicine and buy it. In this case, substitutes have very little impact because they do not perform the exact same function. However, for a product that has elastic demand, such as rounds of golf, a price increase of $25 for a round may create a significant substitute impact. Chapter 11 will deal more in detail with the marketing and pricing of goods; it is sufficient here to say that the presence and power of substitutes need to be considered by the new businessperson. When developing your competitive map, you will need to include those companies that are close substitutes for your product or service and determine how to evaluate a trade-off value.

Ease of Entry or Exit

Another issue that needs to be considered is the ease of entry to and exit from the industry. Once a business is in operation, expenses are being incurred. If those expenses are such that an entrepreneur cannot easily recoup the investment, then the level of competition will be more intense. This is considered an **exit barrier**[10]—that is, a barrier that keeps an entrepreneur from leaving a business she has invested in.

The ease of entering and exiting a business investment is an important detail to consider.

©Ingram Publishing RF

To illustrate an exit barrier, consider the principal investments for a clothing store, the clothes in the store. Clothes tend to be very seasonal. If a piece of clothing is not sold in season, then it likely has limited value in the near future. Think about the value of white polyester suits if you need to be convinced. (Your parents probably wore them.) To close a clothing store is easy, but to recover the initial investment is not. The owner will need to sharply discount the price of the goods just to get as much of their invested money back before they have to close the store.

exit barrier
A barrier, such as investment in capital assets, that keeps a firm from leaving an industry.

In our golf example, the initial investment for the golf course is very high, but the ease of exiting the business is also very high, as the real estate could be converted to another use such as a housing tract; thus, in the case of the golf course, there is no real exit barrier. If a business owner cannot easily exit an industry, then that owner is more likely to use predatory pricing in an effort to generate cash flow and survive. The ability to exit the industry must be taken into consideration when evaluating the competitive threat posed by existing businesses. A clothing store would have a high-intensity competition, whereas a golf course would have somewhat less. In contrast to the clothing store, a liquor store's principal investment is alcohol. If a liquor store is not

ETHICAL CHALLENGE

How far can or should you go to collect information about your competitors? Most competitors will be private companies, and their financial information will not be part of the public record. Is it appropriate to be a customer of your competitor for the purpose of collecting competitive information? At what stage does acting as a customer cross an ethical line? Can you lie about why you are there? Can you hire a private investigator to find out information that is not in the public domain? What if the existing firm is owned by a friend? At what stage can you copy ideas from your friend and still maintain your ethical standards?

QUESTIONS

1. In terms of your own business what information would be useful about your competition as you start your business. List all potential data.
2. Rank this information in order of how easy it will be to obtain.
3. Which of the data do you think would cross the line of ethics?

doing well and needs to close, there is always a secondary market for liquor. There is little need to have deep price discounts to seek to recover the investment. Thus, exit is relatively easy, and competition would be expected to be a bit lower. The ability to exit a business relatively easily tends to limit the intensity of competition in the industry and reduces the threat posed by a new entry.

Benchmarking

benchmarking
Working with and learning from a company outside of your industry that has a particular skill that is potentially critical to your operation.

There may be specific areas in your business that you have identified as potentially providing you a competitive advantage. To strengthen those areas, you may consider **benchmarking** a business that is very successful in that particular arena, but that does not compete in your industry.[11]

The ability to provide a top-flight call center for your business could be dramatically improved by your looking to companies in other industries that have excellent call-center operations. Most companies are more than willing to share their knowledge as long as you are not a potential competitor.

Industry Trends

An overarching part of any analysis of competitors is an understanding of the trends in the industry. These trends shape the long-term prospects of the industry. For example, the United States is moving toward a more self-service economy, and companies that can move that process forward or take advantage of this movement appear to have an opportunity for success. Another example might be restaurant patronage. Whereas the number of people eating at restaurants has not changed dramatically over the past few years, what they eat has been changing in a consistently predictable manner. Healthy, mid-price-range restaurant sales have been increasing dramatically. Thus, the percentage of individuals who are willing to pay a little more than fast-food prices for differentiated product is steadily increasing, while there has been little change in those willing to pay for very high-end restaurants. As a result, a restaurant that enters an emerging market (utilizing the Atkins Diet or another diet craze as a menu theme, for example) may be able to be among the first to enter that niche, and thereby gain an advantage over other firms.

LO4-6

Differentiate between those elements of the business that provide a competitive advantage and those that do not.

Competitive Advantage

competitive advantage
The edge a business has over competing businesses, made up of those things that the business does better than anyone else in the industry.

Once the industry, customer, and competitor issues have been clearly identified, an entrepreneur must develop a deep understanding of the competitive advantage they expect to hold. A **competitive advantage** is made up of those things that your business does uniquely well or better than anyone else in your industry (remember, the industry is defined by you and consists of those businesses in direct competition with you in your area).

Understanding the competitive advantage is the last step in your external analysis. We will discuss competitive advantage in greater detail in Chapter 5; it is important at this point to understand that these advantages (we hope there will be several) will ultimately be the reason that individuals come to your business and not to one of your competitors. Those areas that provide you with competitive advantages are the ones that are valuable—allowing the business to charge a price that exceeds that of its direct competitors—provide a product or service that might be priced the same as competitors but at a lower cost structure, or allow the new business to draw in new customers even if the price and costs are at an equivalent level with your competitors.

A competitive advantage must provide the new business with the opportunity to make money in excess of the competition. Few new businesses perform better than their competitors in all areas, nor should they be concerned about doing so. Instead, there are many functions that a business must perform (and perform well) simply to be a player in the industry. In most industries the new business is similar to its competitors, but there is one (or hopefully, several) fundamental characteristic(s) with which the firm is able to exceed the performance of the industry. These characteristics constitute the business's competitive advantage. In order to be able to define the potential areas for this advantage, it is imperative that you have completed the competitive map and are able to discuss how each of your competitors do business today.

The source of the competitive advantage can be an activity of the firm, such as the type of service or product they provide. It can also be something structural, such as a high-quality location. The new business must be clear about what its own competitive advantages will be, as well as about the current advantages of its competitors. One of the causes of failure for new businesses is a lack of focus on their competitive advantages. Individuals might believe they have a great idea and work hard to implement it, but they may not clearly understand why a customer might choose their business over that of their competitors. Your customers must have reasons to consciously choose your business, and you must know what those reasons are to maintain your advantage.

In thinking about competitive advantage, it is helpful to examine the business as consisting of performance within two areas. The **normal or ordinary parts of the business** must be done and done well, but there is little reason to do any of these things any better than the average in the industry. The **unusual or unique parts of the business** that are central to the firm's competitive advantage over others should be the focus of the energy, money, and time of the business, because they are the means by which a business can differentiate itself from its competitors.[12] What provides a competitive advantage varies by industry, and it varies with time in an industry. The standard practices in an industry move, and they inexorably move to greater and greater heights. For example, when the frequent-flyer program was initiated, it was unusual and allowed the pioneering airline to stand out, gaining customers and profit at the expense of its competitors. However, today virtually every airline has a frequent-flyer program, and indeed, many have shared programs. What starts out as unusual will (if it is effective) lead to imitation, and thus become normal in the industry. That said, we suggest that the new businessperson examine the competitive map carefully. What is normal in the industry—that is, what does virtually everyone do just to be a player in the industry? These are the standard things you will have to provide just to be a business in this arena. What is unusual in your industry? What are competitors doing that varies from one to another? What can you do that is unusual and might form a competitive advantage? The nature of an app is not only crafting an effective technical product but one that is also attractive to customers. The entrepreneur's key issue is effectively pulling themselves out of the mass of applications that are now available.

normal or ordinary competitive factor
Describing those areas of a business that are simply standard practice in the industry and are necessary for the business to be a player.

unusual or unique competitive factor
Describing those areas of a business that are unique or unusual when compared to the standard practices of the industry, and that provide the opportunity for the business to gain value over and above the ordinary returns in the industry.

The need to be complete in this area is critical. Table 4.2 explores the competitive advantage of a new restaurant. Although not complete, it provides a bit of insight into this process.

Even though this chart may appear to be a bit excessive, it is not nearly complete. It would be difficult for us to overemphasize the importance of developing this chart prior to beginning operations so that entrepreneurs are clear

EXERCISE 5

Develop a two-column list for your new business. Label the first column "Normal" and the second "Unusual." In the "normal" column, list everything that you will need to have (physically) and do (actively) just to be accepted by customers in the industry. In the second column, explain what your business will have or do that is rare or unusual compared to your competitors.

NORMAL BUSINESS RESOURCES AND CAPABILITIES	POTENTIALLY UNIQUE BUSINESS RESOURCES AND CAPABILITIES
A storefront	A small, intimate facility
Tables	Fixed tile tables
Chairs	Roller, cushioned chairs
Floor covering	Tile floors
Lights	Mood lighting throughout
Cash register	Card swipe machines at each table
Signs	Custom neon signs
Menu	Touch screen at each table
Kitchen equipment:	
Freezers	
Refrigerators	
Sinks	
Stoves/ovens	
Cookware	
Safety equipment	
Fryers	
Plates, cups, silverware, napkins, salt and pepper shakers, sauce dispensers	
Shelving	
Tables and chairs	
Desk/work area	
Time sheets	
Staff:	
Cook staff	Trained chefs
Waitstaff	Unique outfits; experienced, highly trained staff requirements, formal
Bartenders	
Cleaning crew (tables, etc.)	
Host crew	
Management	
Trash cans (internal and external)	
Utilities	

Table 4.2
Company Evaluation of Resources and Capabilities

as to what might form a competitive advantage for them. We have found few tools more helpful in defining the uniqueness of the potential start-up, as well as defining the potential start-up expenses.

Resource-Based View

To understand the unique resources and capabilities of a business and develop a competitive advantage the new business owner should use a technique generally known as **resource-based analysis** (although it can be found with a variety of acronyms such as VRIN or VRIST). This tool helps the entrepreneur delve deeper into what actually creates an advantage. In the prior list of potentially unique actions for a restaurant that could create a advantage for a restaurant, it was noted that tiles on the table could be a normal business item. However, upon further consideration, the tiles are really just part of a larger resource that relates to the ambiance of the restaurant. The tiles themselves are good, but they need to be part of something more significant to have an impact. Resource-based analysis has been developed over the past 50 years;[13] it has become one of the most effective tools in defining a business's competitive advantages and in differentiating these from their competitors. While we will cover this topic in depth in the next chapter, we feel that some introduction to this topic is warranted in the discussion of positioning relative to your competitors. The focus of resource-based analysis is solely upon the potentially unusual products or services that you will offer in your business, which can be a source of competitive advantage.

resource-based analysis
A theoretical approach and practical methodology that examines the functioning of a business in terms of whether a product or service simultaneously meets the criteria of being rare, durable, nonsubstitutable, and valuable.

To develop into a competitive advantage, the potentially unusual products or services offered by the new business need to meet all of the following criteria: They must be rare, durable, relatively nonsubstitutable, and valuable to develop into a competitive advantage. "Rare" describes a quality that competitors will find difficult to obtain. For example, a particular chef might be unique, or a location may be particularly valued. "Durability" has three elements to it where any one element provides the company with the ability to hold onto the competitive advantage. The first has to do with the length of time that you might be able to gain and hold a competitive advantage. The second is an evaluation of how long would it take for a competitor to imitate you or to wash away your advantage. The third is an evaluation of the desire of your competitors to compete with you with the same potential resource or capability. "Relatively nonsubstitutable" is a determination about whether the product or service may be easily substituted by something else that a competitor could provide. "Valuable" refers to your ability to gain extraordinary returns from your product or service. A product or service might be rare, durable, and nonsubstitutable, but if you cannot obtain returns in excess of your competition from its sale, then it will not provide you with a resource-based advantage.

As you examine your list of unusual products or services for the new business, consider each one along these four dimensions. Those items that meet all four criteria are your primary points of competitive advantage. These are the points on which you should concentrate your resources, time, and effort. These are the areas that will provide you with a competitive advantage relative to your competitors, and will be the reasons that customers choose you over the competition. We will discuss this in much more depth in the next chapter.

SUMMARY

This chapter examined the reasons and methods for the potential entrepreneur to develop a complete, well-reasoned, and personal knowledge of the competitive conditions for their business. This analysis is fundamentally founded upon the idea that the entrepreneur decides what constitutes the "industry." The industry does not include (except in unusual circumstances) the whole country or the world. It is important that the entrepreneur limit the defined "industry" as it relates to the specific business, to effectively analyze the competition and the potential competitive threat. We have provided these highly practical tools for the founders to personally develop their own analysis of the environment and their ability to compete within that environment.

KEY TERMS

benchmarking 74
competitive advantage 74
competitive map 70
elasticity of demand 72
exit barrier 73
fragmented markets 68
industry 64
normal or ordinary competitive factor 75
resource-based analysis 77
substitute 72
unusual or unique competitive factor 75

REVIEW QUESTIONS

1. How would you advise a potential entrepreneur define the industry for a new business?
2. How should a new business develop a profile for its potential customers?
3. Why should a potential entrepreneur research the industry personally?
4. What techniques would you recommend for identifying competitors within an industry?
5. How would you recommend developing a complete analysis of the competitors for a new business?
6. What elements are in a competitive map?

BUSINESS PLAN DEVELOPMENT QUESTIONS

1. What is the industry for your potential business?
2. Who is the customer?
3. Who are the competitors?
4. Develop a competitive map for your business.
5. What do you believe your tentative competitive advantages will be?

INDIVIDUAL EXERCISES

1. Using your map developed for the business plan exercise above, visit (virtually or in-person) the first two competitors on your list and adjust the map according to reality.
   a. What additional items might you add to the map?
   b. What qualitative areas of competition did you add to your map?
2. Using the material that you have developed in the previous exercises, write a two- to three-page description of the competitive environment in which your proposed new business will compete.
3. Develop a competitive map for the restaurants around campus. Discuss in class how everyone else designed their competitive map of this group.

GROUP EXERCISES

1. Look at the list of items for the restaurant in Table 4.2 of this chapter. What would be the resources that would drive the potential sources of competitive advantage?
2. Take the material that you developed outside of class. Break into small groups. Create a final list of resources you will need to develop your competitive advantage for the firm.

ENDNOTES

1. A. Ardichvili, R. Cardozo, and R. Sourav, "A Theory of Entrepreneurial Opportunity Identification and Development," *Journal of Business Venturing* 18, no. 1 (2003), pp. 104–24.
2. F. Delmar, P. Davidson, and W. Gartner, "Arriving at the High-Growth Firm," *Journal of Business Venturing* 18, no. 2 (2003), pp. 189–217.
3. N. Kumar, "The CEO's Marketing Manifesto," *Marketing Management* 17, no. 6 (2008), pp. 24–29.
4. C. Comaford-Lynch, "The Power of Positioning," *BusinessWeek Online,* June 3, 2008, p. 13.
5. H. Corrigan, G. Craciun, and A. Powerll, "How Does Target Know So Much About Its Customers? Utilizing Customer Analytics to Make Marketing Decisions,"

Marketing Education Review 24, no. 2 (2014), pp. 159–66.
6. G. Dess, “Consensus on Strategy Formulation and Organizational Performance: Competitors in a Fragmented Market,” *Strategic Management Journal* 8, no. 3 (1987), pp. 259–79.
7. W. Bogner, H. Thomas, and J. McGee, “A Longitudinal Study of the Competitive Positions and Entry Paths of European Firms in the U.S. Pharmaceutical Market,” *Strategic Management Journal* 17, no. 2 (1996), pp. 85–108.
8. R. Wilden, M. Devinney, and G. R. Dowling, “The Architecture of Dynamic Capability Research Identifying the Building Blocks of a Configurational Approach,” *Academy of Management Annals* 10, no. 1 (2016), pp. 997–1076.
9. D. Teece, G. Pisano, and A. Shuen, “Dynamic Capabilities and Strategic Management,” *Strategic Management Journal* 18, no. 7 (1997), pp. 509–30.
10. M. Porter, *Competitive Advantage* (New York: Free Press, 1985).
11. H. Wang, J. Choi, G. Wan, and J. Q. Dong, “Slack resources and the Rent-Generating Potential of Firm-Specific Knowledge,” *Journal of Management* 42, no. 2 (2016), pp. 500–523.
12. L. Costa, K. Cool, and I. Diericky, “The Competitive Implications of the Deployment of Unique Resources,” *Strategic Management Journal* 34, no. 4 (2013), pp. 445–63.
13. S. Alvarez and L. Busenitz, “The Entrepreneurship of Resource-Based Theory,” *Journal of Management* 27, no. 6 (2001), pp. 755–75; J. B. Barney, “Firm Resources and Sustained Competitive Advantage,” *Journal of Management* 17, no. 1 (1991), pp. 99–120; R. Grant, “The Resource-Based Theory of Competitive Advantage: Implications for Strategy Formulation,” *California Management Review* 33 (1991), pp. 114–35; E. Penrose, *The Theory of the Growth of the Firm* (New York: John Wiley & Sons, 1959); M. Peteraf, “The Cornerstones of Competitive Advantage: A Resource-Based View,” *Strategic Management Journal* 14 (1993), pp. 179–91.

chapter 5

Business Mission and Strategy

learning outcomes

After studying this chapter, you will be able to:

LO5-1 Recognize how mission statements guide a new business.

LO5-2 Explain what constitutes a sustainable competitive advantage.

LO5-3 Identify a new business's assets and capabilities.

LO5-4 Distinguish which of those assets and capabilities are standard and which are unique.

LO5-5 Apply a resource-based analysis approach to arrive at a list of competitive advantages.

LO5-6 Determine a strategy to match the new business mission.

VICTORIA TSAI—TATCHA

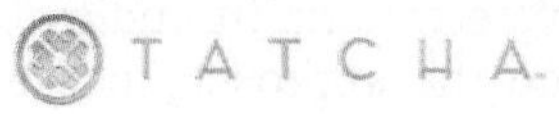

Victoria Tsai initially was a fixed-income analyst at Merrill Lynch in New York City when the 9/11 terrorist attack occurred. Several years later her husband developed a serious illness. These two major events made Tsai realize that life was a precious gift, and she needed to do things that she valued. This revelation led her to go back to school to pursue her MBA from Harvard and look for other opportunities in life. After her MBA she obtained a job introducing new consumer products, particularly women's cosmetics, to China. However, she demonstrated the cosmetics on herself far too much and developed a serious skin condition on her face.

This skin condition led her to realize that makeup made in the United States that she was selling in China was largely an unregulated domain. The U.S. government will only investigate and seek to control what is in cosmetics if something is proven dangerous. The result is that unless there is a very serious problem cosmetics largely go without any government oversight.

Both medicines and natural remedies such as granola proved unsuccessful in treating Tsai's face condition. During her travels in Asia, Tsai came in contact with geisha's in Kyoto, Japan. She instantly noted how beautiful their skin was and was able to learn that one of their beauty activities was to use blotting papers to clean their skin. The specific blotting papers they employed were made of abaca leaf, a plant like a banana leaf. The effect of the blotting papers cured her skin condition.

Building on this understanding, Tsai determined that she wanted to develop a product like this for the U.S. market, around which she would build a business. To build this business, she quit her job but continued to take on special consulting jobs to get capital. She sold her car and engagement ring to help raise funds. Ultimately, she also brought in two partners to help finance the effort.

The various means to raise capital allowed her to develop the product, the proper packaging, as well as the order of 10,000 blotting papers. The initial marketing was limited, and most sales happened through the Internet. The big break came as Tsai sent samples of her product to news outlets such as Oprah's *O* magazine. Ultimately, these samples impressed those she sent them to, which lead to a substantial and very favorable volume of free press. (You can see the nature of this free and very complimentary press at https://www.tatcha.com/.)

The firm remains privately traded but the latest information from 2014 is as follows:

Year Founded: 2009

2014 Revenue: $12 million

3-Year Growth: 10,996%

Sources: T. Byrnes, "How Victoria Tsai Turned a Geisha Secret into a Cosmetics Innovation," *Entrepreneur*, January 22, 2016. https://www.entrepreneur.com/article/269793; B. Helm, "How a Geisha's Secret Helped Me Found My Company," *Inc. Magazine*, September 2015. http://www.inc.com/magazine/201509/burt-helm/2015-inc5000-memoirs-of-a-wannabe-geisha.html; Oprah.com, "Skincare Secrets for a Glowy Complexion," *The Oprah Magazine*, April 2013. http://www.oprah.com/style/victoria-tsai-tatcha-skincare-clear-skin.

mission statement
A brief statement that summarizes how and where a firm will compete.

Defining the new business's mission is one of the most difficult and critical elements in the success of any business. A firm's **mission statement** is a brief statement that summarizes how and where the firm will compete.*

LO5-1

Recognize how mission statements guide a new business.

Mission Statements

Because the mission and strategy together have the power to guide the business as it develops, we believe that an early effort to craft both is warranted. Substantial research has found that as a business grows, it gets progressively more difficult to change its direction. Recall from the lean start-up discussion that our goal is to keep the firm flexible and adaptive. It is hoped that this concept remains constant in the firm although it is hard to do.

Imagine establishing a new business oriented toward high levels of customer service with experts in each area of the business available to help customers. The customers appreciate this extensive expertise, and, as a result, the business grows. However, the founders find that the model they have developed is expensive and they wish to increase their profits. Therefore, despite the company's success, they decide to eliminate the experts and not provide the same level of ability to answer the customers' questions. The negative reaction from their established customer base will likely take place over time. It will not be a dramatic drop in one month, but over time customers will begin to cease doing business with the firm as they seek out other firms, which provide the expertise they desire.

This is precisely what happened to Circuit City. The firm started in 1949 (originally as Wards in Richmond, Virginia) as an entrepreneurial venture based on a well-defined strategy of hiring individuals throughout the company who were experts in the products sold. As a result, the company grew to be one of the largest electronic goods retailers in the United States. The business was crafted around commissioned salespeople who were experts in audiovisual equipment. New management decided to change the approach to use inexpensive, noncommissioned clerks in an attempt to match the cost-conscious model being pitched by the new upstart, Best Buy. A dramatic change over time in the expertise that Circuit City could offer its customers occurred, which led to a loss of Circuit City's traditional customer base and, more important, a loss in its unique positioning in the market. The result was that the entire business closed in 2009, in one of the largest retail store closures in U.S. history.

Smaller electronic stores and chains benefit from hiring employees with a high level of product knowledge.

©Juice Images/Alamy RF

The firm's mission and strategy are central to the new business's ability to maintain a clear vision about what it wants to be and how it will accomplish that plan. Without that consistent guidance, the firm can lose its focus and competitive advantage. Although there is great strength in building into the firm a strong common understanding of the firm's strategy, firms sometimes

*Larger firms might also have a vision statement that is a very broad statement of the firm's direction while the mission statement is a more specific statement. For a new business we believe that mission alone is appropriate. The goal is to help direct everyone who works for or with the firm in its actions and not create unnecessary work. For a new business to try to differentiate between vision and mission would be splitting hairs. Thus, the student should not only recognize their differences in theory but also recognize that here they are treated as the same item.

find that they have to change their mission and strategy. Any business seeking to radically change its fundamental way of doing business as defined by the firm's strategy will find the road ahead difficult. Once the understanding of how to do things is built into the organization it becomes second nature and can be hard to change.

We use the term *mission statement* here, but there are many terms used when creating the overarching goals of an organization. It is quite easy for a businessperson to become consumed in the proper labeling of this statement rather than focusing on the goals of the organization. As a result, you will likely see terms as varied as *company mission*, *vision*, *overall strategy*, *goals*, *simple rules*, and *statement of purpose* to describe what we refer to as the *mission*. The important point for the new business is that the statement is concise and well understood by everyone who will come in contact with the business so that they will understand what the company does and what it does not do.[1]

The firm's mission helps the venture by targeting its efforts in specific arenas and on specific opportunities. No firm can be all things to all people. Instead, the new business needs to focus on performing those activities where it has competitive advantage, or doing some set of activities better than everyone else. The firm's mission helps the new business specify what the business does best in its industry (the industry consists of those businesses you believe are your direct competitors). However, the mission statement also helps the small business stay away from things that opportunistically sound promising, but which take the business away from its principal focus. Realize that if you start wandering off to another area of competition, you will lose focus in your core area of business. If that occurs, there are always single-focused companies in any market that are ready to capitalize on your judgment errors.[2]

To illustrate the benefit of a mission statement in targeting a firm's activities, let's take a look at another restaurant business. The mission statement of this restaurant read as follows (with some minor changes to protect its identity): *The Gourmet Mediterranean (Italian) Meal Experience in the Heart of the City.*

Even though this mission statement is very simple, it ultimately helped the business owner tremendously. The city was opening a new central high school basketball arena and needed someone to run the food facilities. The head of the school board asked the owner of the restaurant to consider running the concessions for the arena. The idea appeared to have the potential to be very profitable. However, the food that would be sold at the arena would be very different from what the restaurant traditionally sold. Thus, the expertise that the business owner held would largely not be applicable. Additionally, new suppliers would need to be located because the concession stands and the restaurant would use different quality inputs. The operation of the concessions would also take the business owner's attention away from what she knew best: running a high-quality Mediterranean restaurant. Thus, even though both the restaurant and the concession stands involved the preparation and selling of food, in reality they were two distinct businesses. A clear mission statement helps the new-business person focus her efforts on her expertise. The ability to be successful with one type of business does not mean that she will be successful with another type of business, even one within the same broad domain. The businessperson's earlier mission statement helped that owner keep the business targeted where it needed to compete. The owner declined the opportunity to run the concession stands in the basketball arena and instead continued to build her restaurant to become one of the most successful in the area.

Yahoo! is a name that is widely known today. But when you think of it, can you really say what Yahoo! does? Yahoo! is another example of the need for a clear mission statement.

KOSHER HOME

Jack and Toby are aware of how important a mission statement will be for their new business. Reflecting on the insights they made on industry and competition, they developed the mission statement below:

Mission Statement: *Kosher Home prepares and ships high-quality, individual kosher meals anywhere in the United States.*

Key Issues This Mission Statement Reflects

Product. The mission statement of Kosher Home positions the firm as unique in a fast growing industry. The prepared meals shipped directly to individuals started with the diet industry. Firms such as NutriSystem report sales close to $460 million a year. Another segment that developed was for the elderly who could not cook. The newest and fastest growing segment caters to those individuals who want to cook in a gourmet fashion but do not necessarily have the time or skills to do such cooking. To date there is no one focusing on kosher segment of this industry.

Positioning. The analysis of the competitive position of simply shipping dry goods seemed to the entrepreneurs too easily copied by anyone if the firm was successful. Beyond that, a typical grocery store can sell over 100,000 dry kosher grocery items. These items are already in most stores, so how could the firm choose which to deal with and then how it is adding value that a typical grocery store does not. The two entrepreneurs also want to focus on serving isolated communities and soon realized that financially they would need to provide much more than just dry goods. The Pew Foundation highlights that 49 percent of the American Jewish population lives in urban areas, 47 percent live in suburban areas, and 4 percent reside in rural locations. Thus, as is often the case the entrepreneurs had to adapt their business plan. Jack had largely grown up in a rural part of Oklahoma. He did not realize how unusual his experience was until he began research for his new firm. This meant they were going to provide their meals throughout the United States, not just isolated communities.

Pricing. The firm has decided to offer a differentiated product that will entail offering a superior product at a price premium. If someone wants to have the lowest price product, the individual can choose not to eat kosher despite religious desires or they can have dry kosher products shipped to them via a number of firms. To eat fresh food that is kosher will mean that the entrepreneurs will have to have a very specific high-quality product and that product costs both the entrepreneurs and ultimately the customers.

QUESTIONS

1. Do you agree with their focus on fresh meals shipped to homes?
2. What do you think of the entrepreneurs substantially changing the initial idea of their business?
3. Do you think their mission statement needs anything else in it?

The nature of change in the industry has swept this what Garry listed. The firm was originally an electronic community that drew people in for many purposes—including e-mail, search engines, online communities, and video streaming. Some of these purposes made money on their own, but most generated revenue through advertising. Advertisers pay to be at the top of a particular search item or to be displayed alongside a search for something closely associated to your search. From these services Yahoo! was able to build a business with over 700 million customers. Yahoo! was one of the pioneers in the industry. As a search engine, they were passed by the ease of Google and Internet Explorer (which was preloaded on most new PCs).

As the Web grew, so did the offering of specialized services. If you want to connect to others with similar interests like yours, you are likely to use Facebook. If you want to buy something, it is not likely that Yahoo! is your first choice. It would be more likely to be a specialty retailer or some broad-based retailer like Amazon. As a result the firm faced severe financial hardships that ultimately led to Verizon offering to buy what was left of the business. As an industry changes, firms must change and adapt.

There are numerous books on the development of mission statements, and the ways suggested to do them are as diverse as the individuals who write the books. There is, in fact, little empirical evidence regarding the most effective type of mission statement. We suggest that an effective mission statement and sustainable competitive advantage are inseparable. It should be recalled from Chapter 4 that the resources of the firm are generally constrained. As a result, it is particularly critical that the new business conserves its resources and focuses them on those areas that have the potential to maximize the firm's success. A key aspect to that success is the firm's **capabilities,** or those resources that combine to allow the firm to perform better than its competitors.

EXERCISE 1

1. Kosher Home originally decided to differentiate itself by offering Kosher food to isolated Jewish populations. Almost by definition this will mean that the firm must charge a premium. The firm will buy in smaller quantities than say a large national chain and then have to ship the goods. Would there have been a way that Kosher Homer could have been a low cost provider?
2. What would be the range of differences in the actions of the firm if the mission statement had been set up with a focus on being the lowest-cost provider?

capabilities
Resources that combine to allow a firm to do things better than its competitors.

Designing a Mission Statement

In developing the mission statement, we believe there are several key characteristics that should drive the new-business founder(s).

1. Keep it short—Make sure it can fit on a coffee mug?
2. Keep it simple—Ensure that everyone in the company can learn and understand what it means and why.
3. Make it applicable—The mission statement should be able to guide every individual in the company each and every day. It should also be something that customers cite as to why they use the company.
4. Be specific—Be so clear that it tells everyone exactly what you do, and by definition, what you do not do.
5. Establish measurable goals—Be able to develop a metric for every part of the statement.

Keep It Short We cannot overemphasize this fundamental aspect of a mission statement. The statement must be understandable and memorable for all those who come in contact with it. While it principally is written to guide the employees of the company, it must also speak to customers, suppliers, and others. It is not a tome that describes everything you have done and might do, and how you will do it, so that the organization can impress external parties. It is a short, direct statement that is designed to guide the organization each and every day.

The mission of a firm is not "to make money"; that is a by-product of a good direction; it is significantly more likely that the organization will indeed make money if the mission statement is clear, succinct, memorable, and widely known by all in the firm.

Keep It Simple A mission statement that is not shared has little, if any, value to the organization. We have watched people spend countless hours crafting a statement only to have it poorly communicated and/or not reinforced by the senior management of the company. The new-business owner must ensure that every employee can understand the statement and how it can be applied to his day-to-day decision making. The key to the ability to communicate a mission easily is that the statement be simple, direct, and appropriate.

As the firm is developed, the founder needs to ensure that the mission statement is at the center of the various activities that are developed. Whether the firm is a new high-technology firm with PhDs on staff or a quick-order restaurant where many employees have no high school education, the workers will come closer to having an understanding of the mission of the organization if the statement is simple. The firm needs to ensure that the words and concepts employed in the statement are straightforward and have a clear meaning to all who hear or read them. A great line in the 2003 Disney movie *Pirates of the Caribbean* illustrates this concept wonderfully. The captain of the ship, somewhat taken aback by the demands and high-brow, patronizing language of his recent captive, responds to her request by saying, "I'm disinclined to acquiesce to your request," pauses for a moment, and turns back to her and says, "Means NO." Avoid the use of lots of adjectives or descriptive language about how the company will accomplish its mission.

Make It Applicable It takes extraordinary care to develop a mission that guides the entire organization, and yet, for the mission to be utilized effectively by every member of the company, it must have direct applicability to even the most entry-level employee. Imagine the employees assigned to handle the customer service lines who are faced daily with customers calling in with concerns and complaints. If the mission of the organization is a long statement that fundamentally says "do good," or if it is like so many and simply exhorts the employees to "act like owners and maximize shareholder value," then what are the customer service employees to do? They will try to follow procedures and not get in trouble. Although large companies can afford to have people who just follow procedures rather than use all of their skills and creative abilities, new businesses cannot afford to limit their employees. The entrepreneurial business needs to align employees in a consistent direction and allow them to use their creativity and skills.

Thus, the mission of the business needs to be actionable. That is, the mission statement needs to help the employees to make active decisions in the moment, without having to refer everything to the founder of the firm. An advantage to a well-developed mission statement is that it is able to guide everyone in the organization toward the goals that the owners have set. A well-developed mission statement helps ensure that everyone in the organization is heading in the same relative direction, so that, although there will be some variance, there will not be decisions made that are counter to what the founder of the new business would choose.

Be Specific In order to accomplish the three keys for mission statements we have noted it is necessary that the mission be so specific that it clearly also tells everyone what *not* to do. Take a look again at the mission statement for one of the restaurants discussed earlier in this chapter: *The Gourmet Mediterranean (Italian) Meal Experience in the Heart of the City.* We know from this statement that it does not serve Chinese, or barbeque, among other items. We also know that it is located in the city and (at least with this statement) should not look to expand into the suburbs. It provides an "experience" that includes ambiance, certain types of wine, food, and service. It should not consider adding American cuisine, French wines, or rap music. The value of this limitation should be clear to everyone every day. Employees are repeatedly faced with decisions that appear to be of little importance, but the cumulative impact of such small decisions that do not lead in a consistent direction is that the firm eventually is trying to be everything to everyone. A strong focus on a single mission statement keeps everyone in the organization constantly striving to achieve the goals of the owners.

metric
A measure to evaluate whether a person or firm is meeting stated goals.

Establish Measurable Goals A **metric** is a measure used to evaluate whether a person or firm is meeting its goals. From the mission statement, a new-business owner should be able to develop a set of metrics that are meaningful to judge if the mission is being accomplished.[3]

Greater specifics on metrics and developing them will be presented in Chapters 7 and 8; however, a few brief comments are appropriate here. We typically recommend that each organization develop between five and eight measures of success for its venture. These are broken up into two categories: (1) quantitative measures—those that are tied to the financial or strategic goals of the organization and are easily measured—and (2) qualitative measures—those that are tied to the strategic goals of the organization but have more to do with the "feel" of the organization. Recall though if these metrics show the firm is not meeting the goal, there must be some significant soul searching by the entrepreneur—do you seek to improve on what you are doing or are there more fundamental changes needed. The lean start-up method we employ here in thinking through a business requires that a firm measures early and often, with a clear vision that the entrepreneur must change and adapt as the results of various measures come in. The feedback loop that leads the entrepreneur to take action is critical.

To illustrate, below are some of the metrics used by our example of a high-end restaurant that we have been discussing:

Mission: *The Gourmet Mediterranean (Italian) Meal Experience in the Heart of the City*

Metrics The Gourmet

1. Number of chefs who have graduated from gourmet schools
2. Ranking in annual Zagat or similar guides
3. Quality of reviews in local papers

Mediterranean Meal Experience

1. Closeness in appearance to actual Mediterranean restaurants
2. Number of employees from Mediterranean region
3. Service measure as compared to actual restaurants in Mediterranean

Heart of the City

1. Proximity to city festivals/events
2. Do people refer to other stores, events, and so on by referring to our restaurant as the starting point (i.e., "Just down the block from XX restaurant")?

Metrics are best established at the founding of the business and are evaluated on a recurring basis. The baseline position is not nearly as important as the vector (direction and level of change) that the metrics are taking. We want to see positive movement on each of the metrics. They are the direct measure of the business's mission, and the more the business improves on each metric, the closer it is getting to its fundamental mission.

Mission Statement Impact

To illustrate the range of decisions that are impacted by the mission of the organization, consider three domains (advertising, location of the business, and staffing) for the Kosher Home example in this chapter and how they are impacted by market choice:

1. If Kosher Home chose to pursue multiple types of client bases at the same time, where would the firm advertise? Each market has substantively different outlets to reach its respective customers. Which magazines do different groups of people read? What endorsements would each group of potential customers consider important? What

organizations (hospice, Ronald McDonald House, and/or AARP) might you support, given your desired customer base?

2. The location chosen for the type of business would differ significantly based on the mission. A company focused on the elderly might want to be positioned near big hospitals if they offer day care for patients. However, because Kosher Home's service is in the customers' homes, the clients and their families never go to the office. Thus, the nature of the office or its location may be unimportant.
3. Personnel and staffing size would vary from firm to firm as well. The style, sophistication, and approach from the staff will vary dramatically with the approach and audience chosen to serve.

Thus, before the founders can begin to build the new business, they must be clear about where and how they will compete. Almost all new ventures have a wide variety of activities that can be pursued. The mission statement should help by clearly specifying in which market the firm will compete, in some cases how broad a geographic range the firm will serve, and the major ways in which it will compete. If these activities are not precisely defined, the new owners will find themselves building an entity that in some ways is targeted to one business and in other ways targeted to another related but inconsistent business. Having everyone in the business moving in the same direction and toward the same group of customers will provide immense benefits to the new firm.[4]

LO5-2

Explain what constitutes a sustainable competitive advantage.

Sustainable Competitive Advantage

It was noted in Chapter 4 that a firm needs to ensure that it has a set of *competitive advantages,* or areas of separation where the firm performs better than anyone else in the market that it serves. Here we will go into more depth on this critical topic and discuss how it impacts the implementation of the mission statement. In particular, we will examine competitive advantages in terms of a **sustainable competitive advantage**—that is, a set of advantages that provides you with the opportunity to make money where other businesses cannot easily copy your advantages.[5]

sustainable competitive advantage

An advantage that others cannot immediately copy.

All individual competitive advantages eventually disappear as industries change and competitors adapt. However, businesses should seek to maintain an advantage for as long as possible by continually refining their business model. A key part of building a competitive advantage is having a deep understanding of your customers' needs.[6] For example, a new business may decide that it will develop its business around the best customer service in the replacement/repair of any item it sells. If customers do not really value the ability to repair the product quickly, then this service (which is quite expensive) will not provide a sustainable competitive advantage. Consider another example: a business that sells and repairs Wi-Fi systems for businesses to use wireless throughout the organization. Having the wireless capability go down during a business day is an emergency at most companies. Businesses have come to rely on wireless to accomplish so many activities in the firm. Focusing attention and effort on the rapid deployment and quick recovery of these systems could provide a substantial competitive advantage for the right entrepreneur. For products like an app, it can be even harder to determine what your competitive advantage will be. It is typically impossible to prevent someone from developing a similar app.

Wind turbines create a reliable and sustainable energy source for future generations and likewise building a sustainable business is critical to long-term success.

Many entrepreneurial businesses find that their greatest source of sustainable advantage is founded in the personal relationships with their customers.[7] The development of a compelling personal relationship is something that large organizations find quite difficult. Building the relationship with a customer for the new firm may be as simple as acknowledging the customer when you see him or as complex as knowing what a customer buys and contacting her when a new shipment arrives. The long-term difficulty for the new-business owner comes from setting expectations now that you will be able to maintain in the future. For an app customer relationships are critical. The entrepreneur may not be able to prevent other entrants, but if you have a loyal customer, the other app will have to be dramatically better or cheaper to have someone switch. Building that customer loyalty before others enter the market is critical.

Prior to developing an effective mission statement, the new business must first develop a detailed list of what might constitute or what will constitute its competitive advantages. There are three steps to the process of identifying a new business's sustainable competitive advantage. Although it is quite tempting to skip ahead, we suggest that the process itself leads to unique insights and will help the founder craft a business that has a long-term opportunity for success.

Identifying a Sustainable Competitive Advantage

Step 1: Develop a list of your business's assets and capabilities (either existing or proposed).

Step 2: Break that list into two groups: standard and unique.

Step 3: Evaluate the unique resources/capabilities.

Step 1: Develop a List of Your Business's Assets and Capabilities

LO5-3

Identify a new business's assets and capabilities.

The owner, or founding team, needs to develop a complete list of all the physical and intangible assets that the company will have at its founding. **Tangible assets** are those hard assets such as equipment or a location. The intangible assets are those things that are not physical but are just as critical to success, such as relationships with key suppliers. A key part of the **intangible assets** are the capabilities and skills of the founders or employees.[8]

tangible assets
Hard assets such as equipment or a location.

intangible assets
Things that are not physical but are just as critical to success, such as a relationship with a key supplier.

Although this inventory process may seem a bit mundane, it is absolutely critical to the later steps and the development of an effective and focused mission for the organization. In evaluating the intangible assets and capabilities, the new-business founders need to develop a clear and precise list that encompasses the breadth of knowledge within the founding team. This list will tend to be long and should include absolutely *everything* that the company has now or will have at the point that it opens for business. See Table 5.1 for a very short example.

Step 2: Split the List into Standard and Unique Assets

LO5-4

Distinguish which of those assets and capabilities are standard and which are unique.

The tangible and intangible assets can be further separated into standard and unique, much in the same way we categorized actions of the entrepreneur and firm earlier as either standard or unique. Most of the assets listed by a firm are standard to be a player in the industry. For Kosher Home those assets might include a wide range of items such as an office, computer systems,

Table 5.1
Tangible and Intangible Assets

TANGIBLE ASSETS	INTANGIBLE ASSETS
Building location	Industry experience
Equipment (list)	Contacts
Initial financing (equity or debt)	Previous start-up experience
Inventory	Education
Patents or patents pending	Unique knowledge of the industry (usually from previous research)
Software and systems for business	Skill set of founders (presentation, innovation, etc.)
Build-out of facility (list detail)-walls, fixtures, built-ins, etc.	Name branding

telephones, and business licenses. These assets allow the firm to operate; they are not, however, things that provide a competitive advantage to the firm.

Similarly, most capabilities, or skills of the founders and employees, are also standard for the industry. For example, serving customers in a timely manner may be done very well by a new business; however, the standard expectation of most customers is that you will have a strong capability to provide such service. Therefore, this capability can only rarely be a source of sustainable competitive advantage, and then so only if it is so far above average that the customer really notices.

There will also be unique assets and capabilities that the entrepreneur or entrepreneurial team possesses. These unique resources and/or capabilities can provide the business a competitive advantage for some period of time. The nature of individuals, and in turn businesses, is that they are driven by inertia. Individuals or businesses are not willing to make a change unless encouraged to do so for some reason. Your unique capabilities will be the source of that motivation to convince customers to change to do business with your new business. The previously discussed personal relationship is just such a unique capability.

An Apple iPad is used to view Netflix, the leading global Internet subscription service for films and TV programs. Netflix offers instant and unlimited access to a broad range of entertainment.

To illustrate, if you were to consider opening a new video store in a strip mall, what would you consider to be your competitive advantages? Why would customers come to it rather than use Netflix or rent via a Redbox vending machine? Would your new firm have different movies when compared to the other choices? Would the firm's movies be rented more cheaply? Would access to the business be easier? If you are going to do the same thing that other firms do, or something that is considered to be a step backward, then why will anyone switch to your store?

The new business must have something that will motivate potential customers to select that business; these are your unique resources and capabilities. It will be these unique assets (or resources, if we consider the term more broadly) and capabilities that form a competitive advantage for new business.

first-mover advantage
The benefit of gaining customer loyalty by being the first firm to market.

followers
Firms that enter a market after the first mover.

There are a wide range of potential resources and capabilities that can be the source of a competitive advantage. For example, customer loyalty can be obtained if customers are driven principally by something other than cost and the firm is the first to market with a differentiating approach. This is referred to as a **first-mover advantage**, and those firms that arrive later are referred to as **followers**.[9] Followers can benefit by learning from the mistakes of the first movers, but they may not be able to obtain the loyalty of customers if there is any to be had. For the new business, this does not mean that you have to be the first to market with the broad concept as long as you bring some unique resource or capability to the idea. A new business could never be the first to market with a general concept such as that of a mid-priced restaurant. However, you may recall from Chapter 4 that new businesses do not compete against the entire industry. Instead, there are limits to how far someone will drive for a restaurant. Therefore, a new business only needs to be the first in the industry that is relevant to that firm. In many fast-growing suburban areas, a restaurant may be the first of its type in the area; it would then be the first mover in that area.

There are other ways that a new business can build a competitive advantage. For example, a firm can have special relationships with suppliers. There are a number of Amish carpenters who make furniture. A small retailer may wish to carry that particular furniture but would need to have a relationship with those specialized suppliers before such opportunities could be arranged. Location can be another source of advantage; those firms with prime locations that have easy automobile access might have an advantage over those businesses that are hard to access. The range of potential sources of a new business's competitive advantage is as wide as there are activities in the firm. A new business's competitive advantage also needs to be defensible. That is, the advantage must be something that is not easily substituted away or matched by established competitors.

EXERCISE 2

Develop a complete list of resources and/or capabilities for your proposed new venture. Then break the list into two sections based on whether each one is standard or unique for the industry as you have defined it.

Step 3: Evaluate Competitiveness of Unique Resources or Capabilities

LO5-5

Apply a resource-based analysis approach to arrive at a list of competitive advantages.

Once you know what resources or capabilities your new business might have that appear to be unique, you will need to examine each before you can claim any of these as a source of competitive advantage. Successful businesses generally have several sources of the competitive advantage. The new business may have a capability or resource that is unique, but as noted before, that may or may not be the best resource on which to center a new business. To illustrate further, in a manufacturing business we may be able to offer 24-hour customer service in an industry that does not value 24-hour operations. The new business needs to focus its efforts on those areas that have the potential in the market to provide the greatest competitive advantage to the business. We refer to the financial gains garnered from an asset or capability that are in excess of the ordinary returns in that particular industry as **economic rents**. Ordinary returns in an industry suggest that you are doing no more nor less than the average of the industry. This average performance should be accomplishable by simply matching the industry average for behavior, location, and the like. Economic rents imply that the new business not only matches the norms for the industry but, in several areas, far exceeds the industry in a manner that allows it to charge well in excess of its additional costs.[10]

economic rents
Financial gains garnered from an asset or capability that are in excess of the ordinary returns in that particular industry.

There are several means with which to analyze these resources and develop a small list of resources and capabilities that truly provide the new business with the potential to obtain a sustainable competitive advantage. The predominant approach by strategists is the resource-based perspective.[11] For new businesses, there are four elements that seem to be most important within this evaluation system. Each and every resource and capability that is listed as potentially unique in the previous step must be subjected to the following four questions. As mentioned at the end of Chapter 4, only those unique resources

ETHICAL CHALLENGE

A business that primarily revolves around an app will find that differentiating itself is very difficult. The number of apps (as we have noted) is enormous. We have also noted social media can be a critical part of the firm pulling itself out of the mass of competitors. A key ethical question that arises then is what you are willing to do to be noticed in social media. Looking at some of the most followed individuals in social media, it is clear that many are famous for nothing more than being famous. There are individuals and organizations that will do almost anything to get noticed and have others reinforce that notice by sharing it with others. Pharrell Williams wore what many called a "Dudley Do-right" hat that was so distinctive that the hat itself ended up with its own Twitter account, while Kim Kardashian attempted to "break" the Internet by tweeting out a risqué picture. The false personality Alex from Target (a real person who was part of an effort by another company to make an average person famous) really did just about break the Internet and provided Target with a lot of great press. There are extreme forms of recognition that may only be possible on social media. Entrepreneurs really have to determine how they will build their social media recognition. What are the ethical approaches that you wish to follow? Do you wish to only communicate about the product? Will you have others follow you for a broader insight on the industry? Will you instead become a brand that is followed as much for the interesting things you do as for the app you may develop?

QUESTIONS

1. Have you developed a plan for social media for your business?
2. What will be your approach to social media?

and capabilities that meet all four criteria are truly the keys to the new business's strategy.

Is It Rare?

You must evaluate the uniqueness of each resource and capability relative to the competitors in your market. Is the resource or capability relatively unique for your industry? If the resource or capability is matched by one of your competitors, it can still be considered rare. However, if it is matched by more than one competitor, then it is not rare and therefore is simply the standard expectation in the industry. These are qualitative judgments based on the research and experience of the founder.

Is It Easily Substituted?

For every resource and capability that you determine to be indeed rare, you should evaluate the market for a close substitute. A substitute is not provided by a direct competitor, but it is something that satisfies the same basic need that is satisfied by your product or service. If we started up a small electronics repair operation, then our direct competitors would be other businesses that repair electronics in our area. Substitutes would consist of self-repairs, manufacturers' warranties, or throwing the item away. As you can see, these are not particularly great substitutes, and that is the question every entrepreneur needs to ask: How close are the substitutes to your unique resource and capability, and are they good substitutes? If there are not good substitutes, then that element of the business is a potential competitive advantage. Some businesses that rely on an app will have many substitutes. Too often entrepreneurs think of their products or services as unique without considering the perspective of the customer.

Is It Durable?

If you have determined that a unique resource or capability is both rare and not substitutable, then the next step is to determine how long you might be able to hold onto those advantages. As noted before, no advantage lasts forever, but the new-business person wants an advantage to last as long as possible. The time lag between the introduction of the competitive advantage and the point where competitors can match your advantage is the window where the new business can earn unique returns. In some industries, a competitive advantage will last only a few months, whereas in other industries, an advantage might last a long time as competitors are slow to adapt.

The evaluation of durability is done by estimating both the amount of time you believe it would take for a competitor to match you in a particular area and whether you believe they would actually try to match you. Many companies have the resources to match the offering of a new business, and yet they do not always try to match the competitive advantage. The entrepreneurs' estimation of the time frame in which they will be able to enjoy the benefits of a unique advantage is a critical element in this evaluation. Said succinctly, "Can a competitor easily copy it? If it can be copied, how perfectly can it be imitated and how long would it take to be copied?"

Is It Valuable?

In order for the resource or capability to be a competitive advantage, the customer must be willing to pay extra because of these unique resources and/or capabilities. A key decision, then, is which resource or capability the customer will pay the most for. It is not uncommon to have a resource and/or capability meet all three criteria above, and yet be unable to attain value in one or more of the three means for doing so: (1) charging more to generate more profit, (2) obtaining more customers, or (3) reducing costs relative to the competition.

Table 5.2 summarizes these concepts.

Table 5.2
Components of Resource-Based Analysis

CRITERION	MEANING	ILLUSTRATION
Rare	Few firms have it.	There are only four corners at an intersection. Once they are used, no other firms can locate there.
Nonsubstitutable	It cannot be replaced by something else easily.	Your firm may be able to supply original auto parts for automobiles from the 1950s. However, newly produced auto parts for such cars would substitute for those parts easily.
Durable	The length of time that the advantages will last before competitors match the offering.	Can firms match what you do in days, months, or years? Do they have the financial means to do so? Do they seem to care about what you are offering?
Valuable	Customers are willing to pay extra and/or it draws in new customers from the competitors and/or it costs the new firm less to accomplish than its competitors.	What you do is something that customers value and so they will pay more than what is charged by your competitors.

LO5-6

Determine a strategy to match the new business mission.

strategy
The broad approaches a small business will use to accomplish its mission.

Strategy

We have presented the content thus far in a sequential manner, but the reality is that much of this is and should be done concurrently. The firm needs to build on its mission and develop an effective **strategy** for the new business. This building process in which the mission is the firm's foundation explains why such extensive attention is given to the development of a mission statement. The firm's strategy is how the firm plans to use the competitive advantages of the business to accomplish its mission. Thus, the mission is the foundation on which the firm's strategy is built. Strategy is a complex field of study, and we do not presume to cover the subject in this text. Our goal is to present the general concepts we believe will be most valuable to a new-business start-up.

If you went into the cupcake-making business, what would you need to do to differentiate your strategy from a large competitor?
©Fuse/Getty Images RF

Michael Porter suggests that there are fundamentally three broad means to view a business's strategy: low cost, differentiation, or focus. A low-cost strategy is one where the firm seeks to be the lowest-cost competitor in the industry. A differentiation approach is one where the firm finds a unique position in the market through product, service, location, and the like. A focus approach seeks to craft a business around a small set of customers, specialty products, or a small geographic approach. Porter goes on to argue that firms can combine their focus approach with one of the other strategies; thus, there could be a focus differentiation or a focus low-cost strategy.[12]

As a practical matter, most new firms pursue a combination of these broad categories. The result is a value strategy in which some combination of cost and differentiation is employed as the firm seeks to serve a focus population of some type. A key reason for this combined strategy is that a new business is only rarely the absolute lowest-cost competitor in an industry (especially in an industry that is well established). Similarly the new business will also find it difficult to be differentiated along all dimensions of a product or service (and actually may not really wish to be). A value strategy that mixes cost and differentiation also can help a firm evolve its strategy as its industry changes.[14]

Thus, many new businesses employ a value strategy and then also seek to employ a differentiation focus strategy. In choosing the elements where they may effectively differentiate, new-business owners should reexamine the prior discussion in this chapter on competitive advantage. The resources and capabilities upon which the new business differentiates itself will constitute the key elements on which the firm builds its competitive advantage. To illustrate, the firm may believe that customer service will be one of its competitive advantages, so that should also be where it builds its differentiation and value strategy.

There are four logical steps in developing the firm's strategy which build on the earlier discussion of the firm's mission statement and understanding of its capabilities.

Step 1: The firm's mission statement is employed to specify where the firm is to compete and how.

Step 2: A detailed strategic plan is laid out specifying a series of resources or capabilities that will be used to meet each part of the mission and strategy. This plan should include the area of the mission that is being addressed, the strategy employed, the specific action, the result desired, the person responsible, and the status of the action. This can be developed in a spreadsheet format for ease of analysis. A brief example is shown in Table 5.3 for our Mediterranean restaurant example.

MISSION	STRATEGY	ACTION	RESULT DESIRED	RESPONSIBLE PARTY	STATUS
Gourmet	High-end, well-known chefs	Hire a chef from one of the top schools	Recognized in community	Founder	
			Has a short spot on TV news show each week	Founder	

Table 5.3
Restaurant example's strategic plan

Step 3: Following the approach outlined previously, the strategy needs to meet the criterion of being defendable for some length of time (depending on the industry, the length of time that would be considered sufficient may vary). The strategy should also provide the founder(s) economic returns above the industry average. If these two criteria cannot be satisfied, then the firm's strategy needs to be reexamined. However, if these two criteria can be met, then the firm should move forward with a focus on those activities that are defendable and have the potential to provide economic rents. The firm does not have to be excellent in all areas. Instead, it needs to have only those two to three competitive advantages that are its means of value differentiation.

Step 4: The firm's strategy needs to be constantly reevaluated. As noted, no competitive advantage or means of differentiation lasts forever. The new business must constantly evaluate its performance and its means of competitive advantage relative to its direct competitors to ensure that they are still relevant. This control function will be discussed in greater detail as we discuss analysis techniques in Chapter 12.

Applying the Strategy

Implementing a strategy is about fit and alignment within the business. Greater detail will be discussed in Chapters 10 and 11 on how to build a consistent set of activities around the strategy of the firm. However, to illustrate the key role that strategy can play for the new business, consider another illustration from the restaurant industry. A restaurant was founded by a Greek immigrant located close to downtown in a large midwestern city.* The principal customers were expected to be the individuals who lived in the apartments and condos that were close to the downtown area. The restaurant started as a café with cheaper Greek entrées, but over time it developed a dinner clientele that kept requesting more sophisticated menu items. So the owners upgraded a number of items on the menu to the point where a standard dinner entrée cost $15. Due to inertia and a desire to hold onto the restaurant's roots, the owner kept several of the original items on the menu. Then the founder wanted to expand his customer base. He noted that Cajun food was gaining popularity in the region, so without regard to his position as a Greek restaurant, he added Cajun food to the menu. The market already had several restaurants, which were part of large chains that offered Cajun food in the downtown area.

Piece by piece the owner of the Greek restaurant was working his business away from what he wanted it to be and muddling the perception that potential

*We have referred to restaurants on several occasions as classic examples of strategic management not because we believe they are the only examples, but because they are well-known types of establishments and their positioning is obvious to even the most casual observer. They also are a classic business type with an owner/manager who typically has high involvement in the business. These businesses can be founded by anyone with a passion for the business and do not generally require the special training that many other types of business might require.

customers had of his establishment. Customers who chose to go to dinner at his restaurant might have found the Greek atmosphere and food appealing. However, as the atmosphere and offerings moved away from this Greek atmosphere, customers were confused by the menu choices and the eclectic nature of the offerings. The restaurant was losing its appeal and becoming undifferentiated in a market that has thousands of choices.

The owner of the restaurant decided that his business was on its way to being a generic restaurant (and would probably need to close if changes were not made). He decided to refocus the organization around a succinct mission statement for the firm and then build a strategy or set of actions consistent with that mission. It had become obvious that although he thought he had seen an opportunity, he had failed to define his true competence and focus. As a result, the owner centered his business strictly on Greek food, eliminating the Cajun offerings. The owner also determined that his fundamental skill set was oriented toward more sophisticated meals, so he chose to offer a differentiated product at a premium price.

The owner then set out to align his business in a manner consistent with the differentiation strategy that would focus on sophisticated Greek food. The simpler, cheaper offerings were eliminated from the menu. This rationalization of the menu also allowed the owner to more efficiently use the food that went into making the products. In this industry, a key success factor, especially for a small restaurant, is control of the cost of inputs. The cost to the firm of ordering a large variety of food items entails significant storage and spoilage expenses in addition to an increase in complexity in virtually every aspect of the business. Thus, focusing strictly on Greek food and eliminating lower-priced items helped the efficiency of the whole organization, as well as situating it in a unique position within the market.

Consistent with this approach on food, the restaurant began offering only Greek wines. Previously the restaurant had served beer, but consistent with its differentiation focus, the owner wanted to focus on wine as the drink of choice, and specifically Greek wines. The hiring of staff also became much more clearly focused. There were a number of Greek immigrants in the city with detailed knowledge of this cuisine who were willing to work in a restaurant. The owner decided to hire these individuals, actually paying them a premium, in order to have highly skilled workers who understood what they were serving.

Finally, rather than advertising in the newspaper that went to all parts of the city and to numerous individuals who would never come downtown or, even if they did, would not patronize a high-end Greek restaurant, the owner began to focus his advertising. These are the specifics:

1. Since the restaurant is a part of the downtown area, the owner began to work with the concierge at the major hotels in the area in order to become one of their suggested specialty restaurants.
2. The Greek community in the city was strongly associated with the local Greek orthodox church. The owner opened a Greek restaurant because that was the food he knew. Only later did he realize that the Greek community was willing to travel from around the city to have good Greek food. Therefore, the owner began to advertise in publications and activities associated with the church to better reach that audience.

The result was that the restaurant built a consistent set of activities around its mission and strategy that helped to focus the firm clearly on what played to its strengths and gave it the best opportunity to make economic rents.

EXERCISE 3

1. As a class, pick several neighborhood bars close to campus or near downtown. Have each person write a mission statement for that bar. Compare the mission statements generated.
2. Discuss the impact each of these mission statements would have on the way the bar is operated.

YRFURN—AN APP FOR FURNITURE

As the team moved forward, they visited the Small Business Assistance Center as well as their entrepreneurship professor to make sure they were thinking of all the key issues they faced. The consistent message the team got was to craft a mission statement to ensure the entrepreneurial venture stayed focused on their key concerns as they moved forward.

The team had learned in their entrepreneurship class that the new venture needed to identify a pain that existed in the marketplace and then come up with the solution to be successful. The team understood the pain in the marketplace they wanted to solve, or more importantly, they knew what technology aspect they wanted to exploit to solve that pain. While they understood technology more than the industry it was being applied to, they struggled to come up with exactly what made them unique.

The team had intimate knowledge with a number of apps and knew that the ease of use was going to be critical to their success. They had decided to focus on consumers so that they also knew the aspects they needed to incorporate that would allow these individuals to not only use the app but also navigate the sales process easily. The technical development would need to be at a high level since the word among consumers spreads quickly if the app does or does not work well.

The founding team began to develop a clearer picture of the firm and its future. The team also examined the resources they needed in terms of technology. Their product needed to be able to take a picture of a room, and then easily remove and add any piece of furniture directly from the photo. They would allow an easy way for that information to be transmitted by consumers to retailers. Finally, the technology needed to be able to easily archive the data so that customers could find items and switch back and forth up to several dozen choices. In addition, if the customer loaded the furniture name into the application, then they would be able to show the exact pieces in all the colors available (this meant they were going to have to work with manufacturer databases that changed seasonally).

With all this in mind the team designed the following mission statement as their first draft.

"Furniture Shopping visually placed in YOUR Room"

QUESTION

1. As you look at the mission statement what becomes clear in terms of:
   a. Industry
   b. Consumers versus retailers focus
   c. Technology

SUMMARY

New businesses are well served by developing a mission statement for the company. A good mission statement that is effectively implemented with a consistent strategy will help everyone involved in the organization to focus on what is needed.

Five elements to keep in mind while crafting a mission statement are as follows:

1. Keep it short—Make sure it can fit on a coffee mug.
2. Keep it simple—Ensure that everyone in the company can learn and understand what it means and why.
3. Make it applicable—It should be able to guide every individual in the company each and every day. It should also be something that customers cite as to why they use the company.
4. Be specific—Be so clear that it tells everyone exactly what you do, and by definition, what you do not do.
5. Establish measurable goals—Be able to develop a metric for every part of the statement.

The strategy puts that mission into action. The steps to identifying a sustainable competitive advantage follow:

Step 1: Develop a list of your business's resources and capabilities.

Step 2: Break the list into two groups: standard and unique.

Step 3: Evaluate the unique resources and/or capabilities.

1. Is the resource or capability rare?
2. Is the resource or capability durable?
3. Is the resource or capability relatively non-substitutable?
4. Is the resource or capability valuable?

KEY TERMS

capabilities 85
economic rents 91
first-mover advantage 90
followers 90
intangible assets 89
metric 86
mission statement 82
strategy 94
sustainable competitive advantage 88
tangible assets 89

REVIEW QUESTIONS

1. What is the value of a mission statement for a new organization?
2. How should a mission statement guide the actions of employees?
3. What makes a good mission statement?
4. What is the difference between a tangible and an intangible asset?
5. Why do resources or capabilities have to meet all four requirements of the resource-based analysis to provide the company with a competitive advantage?
6. Why is it important to identify the standard elements of a new business?

BUSINESS PLAN DEVELOPMENT QUESTIONS

1. What are the core resources and/or capabilities of the business you are contemplating?
2. Which of those resources or capabilities do you believe are just standard expectations in the industry?
3. Which of those resources or capabilities do you believe pass all four elements of the resource-based approach?
4. Given the resources or capabilities you listed in question 3, what mission statement would you write for your new business, and why would it be a good one?

INDIVIDUAL EXERCISES

1. Seek out a locally owned business.
   a. Ask if the owner can provide you with the mission statement of the business.
   b. Ask if the owner can talk about the unique positioning of the business in the market.
2. Seek out a locally owned business and, without talking to the owner, visit the business.
   a. Can you craft a mission statement for the business that aligns with your experience?
   b. What do you believe are the unique elements of the business compared to the competitors?

GROUP EXERCISES

1. Using the Internet, identify three large corporations that are in the same general industry as the business that you are developing. Search their Web pages and record their mission statements. For these corporations, how would you evaluate the mission statements in terms of clarity and fulfilling the goals of a mission statement identified in the chapter?
2. Discuss in your group how these mission statements might be improved.
3. Take one of these organizations and list your best assessment for what might be ordinary and unique at the company.

ENDNOTES

1. K. M. Eisenhardt and D. M Sull, "Strategy as Simple Rules," *Harvard Business Review* (January 2001), pp. 107–16.
2. B. Bartkus and M. Glassman, "Do Firms Practice What They Preach? The Relationship Between Mission Statements and Stakeholder Management," *Journal of Business Ethics* 83, no. 2 (2008), pp. 207–16.
3. M. L. Barnett, N. Darnall, and B. W. Husted, "Sustainability Strategy in Constrained Economic Times," *Long Range Planning* 48, no. 2 (2015), pp. 63–68.
4. T. Powell, "Organizational Alignment as Competitive Advantage," *Strategic Management Journal* 13, no. 2 (1992), pp. 119–35.
5. A. Davis and E. Olson, "Critical Competitive Strategy Issues Every Entrepreneur Should Consider Before Going into Business," *Business Horizons* 51, no. 3 (2008), pp. 211–21.
6. R. McNaughton, P. Osborne, and B. Imrie, "Market-Oriented Value Creation in Service Firms," *European Journal of Marketing* 36, no. 9/10 (2002), pp. 990–1013.
7. I. Chaston, B. Badger, T. Mangles, and E. Sadler-Smith, "Relationship Marketing, Knowledge Management Systems and E-Commerce Operations in Small UK Accountancy Practices," *Journal of Marketing Management* 19, no. 1/2 (2003), pp. 109–31.
8. R. Hall, "A Framework Linking Intangible Resources and Capabilities to Sustainable Competitive Advantage," *Strategic Management Journal* 14, no. 8 (1993), pp. 607–19.
9. M. Lieberman and D. Montgomery, "First-Mover (Dis) advantages: Retrospective and Link with the Resource-Based View," *Strategic Management Journal* 19, no. 12 (1998), pp. 1111–26.
10. T. Stucki, "How the Founders' General and Specific Human Capital Drives Export Activities of Start-ups," *Research Policy* 45, no.5 (2016), pp. 1014–30.
11. M. Sabatier and B. Chollet, "Is There a First Mover Advantage in Science? Pioneering Behavior and Scientific Production in Nanotechnology," *Research Policy* 46, no.2 (2017), pp. 522–33.
12. M. Porter, *Competitive Advantage: Creating and Sustaining Superior Performance* (New York, NY: Free Press, 1985).
13. R. R. Gehani, "Innovative Strategic Leader Transforming from a Low Cost Strategy to Product Differentiation Strategy," *Journal of Technology Management & Innovation* 8, no. 2 (2013), pp. 144–55.

part
3
chapter
6

Analyzing Cash Flow and Other Financial Information

learning objectives

After studying this chapter, you will be able to:

LO6-1 Recognize the fundamental importance of cash flow analysis.

LO6-2 Prepare a cash flow statement and a budget.

LO6-3 Identify other financial tools.

PARTPIC

PARTPIC

Finding the exact replacement part for any machine has always been an exercise in persistence measuring and in some cases trying desperately to read very tiny writing. Replacing a missing screw on the bottom of your laptop computer, the hose clamp on your car, or more importantly the thousands of parts that must be replaced on a yearly basis at most manufacturing plants requires a very precise part and often many hours of work to obtain the part.

PartPic was born out of this frustration by Jewel Burks in 2013 and the opportunity that has been provided by spectacular new smartphone cameras and 3D visualizations. Users use PartPic's app to snap a picture and receive the name of the part they are looking for in seconds. PartPic is developing an extensive database that starts with digitizing the entire replacement part catalogs of suppliers. PartPic crafted a set of algorithms that allows it to narrow the margin of error instantly. They hope to complete the circle with an ability to purchase the part from the supplier right from the user's phone.

The entire operation can be done with a smartphone without ever having to take the offending part to a store. The company won a series of "pitch" competitions and now has four PhDs on staff and has published two peer-reviewed papers about its computer-vision technology. They were able to raise several rounds of seed funding while they were building the algorithms and developing the business model. In 2014, they won The Rise of the Rest pitch competition in Atlanta, which won them a $100,000 investment from AOL cofounder Steve Case, and in 2015 they secured a $1.5 million dollars seed round from a group of 15+ angel investors and venture capitalists.

Questions

1. Do you believe that the company will be able to make money on this business? If so, who will pay them?
2. What do you believe the company will have to achieve to become self-sustaining?

Sources: http://www.partpic.com/#; F. Tepper, "Disrupt Alum PartPic, A System That Identifies Replacement Parts, Raises a $1.5M Seed Round," *TechCrunch* (June 17, 2015). https://techcrunch.com/2015/06/17/disrupt-alum-partpic-a-system-that-identifies-replacement-parts-raises-a-1-5m-seed-round/; A. Glaser, "Searching for a Replacement Part? Just Take a Picture of It," *Wired* (February 23, 2016). (https://www.wired.com/2016/02/partspic-image-recognition/).

At this point in the development of your business, you have generated the basic concept for a business, analyzed the external environment of your proposed business, and determined what strategy the new business will employ. The next step in the due diligence process is to develop an actionable financial plan for the business. In fact, the next analytical step is perhaps the most critical in the due diligence effort, as the financial analysis of the business will most likely determine whether there is actual opportunity. Specifically, a new firm must decide whether there will be sufficient cash flow for the proposed business to survive its early days and then thrive as an established entity. An idea that has passed your evaluations to date but that is unable to generate minimally sufficient cash flow in a reasonable time is not a practical business idea.

cash flow
Actual cash that flows into the firm, minus the cash that goes out of the firm.

It is important to understand that **cash flow** in a business is not the same as profit.[1] A firm obtains profits when its sales revenue is higher than its expenses, including depreciation of assets. However, generating profits does not put cash in the bank today. It is quite common to have high levels of a product or services "sold" with no cash coming into the firm. Credit accounts commonly have terms that range from 30 to 90 days, which means you will not receive payment for your services or goods for 30 to 90 days. In fact, some percentage of these credit accounts will go past due and some will ultimately be uncollectible. Our point is that you may not receive the money for your business at the time of sale. On the other hand, a new business must generally pay in cash for its goods and supplies immediately because it has no credit history. Carrying inventory of any type results in payments for those supplies taking place long before any cash is received by the business. Thus, while many new firms appear to be making a profit, they can be suffering from a negative cash flow. Ultimately, the danger is that the entrepreneurial business will need to make payments in cash for its inputs but will have insufficient cash available from sales to make those payments.*

This cash crunch is actually exacerbated when sales are growing. A doubling in orders in a single month sounds great, but it means that twice the inputs must be ordered and paid for while there is no cash coming into the firm to pay for the dramatic increase of inputs needed until those goods are paid for by the customer. The outcome is that rapid growth by a new entrepreneurial business is actually one of the most dangerous times for that business. An entrepreneurial firm must understand and monitor its cash flow as it is typically the absence of sufficient cash flow that is the greatest reason that an entrepreneurial business fails.[2]

To prevent such a cash crunch, it is important for a new entrepreneurial business to carefully, thoughtfully, and accurately forecast its real cash flow. In its simplest form, a cash flow statement is a comparison of cash inflows to cash outflows. In this chapter we will present a thorough method that will help ensure that the business has a clear picture of its cash flow situation.

LO6-1

Recognize the fundamental importance of cash flow analysis.

Importance of Cash Flow Analysis

The role of the cash flow statement developed in the due diligence stage of a new entrepreneurial venture is substantially different from the financial analysis developed for an ongoing firm. An established business will develop a series of financial reports for either themselves or for investors over some time period such as a month or a quarter. The data generated not only will include an actual cash flow statement but will also include a balance sheet, an income statement, and a small series of industry-specific reports. Each of these financial statements provides a unique look at the operation of the business, and

*For a good case regarding cash flows see T. G. Canace and J. E. Wilkerson, "A Practice Based Statement of Cash Flows Learning Experience: An Initial Public Offering for Contempri Homes?" *Issues in Accounting Education,* 29, no. 1 (February 2014), pp. 195–216.

KOSHER HOME

To illustrate the fundamentals of cash flow analysis, consider Kosher Homer as the two friends evaluated the potential financial viability of the new venture. The initial analysis the founders made of their projected cash flow is below. The cash flow statement reflects the firm's plan for $100,000 of equity investment by the two founders and the acquisition of a bank loan in September. The founders tried to include every actual expense for the first six months of operation—a time that would be relatively small. They estimated the receipts by seeking as much information as they could from similar firms doing an Internet food business. They obtained an estimate of operational expenses by talking with owners of firms that have started shipping perishables via Internet orders. The two largest expenses for the firm will be advertising and the cost of the personnel who will work for the business. The advertising is critical because Kosher Home will have to educate their target consumer (individuals who keep kosher) about prepared kosher meals shipped to their home and their value. The marketing will be examined in Chapter 11. The personnel costs include the benefits offered to each employee.

The equipment is for computers and related software. The smaller amounts in later months relate to software that is assumed will be needed although exactly what that is unknown at this stage. The product development fees are the cost to develop new products. Before starting, the firm will have a set of 25 meals. The entrepreneurs assume that individuals will not buy a prepackaged meal every night, but it would be several times a week. However, there is a continuing need to update the meals. Conference costs are to attend conferences related to Jewish concerns to build relationships and knowledge of the firm. There are three key conferences that they both felt were important to their business. The first one both Jack and Toby will attend, while only one of the founders will attend each of the other two.

QUESTIONS

1. Do you see major expense items that the entrepreneurs have forgotten?
2. Do you believe the entrepreneurs are too optimistic in their expectations?

	JULY	AUGUST	SEPTEMBER	OCTOBER	NOVEMBER	DECEMBER	TOTAL
Receipts(Sales), $	$ 0	$ 0	$ 31,000	$55,000	$78,000	$ 91,000	$25,000
Debt Financing, $	0	0	50,000	0	0	0	50,000
Equity Financing, $	100,000	0	0	0	0	0	100,000
Equipment Purchases, $	22,250	3,850	2,500	500	1,500	0	30,600
Salaries, $	4,167	22,167	40,167	48,000	55,500	63,500	233,501
Payroll Taxes, $	375	375	375	675	675	675	3,150
Product Development, $	900	900	900	1,350	1,350	1,350	6,750
Conference, $	5,000	2,500	0	2,500	0	0	10,000
Office Lease, $	5,208	5,208	5,208	5,208	5,208	5,208	31,248
Utilities, $	750	500	500	550	600	750	3,650
Shipping Product, $	0	850	900	1,000	1,000	1,000	4,750
Insurance, $	1,350	0	0	1,350	0	0	2,700
Advertising, $	0	7,500	4,250	2,500	4,250	7,000	25,500
Office Supplies, $	500	1,000	250	250	500	500	3,000
Interest, $	0	0	0	417	417	417	1,251
Taxes, $	0	0	0	0	0	1,695	1,695
Beginning Balance, $	$ 0	$57,000	$ 12,150	$ 30,100	$ 31,300	$38,300	
Cash In, $	100,000	0	81,000	55,000	78,000	91,000	
Cash Out, $	43,000	44,850	63,050	53,800	71,000	82,095	
Net Cash Flow, $	57,000	44,850	17,950	1,200	7,000	8,905	
Ending Balance, $	$ 57,000	$ 12,150	$ 30,100	$ 31,300	$38,300	$ 47,205	

EXERCISE 1

1. What additional items would you like to see included in the Kosher Home cash flow statement?
2. Do you believe that the numbers above are realistic? Explain.
3. For which items would you like to have additional information? How might this be best presented?
4. Solely based on the cash flow statement, would you believe that this venture was worth investing in if you were an investor? Why or why not?

each is valuable in its own right. We will briefly examine these statements in this chapter, and then in Chapter 8, we will provide a detailed examination of the means to use such financial reports once the business is up and running. For a proposed business, the financial analysis focuses almost exclusively on its ability to generate positive cash flows in the shortest time possible.

The focus on cash flow is due in part to the fact that in the new business, the management of the firm will also be the owners of the firm. Profitability is applauded in the public investing community, where the members of management are generally not the majority owners, and therefore, there is a split in ownership and control. When there is a separation between management and ownership, profits are a useful measure as a means to evaluate performance, inasmuch as such firms are typically larger and have numerous slack, or excess, resources. However, for owners of a new entrepreneurial firm, the focus is on the viability of the business, and the viability of the firm will be decided by cash flow, not profitability. The ability of the new business to generate strong profits on each item sold is indeed important; however, profit should not be the principal focus in the analysis of a potential new business. Profits have little to do with whether the business will be viable over the long term. The key to the success of a new venture (as simple and obvious as it seems) is its ability to bring in more cash each month than it spends and, more importantly, to bring that cash in on a cycle that is faster than the payout cycle.

equity
Investment into the entrepreneurial business by the owners of the firm.

We once assisted a start-up company whose founders had developed a product that sold for $199 and was used in the construction industry. The founders and their investors had invested almost $80,000 in the business (the firm's **equity**). This entrepreneurial business had been in operation for approximately four months when the founders asked us to come to the office for a celebration. Upon our arrival there were drinks and balloons to celebrate the first sale of the product produced by the firm. One of the founders proudly announced he had just made $100, a profit margin of about 50 percent on this first sale of their product. The owners were totally focused on that profit margin and had visions of a business that would now grow and provide them a solid living for the rest of their lives. However, the owners had burned through almost $38,000 to make that $100. Total cash that had flowed into the company was $199; total cash outflow had exceeded $38,000, for a net cash flow of a negative $37,801.

Similar to homeowners, business owners invest their own money with the hopes that there will be a big pay off over time.

©Ingram Publishing/age fotostock RF

Regardless of the profit margin of a company's product, there is a need to bring in sufficient cash to pay all of the bills. That entrepreneurial business was going to have to generate many more sales to have any potential for staying in business. Although the firm generated lots of interest and started to gain contracts for its product, it went through all of its cash reserves before it could bring in sufficient cash from sales for the firm to survive. Unfortunately, this occurs to many new entrepreneurial firms. This was another great idea that had lots of potential and a good profit margin but ran out of cash from loans and equity before it could generate a positive cash flow.

Of course, an entrepreneur wants to make a profit, but cash pays the bills and the payroll. As we stated earlier, a new entrepreneurial business will have to pay its vendors cash. Even after an entrepreneurial business is well established, it may have only 30 days to pay vendors, whereas its customers, particularly if they are large firms, may take upward of 90 days to pay their bills. The entrepreneurial business has to cover that period of 60 days between when it had to deliver the product and when it receives payment. It may even be a longer period if your customer was a government entity of some type.

This situation represents an important concept or term in cash flow analysis: **float**. Float is the difference between when the money goes out and when it comes in.[3] Banks commonly use float to their benefit. You as a business owner may deposit a check or receive an electronic transfer from an out-of-state buyer. For some period of time your bank account reflects no or just a token inflow to you. However, the bank generally receives the money for that check within 24 hours. This is because the bank is legally allowed to hold a check for clearance for preassigned time periods. The bank has free use of the money during the period from when it has received the cash but is not yet required to reflect it in your account. Even though the float from one check may be very small, when those amounts are aggregated by large banks, they can involve millions or billions of dollars they have the ability to use at no cost to themselves during a year.

float
The difference between when the money goes out and when it comes in. For example, if you deposit a check or receive an electronic transfer today in payment for some good, you typically do not receive cash when you deposit it. Instead there is a period of float before it is credited to your account.

The entrepreneur can also benefit from float. Credit card charges (not including cash advances) are typically a free form of cash float, as the new-business owner does not have to pay interest unless the bill is not paid in full each month. For anywhere up to 25 days a month, the owner has use of the funds without having any outflow to pay the bill. This is a positive cash flow situation for the entrepreneur.

Cash Flow Versus Budgets

A cash flow statement is not a budget and should not be confused with a budget.[4] A **budget** projects all the costs that will be incurred by the organization over some period of time (a year, for instance) and allocates that expense evenly over the relevant time period. This is similar to what you might do for your household expenses as you set aside money each month to pay the annual life insurance payment or school tuition. At any one time the account for that expense usually has excess funds (except for the month in which the bill comes due). An example might be an insurance payment. The annual cost might be $1,800; thus, the budget would reflect $150 per month.

budget
Statement that projects all the costs that will be incurred by the organization over a period of time and allocates those expenses evenly over the relevant time period.

An example budget for a start-up firm that sells software is shown in Table 6.1. This is the actual budget prepared by a new business that sold software and consulting services to other small- to medium-sized businesses (the founders had developed a small software package and sales consisted of a software download). This budget was what the firm relied on as it started its business, and it showed that the business should have consistent positive cash balances. Note that virtually all of the amounts in each category were the same from month to month.

A cash flow statement does the exact opposite of a budget. In the example above of an insurance payment, in each month in which no actual cash outflow occurs, the category receives a zero, and then in the month that the payment is due, the account will record a cash outflow of $1,800. Although budgets are helpful for planning purposes, nothing brings home reality like the recognition that the company must have X amount of actual cash in order to pay this month's bills.

Compare the example firm's budget with its actual cash flow statement in Table 6.2.

The firm started tracking actual cash flow after several months of operation, when it became clear that the budget document was not proving helpful in the management of the firm's cash. The cash flow statement that was developed for the company showed some shortfalls that should scare a firm founder. The company (which started with $10,000 from the founders) was

BUDGET

Receipts:		January	February	March	April	May	June	Total
	Sales, $	$ 1,000	$ 2,500	$ 3,000	$ 5,000	$ 7,000	$10,000	**$28,500**
	Consulting, $	5,000	5,000	5,000	10,000	10,000	10,000	**45,000**
Total Receipts, $		$ 6,000	$ 7,500	$ 8,000	$15,000	$17,000	$20,000	**$73,500**
Disbursements:								
	Salaries, $	$ 4,000	$ 4,000	$ 4,000	$ 5,500	$ 5,500	$ 5,500	**$28,500**
	Travel, $	1,000	1,000	1,000	1,000	1,000	1,000	**$ 6,000**
	Car Leases, $	1,000	1,000	1,000	1,000	1,000	1,000	**$ 6,000**
	Rent, $	900	450	450	450	450	450	**$ 3,150**
	Payroll Taxes, $	300	300	300	300	300	300	**$ 1,800**
	Insurance, $	121	121	121	121	121	121	**$ 725**
	Fuel/Maint., $	150	150	150	150	150	150	**$ 900**
	Benefits, $	350	350	350	350	350	350	**$ 2,100**
	Advertising, $	300	300	300	300	300	300	**$ 1,800**
	Inventory Inputs, $	50	50	50	50	50	50	**$ 300**
	Utilities, $	200	200	200	200	200	200	**$ 1,200**
	Misc., $	250	250	250	250	250	250	**$ 1,500**
Total Disbursements, $		$ 8,621	$ 8,171	$ 8,171	$ 9,671	$ 9,671	$ 9,671	**$ 53,975**
Beginning Balance, $		$ 0	$ 7,379	$ 6,708	$ 6,538	$ 11,867	$ 19,196	
Equity Investment, $		10,000						**10,000**
Net Profit, $		(2,621)	(671)	(171)	5,329	7,329	9,196	**18,392**
Ending Balance, $		$ 7,379	$ 6,708	$ 6,538	$ 11,867	$ 19,196	$ 28,392	

Table 6.1
Example Budget for Start-Up Software Firm

completely out of cash by March and had a negative cash position of almost $2,000 in April. The firm actually covered this shortcoming with credit card cash advances and was able to survive. Note that the company founders did not account for the interest on those advances which accrued from the date of the transaction—a cost they should have accounted for to better understand the firm's financial standing. One of the fundamental realities of starting a new business is that it takes a period of time for the new venture to ramp up sales and then to obtain cash from those sales. Much of the difficulty with this business could have been avoided with a cash flow projection prior to deciding whether to pursue the business or not, and then with use of that cash flow projection to ensure an increase in the initial equity position of the new firm.[5]

We utilize a rule of thumb (and it is only a rule of thumb) when examining the initial equity needs of a new venture that has proved to be very helpful in ensuring that the new venture has sufficient cash to achieve a market position. Calculate your entire cash flow projection without adding in any equity investment, and look for the point where the ending balance is at its lowest point. Take that number and multiply it by 150 percent. We argue for multiplying by 150 percent because it always takes more cash than

CASH FLOW STATEMENT

Receipts:		January	February	March	April	May	June	Total
	Sales, $	$ 350	$ 550	$ 1,200	$ 9,400	$12,200	$13,000	**$36,700**
	Consulting, $	3,000	3,500	5,000	0	3,000	3,500	**18,000**
Total Receipts, $		$ 3,350	$ 4,050	$ 6,200	$ 9,400	$15,200	$16,500	**$54,700**
Disbursements:								
	Salaries, $	$ 4,000	$ 4,000	$ 5,000	$ 5,000	5,000	$ 5,000	**$28,000**
	Travel, $	2,304	365	558	846	1,368	1,104	**$ 6,545**
	Car Leases, $	1,000	1,000	1,000	1,000	1,000	1,000	**$ 6,000**
	Rent, $	900	450	450	450	450	450	**$ 3,150**
	Payroll Taxes, $	240	240	300	300	300	340	**$ 1,720**
	Insurance, $	0	0	0	1,450	0	0	**$ 1,450**
	Fuel/Maint., $	13	21	46	361	468	502	**$ 1,412**
	Benefits, $	350	350	350	350	350	350	**$ 2,100**
	Advertising, $	28	44	96	752	976	0	**$ 1,896**
	Credit Card, $				500	2,000		**$ 2,500**
	Supplies, $	17	20	31	47	76	112	**$ 303**
	Utilities, $	174	213	208	189	132	188	**$ 1,104**
	Misc., $	67	81	124	188	304	764	**$ 1,528**
Total Disbursements, $		$ 9,093	$ 6,784	$ 8,163	$ 11,433	$ 12,424	$ 9,810	**$ 57,708**
								$ 0
Beginning Balance, $		$ 0	$ 4,257	$ 1,523	$ 60	$ 27	$ 2,802	
Equity Investment, $		10,000						**10,000**
Credit Card Advance, $				500	2,000			
Net Cash Flow, $		(5,743)	(2,734)	(1,963)	(2,033)	2,776	6,690	**(3,008)**
Ending Balance, $		$ 4,257	$ 1,523	$ 60	$ 27	$ 2,802	$ 9,492	

Table 6.2
Example Cash Flow Statement for Start-Up Software Firm

you expect to start the business. (It also takes more time than you expect.) That number is what we would recommend for the initial equity or equity-plus-debt investment.

For example, we take the exact cash flow statement from Table 6.2 and remove the equity-plus-debt investment from the projection to produce Table 6.3.

Notice that in Table 6.3 in April the low point for the ending balance is ($12,473). Multiplying that number by 150 percent yields a recommended initial investment of $18,709, or roughly $19,000. With that number inserted into the initial equity investment for the firm, we see that the cash balance remains well above zero. This provides a cushion to the new firm, which enables it to pursue options it did not consider at founding, more easily handle rapid growth, and/or handle unexpected external shocks to the organization. See Table 6.4.

In developing a cash flow projection, the new-business owner should contact vendors and suppliers to ask about payment terms and also check with credit card companies to get exact information about when accounts will be

CASH FLOW STATEMENT

Receipts:		January	February	March	April	May	June	Total
	Sales, $	$ 350	$ 550	$ 1,200	$ 9,400	$12,200	$13,000	**$ 36,700**
	Consulting, $	3,000	3,500	5,000	0	3,000	3,500	**18,000**
Total Receipts, $		$ 3,350	$ 4,050	$ 6,200	$ 9,400	$15,200	$16,500	**$ 54,700**
Disbursements:								
	Salaries, $	$ 4,000	$ 4,000	$ 5,000	$ 5,000	$ 5,000	$ 5,000	**$28,000**
	Travel, $	2,304	365	558	846	1,368	1,104	**$ 6,545**
	Car Leases, $	1,000	1,000	1,000	1,000	1,000	1,000	**$ 6,000**
	Rent, $	900	450	450	450	450	450	**$ 3,150**
	Payroll Taxes, $	240	240	300	300	300	340	**$ 1,720**
	Insurance, $	0	0	0	1,450	0	0	**$ 1,450**
	Fuel/Maint., $	13	21	46	361	468	502	**$ 1,412**
	Benefits, $	350	350	350	350	350	350	**$ 2,100**
	Advertising, $	28	44	96	752	976	0	**$ 1,896**
	Credit Card, $				500	2,000		**$ 2,500**
	Supplies, $	17	20	31	47	76	112	**$ 303**
	Utilities, $	174	213	208	189	132	188	**$ 1,104**
	Misc., $	67	81	124	188	304	764	**$ 1,528**
Total Disbursements, $		$ 9,093	$ 6,784	$ 8,163	$ 11,433	$ 12,424	$ 9,810	**$ 57,708**
								$ 0
Beginning Balance, $		$ 0	($ 5,743)	($ 8,477)	($10,440)	($ 12,473)	($ 9,698)	
Equity Investment, $								**0**
Credit Card Advance, $								
Net Cash Flow, $		(5,743)	(2,734)	(1,963)	(2,033)	2,776	6,690	**(3,008)**
Ending Balance, $		($ 5,743)	($ 8,477)	($10,440)	($12,473)	($ 9,698)	($3,008)	

Table 6.3
Modified Example Cash Flow Statement for Start-Up Software Firm

processed and what percentage will be charged to the company for each transaction. These interactions also allow the new-business owner to seek out the best terms possible from vendors and suppliers. In the next section of this chapter, we will suggest specific items to be accounted for as you develop your cash flow statement. Once the venture begins operations, actual cash flow should be compared monthly to the projected cash flow statement in order to produce a **deviation analysis**, an analysis of how the predicted and actual cash flows differ. This will not only assist the entrepreneur in developing realistic forecasts for the business in the future but also point out differences between actual performance and predicted performance at a point in time. Taking the time each month to examine this allows the new-business person maximum flexibility in making changes to the business as it grows (a habit that will help keep the venture responsive as the venture develops). Chapter 8 will go into greater detail on such comparisons and how to analyze and respond to the deviations that are identified. To illustrate, you can see in

deviation analysis
Analysis of the differences between the predicted and the actual performance.

CASH FLOW STATEMENT								
Receipts:		January	February	March	April	May	June	Total
	Sales, $	$ 350	$ 550	$ 1,200	$9,400	$12,200	$13,000	**$36,700**
	Consulting, $	3,000	3,500	5,000	0	3,000	3,500	**18,000**
Total Receipts, $		$ 3,350	$ 4,050	$ 6,200	$9,400	$15,200	$16,500	**$54,700**
Disbursements:								
	Salaries, $	$ 4,000	$ 4,000	$ 5,000	$5,000	$ 5,000	$ 5,000	**$28,000**
	Travel, $	2,304	365	558	846	1,368	1,104	**$ 6,545**
	Car Leases, $	1,000	1,000	1,000	1,000	1,000	1,000	**$ 6,000**
	Rent, $	900	450	450	450	450	450	**$ 3,150**
	Payroll Taxes, $	240	240	300	300	300	340	**$ 1,720**
	Insurance, $	0	0	0	1,450	0	0	**$ 1,450**
	Fuel/Maint., $	13	21	46	361	468	502	**$ 1,412**
	Benefits, $	350	350	350	350	350	350	**$ 2,100**
	Advertising, $	28	44	96	752	976	0	**$ 1,896**
	Credit Card, $				500	2,000		**$ 2,500**
	Supplies, $	17	20	31	47	76	112	**$ 303**
	Utilities, $	174	213	208	189	132	188	**$ 1,104**
	Misc., $	67	81	124	188	304	764	**$ 1,528**
Total Disbursements, $		$ 9,093	$ 6,784	$ 8,163	$ 11,433	$ 12,424	$ 9,810	**$ 57,708**
								$ 0
Beginning Balance, $		$ 0	$ 13,257	$ 10,523	$8,560	$ 6,527	$ 9,302	
Equity Investment, $		19,000						**19,000**
Credit Card Advance, $								
Net Cash Flow, $		(5,743)	(2,734)	(1,963)	(2,033)	2,776	6,690	**(3,008)**
Ending Balance, $		**$13,257**	**$10,523**	**$8,560**	**$6,527**	**$ 9,302**	**$15,992**	

Table 6.4
Finalized Example Cash Flow Statement for Start-Up Software Firm

Table 6.5 the cash flow deviation analysis from the software firm we have been discussing.

In this example, the software company's revenues fell $2,650 short of the owners' predictions, and their expenses were $693 more than they had expected. Although the firm will still have positive cash balance, this type of cash analysis provides valuable information to the owners of this new company. Why were sales so far below expectations? Why was travel more than double the projection? We note that the firm did virtually no advertising; perhaps this is why sales were less than expected. Some expenses need to be made in order to increase the opportunity for success on the revenue side, so we are not suggesting that the new venture attempt to cut its way to success; instead we suggest a careful monthly analysis of all actual revenues and expenses.

©Panther Media GmbH/Alamy RF

Table 6.5
Example Deviation Analysis for Start-Up Software Firm

DEVIATION ANALYSIS

Receipts:		January –Predicted	January –Actual	Difference
	Sales, $	$ 1,000	$ 350	($ 650)
	Consulting, $	5,000	3,000	(2,000)
Total Receipts, $		$ 6,000	$ 3,350	($2,650)
Disbursements:				
	Salaries, $	$ 4,000	$ 4,000	$ 0
	Travel, $	1,000	2,304	1,304
	Car Leases, $	900	1,000	100
	Rent, $	900	900	0
	Payroll Taxes, $	300	240	(60)
	Insurance, $	0	0	0
	Fuel/Maint., $	150	13	(137)
	Benefits, $	350	350	0
	Advertising, $	300	28	(272)
	Supplies, $	50	17	(33)
	Utilities, $	200	174	(26)
	Misc., $	250	67	(183)
Total Disbursements, $		$ 8,400	$ 9,093	$ 693
Equity Investment, $		10,000	10,000	0
Net Cash Flow, $		(2,400)	(5,743)	(3,343)
Ending Balance, $		$ 7,600	$ 4,257	($3,343)

LO6-2

Prepare a cash flow statement and a budget.

Developing Cash Flow Statements and Budgets

There are several key issues that should be noted in developing a cash flow statement. The first is that a cash flow statement for a new business is substantially different from the typical publicly traded corporate annual report that you may have seen. New businesses, unlike established companies, are unlikely to have either investing activities or financing activities (interest on notes/loans is included in the operations section of new-business cash flow statements). New entrepreneurial ventures typically have only one type of activity: operations. Everything that involves cash in/cash out is related to the operation of the business.

The cash flow statement is used to describe all of the activities that provide and use cash during the period being examined (we would recommend that the statement be done monthly until the business is well established). Used effectively, this statement helps the owners accurately keep track of the overall cash position of the business and provides a well-respected and accepted means of displaying the ability of the company to meet its obligations. As the business grows, a well-developed, accurate long-term track record of cash flow statements and the comparison of the planned cash flows to reality will go a long way toward assisting the company with loans, credit lines, infusions of equity capital, and even valuation, should the businessperson want to sell the company.

Generating the cash flow statement should actually begin with the expenses of the organization, for the very simple reason that they are easier to accurately forecast than are revenues. Expenses fall into a number of categories that are inclusive of, but not limited to, the following list:

- Salaries
- Basic Benefits
- Taxes/Fees
  - Payroll
  - Income
  - Local
  - State
  - Business
  - Licenses
- Cost of Goods Sold
  - Manufacturing/Development
  - Packaging
  - Direct Labor
  - Shipping
- Utilities (Electricity, Gas, Phone Service, etc.)
- Security Systems
- Tools/Machinery/Computers
- Office Supplies (a big and often underestimated expense)
- Travel Expenses
- Insurance
- Advertising
- Furniture
- Cell Phones
- Maintenance of Equipment
- Cleaning (either a service or supplies for your use)
- Rent/Mortgage Payments

In short, all actual expenses must be accounted for in the cash flow statement. If your specific business has unique expenses that do not fit into these categories, note that you also need to add those expenses to this list.

Revenues (cash inflows) should be separated into as many categories as possible in order to provide maximum insight to the owner. The firm's revenues can come from a wide variety of sources that may not automatically be recognized. A new firm may sell computers, but it may actually make more money from servicing those computers. Separating out revenue lines aids both in predicting where the firm's revenues will come from and in analyzing the actual revenue sources for the new entrepreneurial firm. Once there is a fine-grained understanding, then those categories can be collapsed together if a more general-level categorization is desired.

To illustrate further, a lawn care company found from its cash flow analysis that its cash inflow was more positively impacted by what appeared to be an ancillary portion of the business (planting the flowers for a commercial building). The firm had to have the contract to mow the lawn to get the business, but it was planting the flowers that actually had a greater positive impact on the cash flow. Thus, the firm reexamined its pricing and priced the mowing so that the firm was certain to get the lawn-mowing contract, with flower planting and other landscaping activities providing the substantial portion of the positive inflow of revenues.

Several examples of the breakout in revenues that we have seen are listed in Table 6.6. These include revenue statements from a restaurant, a SaaS, and a retail office supply operation. Note that these examples focus only on revenues to provide you an idea of how to develop this aspect of cash flow statements.

As the examples above suggest, generating a cash flow statement should be tailored to the information needs of the new venture. The lists above are not meant to be exhaustive. In general, we recommend that each unique area of the business that generates income should be given a separate revenue line item.

sensitivity analysis
An examination of the best- and worst-case cash flow scenarios.

A final comment regarding cash flow statements concerns the development of a **sensitivity analysis**.[6] The cash flow statement developed thus far could best be labeled a "most-likely case" scenario. It is also quite prudent to look at a worst-case and a best-case scenario to examine the sensitivity of the potential cash flow to dramatic changes in the revenue or cost stream when conducting due diligence on a business idea. The sensitivity analysis is a judgment call by the new-business person about whether the business could survive the worst-case or successfully carry out the best-case scenario.

To better understand your financial situation, our advice is that you take the revenue figures developed in your most-likely scenario and create two new cash flow statements. One increases monthly revenue by 25 percent and the other decreases monthly revenue by 25 percent. In addition, you will need to adjust the expenses of the business to match these new revenue numbers. What is the effect upon your net cash flow? Could your new venture survive either of these situations? What changes might you make to accommodate the new outcomes?

There are several ways an entrepreneur can help to manage their cash flow. Clearly seeking the longest time to pay for any inputs will help the firm. However, the entrepreneur can also choose to pay their hourly employees in arrears (that is after they have worked the time to be paid) on the 15th and the 30th rather than the 1st and the 15th. The delays of several weeks help the entrepreneur to delay those payments. One thing that entrepreneurs should also consider if their cash flow is too low is that they simply may not be charging enough for their product. Another option is for the firm to use a business credit card to pay some expenses, which can allow up to a 25-day delay in paying expenses. The ability to barter for services can also save the new company extra cash.

To illustrate the benefits of cash flow analysis, the owners of a new print shop developed best- and worst-case scenarios of their cash flow projections. The insight led the founders to realize that if things continued as they were the business might not survive. This did not lead the entrepreneurs to give up. Instead, they worked to control their immediate costs through methods such as negotiating with their landlord to pay lower rent until they reached the break-even point. Additionally, this situation encouraged the founders to secure several definitive contracts from the city for printing. The result was that the founders were able to revise their cash flows such that even a worst-case scenario would be survivable.

EXERCISE 2

1. To help Toby and Jack work on their cash flow statements for Kosher, consider their expenses—what would be the principal expenses?
2. Estimate the relative percentage of costs to food inputs, shipping, and personnel.
3. Develop a cash flow statement that incorporates your estimates of both receipts and expenses for Kosher.

RESTAURANT CASH FLOW STATEMENT

Receipts:		January	February	March	April	Total
	Food, $	$1,300	$1,800	$2,300	$2,400	**$ 7,800**
	Drink, $	350	490	600	605	**$ 2,045**
	Alcohol, $	450	770	780	810	**$ 2,810**
	Misc., $	110	200	205	399	**$ 914**
Total Receipts, $		$ 2,210	$3,260	$3,885	$ 4,214	**$13,569**

SAAS CASH FLOW STATEMENT

Receipts:		January	February	March	April	Total
	Initial Online Sale, $	$1,100	$ 900	$ 880	$ 850	**$ 3,730**
	Renewals, $	800	1,300	3,900	4,010	**$10,010**
	Telephone Sales, $	210	800	1,460	1,503	**$ 3,973**
	Consulting Services, $	0	130	468	890	**$ 1,488**
	Customizations, $	35	473	608	950	**$ 2,066**
Total Receipts, $		$2,145	$3,603	$7,316	$8,203	**$ 21,267**

OFFICE SUPPLY STORE CASH FLOW STATEMENT

Receipts:		January	February	March	April	Total
	Paper, $	$ 110	$ 400	$ 900	$ 1,450	**$ 2,860**
	Calculators, $	0	340	0	110	**$ 450**
	Computers, $	0	4,060	1,300	9,400	**$ 14,760**
	Peripherals, $	460	2,389	1,600	2,450	**$ 6,899**
	Furniture, $	0	0	0	199	**$ 199**
	Writing Instruments, $	280	300	460	730	**$ 1,770**
	Presentation Materials, $	505	695	803	477	**$ 2,480**
	Impulse Display Items, $	34	79	672	309	**$ 1,094**
	Cards, $	250	150	172	220	**$ 310**
	Services, $	120	420	1,200	1,833	**$ 3,573**
	Other, $	96	388	700	271	**$ 1,455**
Total Receipts, $		$1,855	$ 9,221	$ 7,707	$ 17,449	**$35,850**

Table 6.6
Revenue-Side Examples for Three Different Businesses

YrFURN—AN APP FOR FURNITURE

The team thought through all the key details for the business including hiring contractors to help write the initial code for the application, their business strategy, and key operational issues. However, despite the fact that all three entrepreneurs took an elective class in entrepreneurship, they initially developed only a very simple budget for the business.

When they went to the Small Business Assistance Center to vet their plan, they were told that a budget was simply not enough. The team had to develop a cash flow statement to be able to track the outflow of cash. With their business, there was going to be a long stretch of outflow before any money comes in. In fact, as the team started to think of cash flow, it was clear they were not sure how they were going to make money. They planned to sell the app for a very low price and had considered other revenue streams such as selling advertisements or selling data from those that used the app.

The team agreed that Brad should craft the cash flow statement. He started with an overall assessment of expenses. Here is what he came up with as a start:

Office Rent	$ 1,500	Paid Monthly
All Utilities	$ 600	Paid Monthly (Various dates)
Coding Contractors	$ 50,000	Beginning of First Month
	$ 25,000	Beginning of Second Month to Alpha Testing
	$ 75	Per coder per hour—Alpha Results Onward-End of each month
Marketing Agency	$ 5,000	Per Month for 3 months starting with Alpha Testing
Salaries	$ 2,000	Per Month for each of the Founders
Travel to Find Investors	$ 3,000	Per Month
Hire IT Director (Includes Benefits)	$ 9,500	Per Month—Hire at Alpha Testing Point and Forward

The cash flow would help the group realize very quickly that they were going to have to raise some new funds quickly. Their $300,000 initial investment would be gone long before they would achieve a viable product.

QUESTIONS

1. As you look at the cash flow are their items you would include they did not?
2. Are there areas in the basic expense where they could save money?

LO6-3

Identify other financial tools.

Other Financial Tools

pro forma

A term describing estimates of what the balance sheets and income statements will look like in the future.

The focus thus far in this chapter has been exclusively on cash flow. This focus is consistent with the view that cash is king in an entrepreneurial business. However, there are other financial tools that are very helpful in analyzing a new business idea. Specifically, a new business will likely want to create **pro forma** balance sheets and income statements. The term *pro forma* (Latin, meaning "as a matter of form") simply means that the entrepreneur estimates what the balance sheets and income statements will look like in the future, in order to plan well.

Balance Sheet

balance sheet

A summary of the assets and liabilities of the entrepreneurial business.

A **balance sheet** is a summary of the assets and liabilities of the entrepreneurial business. It is useful for the new business to analyze and understand the types of assets and liabilities the business can expect. Once the firm is up and running, the pro forma balance sheet is also useful as a comparison in order to understand how assets are being used. The analysis of balance sheets in an ongoing business will be discussed more in Chapter 7. There are two basic types of assets that should be included as separate items in the balance sheet:

Current assets: Assets such as cash or those assets that can easily be converted to cash, such as accounts receivable and notes receivable.

Fixed assets: Assets that have a physical presence, including land, buildings, office equipment, machinery, and vehicles.

The balance sheet should include separate lines for each relevant type of current and fixed asset. The level of detail in this type of document is exclusively up to the entrepreneur; however, we would suggest that one err on the side of more detail early on in the life of the new venture.

On the other side of the equation there are two types of liabilities: current liabilities and long-term liabilities. The definitions of these two types of categories and explanations of what constitutes each are as follows:

Current liabilities: Liabilities or debts that the entrepreneurial business has to pay within one year. These include accounts payable, notes payable such as bank notes, and accrued payroll.

Long-term liabilities: Liabilities that are owed by the business and are ultimately due more than a year from the current date. These include mortgages payable, owners' equity, and stockholders' equity (the latter two are the investment by these individuals in the business).

The assets minus the liabilities of the firm reflected in the balance sheet should total to zero. Thus, the assets and liabilities balance each other. A balance sheet is a snapshot of a firm at some point in time. For a new start-up small firm, the balance sheet is a pro forma projection of what is expected in the future. The estimate of the firm's current assets will be quite limited, as the firm will not yet have any operations. The fixed assets and liabilities can be more exact and should be estimated with some care, since the cost of items can be reasonably estimated, and issues such as debt should be well known. Since the firm is a start-up, there will generally not be depreciation of items such as machinery. The text will discuss issues such as depreciation in Chapter 8, but for now you should know that it is basically a percentage of the value of equipment that is seen as the loss of value of an asset due to wear, tear, age, or obsolescence. The current assets minus the current liabilities are referred to as the working capital, which is in effect the liquid assets the firm could call upon quickly to meet needs that arose. Table 6.7 shows the balance sheet for a small manufacturing firm.

current assets
Assets such as cash or those assets that can easily be converted to cash, such as accounts receivable and notes receivable.

fixed assets
Assets that have a physical presence, including land, buildings, office equipment, machinery, and vehicles.

current liabilities
Liabilities or debts that the entrepreneurial business has to pay within one year. These include accounts payable, notes payable such as bank notes, and accrued payroll.

long-term liabilities
Liabilities that are owed by the business and are ultimately due more than a year from the current date. These include mortgages payable, owners' equity, and stockholders' equity (the latter two are the investment by these individuals in the business).

ETHICAL CHALLENGE

We have noted that banks are able to accept a check (whether it was deposited at a branch or deposited online through an app), and yet they do not have to place those funds in your bank account for a period of up to 10 days, even though the bank may actually obtain those funds earlier. The banks benefit from the float. Although this is a historic element of the business and certainly an element of the business model for banks, what is your opinion of the practice? Many entrepreneurial businesses use the same type of float to their advantage when they use credit cards during the month, knowing that they will pay off the balance before any finance charge is due.

QUESTIONS

1. How could banking and businesses adjust this practice and gain a competitive advantage?
2. Should other tools be employed along these same lines?

Income Statement

income statement
Revenue of the firm minus expenses.

A pro forma **income statement** projects the future income of an entrepreneurial firm. The focus of the income statement is profit rather than cash flow. Whereas we emphasize cash flow as a foundation for analyzing the potential viability of the new business, we believe an understanding of profit allows the projected business to understand its overall cost picture. It is not unusual for a new entrepreneurial business to take a significant amount of time to reach overall profitability.

One of the keys to developing an income statement is predicting sales for the entrepreneurial firm. Even though there is much more art than science to this process, there are some techniques available to assist the entrepreneur. The entrepreneur should initially look to similar enterprises and attempt to estimate or research their sales levels. If a restaurant with a format similar to yours is available, for example, you can estimate its sales by taking the average ticket price and multiplying that by the traffic flow through the restaurant. You can estimate traffic flow to the restaurant by sitting in the parking lot at strategic times keeping a count of how many customers go in the door. The ability to talk with entrepreneurs in the same domain against whom you will not compete was cited in Chapter 3 (identifying the idea) and in Chapter 4 (external analysis) as excellent sources of information. These same individuals

Table 6.7
Pro Forma Income Statement

Assets			
Current Assets			
Cash, $			$ 50,000
Acct Receivable, $			0
Total Current Assets, $			$ 50,000
Fixed Assets, $	Land	100,000	
	Buildings	150,000	
	Office Equipment	15,000	
	Machinery	75,000	
Total Fixed Assets, $			340,000
Total Assets, $			**$390,000**
Liabilities			
Current Liabilities			
Accounts Payable, $		35,000	
Notes Payable (less than a year), $		4,500	
Accrued Payroll, $		15,000	
Total Current Liability, $			$ 54,500
Long-Term Liabilities			
Mortgage, $		200,000	
Total Long-Term Liability, $			$ 200,000
Owner's Equity, $			$ 135,500
Total Liabilities/Owner's Equity, $			$ 390,000

are excellent sources of information on what sales levels could be expected at various stages in the growth of new business. The key is to be conservative, because the reality is that things never happen as fast or as smoothly as you would hope in founding your business.

Correctly predicting a business's performance can help secure better terms with vendors and suppliers.

©Nonwarit/Shutterstock RF

The entrepreneur may come to the conclusion that there are 25,000 people who live in the area around her appliance rental store who are potential customers. The store owner cannot (and should not) assume she will get all or even a majority of those customers. It is better to be very conservative and underestimate demand for a product or service than to overestimate demand. What percentage of the general population rents appliances on a weekly basis? What are the demographics of the typical appliance rental customer? How far will the typical appliance rental customer drive to rent an appliance? What are the primary drivers for the rental of appliances versus the purchase of them? How is the industry tracking? These and many other questions will assist the new-business person in estimating the potential sales of her new venture. Additionally, the entrepreneur needs to realize that sales growth is a function of time and should not assume that the new venture will reach an established company's sales volume in the short run. The new business venture needs to make conservative predictions regarding demand. Again, discussion with successful entrepreneurs is the new-business person's best resource. Table 6.8 illustrates the income statement developed for the computer sales and service firm.

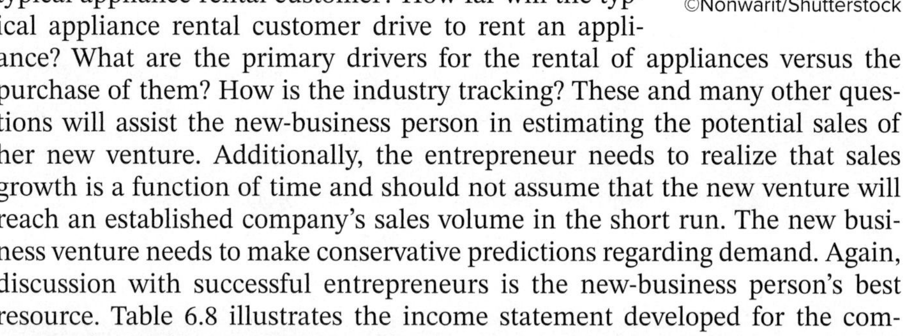

The income statement provides both the gross and the net profit figures for the firm. In its simplified form, gross profit generally equals the sales of the organization minus the cost of goods sold. The firm then calculates all other expenses, such as salaries and benefits, to reach a total expense for the firm. Gross profit minus all other expenses yields net profit before taxes. Lastly, estimated taxes are calculated and subtracted from net profit, to determine the company's net profit after taxes. Note that the cost of goods sold is very small, in that producing a computer disk and a manual are very cheap activities from the production standpoint. If this were a restaurant, the cost of goods sold would be much higher.

Break-Even Analysis

Now that you have developed a pro forma cash flow statement, income statement, and balance sheet for your proposed new venture, it is time to look at one additional analytical tool. The initial effort to project the cash flow is critical. However, the firm needs to extend this analysis. Specifically, what are the opportunities for the new venture to generate significant returns for the owners? Individuals have numerous alternatives to starting a new venture, and we want to suggest that a **break-even analysis** of the projected position of the company will go a long way toward determining not only the viability of the new venture but also the realistic assessment of whether this is the best path for the entrepreneur to embark upon. A break-even analysis provides some judgment about when the firm will reach a point of being self-sustaining after the business is begun.[7]

break-even analysis
Tool for the estimation of when a business's income exceeds its expenses.

fixed costs
Costs that must be paid no matter how many goods are sold, such as rent for the building.

variable costs
Costs that vary according to how many goods are produced.

The break-even analysis recognizes that the growth in sales does not occur all at once. Instead, the sales of the business will grow incrementally once the firm starts. However, many of the expenses of the firm will start months before the first sale. Specifically, there are **fixed costs** (e.g., rent, utilities, equipment leases), which must be paid regardless of the sales level. There are also **variable costs** that will fluctuate according to how many goods are

INCOME STATEMENT

Receipts:		January	February	March	April	May	June	Total
	Sales, $	$ 350	$ 550	$ 1,200	$9,400	$12,200	$13,000	$36,700
	Consulting, $	$3,000	3,500	5,000	0	3,000	3,500	18,000
Total Income, $		$3,350	$4,050	$ 6,200	$9,400	$15,200	$16,500	$54,700
Cost of Goods Sold								
	Inventory Inputs, $	17	20	31	47	76	112	303
Gross Profit, $		3,333	4,030	6,169	9,353	15,124	16,388	54,397
Other Expenses								
	Salaries, $	$4,000	$4,000	$5,000	$5,000	$5,000	$5,000	$28,000
	Travel, $	2,304	365	558	846	1,368	1,104	6,545
	Car Leases, $	1,000	1,000	1,000	1,000	1,000	1,000	6,000
	Rent, $	900	450	450	450	450	450	3,150
	Payroll Taxes, $	240	240	300	300	300	340	1,720
	Insurance, $	0	0	0	1,450	0	0	1,450
	Fuel/Maint., $	13	21	46	361	468	502	1,412
	Benefits, $	350	350	350	350	350	350	2,100
	Advertising, $	28	44	96	752	976	0	1,896
	Utilities, $	174	213	208	189	132	188	1,104
	Misc., $	67	81	124	188	304	764	1,528
Total Expenses		$ 9,093	$ 6,784	$ 8,163	$10,933	$10,424	$ 9,810	$ 55,208
Profit Before Taxes, $		(5,760)	(2,754)	(1,994)	(1,580)	4,700	6,578	($ 811)
Taxes, $		0.00	0.00	0.00	0.00	0.00	0.00	0.00
Profit After Taxes, $		($5,760)	($2,754)	($1,994)	($1,580)	$4,700	$ 6,578	($ 811)

Table 6.8
Example Income Statement for Computer Sales and Services Firm

produced. For example, if you manufacture something packaged in plastic bottles, you will have increasing costs as you produce more products, since you will need more bottles.

The traditional Fortune 500 approach to break-even analysis would suggest that once revenues exceed the total of the fixed costs plus the variable costs, then the firm has reached breakeven. In this approach, the profit margin from each sale adds to the net profit for the firm. For firms operating in a project-by-project environment, this type of analysis is relatively effective. These firms are simply trying to compare an investment in one project to an investment in another, as shown in Figure 6.1.

However, entrepreneurial ventures need to operate in a fundamentally different manner, and we calculate breakeven using cash flow rather than profit. The initial investment in the new venture is an item of concern that is not normally included in most corporate cash flow analyses. Accounting for the initial investment allows the new firm to discuss the true economic returns, or economic benefits, from the business. (Recall that we discussed earlier that the entrepreneur wants to be sure that her business is providing the economic return she envisioned and that she is not working essentially for free.) Figure 6.2 demonstrates this relationship. We begin this diagram with an initial investment

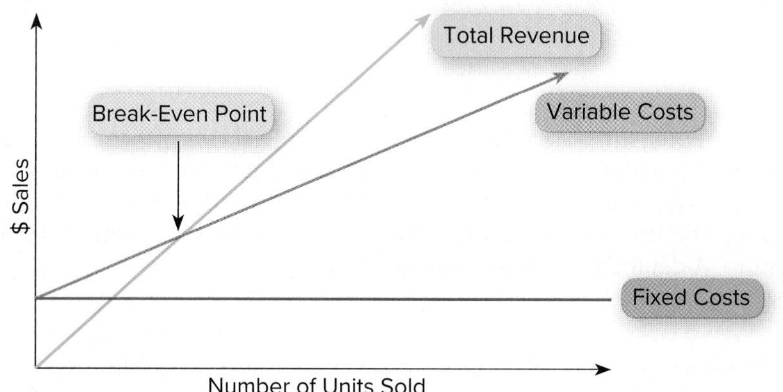

Figure 6.1
Classic Break-Even Diagram

level. As the new firm begins operations, it is burning cash (from both a fixed- and a variable-cost standpoint) and reporting a negative net cash flow. Depending upon the venture and the industry in which it is operating, this negative cash flow can go on for some time. However, at some point a successful business turns the corner and begins producing positive cash flows. This has been called the break-even point for the company, that is, when the firm's costs equal its sales. However, we believe that until the new venture's positive cash flow exceeds the initial investment, **entrepreneurial breakeven** has not been achieved. This analysis can be further enhanced by taking into consideration the issue of time value of money.[8] There are other uses of your investment dollars and your raw time. With inflation, $1,000 received today is far more valuable than $1,000 will be if received 10 years from now. Thus, if you invest in a business today, you will want it to produce a return that is greater than the return you could have made if you simply had put the money in a savings account. Calculating the **time value of money** gives the initial investment line in Figure 6.2 an upward slope and creates an entrepreneurial break-even point that is farther out, but infinitely more realistic from an investor point of view.

entrepreneurial breakeven When a new venture's net cash flow exceeds the initial investment plus the time value of the money invested.

time value of money The value of money over time at a given rate of inflation or other type of return. Calculated as the value of your investment in time and money if you did not do the proposed venture.

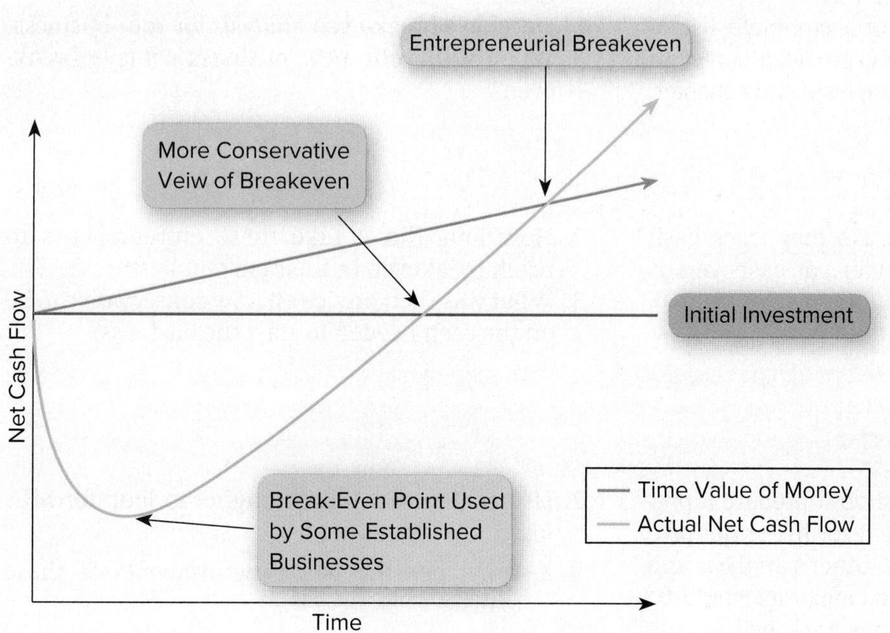

Figure 6.2
Entrepreneurial Break-Even Diagram

SUMMARY

The decision process for starting a new entrepreneurial business is fraught with the unknown. This chapter has focused exclusively upon the analysis tools that are the most critical in determining the financial viability of the proposed new venture. A detailed examination of cash flow, its inputs, and its uses was provided. A brief examination of the balance sheet and income statement were provided, and finally we discussed the unique nature of an entrepreneurial break-even analysis.

KEY TERMS

REVIEW QUESTIONS

1. Why is cash flow so important for a new business?
2. How are cash flow and profit related?
3. What are the basic elements of a cash flow statement for an entrepreneurial business?
4. Why is a budget statement not a cash flow statement? How do they differ?
5. How does float affect a cash flow statement?
6. How does a balance sheet relate to a cash flow statement?
7. Why is break-even analysis so important to a new business?
8. What elements make up a break-even analysis?
9. How is an income statement used by new business?
10. What is Entrepreneurial Breakeven?

BUSINESS PLAN DEVELOPMENT QUESTIONS

1. You have all the basic tools now to create a projected cash flow statement for your proposed business. Categorize all of your income-generating areas and carefully develop a complete list of your expenses (review the list provided earlier in this chapter). Using the examples in this chapter, develop a projection that shows when the business is self-sustaining and then present it to a group of your peers.
2. Develop a break-even analysis for your business.
3. When will your new business achieve breakeven?

INDIVIDUAL EXERCISES

1. Talk to two entrepreneurs. Do they track cash flow? If so what is their view of cash versus profit in their business.
2. How long did it take these entrepreneurs to reach breakeven in their current business?
3. What was their advice on how conservative to be on the cash needed to start the business?

GROUP EXERCISES

1. Each person on the team should prepare a preliminary cash flow statement for his or her proposed venture. Look at each other's analysis and discuss what other revenue categories could be developed to better focus sales tracking?
2. Use an Internet search engine to look for SBA loans.

   a. What are the basic requirements of these loans?

b. Why do you think the government supports such loans for entrepreneurial business?

c. What insights does this provide each person on the team about his or her own proposed ventures?

ENDNOTES

1. J. Kelly and J. O'Connor, "Is Profit More Important Than Cashflow?" *Management Accounting* 75, no. 6 (1997), pp. 28–30.
2. S. Allen, "Cash (Flow) Really Is King," The Balance, July 12, 2016, https://www.thebalance.com/cash-flow-really-is-king-1200759.
3. C. E. Chastain, S. Cianciolo, and A. Thomas, "Strategies in Cash Flow Management," *Business Horizons* 29, no. 3 (1986), pp. 65–74.
4. H. Whited, "Constructing a Cash Budget and Projecting Financial Statements: An Exercise of Short-Term Financial Planning for Entrepreneurs," *Review of Business and Financial Studies* 5 (2013), pp. 102–12.
5. K. Klein, "How Small Business Owners Can Cope with the Crisis," *BusinessWeek Online,* October 13, 2008, p. 14.
6. R. B. Lorance and R. V. Wendling, "Basic Techniques for Analyzing and Presentation of Cost Risk Analysis," *Cost Engineering* 43, no. 6 (2001), pp. 25–32.
7. D. White and P. White, "How to Calculate 'Breakeven,'" Entrepreneur, May 24, 2016, https://www.entrepreneur.com/article/276296.
8. R. R. Crabb, "Cash Flow: A Quick and Easy Way to Learn Personal Finance," *Financial Services Review* 8, no. 4 (1999), pp. 269–83.

chapter 7

learning objectives

After studying this chapter, you will be able to:

LO7-1 Identify key financial issues involved with starting a business.

LO7-2 Discuss the basics of funding a business.

LO7-3 Explain the importance of proper accounting when starting a business.

Financing and Accounting

CHRISTOPHER GRAY—SCHOLLY

Christopher Gray wanted to break out of his circumstances and go to a top college, but he needed to find scholarships to fund the effort. He did not have the resources to attend the schools he was interested in as his mom was unemployed in Birmingham, Alabama, during the worst recession to hit the United States in six decades. He went on a hunt to find scholarships that would allow him to attend and found that the information on scholarships was disorganized and poorly articulated the requirements for the various scholarships. Christopher spent eight months crawling through the Internet and filing out applications (often on his cell phone as his family did not have web access at home). He found "[s]earching for scholarships became like looking for a needle in a haystack. There was information online, but it was scattered all over, and often outdated." Ultimately, his efforts resulted in winning over $1.3 million in scholarships, including scholarships from the Bill and Melinda Gates Foundation and the Coca-Cola Scholars Foundation. Christopher was able to take these funds and study finance and entrepreneurship at Drexel University.

While at Drexel he founded Scholly along with two friends as an app that would allow people seeking scholarships to find them easily and apply for them directly. By 2015 the three entrepreneurs had helped students obtain $9 million in funding. The three applied for and won a spot on the popular TV show ***Shark Tank***. The team was awarded $40,000 for 15 percent by the sharks and then had to wait eight months for the show to air (without being able to say anything).

As the entrepreneurs waited for the show to air, they prepared for what they hoped would be an onslaught of activity once the show aired. They were rewarded. When the show aired, their site was getting over 8,000 hits a minute. For the next three weeks, Scholly was the #1 app on both the Apple and Google Play stores. The app is available on iPhone and Androids phones and costs $2.99. The success allowed the company to bring on seasoned management in the field and got Jesse Williams from the TV show *Grey's Anatomy* to be a spokesperson for the business.

By 2017 their platform had helped literally hundreds of thousands of students obtain over $50 million in scholarships.

Questions

1. Besides charging the nominal price for the app, how would you recommend they make money on their efforts?
2. What other areas for expansion would seem to fit with Scholly's capability set?

Sources: https://myscholly.com/story/; A. Field, "Life Post-Shark Tank at Scholarship App Startup Scholly," *Forbes*, March 24, 2015. http://www.forbes.com/sites/annefield/2015/03/24/life-post-shark-tank-at-scholarship-app-startup-scholly/#710ae0f424f8; M. Simon, "Jesse Williams Backs 'Scholly' App for College Scholarships," NBC News, September 14, 2016. http://www.nbcnews.com/news/nbcblk/jesse-williams-backs-scholly-app-college-scholarships-n648381.

Financing the start of a new business and establishing the accounting systems are central operational concerns in the start-up of a new business. In Chapter 6 we examined the basic financial analysis (on a pro forma basis) that should be used to evaluate the decision to start a business. The next issue to develop is the specific financing and accounting issues that impact the operational start-up of the business. Specifically, three questions are examined in this chapter:

1. How will the entrepreneur or entrepreneurial team fund the new business, and what funding level is really needed for the new venture?
2. What accounting records should be maintained, and how will they be maintained?
3. How should the business manage the information flow of information for the new company?

All of these issues are directly related to the successful establishment of the financial structure and record keeping of the new company. Too often new businesspeople put these issues at the bottom of their priority list (both during and after start-up) and do not devote much time to them. However, it is far easier to establish items such as a sound system to account for the transactions of the business at the beginning of the venture. Some forethought on the process will save lots of frustration after the business is up and running.

LO7-1

Identify key financial issues involved with starting a business.

Key Financial Issues Involved with Starting a Business

There are a wide range of issues that new businesses need to be aware of that are related to financing of the start-up. The issues we address in this chapter are not ordered by their importance; instead these issues are intertwined with each other. The first is the funding and funding level of the firm. The next is the establishment of an accounting system. Finally, the flow of information in the new business needs specific attention. If the new business does not address all of these issues very early on in the effort, then the owners will constantly be putting out fires related to these items rather than focusing on building the firm.

Entrepreneurial firms often face such opportunities—ones that may or may not be beneficial to the entrepreneur. However, the entrepreneur needs to evaluate clearly the pros and cons of any such major shift to their business plan.

Extra expenses, especially early on in a business's life when no (or virtually no) income is coming in, can quickly use up the cash intended to found and grow the business. How much initial funding does a business need to survive the first year of operation? What type of financial cushion should be in place to help buffer the business when an unexpected cost arises? Central to a financial cushion is the nature of the firm's funding. When considering funding, the firm needs to evaluate not only the amount provided but also the sources of that funding. A key aspect of how the funding will be used is found in the information provided by the business, and that comes through the accounting system and the data flow management.

LO7-2

Discuss the basics of funding a business.

Basics of Funding a Business

Funding for almost any new business starts with the founder(s) and his or her personal resources. However, at some stage (often prior to actual start-up), the firm may need to find other sources of funding. These sources may be small and may or may not be tied to an equity (ownership) interest in return for the funding.

KOSHER HOME

Kosher Home was continuing on its path to make the new business a reality. The owners had established a banking relationship with the region's largest bank and found a place they would operate out of that included a large, commercial kitchen that could be arranged to meet kosher requirements and cold storage. They discovered they would need licensing as a food distributor and had put that in place.

The two founders decided to run a small experiment with their products locally before moving to national distribution. Their focus was on those who attended a single orthodox synagogue. (Judaism in the United States has three major branches—Reformed that normally does not follow kosher, Conservative that may follow Kosher typically, and Orthodox that always follows Kosher.) The team would develop new meals, sell them for a reduced price to members, and obtain feedback on the products delivered. The two entrepreneurs quickly discovered that in the process of spending money and receiving invoices, they needed a means to track their transactions. For the first few weeks, they simply kept a classic accounting T-chart with all the expenses on one side and all the income (of which there was very little) on the other.

During this time, they also received their first bank statement and, more importantly, a call from a local businessman who had learned of their new operation. The businessman had a restaurant and wanted to partner with the two entrepreneurs. He stated that he had thought of starting a similar business but since they were up and running, it could be a win-win for all if he simply bought into the firm.

The founders met with the businessman and were excited that someone thought their idea would be viable and could be very profitable. Jack and Toby were thrilled with the prospect of joining with an established businessman since they assumed this person would have the expertise to handle much of the basic business aspects of their venture. Jack and Toby could then focus on promoting the business and the technical aspect of setting up an Internet business.

At the synagogue there was a businesswoman who was friends with Toby's aunt. Both women had offered to provide any advice he may need. Toby and Jack called on the businesswoman. As she looked at the terms of the deal, she highlighted to Jack and Toby that the businessman was putting in money to the venture. However, the terms would mean he would have effective control of the firm. She also highlighted that Jack and Toby would be responsible for the debt incurred not the businessperson. Jack and Toby began to realize that the offer was not as good as they initially assumed.

This episode made the entrepreneurs realize they needed not to rely on someone else to help with the business aspect of the firm but instead to immerse themselves in these details. They informed the businessman that they had decided not to take his offer of investment. The two entrepreneurs then set about studying the detail of the costs of inputs and the profit on each product they sold. In the process of reviewing the costs of their products and their pricing, the entrepreneurs came to see that their business was much more complex than they had initially thought, and they needed to have a much better system to track all of their finances. The realities of the business were confronting them.

Jack and Toby called a local accountant they found online. This accountant told them that maintaining accurate records was going to be critical, and the sooner they got a computer accounting package and used it, the better. The accountant recommended a straightforward package that was available at most office supply stores and was easily understood. The entrepreneurs quickly acquired the software and went about learning it and setting up all of the business records. The result was that they were learning how to use the system and seeking to adapt it to their needs while, at the same time, preparing to run the business.

QUESTIONS

1. How important will inventory control be to this business? What do you recommend?
2. What do you think the most critical cash flow issues will be with the business?
3. What do you recommend the founders do to manage cash flow?

In contrast, other investors will make **equity investments**, where someone provides funding in return for some ownership in the new business. Each of these types of funding will be reviewed in turn. First, we review those funding sources that do not require equity in the firm, followed by a review of equity investments, and wrap up with alternative sourcing tools, such as

equity investment
Funds received by a business in exchange for a percentage ownership of the business.

crowdfunding

Funds received by a business by soliciting a large number of very small investors usually via the Internet.

crowdfunding, that have become so popular.[1] Separately we will discuss a means for determining the actual amount of funding a new business should seek, to ensure it has sufficient resources at the outset of the business.

Nonequity Funding

There are several sources for nonequity capital to start a business. Debt is a major source of such nonequity financing and can come from banks, credit cards, asset leasing companies, individuals, and/or suppliers. Grants and winnings from business plan competitions are another type of nonequity funding to which some businesses may have access. A grant may come from the government or a nonprofit agency; it is simply money designed to help the new business begin operations with no expectation of repayment.

debt

A generic term to describe any type of nonequity funding tied to the business.

Debt. A firm can obtain **debt** in many forms, each with positives and negatives for a new business. Debt is any form of capital infusion that must be paid back with interest. Debt allows the new business to manage its cash flow through the various peaks and valleys in the operation of a business or, more importantly, to handle the disparity between when goods must be purchased and when money will be received from a customer to pay for those goods. The most common forms of debt for new businesses can be classified as follows:

1. Loans from
   a. Bank or finance company
   b. Individuals
   c. Founders
2. Credit cards
3. Supplier credit

loan

Contractual agreement whereby the firm receives some amount of money that must be repaid over a specified period of time at a specified interest rate.

Loans. A **loan**, regardless of its origin, involves a contractual agreement whereby the business receives some amount of money that must be repaid over a specified period of time at a specified interest rate. Loans are most often repaid monthly from cash flow and, especially early in the life of a business, are secured by assets or a personal guarantee. In the case of business failure, debt must be paid back prior to any equity investors receiving a distribution.

Banks have traditionally been a major source of funds for established firms but are quite restrictive in their lending to start-up firms, as the risk is perceived to be too high. However, there are some specific ways that banks lend to new businesses. For example, banks will make loans for the purchase of some types of equipment. In this type of lending, the bank will estimate the residual value of the equipment if the bank had to repossess the equipment and then lend the business a percentage of the difference between that number and the sale price. This discount is typically quite significant. This type of lending is referred to as **asset-based lending**. As will be discussed in Chapter 12, a relationship with a bank is critical to the new business's ability to obtain bank financing.[2]

asset-based lending

A loan provided for the purchase of a necessary asset for the business.

Banks will also lend money for the establishment and maintenance of inventory by arranging a revolving line of credit. A lender will periodically perform an on-site examination of the inventory to ensure that the inventory is being accounted for properly. A particular problem with lines of credit for inventory is that a firm may have old inventory that has not been sold for a period of time. Such inventory needs to be discounted, as its value in the market has shrunk. Too often firms still reflect that old inventory on their books at full market value.

A classic source of entrepreneurial finance is friends and family. Although the conditions for borrowing from friends and family may be a bit more relaxed, the new business owner should view the loan as he would one from a bank. One issue to consider in such loans is that if the business fails, the inability to repay such loans can permanently rupture the family relationship or friendship.

The founder(s) of the business may also choose to personally lend money to the new business. Even though it may strike some as odd to lend money to your own business, debt is a secured investment. Therefore, if you lend your firm $1,000, then you, along with the other debt holders, have the right to the firm's assets if the firm fails to pay off that debt. An equity investor generally receives only those proceeds that are left after paying off all other debts.

credit card
Card entitling one to revolving credit that is not tied to any particular asset, does not have a set repayment schedule, typically has a set upper limit, and is usually tied to a much higher interest rate than that of a bank loan.

Credit Cards. Credit cards are another form of nonequity investment. A **credit card** is simply another type of credit. However, a credit card is not tied to any particular asset, nor does it have a set repayment schedule (other than a minimum payment).

We have worked with a number of new businesses that decided early on to finance their operations with credit card debt. One new businessperson running an advertising agency would, when faced with a new bill for the company, go to the center desk drawer to look through more than 60 active credit cards to decide which one should be used to pay the bill. Not only is this a very poor management system that is extremely expensive, but it is also one where the debt is almost always tied personally to the founder(s), thus exposing them to personal bankruptcy. That said, credit cards can be a wonderful short-term method of managing your cash flow, especially during peak times in the early stages of the business. If paid off each month, business-issued credit cards provide the company with an excellent financial tracking system that can be divided up by individuals within the company, and payment can be delayed by up to 25 days, allowing for a unique positive cash flow situation. However, the new business must be able to manage such debt carefully if it is going to be employed. The interest rates can easily exceed 30 percent and will quickly bankrupt a firm if allowed to build.

What are the risks and rewards of using credit cards when financing a business?

©studiocasper/iStockphoto/Getty Images RF

supplier credit
Another form of nonequity funding that is available. Suppliers often will provide credit on both physical assets (refrigerators, molding equipment, etc.) and the actual supplies provided.

Supplier Credit. **Supplier credit** is another form of nonequity funding that is available.[3] Suppliers will generally provide credit on both physical assets (refrigerators, molding equipment, etc.) and the actual supplies purchased. A firm such as IBM Credit LLC is an example of a firm that you may be familiar with that exists primarily to fund the acquisition or lease of IBM products and services although they also finance purchases from other organizations. The credit terms offered by such firms can be quite generous, but they are a liability for the company and need to be managed as such. Accepting supplier credit can tie you to that supplier, limiting your ability to shop around for a cheaper source. The terms can be quite generous, and the rates are usually more competitive than those available from traditional bank sources.

grants
Special funds that do not require repayment and are designed to aid businesses in specific areas.

Grants. The new business should also explore **grants** from both governmental and private foundation sources. There are special funds that are neither equity nor debt funds that are designed to aid businesses in specific areas. These grants typically target disadvantaged groups, economic areas, or particular industries. There are also grants for target groups such as veterans and women-owned businesses. The presence of such grants vary widely based on the given funding year and where you live. Grants should be explored through groups such as your local Small Business Assistance Center.

Equity Funding

The new business should employ all nonequity funding mechanisms available to it. In the long run (assuming a successful business operation), the cost of such capital is generally less than that of equity investment. However, a growing business might need to seek equity funding beyond founders' capital.

In the founding process, the business generally receives funds from the founder(s) as well as other investors. An evaluation is needed to determine the percentage of ownership each founder will have in the business and the percentage that will be reserved for investors. We will cover valuation of the business in Chapter 13, and we recommend that prior to allowing any non-founder to invest in your new business, you have a fair and valid estimation of the value of your company. That said, we would like to address several key issues related to equity financing of the new business with outside sources.

Obtaining equity investment from investors has a number of potential operational impacts. Investors can be active or passive, majority or minority, companies that might ultimately wish to buy the whole new venture, and/or suppliers looking to add new volume for their products. Each of these potential sources has characteristics that can have a major impact on your business. Additionally, accepting an equity stake from an outside investor adds a dimension of accountability to the founding of a new business and opens the new venture up to new concerns. Therefore, seeking outside funding is a significant decision.[4]

To illustrate the impact of outside investors, we worked with an entrepreneur who started a new high-end restaurant. The initial investment needed to make the venture work was substantial and well more than the founder could invest. She sought outside investors for the business from her country club, social friends, and business acquaintances. She ended up with 47 total investors with separate investments that varied from $8,000 to $110,000. The restaurant was built and opened to great fanfare. Thursday, Friday, and Saturday nights were packed, with an average wait for a table of two hours. The founder worked nonstop on those evenings, but had continuous problems with her fellow "investors."

A number of these investors believed that they deserved preferential treatment at the restaurant because they were "owners." Many of them demanded special favors, such as being placed first on the wait list for a table; walking through the kitchen with guests (not a helpful thing to do on busy nights); talking to the chefs about their ideas; or even having their meals "comped" (received for free). Some investors similarly felt free to discuss employee performance with the individual employees. These investors would also call at will to talk to the founder about the restaurant's direction, as well as expecting to be able to meet with the founder at their convenience.

The founder finally had a meeting with all of the investors to lay out the problems involved with their behavior and the disruption to the success of the business. Several of the investors were indignant and demanded their investment be returned. This was not something that the business could afford at this early stage, and legally it did not have to comply with their request. The result was fractious relations with some investors, and an enormous amount of time being taken away from the business to handle "bruised egos." A little care in the initial setup of these relations could have prevented a series of problems later in the operation. Eventually each of the upset investors was bought out and all of the other investors agreed to end their disruptive behavior.

Equity investment traditionally involves selling a percentage of the business to an outside party. This should be done in consultation with an attorney who is well versed in this area of the law. The founder(s) must be very clear that in the case of dissolution, each investor is entitled to the percentage of the break-up value (after all debts and obligations are paid) equal to their investment percentage of ownership. However, even more critical to the success of the business is to carefully and clearly outline what rights and expectations each investor has as the business grows. Equity investment does not necessarily carry with it an equivalent percentage of control in the firm. An entrepreneur needs to clearly specify how ownership will be handled. Similarly, the entrepreneur needs to clearly specify how the profits of the business will be handled. Will the new venture divide up all profits at the end of each year? What will be retained in the business for future growth? How can each investor "sell" his or her shares? Does the company have first right of refusal in any share sale? Working with an attorney to develop a clear document that details all of the concerns about an equity investment should be completed prior to approaching a potential investor.

As previously mentioned, the sources of equity investment include other firms, venture capitalists, and business angels.

Businesses as Equity Investors. Many established businesses are willing to make equity investments in other start-up firms. Large firms such as Microsoft, Intel, and Cisco have traditionally been among the most active equity investors in new start-up firms in the technology sector; corporate venture capital from these firms is actually one of the leading sources of venture capital in the United States. (Venture capital is discussed in greater detail below.) There are two scenarios that we have dealt with regularly in the funding from such firms. The first involves a company that will invest in a new venture with the idea of ultimately purchasing the operation. The second type is a large supplier that is willing to invest in a new operation as an additional outlet for its products.

The company that invests with the idea of an ultimate purchase does so because it is one of the least expensive means for trying out new ideas/products/methods and for maintaining access to the latest thinking in the field. For the established company to try to develop every idea in-house, it would have to redirect significant resources away from the core focus of its business. Instead, the large business invests in a series of businesses that are trying new things within its industry, and in effect, it has taken out a series of strategic options without having to detract from its core business.[5] Those options that turn out to be successes are then purchased and brought into the core organization. This can be a wonderful harvest strategy for the entrepreneur to capture the value in a newly founded business; however, the founder(s) may not wish to sell the business at the exact point in time that the larger company wishes to close the sale. Depending on the nature of the investment, the founder(s) may not have the option to decide when the business is sold.

What are the pros and cons of equity investment from an established, larger firm in a new small business?

©stevecoleimages/Getty Images RF

Having a supplier invest in your new business is somewhat simpler, in that the supplier is generally not trying to run your business, nor looking to take the business over if it does particularly well. Instead, the issue with this type of equity investment is one of restriction. The deal usually involves an exclusivity agreement to use only that supplier's products. This can be a significant (and in some cases a business-killing) proposition. The founder(s) must be careful not to trap themselves into an agreement that prevents flexibility that may be needed in the future.

Venture Capital (VC). A form of equity investment that seems to garner considerable press because of the sheer size of their investments is venture capital. A **venture capital fund** is a fund that is usually organized as a limited partnership.[6] Limited partners in the fund, which may include very wealthy individuals, insurance companies, other businesses, and retirement funds, invest in such funds seeking high returns. The general partner in the fund is the venture capitalist, who then investigates and invests in each new business. Venture capitalists might invest in less than one out of the thousand business plans they see in a year. They are seeking extremely high-growth businesses that have an opportunity to "cash out" with an IPO or sale to a larger company within a set period of time. VCs are looking to make a significant investment, generally something greater than $2 million. As such, they are not a source of funding for very many new businesses, and we spend very little time in this text on venture capital.*

venture capital fund
A fund that is organized to make significant equity investments in high-growth new ventures.

Business Angels. Business angels are a form of equity investors that are more widely available to new businesses. **Business angels** are high-net-worth individuals that invest widely in businesses.[7] These individuals may include entrepreneurs who have built one or more businesses and have cashed out (i.e., sold their businesses and have the excess cash in hand), executives with large organizations that have high incomes, professionals such as doctors and lawyers, and individuals with significant inheritances. These individuals can be very helpful sources of expertise and contacts in the area. However, the new businessperson should seek individuals who have relevant knowledge (not just money) to add to the firm. When seeking investment from such individuals, we suggest that you evaluate the nature of their advice, how intrusive they will be, the nature of their business experience, and what other contacts and relationships the angels may have that can help the new firm.

business angels
High-net-worth individuals who invest in businesses not as a business but as an individual.

Crowdfunding. Crowdfunding is a relatively new means for raising capital that may result in either an equity approach or an in-kind exchange for the firm. Companies seeking to raise capital without using the traditional approaches have found that the Internet is an excellent means to try to reach out to potential investors.[8] Internet sites such as Kickstarter.com, EquityNet.com, Indiegogo.com, and others have systematized the process. Entrepreneurs seeking capital make their pitch on the site and let potential investors know what they will receive for their funding. This might be equity (depending upon the size of the investment) but is more often a product/ service, or gift.[9]

Other Financing Tools

Several other financing tools are available to the new business as it starts. These mechanisms include asset leasing and factoring.

Asset Leasing. A form of funding for a new organization is an **asset lease** arrangement. Similar to leasing a car, many of the assets needed by the new business can be leased from the manufacturer or from a third-party reseller. Instead of owning the assets, the company simply leases what it needs. In fact, there are companies (third-party resellers) that have a significant part of their inventory in equipment that they lease to other companies. The advantages are relatively straightforward. The new business is able to acquire the assets that it needs to begin operations with a minimal cash outlay. The company pays the lease from production that is a direct result of using the equipment that it has leased. Furthermore, it is not stuck with an aging asset. As newer, higher-quality machines become available, the entrepreneur is able to trade up.

asset lease
A form of lease tied to a particular asset used by a business to conserve cash and maintain the latest versions of whatever equipment is available.

*If the student wishes to locate more information on venture capital and venture capitalists in his or her area, the National Venture Capital Association is an excellent source of information.

The big disadvantage to leasing is that over time the new business may spend more money for the equipment than if it had bought the unit outright. However, the net present value of the lease may actually work out to a net positive as the new businessperson does not have to put as much cash initially into the lease as in a purchase. Therefore, the decision maker should evaluate two areas: (1) How much cash does the new business have to invest in equipment as the firm starts? and (2) Given the pace of equipment obsolescence in that industry, would it be more advantageous to lease or own the equipment needed to operate the business?

Factoring. With the exception of new businesses that operate strictly on cash, as the business begins to make sales it will generate accounts receivable—that is, sales that have been made but not yet paid for. If the firm needs to generate cash in the short run, these accounts can be sold at a discount via a technique known as **factoring**.[10] Numerous businesses provide this service. These firms will discount the dollar amount of such accounts based on the quantity and quality of the receivables. The quality of the receivables is determined by such issues as: (1) who owes the new business money; (2) the debt age; (3) the size of the transaction; and (4) the debtor's credit rating. For example, if a blue-chip firm such as ExxonMobil or a government entity owes you the money, there is a virtual 100 percent chance of being paid. In contrast, if your accounts receivables are from a small building contractor (an industry segment with a considerable history of turnover), then the accounts will be more heavily discounted. The benefit for the entrepreneur is that the new business gets the money from the accounts receivable immediately. Aside from obtaining the cash up front, the new business does not have to spend time and effort trying to collect the accounts receivable. The negative is that the new business will not receive the full amount of the debt that is due to it.

factoring
Accounts receivable that are sold at a discount to another company to receive immediate cash.

Initial Funding

The new businessperson needs to calculate how much money will be needed to start up the business. Although it would appear that more initial funding would be somewhat better than less, it must be tempered by what the founder has to give up to obtain the money. In Chapter 6 we examined the financial issues associated with breakeven and basic cash flow analysis. The complexity of capital funding increases substantially as the new business requires external investment to begin operations.

To calculate the maximum amount that you may wish to obtain in outside financing, recall from Chapter 6 that we recommend the entrepreneur calculate the entire cash flow projection without adding in any equity investment and look for the point where the ending cash balance is at its lowest point. A safe rule of thumb suggests taking that number and multiplying it by 150 percent. The resulting amount is what we recommend for the initial equity or equity-plus-debt investment. The new businessperson then connects this amount with the percentage of the firm that was previously determined would be made available to other investors. The two points frame the new businessperson's investment parameters. Consider the following example:

Value of the Firm Prior to Beginning Operations (See Chapter 14)	$100,000
Lowest Point in Projected Cash Flow	$ 20,000
Required Investment	$ 30,000
Amount Invested by Founder	$ 10,000
Amount Needed from Outside Investors	$ 20,000
Potential Percentage of the Business to Be Expected by Investors (20,000/100,000)	**20%**

EXERCISE 1

1. How much funding will you need for your new business?
2. How do you plan to fund the new business?
3. What assumptions have you made regarding your funding?

It is important to remember that negotiations between the founder(s) and your investor are just that, negotiations. It takes two willing parties to reach an agreement. You may see the investment in your firm as worth X, whereas an investor sees it as worth Y. It will take negotiation to determine the ultimate value. A review of Chapter 13's discussion of valuation and negotiation should be helpful in conceptualizing these issues.

LO7-3

Explain the importance of proper accounting when starting a business.

Importance of Proper Accounting When Starting a Business

We do not presume in the next few pages to show you how to do all of the accounting that you will ever need to know to manage your business. There are many fine texts and courses available that focus tightly on this huge and complicated area of business. Furthermore, we covered the basics regarding the balance sheet and income statement in Chapter 6. That said, we would like to suggest that the needs of most new entrepreneurs are very straightforward and can best be met with one of the numerous computer software programs available.

The new businessperson will need to quickly decide whether she will use a cash- or accrual-basis accounting system. In its simplest form, cash-based accounting recognizes expenses as they are paid and recognizes revenue as it is generated. Accrual-based accounting is the more typical form of accounting used, with expenses and revenues recorded when they actually occur, regardless of when the cash is received. Accrual accounting must be used if you have inventory; if you have to report your financial statements; and if your business is a Subchapter C corporation, partnership, or trust. The end result is that only the smallest businesses use cash-basis accounting.

The new businessperson will need to carefully evaluate which accounting program would be the best for his business. Choosing a package that will be useful for your business is a process of understanding your new business first and then finding a package that will accommodate your needs with the least impact on the business. Most of the packages will provide any report that could be demanded by the owner(s), potential investors, auditors, or loan officers. Some of the key reports that the new businessperson should be prepared

ETHICAL CHALLENGE

You have seen in this chapter that there are different types of investors, and there can be different levels of investment. These investors come into the business facing potentially different types of risk and return.

QUESTIONS

1. Think about and discuss the ethical obligations you have to early-stage investors versus later-stage investors. Do you promise more returns to someone who shows faith in you at an earlier stage?
2. What are the ethical obligations if some investors are family members and some are not? Do family members deserve different investor treatment?

to generate include (1) chart of accounts, (2) petty cash register, (3) check register, (4) expense accounts, (5) inventory accounts, (6) accounts payable, and (7) payroll.

Chart of Accounts

The chart of accounts is the master system for tracking the activity of the business. It requires a bit of care up front in its establishment and will need updating as the business grows. This chart is not complex; however, the new businessperson needs to ensure that the system designed provides the information necessary to analyze the business and its performance. This topic will be discussed more in Chapter 8 as we examine business performance of the going concern and ensure that the firm is performing as desired.

A chart of accounts is simply a listing of each type of activity (income or expense) and each type of asset within the company. The account number used is completely at your discretion, but income categories are usually first, expense categories next, and asset categories last. You may use two-digit or three-digit numbers as you wish and in accordance with the level of detail you anticipate in the future. There are usually far more expense categories than there are income categories. Table 7.1 shows the chart of accounts of an electronics manufacturer, which displays some of the expense categories for the firm.

EXERCISE 2

1. Develop a preliminary chart of accounts for your new business.
2. Have fellow classmates review the chart and add or delete as necessary.

The new businessperson will want to leave room for new account detail to be put into the chart of accounts. As the business develops, you will find that you want to obtain additional detail, as new income/expense categories will appear. Notice that the chart tracks not only income and expense accounts but also asset accounts.

Table 7.1
Chart of Accounts—Electronics Manufacturer

ACCOUNT NUMBER	CATEGORY	ACCOUNT NUMBER	CATEGORY
10	Basic Tube	142	Office Supplies—Other
20	Premium Tube	150	Internet Supplier
30	Basic Service	160	Auto Leases
40	Unlimited Service	170	Insurance
101	COGS*—Wooden Tubes	180	Advertising
102	COGS—Diodes	200	Payroll
103	COGS—Circuit Boards	201	Benefits
104	COGS—Resistors/Capacitors	210	Telephone (Cell and Office)
105	COGS—End Caps	220	Licenses
106	COGS—Packaging	300	Production Machinery
107	COGS—Shipping	310	Tools
120	Utilities	400	Building Mortgage
130	Security System	500	Payroll Taxes
140	Paper	510	State Taxes
141	Letterhead/Business Cards	520	Federal Taxes

*Note: COGS = cost of goods sold.

Petty Cash Register

There are numerous expenses that are simply too small to write a check for, and there are times when a check is simply inappropriate (for example, if you had pizza delivered for everyone because the whole group was working late to meet a deadline). A petty cash fund operates much like a bank savings account. The founder purchases a small lockbox and writes a check to "Petty Cash" for whatever amount they would like to keep on hand (this is not the same as cash register money, which should be handled as a separate deposit/expense account). A register is maintained to track the amount of money in the box, much like a savings account register. For example, if you decide that $100 is the amount that you would like to have on hand, you would start the box off with $100. As withdrawals are made, each is recorded and all change is put back in the box. The founder should be able to glance at the register and know exactly how much money is in the petty cash fund at any point in time, as well as know how the money has been spent. As it depletes, a new check should be written to "Petty Cash" to fill the box back up to the $100 level.

A young woman looking at the First Direct Bank website. Online banking is not only efficient but convenient.

©Jamie Grill/Blend Images/Getty Images RF

Check Register

As simple as it sounds, it is important to create a listing of all checks that have been written and all that have cleared through the bank. Today, with online banking and thc ability to transfer data directly, this process has become quite easy. Regardless of how the entrepreneur might maintain her personal checking account, it is very important to record and balance the company account on at least a monthly basis.

Expense Accounts

Depending on the volume of business that your venture processes, you will have either a daily or a weekly listing of expenses. These will allow the entrepreneur to perform a monthly tracking of expenses and ultimately form an annual record of all expenses. The process requires you to have both your check register and your petty cash register available to record all outflow of funds. Credit card payments should be handled by recording the interest as an interest expense, recording the payment made to the account, and then recording each line item with a notation of "Visa," "MC," "Am. Ex.," and so on, next to the expense. The only other expenses that are truly handled in a different manner are those related to travel. The IRS has very specific requirements related to the record keeping necessary to deduct these expenses. You should be sure to familiarize yourself with the latest rules regarding these expenses.

Inventory Account

Any business that has even a small inventory should maintain an inventory record that lists a description of the item, the quantity, an item number, a unit cost, and a total cost. Inventory should be taken at scheduled times during the year and an exact match should be completed between starting inventory, units sold, and ending inventory. A second record should be kept to track inventory ordered and inventory received. It is a fact of business that **shrinkage** will occur. This reduction in inventory can come from poor record keeping on any of the fronts mentioned previously but can also result from either employee or customer theft.

shrinkage
The difference between what is sold and what was brought into the business.

Accounts Payable

A separate accounts payable record should be maintained for each creditor. All invoices received should be recorded and a record of payment toward each invoice should be included (Date Paid, Amount Paid, and Check Number/Transfer Tracking Number).

Payroll

A payroll record should be maintained for every employee, tracking time for hourly employees and attendance for exempt (salaried) employees. Additionally, an employee record should be maintained that tracks every payroll check (electronically or in paper form) issued to the employee. This record will list all of the items that make up the check:

- Date
- Check number
- Number of hours worked (or 40, for exempt employees)
- Base pay
- Overtime hours worked
- Overtime pay rate
- Gross pay
- Taxes (federal, state, local, Social Security, and Medicare)
- Benefit deductions (if appropriate)
- Net pay

Table 7.2
Profit and Loss Statement

PROFIT AND LOSS STATEMENT					
Period:		Month			
Income, $	Gross Sales		$114,560.00		
	Less COGS		34,900.00		
	Net Sales			79,660.00	
	Other Income			13,400.00	
	Total Income			**$93,060.00**	
Expenses, $	Acct No.	120	$ 1,084.00		
	Acct No.	130	35.00		
	Acct No.	140	110.00		
	Acct No.	141	320.00		
	Acct No.	142	45.00		
	Acct No.	150	79.00		
	Acct No.	160	1,340.00		
	Acct No.	170	367.00		
	Acct No.	180	1,100.00		
	Acct No.	200	47,900.00		
	Acct No.	201	14,370.00		
	Total			66,750.00	
	Misc. Expenses			1,780.00	
	Total Expenses			**$68,530.00**	
	Profit (Pretax)				**$24,530.00**

Accounting software packages the entrepreneur may buy have the ability to produce all of these records plus many more. These become both the control records and the input records to produce your financial statements (Cash Flow, Balance Sheet, and Statement).

One additional statement is a must-have for most businesses and comes directly from the effective collection of all this information: the **profit and loss statement (P&L statement)**. This statement represents your business performance over time. It is a brief, easily understood document that should be prepared monthly. An example is shown in Table 7.2.

profit and loss statement (P&L statement)
A financial statement that summarizes the revenues, costs, and expenses incurred during a specific period of time.

Developing and maintaining effective records is essential in the operation of a business, and some forethought to the process and needs of the business will pay off in the knowledge and understanding developed by the founder(s). We will examine a number of analysis tools in Chapter 8, but for analysis to have any value, good records must be kept.

Managing Information Flow

The entrepreneur needs to recognize that new businesses will differ in the time frames that they need to obtain data based on their industry and experience.

YrFURN—AN APP FOR FURNITURE

As they began to seek to raise the necessary funds, the three founders spent several weeks visiting an extensive line of relatives, friends of their families, and a referral to an angel investor, who was an alumnus of their university. Over that period of time, they were able to put together additional investments of $500,000, which the team felt would ensure survival of the business to the point where they would be able to have proof of concept and be able to raise additional capital. The team raised the money with just eight investors. Three of the investors had put in $100,000 each while the other four investors each put in $50,000. Kyle, Brandy, and Brad each took a 15 percent stake in the business; the three $100K investors each took a 10 percent stake; while the four $50K investors each got 3 percent each. The remaining 23 percent of stock was held for use in the future as incentives for valuable employees.

Having raised enough for the firm to bring the product to market, the team faced a significant issue in the design of financial statements and tracking of funds in the business. The three entrepreneurs had no formal accounting training, and during several conversations with other entrepreneurs, they had been told repeatedly to purchase an accounting software package—which they did. Not knowing what they might need for the business, the team decided to set up some rudimentary categories and then add new ones as needed.

The team at the same time hired a small software design company to help then with coding both the new app and the support system for the app. The entrepreneurs established an office, and each started working on various things they knew needed to be done. The office location came with nothing in it and needed a lot of work. Thus, the team set about buying everything they thought was needed, painted the walls, put in new floors, and had some handymen hired via Craigslist to put up walls and do finishing work.

As the equipment, furniture, and supplies began arriving, Brad was simply too busy trying to set everything up to spend time entering all of the information into his accounting package. He was not worried because he had a good head for numbers and knew that he was right on track for what he had predicted for the business. He thought that he might try to enter the information from the invoices over the weekend. After three weeks of almost constant work, the team had a meeting one morning partially to take a look at the invoices; the three of them quickly realized that Brad's temporary system was not working. There were bills that did not appear to be accurate, but no one had asked about them when the shipment of supplies came in. There were also a few bills that had already gone past due.

QUESTIONS

1. How could Brad have done a better job setting up the accounting system?
2. What kind of data flow system should Brad use to track their business?

The founder(s) should seek to visit with other similar firms and find out what reasonable time frames might be for the monitoring of data. The experience of other firms can be very helpful in the start-up phase of your business.

Well-established firms have aggressively moved to using just-in-time (JIT) inventory. This method of inventory control seeks to minimize excess capital investment in inventory. These firms seek to have inventory present only shortly before it is used. New firms do not have the same complex information measurement methods of large firms, but they should be driven by the same basic philosophy. The key to this ability is obtaining data in a timely manner that is tied to the strategic needs of the organization. The lean start-up approach suggests that a new company's data needs are unique compared to an established organization. As the new company has no or a very small presence in the marketplace, they should seek to experiment in very small, fast past batches. A test, evaluation, modify approach to data collection suggests that the new business needs to be very purposeful in its data collection efforts as well as management practices. The goal is to find what works best with customers in the fastest approach possible. We worked with a restaurant that wanted to serve fresh vegetables and meats; however, the owner wanted to perform his inventory check only once a week. "Freshness" as a strategic position would dictate that the data collection cycle should be shortened. If deliveries are constant, then a high-turnover firm should monitor its inventory needs on a daily or every-other-day basis. The accounting system of a firm is a powerful tool asset that should be used as a fine-grained tool to provide data about when and how inventory is needed.

EXERCISE 3

1. How will you set up your business to track its early performance?
2. Design a preliminary P&L statement for your proposed business.

SUMMARY

This chapter examined two important operational issues directly tied to the start-up of a new venture. Obtaining sufficient initial funding is a key method to allow for the variances inherent in any business. We examined several means of obtaining that financing. We then examined the development of the firm's accounting system and method of data gathering and handling. Establishment of a quality method for data gathering at the outset will allow the founders to focus their efforts on the running of the business.

KEY TERMS

asset-based lending 126
asset lease 130
business angels 130
credit card 127
crowdfunding 126
debt 126
equity investment 125
factoring 131
grants 127
loan 126
profit and loss (P&L) statement 136
shrinkage 134
supplier credit 127
venture capital fund 130

REVIEW QUESTIONS

1. How can using loans help the new business grow?
2. Explain the best use of credit cards in a new business operation.

3. What are the negative impacts of supplier credit on the new business start-up?
4. How can a new business take advantage of grants?
5. Why should a new businessperson be wary of equity investments by other companies?
6. How will venture capital impact a growing business?
7. What are the pros of having angel investors in a new business?
8. How can asset leases be used to improve the income generation of a new business?
9. Why might a business choose to factor its accounts?
10. How might an entrepreneur find out how much a business is worth?
11. What factors impact how much equity a new business gives away for a set dollar investment?
12. How does a new businessperson use a P&L statement?
13. Why should a new business spend time setting up a chart of accounts?

BUSINESS PLAN DEVELOPMENT QUESTIONS

1. At this point in your business development, what mix of equity and debt are you planning on using? Why?
2. Develop a plan for fundraising. Make a list of who you will approach and why.
3. Create a potential chart of accounts for the new business.

INDIVIDUAL EXERCISES

1. Given the needs of your business, examine at least two widely available accounting packages and choose one for your business.
2. Why did you choose that one and not one of the others?
3. How robust is the package that you chose? Will it still be useful if your sales reach $1 million per year?

GROUP EXERCISES

In a group, take one of the companies that a group member is designing (or alternatively, use the YRFurn business) and set up a spreadsheet in Excel (or other similar program) that will form the basic accounting system for the company. To follow are suggestions for such a project.

1. Start with the Cash Flow Statement:
    a. Create a worksheet (tabs) for each of the 12 months and label each one.
    b. Enter all sources of income and all expenses that you can think of for January.
    c. Put in a formula to subtract expenses from income and determine the net cash flow.
    d. Copy January's data to the other 12 months and then modify any month that needs to be adjusted. Remember, this is just the start of the effort. You will have plenty of time to modify this spreadsheet as you develop the company.
    e. Create formulas on the Summary sheet to capture the data from the 12 months.
2. Repeat this process and create a Cash Budget.
3. Repeat this process again to create an Income Statement.

ENDNOTES

1. R. J. Shiller, "Capitalism and Financial Innovation," *Financial Analysts Journal* 69, no. 1 (January/February 2013), pp. 21–25.
2. R. Cole, L. Goldberg, and L. White, "Cookie Cutter vs. Character: The Micro Structure of Small Business Lending by Large and Small Banks," *Journal of Financial & Qualitative Analysis* 39 (2004), pp. 227–52.
3. N. Wilson and B. Summers, "Trade Credit Terms Offered by Small Firms: Survey Evidence and Empirical Analysis," *Journal of Small Business Finance & Accounting* 29 (2002), pp. 317–52.

4. R. Johnson and C. Oshan, "Equity 101: 3 Things Every Founder Needs to Know Before Giving Away a Piece of Their Startup," *Forbes*, February 7, 2017, http://www.forbes.com/sites/break-the-future/2017/02/07/equity-101-3-things-every-founder-needs-to-know-before-giving-away-a-piece-of-their-startup/#4692bf9b155f.
5. R. McGrath, "A Real Options Logic for Initiating Technology Positioning Investments," *Academy of Management Review* 22, no. 4 (1997), pp. 974–96.
6. D. DeClercq, V. Fried, O. Lehtonen, and H. Sapienza, "An Entrepreneur's Guide to the Venture Capital Galaxy," *Academy of Management Perspectives* 20, no. 3 (2006), pp. 90–112.
7. S. Prowse, "Angel Investors and the Market for Angel Investments," *Journal of Banking & Finance* 22 (1998), pp. 785–83.
8. Crowdsourcing Industry, "Will the Rise of Crowdsourcing and Crowdfunding Help Unemployed Young Americans?" www.crowdsourcing.org/editorial/will-the-rise-of-crowdsourcing-and-crowdfunding-help-unemployed-young-americans/32881
9. E. Weitzman, "Crowdfunding Sites Are Making Hard-to-Finance Indie Films Easier to Achieve," *New York Daily News*, July 13, 2014, www.nydailynews.com/entertainment/movies/crowdfunding-indie-films-easier-finance-article-1.1859003.
10. M. Wood, "Step-by-Step Guide to Accounts Receivable Factoring," AllBusiness, September 27, 2016, https://www.allbusiness.com/step-step-guide-accounts-receivable-factoring-108183-1.html.

chapter 8

learning objectives

After studying this chapter, you will be able to:

LO8-1 Explain the use of hypothesis-driven experimentation.

LO8-2 Describe the importance of a solid financial foundation in an entrepreneurial business.

LO8-3 Discuss techniques for measuring performance.

LO8-4 Explain ratio analysis.

LO8-5 Explain deviation analysis.

LO8-6 Explain sensitivity analysis.

LO8-7 Describe the use of short surveys in business.

LO8-8 Analyze the importance of having a measurement focus.

Business & Financial Analysis

TOM SZAKY — TERRACYCLE

TerraCycle was born from the idea that all waste should be recycled. Tom Szaky was a freshman at Princeton University when he visited a friend who was feeding kitchen scraps to red worms in outside containers and using the resulting fertilizer to feed their indoor plants. He liked the concept so much that he decided to use the same approach to recycle as much food waste as he could back in New Jersey.

He created TerraCycle from that basic idea and built a small farm of worm bins. Trying to figure out how to package the fertilizer, Tom decided to repurpose old plastic bottles. The success of that program led him to the conclusion that recycling in general should be the goal of the organization. Rather than just be another recycler, he reset the goal of the organization to reduce waste to zero by recycling the hardest to recycle products.

Over the next few years, this has led the organization into collecting a wide variety of waste while creating a laboratory to figure out how that waste could be repurposed. He started waste collection campaigns that literally paid people to collect soda bottles, cigarette butts, plastic bags, drink pouches, deodorant canisters, yogurt cups, K-cups, and other types of waste.

The company has been honored many times over the years for its success in recycling. The business now has its own TV show called *Human Resources*, which is a reality show aimed at not only showing how the company recycles/upcycles but also how creative effort is used to solve somewhat intractable problems. In 2017 the company founded a program to get people to clean up waste from the beaches in Europe, put it in his Zero Waste Boxes, and use it to create new recyclable shampoo bottles for Head & Shoulders. The company now operates in 24 countries.

Questions

1. Why do you believe large companies are purchasing recycled products for their packaging?
2. What metrics would you suggest investors use for evaluating TerraCycle performance?

Sources: https://www.terracycle.com/en-US/about-terracycle/history; "TerraCycle Is Transforming Ocean Waste into Recyclable Shampoo Bottles," Waste360, January 31, 2017, http://www.waste360.com/waste-reduction/terracycle-transforming-ocean-waste-recyclable-shampoo-bottles; T. Szaky, "Will a Trump Administration Affect TerraCycle?" *Huffington Post*, February 17, 2017, http://www.huffingtonpost.com/entry/will-a-trump-administration-affect-terracycle_us_58a7515de4b0fa149f9ac576; A. Hall and K. Ellman, "The Sustainable MBA TerraCycle CEO Tom Szaky Makes Garbage the Hero," GreenBiz, November 18, 2016, https://www.greenbiz.com/article/terracycle-ceo-tom-szaky-makes-garbage-hero; T. LaGorce, "Human Resources: Reality TV about a Recycling Company," *New York Times*, August 20, 2015, https://www.nytimes.com/2015/08/23/nyregion/human-resources-reality-tv-about-a-recycling-company.html.

With the new business up and running, the focus of the firm shifts from developmental activities to day-to-day operations. In starting a successful business, good initial development is important, but perhaps as important are the efforts of the business as it grows. Once in operation, the business exists within the competitive marketplace and is subject to competitive attack, customer response to the product offering, supplier problems, inventory management issues, collections issues, and more. No operating business ever matches the proposed business exactly. The new firm will be iterative in its approach to the customer—testing new ideas on small sets of customer, refining the product, and releasing again. The reality of operations and the ability to adjust to those realities is the key to managing a successful business. Adjusting requires an in-depth analysis of the firm's progress, particularly its financial progress.[1]

LO8-1

Explain the use of hypothesis-driven experimentation.

Hypothesis-Driven Analysis

A core element of the lean start-up approach is the use of many small experiments with customers in order to refine the product/services offering. The model requires a significant amount of care, experiment design, measurement, and refinement.

Every entrepreneur has a hypothesis as to what a customer really desires. The problem with asking customers is that the information is gathered through the lens of what exists now as opposed to what you are bringing to the table. Rather than trying to craft up the entire business model and delivering to the customer with the hope that it will meet their needs and cause them to purchase your offering, the lean model suggests that you effectively experiment with customers.

This is done in small batches.[2] At many points in the life of a business, there are crucial decisions that must be made. Rather than relying on the internal beliefs of the entrepreneurial team, we craft up a solution and then see how customers react to it. The best reaction (metric) is a purchase decision. However, to make the experiment have the most value, we actually keep our product or service the same for some customers and change it for other. Then we track the results.

Imagine a business operating in the cloud providing services to other businesses (B2B). There is always a backlog of updates, fixes, or new offerings that the business would like to provide. In this model rather than waiting for big release of many changes, they make changes daily or even hourly to the software. However, this is done in a very systematic way with customers and potential customers. Some customers get the new change while others do not. The impact or results are tracked for a short period of time to determine if the change should be accepted across the whole platform or not.

The exact same approach can be done in a:

1. Retail space (with different store offerings, prices, or placement)
2. Services operation (testing out new service offerings or changes to current practices)
3. Manufacturing (offering updated products or features to categories of customers)

A chart might be developed as shown in Figure 8.1.

This type of analysis allows the company to move very quickly and make changes in rapid fashion to react to customers. This type of split analysis can be extended to test different aspects of the product or service on different cohorts of customers and observing the difference in sales, engagement, time spent, or other metric of interest. In order to build up credibility in your business model, you should use experiments to test as many aspects of the business as you can. Credibility will help you with funding, operational improvement as well as your relations with suppliers.[3]

Product/Service	Customer Group	Release Date	Metric	Close Date	Result	Move Forward or Pivot?
In-Line Login						
Separate Login						
Outside Login						
2 Item Login						
3 Item Login						
4 Item Login						
5 Item Login						

Figure 8.1
Hypothesis Testing Example

Importance of a Solid Financial Foundation in an Entrepreneurial Business

LO8-2

Describe the importance of a solid financial foundation in an entrepreneurial business.

The evaluation of a firm starts with the mission of the organization and is (as was pointed out in Chapter 5) always relative to the industry in which the firm competes. The key measures of the firm should focus on the key aspects with which the firm hopes to build its competitive advantage. For example, if the mission of the organization is to be a low-cost operation, then rigorous control of expenses would be the focus. This would suggest that very little money would be spent on such activities as research and development, or new product introductions. The firm's outcomes would be measured at intervals that were relevant to the business, which, in the case of evaluating cost savings, might mean measuring such items very frequently, perhaps even daily. To illustrate, consider a restaurant that plans to have broccoli as a side dish this week and receives its order of fresh broccoli on Monday. Unfortunately, the sales of broccoli during the week are significantly less than expected. If the firm accurately monitors its broccoli supply, it can determine that it needs to offer broccoli soup as an option on Thursday and Friday. Hopefully, this will result in a significant reduction in the waste of the broccoli. (The development of potato skins as a snack food that appears at so many restaurants is a direct result of the way the potatoes that were used for mashed potatoes from the prior day were used to prevent wastage.) Poor monitoring of the situation will result in waste for the business and the same mistake being made week after week.

In this chapter we will examine the development of the various metrics (measures) that should be used to evaluate the business. These analytical techniques are easily available and easily understandable by any business owner.

Techniques for Measuring Performance

LO8-3

Discuss techniques for measuring performance.

There is virtually an unlimited number of items upon which you could perform an analysis of your business, its activities, and its performance. However, taking the time to do this analysis means time away from running the business, and we, therefore, like to limit the analysis to those areas that are critical to the business's ability to make real profits. Any company analysis, large or small, should proceed from the general and move toward the specific.

KOSHER HOME

Kosher Home had been in business for almost six months although at a reduced level of operation where the founders are largely experimenting with products and systems to ensure all was in place before they expanded to compete more broadly. The owners had experimented and found a solid product offering. However, they soon realized they needed a major review of their operations. As they examined their costs, they realized that they were buying far more than they were selling; an insight working with their accountant helped them to identify.

The entrepreneurs did not think people were stealing from them, but they did think employees were being sloppy in recording what they used and when. The system they had in place was very simple: the employees wrote down what they removed from the storeroom and for which order it was assigned. The invoice for the order was entered at the time the meal was shipped, but the inputs into that meal were only entered into the accounting software each week.

After pondering the alternatives, the founders decided they would buy a new software package for the computer system in which all products would receive scan codes, and employees would scan the goods as they were removed from the storeroom. Jack and Toby intended to be in business for the long run, and as such they wanted to have the best operating procedures possible.

Through a well-known businessperson and friend, the founders arranged to meet with the national sales representative from the leading supplier of the software. The system they desired cost approximately $75,000 as they needed both the software and the equipment for scanning the goods. However, rather than closing the deal that night, the saleswoman seemed almost hesitant.

The next day the personal friend of the founders and the saleswoman came to see Jack and Toby. The friend began to question the entrepreneurs as to whether they could really afford the total package they had picked out. The friend asked pointed questions about their true returns and whether this included the cost of capital. What was the depreciation on their existing equipment? What was the nature of the financing they would rely on for the new system? When this friend asked the owners to think about whether they actually were profitable, they realized they had performed no real analysis of the business to date.

Jack and Toby were attracting customers in their local region and their checking account had maintained a nice balance; they were making payroll every month; they had money to make the payments on their loans, and they felt that things were good. Unfortunately, they did not really know how much profit they were making, nor did they really know if the business could continue to expand. The reason that the mutual friend had come to ask these hard questions was that the salesperson selling the system had told him she had seen the scenario many times. A new business starts to do particularly well, and the founders decide to splurge. However, too often the owners of the business are not making as much money as they believe they are, and the new system contributes to the business failing. As a salesperson, she felt she could not say she would not sell them the system, but she had asked their mutual friend to visit with Jack and Toby to ensure they knew the implications of making such a large purchase on credit.

The questions asked helped the founders of Kosher Home realize that the time had come for them to start doing some serious analysis of their business in order to determine how they could proceed.

QUESTIONS

1. As you think about Kosher Home, what other options do they have to the simple system of individuals signing out goods or buying the expensive software program?
2. How does a firm create incentives to help the firm watch its costs?
3. The Kosher-for-Passover menu is different than their normal menu since Jews can't eat any leavened bread or legumes during Passover. How will they adjust operations when a totally separate menu must be prepared?

In that light, we review four analysis techniques prior to our discussion of designing and monitoring the core metrics for a particular organization. These four classic techniques are as follows:

1. Ratio analysis
2. Deviation analysis
3. Sensitivity analysis
4. Short surveys

Figure 8.2
Balance Sheet

BALANCE SHEET (in U.S. dollars)	12/31/2016	12/31/2017	Difference
Assets			
Current Assets			
Cash	$ 50,000	$ 61,000	$ 11,000
Acct Receivable	12,400	16,700	4,300
Inventory	29,000	31,000	2,000
Total Current Assets	**$ 91,400**	**$ 108,700**	$ 17,300
Fixed Assets			
Land	$ 100,000	$ 100,000	$ 0
Buildings	150,000	150,000	0
(Accumulated Depreciation)	(15,000)	(30,000)	(15,000)
Office Equipment	75,000	82,000	7,000
Machinery	45,000	45,000	0
(Accumulated Depreciation)	(3,500)	(7,000)	(3,500)
Total Fixed Assets	**$ 351,500**	**$340,000**	($ 11,500)
Total Assets	**$453,000**	**$430,000**	($23,000)
Liabilities			
Current Liabilities			
Accounts Payable	$ 35,000	$ 42,000	$ 7,000
Notes Payable (less than a year)	4,500	7,000	2,500
Accrued Payroll	15,000	23,000	8,000
Total Current Liabilities	54,500	72,000	17,500
Long-Term Liabilities			
Mortgage	200,000	192,000	(8,000)
Bank Loan	35,000	30,000	(5,000)
Total Long-Term Liability	**$ 235,000**	**$ 222,000**	($ 13,000)
Owner's Equity	**$ 163,500**	**$ 136,000**	($ 27,500)
Total Liabilities/Owner's Equity	**$453,000**	**$430,000**	($23,000)

Before examining these four techniques of analysis, students should quickly review the sample balance sheet in Figure 8.2 and the income statement in Figure 8.3. This data will be employed to illustrate the financial analytical methods.

Figure 8.3
Income Statement

INCOME STATEMENT (in U.S. dollars)			
Receipts:		2016	2017
	Sales	$ 178,790	$ 241,650
	Less Returns	4,000	7,000
	COGS	54,700	67,662
	Gross Profit	**$ 120,090**	**$ 166,988**
Expenses			
	Salaries	$ 28,000	$ 37,000
	Travel	6,545	7,650
	Car Leases	6,000	6,000
	Rent	3,150	3,600
	Payroll Taxes	1,720	2,450
	Insurance	1,450	1,800
	Fuel/Maint.	1,412	1,733
	Benefits	2,100	3,600
	Advertising	1,896	3,000
	Utilities	1,104	1,946
	Misc.	1,528	1,255
Total Expenses		**$ 55,208**	**$ 70,034**
Operating Income		**$ 64,882**	**$ 96,954**
Interest		11,975	13,800
Taxes		14,274	22,299
Profit After Taxes		**$ 38,633**	**$ 60,855**

LO8-4

Explain ratio analysis.

ratio analysis

A series of ratios along four areas of company performance (liquidity, activity, leverage, profitability) that provides a picture of the health of the company.

liquidity ratios

Ratios that measure the short-term ability of the firm to meet its obligations.

Ratio Analysis

Ratio analysis is a tool for the entrepreneur to use for examining the overall health of the organization.[4] Ratios by themselves are of little value. Instead the ratios for any given firm need to be evaluated in comparison to other similar organizations, an industry average, or simply the previous month's or year's performance.[5] We will discuss four basic categories of performance ratios: liquidity, activity, leverage, and profitability (Figure 8.4). We will first provide the means by which these ratios are calculated and then provide some insights that each brings to the business owner.

Liquidity Ratios

Financial liquidity is critical to the success of the firm.[6] **Liquidity ratios** measure the short-term ability of the firm to meet its obligations. These obligations would include debt or accounts payable that must be paid by the business in the near term.[7] Financing institutions generally require that liquidity ratios be kept within certain ranges. If the business drops below the lower bounds of

Figure 8.4
Commonly Used Ratios

Liquidity Ratios		
	Current (Note: current assets = cash + accounts receivable + inventory)	*Current Assets* / *Current Liabilities*
	Quick (or Acid Test)	*Current Assets – Inventory* / *Current Liabilities*
Activity Ratios		
	Inventory Turnover	*Cost of Goods Sold* / *Inventory*
	Accounts Receivable Turnover	*Net Credit Sales* / *Accounts Receivable*
	Total/Fixed Asset Turnover	*Net Sales* / *Fixed Assets*
Leverage Ratios		
	Debt to Equity	*Total Liablities* / *Total Assets – Total Liabilities*
	Debt to Assets	*Total Liablities* / *Total Assets*
	Times Interest Earned	*Operating Income* / *Interest*
Profitability Ratios		
	Gross Profit Margin	*Gross Profit* / *Net Sales*
	Operating Profit Margin (or EBIT)	*Operating Income* / *Net Sales*
	Net Profit Margin	*Net Profit* / *Net Sales*
	ROA (return on assets)	*Net Profit* / *Total Assets*
	ROE (return on equity)	*Net Profit* / *Equity*

its liquidity level, then the bank may limit the line of credit to the firm or require a higher interest rate on the debt, as the risk position of the firm will have increased. Even for companies that appear to be growing well and have good prospects, the ability to meet the short-term obligations of the firm is a significant concern. Two specific types of liquidity ratios are of interest: current ratio and acid ratio.

Current Ratio: Current Assets divided by Current Liabilities. The current ratio measures those assets that can be quickly turned into cash and used to pay for

EXERCISE 1

1. Using the information from the income and balance sheet provided to you, calculate each of the ratios in Figure 8.4 for 2017.

immediate liabilities. In general, this is the cash balance of the firm plus inventory divided by all short-term liabilities.

Quick (Acid) Ratio: Current Assets minus Inventory divided by Current Liabilities. The quick ratio removes the ability to sell inventory and examines the pure cash position relative to the current liabilities. The term used here is *quick ratio*, but it is also sometimes referred to as an *acid test*.

Calculating Liquidity Ratios. Using the balance sheet (Figure 8.2), let's take a look at these two calculations. Look for the lines labeled Current Assets, Current Liabilities, and Inventory.

Current Ratio	2016	$91,400/$54,400 = 1.68
	2017	$115,362/$72,000 = 1.602
Quick Ratio (or Acid Test)	2016	$91,400 - $29,000/$54,400 = 1.147
	2017	$115,362 - $31,000/$72,000 = 1.079

Interpreting these items relative to each other, you can see that this business has held relatively constant over these two years in its ability to meet its short-term obligations. The current ratio is over 1.0, which tells us that the company has enough money to meet all of its short-term obligations. The quick ratio tells us that the firm has slightly decreased in its ability to pay cash for its short-term liabilities. However, the firm relies extensively on inventory to pay its current liabilities. That is not a concern in and of itself, but it can be problematic if the inventory in this industry becomes dated quickly. Therefore, it would be useful to evaluate the firm's ratios against the ratios for the industry (if available). An important issue in ratio analysis is ensuring that you are comparing apples to apples. However, often the ratios you find are based on Fortune 500 firms, and these will have little or no relevance to an entrepreneurial business. We suggest for comparison purposes that an entrepreneurial business use sources such as the data published by the Risk Management Association (RMA). This alliance of community banks gathers data from the portfolios of all of its member firms and then provides typical ratios by industry. The firms in the database are generally smaller than those in most other generic data sources. For our example firm, the data show that the quick ratio is very consistent with the industry averages.

There are numerous online sources of information that you might find useful. These include: Mergent Online, Factiva, S&P Net Advantage, OneSource, Research Insight and Bizminer. Many of these sources may be available to you for free through your University's library site.

©Romantiche/Alamy RF

Activity Ratios

activity ratios
Ratios that measure the efficiency with which the entrepreneur is handling the resources of the business.

Activity ratios measure the efficiency with which you are handling the resources of the business. They are particularly helpful as the business develops, since you will be able to compare from month to month (or more often if you wish). There are three specific ratios in which we are interested.

Inventory Turnover: Cost of Goods Sold divided by Inventory. Cost of Goods Sold is the direct costs involved with a product. As this inventory turnover rises, the firm is getting closer to a just-in-time system. There are pros and cons to operating in a just-in-time system, and in some cases, the reality of the industry means that this is not a reasonable approach. Generally, an inventory turnover ratio that is better than the industry average or one that is improving each month means that the firm is operating more efficiently.

Account Receivable Turnover: Credit Sales divided by Accounts Receivable. This metric examines how fast the company turns credit sales into cash. The faster the firm is able to turn credit sales into cash, the better the cash flow position of the firm is. Credit sales should also be aged into categories based on how long it has been since the sale. Unfortunately, this is necessary because the older the debt is, the less likely it is that you will be paid. Almost all debt 30 days and under is considered highly likely to be paid. After 90 days past due, however, only a small percentage of the debt will be realistically recovered. We will discuss this topic more when we examine collections at the end of this chapter.

Total/Fixed Asset Turnover: Net Sales divided by Fixed Assets or Net Sales divided by Total Assets. Entrepreneurial businesses will likely use one of these numbers more often than the other. The difference principally turns on whether or not the business has large amounts of fixed assets. For example, a small manufacturer will want to focus on the productivity of its fixed assets. How efficiently the business is in using those fixed assets is crucial in determining how competitive the firm is in the marketplace. In contrast, a retail store will be more interested in total assets. Such a firm has limited fixed assets but does have extensive inventory. In either case, the founder is attempting to examine the ability to generate sales from the assets employed by the organization. As this number increases, the firm is being more efficient. New businesses should try to minimize the amount of both fixed and total assets in order to conserve cash.

Calculating Activity Ratios. To calculate activity ratios requires information from both the balance sheet and the income statement. For example, the inventory turnover ratio derives the numerator (cost of goods sold) from the income statement, while the denominator (inventory) comes from the balance sheet. Using the numbers provided in Figures 8.2 and 8.3, we calculate the following activity ratios.

Inventory Turnover	2016	\$54,700/\$29,000 = 1.88
	2017	\$67,662/\$31,000 = 2.18
Accounts Receivable Turnover	2016	\$178,790/\$12,400 = 14.42
	2017	\$241,650/\$16,700 = 14.47
Total Asset Turnover	2016	\$178,790/\$453,000 = 0.39
	2017	\$241,650/\$430,000 = 0.56
Fixed Asset Turnover	2016	\$178,790/\$351,500 = 0.51
	2017	\$241,650/\$340,000 = 0.71

To interpret these numbers (in the absence of industry comparisons), the entrepreneur should focus on the relative change. Such a comparison would tell the business that the inventory turnover rate has gone up in 2017. The business then would want to determine the cause for this greater efficiency. The firm could have been inefficient in 2016 and may be just now gaining the experience necessary to gain the efficiencies of more mature firms. However, another reason might be that the firm has discovered some activity or method that provides the firm a level of efficiency greater than those of its competitors. If this is the case, the business will want to identify that source of competitive advantage and nurture it. Therefore, the business will likely want to have industry information on industry turnover. The evidence from the RMA suggests that the business is more efficient than its peer group in that region of the country.

The other ratios changed little over the time period and appear consistent with those of other similar firms in that region of the country. Therefore, the entrepreneurial business probably does not want to focus its attention on those issues.

Many of the classic ratios that are used for business evaluation are designed for traditional business operations. For service firms or even more importantly for those that operate in the cloud, some of these ratios will have no real value. In all cases, use your discretion in deciding which ratios will provide you with the insight you seek in the business.

EXERCISE 2

1. Using the pro forma statements that you developed for your business (as discussed in Chapter 6), calculate each of the liquidity and activity ratios for your business.
2. How do these compare with the industry averages?
3. If this causes you to reexamine your forecasts, explain why.

Leverage Ratios

leverage ratios
Ratios that are used to examine the relative level of indebtedness of the entrepreneurial business.

Leverage ratios are used to examine the relative level of indebtedness of the entrepreneurial business. Specifically, all creditors (whether they are suppliers of goods or banks with outstanding loans) want to ensure that the entrepreneurial business has the ability to generate sufficient funds to pay the supplier or repay the loans. High levels of debt are dangerous when the economy turns down, as we have all seen these past few years. Three ratios are commonly used to evaluate the relative level of indebtedness of a business.

Debt-to-Equity: Total Liabilities divided by Total Assets minus Total Liabilities. The denominator of this equation (Total Assets minus Total Liabilities) is effectively the owner's equity. This ratio provides the information on the portion of the business owned by the lenders and that portion owned by the founder(s).

Debt-to-Assets: Total Liabilities divided by Total Assets. A slight variation of the debt-to-equity ratio, this measures the percentage of the assets of the firm that are actually owned by the creditors.

Times Interest Earned: Operating Income divided by Interest. This figure estimates the number of times that the firm could repay the current interest owed on its debts. The higher this number is, the more capable the firm is of servicing its debt load.

Calculating Leverage Ratios. The information for most of the leverage ratios will come from Figure 8.2, the balance sheet. However, calculating times interest earned will require information from both the balance sheet and Figure 8.3, the income statement. Using the data for our firm, we can generate the following data.

Debt-to-Equity Ratio	2016	\$289,500/\$163,500 = 1.77
	2017	\$294,000/\$136,000 = 2.16
Debt-to-Assets Ratio	2016	\$289,500/\$453,000 = 0.64
	2017	\$294,000/\$430,000 = 0.68
Times Interest Earned	2016	\$64,882/\$11,975 = 5.42
	2017	\$96,954/\$13,800 = 7.02

In calculating these ratios, what appears is a pattern with a significant change in the debt-to-equity ratio between 2016 and 2017. Similarly, the times interest earned appears to have undergone a significant shift that year.

These areas should attract the businessperson's immediate interest. The businessperson would want to compare these numbers to the industry to identify if this was an industry-wide pattern. In the case of times interest earned, the industry-wide numbers are very similar to what our sample firm experienced. The reason for this was the overall drop in interest rate costs in the United States during that time. The increase in debt-to-equity is more troubling. The industry averages are closer to 1.15 than they are to 2.16. Even more disturbing is that the increase in debt-to-equity ratio appears to be due to lower equity in the firm. This raises a troubling picture. It appears that the business is slowly eating away the equity position of the firm. In other words, more is being taken out of the firm than is being put back into it. This may be the result of a negative net cash flow or something as simple as the founders' drawing more off in salary than the business can support. The result is not an immediate failure of the business but a slow spiral downward that ultimately results in failure. In a normal business that has achieved a break-even position, we would expect the equity position of the business to increase over time, not decrease. Therefore, the entrepreneur should flag this result and question what type of long-term pattern of performance is being established.

Profitability Ratios

Although profitability is the focus of much of the business press, it should be recognized as an outcome of the business's other activities. Thus, profitability is a result of effectively managing the assets and cash flow of the firm, not the activity of focus itself. **Profitability ratios** examine the performance of the firm and its ability to make economic returns over and above its costs. There are five profitability ratios that generate the greatest attention.

profitability ratios
Ratios that examine the performance of the firm and its ability to make economic rents over and above its costs.

Gross Profit Margin: Gross Profit divided by Net Sales. This ratio is used to determine the overall profit that is obtained from all sales during the period being evaluated. Gross profit is a category created by taking the total net sales of the firm and subtracting returned merchandise as well as the direct cost of the goods sold. This is the most basic of the profitability measures.

Operating Profit Margin: Operating Income divided by Net Sales. A finer-grained measure, this looks at the gross profit minus all of the operating expenses. This figure is also known as Earnings Before Interest and Taxes (EBIT) and represents the operating efficiency of the organization.

Net Profit Margin: Net Profit divided by Net Sales. Net profit is the bottom-line calculation from the income statement. This figure presents a picture of the relative margin earned after all obligations and expenses are considered.

Return on Assets (ROA): Net Profit divided by Total Assets. This is one of the two overall calculations that are standards in almost any industry. This ratio examines the ability of the firm to return an overall profit compared to the amount of assets that the firm has invested into the effort.

Return on Equity (ROE): Net Profit divided by Equity (Total Assets minus Total Liabilities). This ratio is used to provide all investors with an evaluation of how much each dollar of their investment is generating in profit.

Calculating Profitability Ratios. The calculations for the first three profitability ratios come from Figure 8.3, the income statement. The last two ratios combine information from both Figure 8.2, the balance sheet, and Figure 8.3, the income statement. Using the information from our sample firm, the following calculations are generated.

Gross Profit Margin	2016	\$120,090/\$178,790 = 0.67
	2017	\$166,988/\$241,650 = 0.69
Operating Profit Margin	2016	\$64,882/\$178,790 = 0.36
	2017	\$96,954/\$241,650 = 0.40
Net Profit Margin	2016	\$38,633/\$178,790 = 0.22
	2017	\$60,855/\$241,650 = 0.25
Return on Assets	2016	\$38,633/\$453,000 = 0.085
	2017	\$60,855/\$430,000 = 0.141
Return on Equity	2016	\$38,633/\$163,500 = 0.24
	2017	\$60,855/\$136,000 = 0.45

The profitability ratios present a firm that appears to be improving in all aspects. All of its margins increased nicely year after year. Its ability to make a profit on the assets and owners' equity provided improved ratios. This was partially due to a reduction in the value of the asset base and partially due to a very pleasant increase in sales without an equivalent increase in expenses. However, it was also due to a serious erosion of owners' equity in the business. Although it is nice to efficiently use the equity, we would normally look for owners' equity to increase as sales were growing. This needs to be looked into and given serious consideration by the founders.

Summary of Ratios

The ratios provided in this chapter can be valuable tools to the firm. All of the statements necessary to calculate these ratios are standard with any accounting package that you might choose. In fact, most of these accounting packages will automatically calculate these ratios. As an owner of an entrepreneurial business, you will likely choose only one or two of the ratios in each category (liquidity, activity, leverage, and performance or profitability) to use for examining the company, because you can be buried in data if you do not. It is important to understand the broad indicators of the different types of ratios to be able to pick them intelligently. Establishing a good data collection system is necessary for any of this analysis to be useful or effective for the entrepreneur. Finally, it is important in analyzing ratios that the entrepreneur remember that it is only through the comparison of those ratios over time or compared

Even though businesses vary, the core concepts involved in a healthy financial endeavor are universal. What are some of the similarities and differences between the financials for a restaurant versus a clothing store?

(left): ©Hero Images/Getty Images RF; (right): ©John Lund/Marc Romanelli/Blend Images LLC RF

to some other firm or group of firms that the ratios can be interpreted. The ratios by themselves are interesting but do not provide much insight.

Deviation Analysis

LO8-5

Explain deviation analysis.

deviation analysis
Analysis of the differences between the predicted and the actual performance.

A second analysis method that is valuable for examining the firm, its activities, and its performance is a **deviation analysis**. This type of analysis is simply a chart tracking various performance measures from one time period to the next (month to month or year to year). The deviation chart has two additional columns, one showing the actual change and the other showing a percentage change. A deviation chart should be maintained for all important metrics. These might include several of the ratios listed above as well as other metrics that the organization deems to be important. An example is shown in Figure 8.5.

Notice that whether a particular item is good or bad for a company depends on the direction desired by the entrepreneur. As you can see, the drop in current ratio from 2016 to 2017 is a negative event, whereas the drop in number of complaints during this period, from 27 to 21, is a positive event. A deviation analysis allows the entrepreneur to quickly evaluate the performance of the organization on those items that are considered most important to the success of the firm.

Although this particular example shows only data from one year to the next, significantly greater insight would be gained by comparing data on more frequent intervals. The resulting picture of the firm's trends is always more revealing about how the company is performing. The business is encouraged to develop a chart using shorter time periods so that the patterns and deviations can be observed and used in the analysis of the business. As a result, we suggest that this chart be maintained at least monthly. Most businesses have some type of seasonality that could be significant for ordering, staffing, advertising, and more. In addition, an annual chart should also be prepared that allows comparison across the years as the firm matures.

In this particular example, we also included several metrics that went beyond the basic financial ratios. As will be discussed shortly, we believe that measuring the performance of a business goes well beyond the financial aspects. The success of the company in pursuing its strategy should be a part of the analysis maintained by all companies.

EXERCISE 3

1. Prepare a deviation analysis for your business using your financial forecasts.
2. What unique items might you include in your deviation analysis that go beyond the basic ratios?

Figure 8.5
Deviation Analysis

ITEM	2016	2017	ACTUAL DIFFERENCE	% DIFFERENCE
Current Ratio	1.147	1.079	−0.068	**−5.90%**
Inventory Turnover	1.88	2.18	0.2	**10.60**
Gross Profit Margin	0.67	0.69	0.02	**2.90**
Net Profit Margin	0.22	0.25	0.03	**13.60**
No. of Complaints	27	21	6	**22.20**
Hours of Operation/Week	42	56	14	**33.30**
No. of Employees	2	7	5	**250**
No. Who Say We Are Their First Choice	47	117	70	**148.90**

LO8-6

Explain sensitivity analysis.

sensitivity analysis

A chart using current cash flow statement, income statement, or balance sheet to create a pro forma projection based on a dramatic increase in sales, a dramatic decrease in sales, or the complication of a major change in the business.

Sensitivity Analysis

A third method of examining the ability of the organization to handle changes in the future is for the firm to perform a **sensitivity analysis.**[8] This type of analysis involves taking the current cash flow statement, income statement, or balance sheet and making projections based on a dramatic increase in sales, a dramatic decrease in sales, or the business undergoing a major change. This method of examination allows the entrepreneur to look at how sensitive the business is to various factors. In the example on pages 155–157, we use a cash flow statement to contemplate the impact of a dramatic sales increase or decrease. If the firm experiences a sudden 50 percent increase or decrease in sales, what will the impact be on the overall organization? In the case of an increase, how many new staff must be hired to accommodate these sales? What might the impact be on travel or insurance? First we list the projected cash flow statement for the firm (Figure 8.6 on page 155), and then we provide one with a 50 percent increase (Figure 8.7 on page 156) and another with a 50 percent decrease in sales (Figure 8.8 on page 157).

Under the rapid increase in sales scenario, the firm is hurt during its first two years but then recovers for an extraordinary third year. The firm will need

YrFURN—AN APP FOR FURNITURE

After six months of coding, testing, and recoding work, the YrFurn app went live. The company paid a search engine optimization company (SEO) to have the app pop up as one of the first items whenever someone searched for "view furniture." The SEO effort forced the firm to develop a clearer rational for what they wanted. If they focused just on terms like "furniture," major retailers and manufacturers names came up. YrFurn realized they could never compete effectively so broadly, so they chose the term and concept of viewing the furniture.

In addition, over the course of the past six months, each of the founders visited furniture stores and ran training sessions for salespeople to learn about the app when customers came in using it. They had more than 100 visits completed before the app went live and planned on continuing the pace for a few months. One chain decided to include promotions for the app in all their advertising and marketing literature in exchange for a monthly fee from YrFurn.

The company applied and was accepted into the Apple Store. The idea of the app received quite a bit of free press especially on technology blogs. This resulted in a quick ramp-up of people downloading and using the app that was ahead of their predictions. The firm started selling the app for $3.99 and noted that they were getting several hundred downloads a day. However, only 20 percent of those who downloaded the app appeared to be using it during the next few weeks after download.

Sales got a big jump when a national chain of furniture stores started recommending the app to their in-store customers as a means to view potential furniture options. In the meantime, they were making dozens of changes to the program per week as issues came up and customer recommendations and complaints poured in. The team had to hire two full-time people to manage the customer calls alone.

At the end of the second month, Brad printed out the totals of a few basic items for the month including total sales, revenue received, receivables, total expenses, the amount actually paid out on bills, and outstanding bills. The team was very happy to be able to see the numbers but quickly realized that they did not know if the numbers were good or bad for their industry. Brad had printed out a basic tracking and ratio performance chart like the one below:

	MONTH 1	MONTH 2	CHANGE
Current Ratio	1.147	1.079	−0.068
Gross Profit Margin	0.65	0.70	0.05
Net Profit Margin	−0.084	−0.125	−0.41

This triggered a conversation with the team about how the business was doing and what these numbers really meant.

more funding if this scenario occurs and should have a plan for handling such situations. Under the decrease in sales projection, not only is the firm not making any positive net cash flows, but the net cash flow number is actually increasingly negative. For the firm to miss its projections by this amount would be devastating for the future of the business. Sensitivity analysis provides the businessperson an opportunity to test out assumptions and view the potential impact of those assumptions prior to committing any new resources.

EXERCISE 4

1. What do these numbers mean for YrFurn?
2. What information would you need to be able to analyze these numbers?
3. Using data that you can obtain on the Internet about apps, compare the business performance for the first two months to those averages.
4. If the business had gone live in June and these numbers reflect June and July, how might that impact your analysis?

Use of Short Surveys in Business

LO8-7

Describe the use of short surveys in business.

The fourth means to analyze the business, its activities, and its performance is the survey. The prior three methods examined (ratios, deviation, and sensitivity) focused on financial data. As has been mentioned several other times in this text, the new businessperson should also recognize that there are nonfinancial

Figure 8.6
Cash Flow—Projected (in U.S. dollars)

	YEAR 1	YEAR 2	YEAR 3
Receipts:			
Sales, $	$ 25,000	$325,000	$675,000
Consulting, $	20,000	20,000	60,000
Total Receipts, $	$ 45,000	$345,000	$735,000
Disbursements:			
Salaries, $	$ 45,000	$ 95,000	$210,000
Travel, $	4,050	31,050	66,150
Car Leases, $	4,000	6,000	7,500
Rent, $	900	6,900	14,700
Payroll Taxes, $	2,700	5,700	12,600
Insurance, $	5,500	6,000	7,500
Fuel/Maint, $	960	4,500	8,000
Executive Comp, $	64,000	72,000	78,000
Benefits, $	13,500	28,500	63,000
Advertising, $	2,000	26,000	54,000
Supplies, $	225	1,725	3,675
Utilities, $	3,150	24,150	51,450
Misc, $	900	6,900	14,700
Total Disbursements, $	$ 146,885	$ 314,425	$ 591,275
Beginning Balance, $	0	98,115	128,690
Equity Investment, $	200,000		
Net Cash Flow, $	(101,885)	30,575	143,725
Ending Balance, $	$ 98,115	$ 128,690	$ 272,415

Figure 8.7
Cash Flow—50 Percent Increase in Sales (in U.S. dollars)

	YEAR 1	YEAR 2	YEAR 3
Receipts:			
Sales, $	$ 37,500	$ 487, 500	$1,012,500
Consulting	30,000	30,000	90,000
Total Receipts	$ 67,500	$ 517,500	$1,102,500
Disbursements:			
Salaries	$90,000	$ 190,000	$420,000
Travel	6,075	46,575	99,225
Car Leases	8,000	12,000	15,000
Rent	1,350	10,350	22,050
Payroll Taxes	5,400	11,400	25,200
Insurance	7,500	8,500	10,000
Fuel/Maint.	2,200	6,000	10,200
Executive Comp	64,000	72,000	78,000
Benefits	27,000	57,000	126,000
Advertising	3,000	39,000	81,000
Supplies	338	2,588	5,513
Utilities	4,725	36,225	77,175
Misc.	1,350	10,350	22,050
Total Disbursements	$220,938	$ 501,988	$ 991,413
Beginning Balance	0	46,563	62,075
Equity Investment	200,000		
Net Cash Flow	(153,438)	15,513	111,088
Ending Balance	$ 46,563	$ 62,075	$ 173,163

methods of analysis that are critical to our understanding and growth of the business. So much of what we would like to know about our customers, suppliers, and employees is contextual information that is not easily categorized and is subject to interpretation.[9] This is the ideal reasoning for using a survey to gather information. Although survey methodology is virtually a science unto itself, we believe that anyone can develop an effective survey with just a little care.

Short surveys can be given to any party to a transaction with your business and provide you with the opportunity to evaluate your company's performance on dimensions that may lead to financial success. If there is a very large set of customers, the entrepreneur may choose to sample every third customer. This is a type of random sample, and the expectation is that this subset of the total customers (presuming that the sample is sufficiently large) will in fact reflect the opinions of all customers (within a small margin of error). Alternatively, an entrepreneur may choose to try to survey all of his customers.

In either case there will be some bias in your survey, since only those individuals who wish to fill out the survey will do so. Therefore, the information from the survey can be useful, but judgment is still required to interpret the results. The questions on the survey should be designed to answer questions

	YEAR 1	YEAR 2	YEAR 3
Receipts:			
Sales, $	$ 12,500	$ 162,500	$ 337,500
Consulting, $	10,000	10,000	30,000
Total Receipts, $	$ 22,500	$ 172,500	$ 367,500
Disbursements:			
Salaries, $	$45,000	$ 95,000	$ 210,000
Travel, $	2,025	15,525	33,075
Car Leases, $	4,000	6,000	7,500
Rent, $	450	3,450	7,350
Payroll Taxes, $	2,700	5,700	12,600
Insurance, $	5,500	6,000	7,500
Fuel/Maint, $	480	4,500	8,000
Executive Comp, $	64,000	72,000	78,000
Benefits, $	13,500	28,500	63,000
Advertising, $	1,000	13,000	27,000
Supplies, $	113	863	1,838
Utilities, $	1,575	12,075	25,725
Misc, $	450	3,450	7,350
Total Disbursements, $	$140,793	$ 266,063	$ 488,938
Beginning Balance, $	0	81,708	(11,855)
Equity Investment, $	200,000		
Net Cash Flow, $	(118,293)	(93,563)	(121,438)
Ending Balance, $	$ 81,708	($ 11,855)	($ 133,293)

Figure 8.8
Cash Flow—50% Decrease in Sales (in U.S. dollars)

directly related to the mission or strategy of the company. Some examples of questions for a high-end manufacturer are as follows:

1. How do you rate our prices:

Lower than most		**Same**	**Higher than most**	
1	2	3	4	5

2. Is the quality of our product:

Lower than most		**Same**	**Higher than most**	
1	2	3	4	5

3. The nature of our service is:

Lower than most		**Same**	**Higher than most**	
1	2	3	4	5

This particular sample firm wants to be competitive in most regards but, given its goals, wants to be better than competitors on both service and quality. Ideally each survey will have several questions that look at various aspects of the same issue. We would want to see some consistency in the pattern of answers within the survey as well as between surveys.

Survey data can be tabulated and examined with some fairly simple statistical techniques, such as percentages. Therefore, a fact as simple as "only 55 percent of your customers indicated that your service is better than the service of your competitors" would be a trouble signal for a firm where service was presumed to be a key competitive advantage. However, with just a slight increase in sophistication in the analysis techniques, quite a bit more can be learned from the data. Cross tabulation of related items and simple regressions can form a picture of the organization that leads it beyond its competitors. Both of these are available in virtually every spreadsheet package, and while the level of statistical sophistication can get quite complex, the basics are relatively easy to use and comprehend. A cross tabulation displays the distribution of two or more variables in columns. Thus, you could see, for example, how your drinks matched your entrées in a restaurant.

	MEAT DISH (%)	SALAD ONLY (%)
Wine	35	25
Beer	40	15
Coffee	5	60

A regression is a more complex analysis and concerns how well points of information fit along a line. The results allow you to see how different variables explain the impact of a given measure, such as profits.

LO8-8

Analyze the importance of having a measurement focus.

Importance of Having a Measurement Focus

This understanding of your key competitive advantages and the ability to develop measurements that ensure you are fulfilling your strategic goals is worth greater focus. Remember from Chapter 5 that there are two aspects to any business, the standard and the unique. The standard parts of a business are those that must be done just to be considered a part of that particular industry, whereas the unique represents those areas where the business really tries to differentiate itself. A business needs to do the standard and they need to do it well, but only as well as the rest of the industry. Thus, the standard parts of the business should be managed in the simplest way possible, with very little extra analysis. As long as the firm is performing as well as the rest of the industry, then sufficient effort has been placed in these areas.

A very simple example illustrates just how easy it is to overinvest in the standard. An owner of a bus tour company said he was contemplating getting a postage machine. The natural question to ask the owner was how many pieces of mail he sends out in a day. Putting stamps on more than about 10 pieces a day easily justifies a postage machine, if for no other reason than the savings in time spent purchasing stamps, maintaining a supply, and putting stamps on envelopes. This company was sending out between 170 and 225 pieces of mail a day. This is a standard activity for a company. That said, the founder decided to make a project out of this decision. He invited three companies to meet with him and demonstrate their machines. He analyzed the amount of time it took to place stamps on the envelopes (about 20 minutes a day) and added in the time for traveling to and from the post office (another 20 minutes or so a week). After all the analysis, the company decided to get a postage machine. The owner wanted to track the success of the decision by having the person who ran the envelopes through the machine record the amount of time it took each day and to include the time it took to periodically recharge the machine. This type of analysis is of no value to the ultimate success of an organization. Not only did it waste the time of the people involved, but it also meant that they were not doing their core jobs during this time. Unfortunately, it is very easy to become consumed with the minutiae of analyzing a business and fail to focus on those operations that are most critical for the customer.[10]

©Paul Rapson/Alamy RF

The focus should be on those areas that provide competitive advantage to the firm. In the example of the bus tour agency, there was no competitive advantage to be gained from either a stamp or an imprint. This firm made large segments of its income from arranging annual foliage bus tours for senior citizens to look at the changing colors of the leaves in the mid-Atlantic states. Therefore, measuring the efficiency of the buses employed, the advertising dollars spent reaching that population, the experience on each tour, and the time spent to secure each account would be much more critical. Concentrating the analysis efforts on those areas that are unique puts the founder's focus on those areas that can create a differentiation for the business compared to those of the competitors.

ETHICAL CHALLENGE

Having just completed a contentious meeting with your board of directors, which included three of your biggest investors, you have been charged with making some significant progress on improving your net profit margin, eliminating some of the late payments from customers, and dramatically improving the customer satisfaction scores.

As you ponder how this can be done, one of your closest advisors calls you and suggests that this can all be done without major changes to the operation of the business. He tells you that you are just categorizing items in a way that hurt your numbers. He points out to you that the board doesn't really have any idea how these numbers are crafted. He knows that some of things he suggests don't conform to generally accepted accounting principles, but he also says that only later will the business ever need to have certified financials. For now, it is about survival and support.

QUESTIONS

1. Are the items that are recorded for a particular category open to interpretation?
2. How open do you believe you should be about the details of the business operation?

SUMMARY

Entrepreneurial businesses have very few slack resources relative to their larger competitors. The result is that a large firm can make a series of mistakes and still maintain a going concern. With a much tighter margin of error, an entrepreneurial business should actively monitor its performance relative both to itself and to its competitors. This chapter provided a series of relatively quick, easily maintained techniques for developing and maintaining an effective picture of the company.

KEY TERMS

activity ratios 148
deviation analysis 153
leverage ratios 150
liquidity ratios 146
profitability ratios 151
ratio analysis 146
sensitivity analysis 154

REVIEW QUESTIONS

1. What are the four means to evaluate the firm, its activities, and its performance?
2. What do liquidity ratios seck to measure? What are the major types of liquidity ratios?
3. Why are industry averages important to the interpretation of ratios?
4. What do activity ratios seem to measure? What are the major types of activity ratios?
5. What do leverage ratios seek to measure? What are the major types of liquidity ratios?
6. What do performance ratios seek to measure? What are the major types of performance ratios?
7. List two performance measures and explain their significance.
8. How is a deviation analysis used by a business?
9. How is a sensitivity analysis used to protect a business?

BUSINESS PLAN DEVELOPMENT QUESTIONS

1. Throughout this chapter you have done a variety of financial exercises related to your business. Which of these would be the most useful for you to track on a weekly basis?
2. Are there other data you would follow on a monthly or quarterly basis?
3. What is the specific industry you wish to compare your performance to in order to judge how you are doing?

INDIVIDUAL EXERCISES

Locate an entrepreneur in your area who would be willing to discuss the method he or she uses to track financial performance. (Note the entrepreneur will likely not give specific information such as profits, but he or she will discuss general concepts.)

1. What financial ratio does the entrepreneur focus on most often?
2. How frequently does the entrepreneur sit and analyze the business's performance?
3. Are there specific warning signs the entrepreneur focuses on as he or she does financial analysis?

GROUP EXERCISES

Go to the Internet and pick one of the following large firms: Coca-Cola, Facebook, or Home Depot. Conduct a ratio analysis for this firm using at least six key ratios. Ensure that you find comparable ratios for its industry. Have the other members of the group do the same company. Compare your findings.

1. Which ratios did you pick and why?
2. What was the financial performance for this firm in 2017?

3. Predict what you believe the financial performance of the company will be based on the pattern of performance in 2017 and before.
4. What was the actual performance of the firm last year?

ENDNOTES

1. "Understanding Financial Ratios For Entrepreneurs," *Inc42*, http://inc42.com/resources/understanding-financial-ratios-entrepreneurs/.
2. E. Ries, *The Lean Startup: How Today's Entrepreneurs Use Continuous Innovation to Create Radically Successful Businesses* (New York: Crown Business, 2011).
3. M. Zwilling, "Traction Metrics Seed Real Startup Funding and Growth," *Forbes*, June 24, 2016, http://www.forbes.com/sites/martinzwilling/2016/06/14/traction-metrics-seed-real-startup-funding-and-growth/#5953bba822a7.
4. P. Back, "Explaining Financial Difficulties Based on Previous Payment Behavior, Management Background Variables, and Financial Ratios," *European Accounting Review* 14 (2005), pp. 839–68.
5. M. Bujaki, "Industry Identification Through Ratio Analysis," *Accounting Perspectives* 11, no. 4 (Winter 2012), pp. 315–22.
6. O. Sharifi, "Financial Risk Management for Small and Medium Size Enterprises (SMEs)," *International Journal of Information, Business and Management* 6, no. 2 (May 2014), pp. 82–94.
7. W. Davidson III and D. Dutia, "Debt, Liquidity, and Profitability Problems in Small Firms," *Entrepreneurship Theory & Practice* 16 (1991), pp. 53–65.
8. C. Praag, "Business Survival and Success of Young Small Business Owners," *Small Business Economics* 21 (2003), pp. 1–17.
9. S. Horng-Cherng, "A Study of the Practical and Theoretical Applications of Second Order Customer Perceived Value Analysis," *International Journal of Organizational Innovation* 6, no. 4 (April 2014), pp. 160–73.
10. I. MacMillan and R. McGrath, "Discovering New Points of Differentiation," *Harvard Business Review* (July/August 1997), pp. 154–56.

learning objectives

After studying this chapter, you will be able to:

LO9-1 Discuss the various legal forms of business to determine the best design for a proposed new business.

LO9-2 Explain the basics of contracts.

LO9-3 Define the role of leases in the legal formation of the new business.

LO9-4 List how laws, rules, and regulations benefit new businesses.

LO9-5 Explain the importance of copyrights, trademarks, and patents to a new business.

LO9-6 Define the role that insurance plays in the risk portfolio of the new business.

LO9-7 Discuss how to develop an effective board of advisors or board of directors.

Legal Issues with a New Business

MARCELA SAPONE AND JESSICA BECK—HELLO ALFRED

Marcela Sapone and Jessica Beck were friends and fellow messy apartment renters while they were at the Harvard Business School. They decided to hire someone to come in once a week to clean and restock groceries for each of their apartments so that they could focus on their studies. They hired someone from Craigslist and had the idea about how this could all be done better and more sustainably. They were frustrated by the difficulty of finding someone on the very plain Craigslist website and they knew that there were no assurances about the quality.

The two women built on this experience to found Hello Alfred (www.helloalfred.com). The new firm was different than Craigslist since it was not based on a shared economy model (peer-to-peer transactions with little or no oversight). In their model the firm hires all of the "Alfred's" (as they call them) as employees of the firm paying them $16/hour with benefits to help people with their lives. They crafted together a careful plan to make every trip made for a client profitable and to grow only as fast as they could develop the people to provide the kind of service the firm promised. Hello Alfred provides personal services to allow customers to live the life they want. Cleaning your place, buying groceries, picking up packages, or picking up cleaning, the goal is to free the client from simple chores.

Following the principles of a lean startup they decided to systematically test their business idea while they were still students in Boston. For six months they tested prices and services with customers. They systematically offered customers different levels of services in order to determine the best offerings. They tested out different web page designs and took surveys of potential customers. They also poured through entries on Craigslist looking for common requests. They finally launched the official business after validating and nullifying findings.

The average Alfred customer spends $415 per month with Hello Alfred and the company has grown to 26 corporate employees in its New York headquarters. The company has been a magnet for Venture Capital funding having raised over $12 million. The business has been growing 30 percent month over month for some time with the founders really holding the business back to ensure that each element of it is financially sustainable. Since they hire and train each employee, the process takes longer yet they believe it ensures that the business strategy will be implemented consistently.

Questions

1. How different would the business model be if Hello Alfred used contractors instead of employees?
2. What are the legal concerns of Hello Alfred employees entering the homes of their clients?

Sources: https://www.helloalfred.com/our-story#founders; Curt Woodward and Katie Johnston, "New Rules for a New Economy," *Boston Globe*, April 23, 2016 (https://www.bostonglobe.com/business/2016/04/22/uber-settlement-seen-win-for-gig-economy/qKjBGoXR6s97aKLPNkBKHI/story.html); Maya Kosoff, "2 Harvard Students Built a Company That Will Do Your Chores for You, and It's Made Money Since Day One," *Business Insider*, February 11, 2016 (http://www.businessinsider.com/how-alfred-founders-built-an-operationally-profitable-startup-2016-2); Bryan Elliott, "How the Developers of Hello Alfred Created a Personal Butler," *Entrepreneur*, June 21, 2016 (https://www.entrepreneur.com/video/277785).

Legal issues are critical for any new business to consider. Even though we present issues sequentially in this text, you should recognize that often things happen simultaneously. Thus, legal issues may occur at the same time as some of the financial issues discussed earlier in the book and, in fact, may impact your financial decisions. In addition, the information in this chapter is not meant to be definitive or exhaustive of all the legal concerns related to starting a new business. The material is factually correct; however, we strongly believe that you should hire a qualified attorney to assist you in building the foundation of the new business. The laws in each state vary, and the consequences are often serious enough that you will want to ensure you have a full and complete understanding of the legal issues related to the business.

In the previous chapters we set out a means for you to develop the type of business you want to create, determine its strategy and/or mission, and perform a detailed analysis of the potential cash flow position for the new firm. However, prior to the beginning of any actual operations, the founder(s) must ensure that the proper legal foundation for the business is established.

Mature economies are based upon laws.* To fully appreciate the reliance in the United States on the legal institutions, one need only compare the United States to China.[1] There is a legal system in China, but in most cases this system is one that is evolving. Often the laws are on the books in China but will be enforced only sporadically or in an inconsistent manner. How those laws are enforced and the penalties for violations of those laws will vary widely across the country. Whether laws and their enforcement are the concern of the central government, province, or city is often unclear; instead, there are competing authorities who may interpret what is to be done very differently. To work in this environment, a business survives by developing good relationships with administrators, regulators, and/or the police. It will be the relationship between these individuals and the entrepreneur that determines if the laws are enforced and, if so, how they are enforced. The relationship between a businessperson and government officials may originate from a variety of sources, such as being related by blood or marriage, going to school together, or making a payoff, but without such relationships the new businessperson will most certainly find that he has significant legal problems.[2]

In contrast, the laws of the United States, and many other mature economies, are relatively clear, reasonably well enforced, and the amount of corruption is relatively low. As a result, legal conflicts are decided based on the facts, not on who you know. This does not mean that the legal system in a nation such as the United States is not a source of irritation for businesspeople. For example, obtaining a license to sell alcohol at your premises involves approval from numerous independent authorities—local, state, and federal (the federal agency is the ATF—the Bureau of Alcohol, Tobacco, Firearms, and Explosives).

Although they are frustrating, entrepreneurs must realize that legal structures in society are critical for businesses. The abilities to collect money owed, to trust that contracts will be honored, to operate without fear of being arbitrarily shut down, and to prevent ruinous interventions by the government are all the result of laws. Indeed, in a developing country, or in one recently ravaged by war, one of the first major steps in building the nation's

*The law present in a country is referred to as an *institution*. Other issues such as culture and ways that a given profession may conduct business are also institutions. These institutions shape the way business is conducted in subtle and pervasive manners. To fully understand how business is conducted in a given area, such institutions must be understood.

economy is to establish the police and the courts so that basic business can be transacted.

There are many unique areas of business that will require the new entrepreneurial team to have solid legal advice. A great example is the legal issues surrounding an app. While an app must comply with all the laws of the location of the business, there are a number of additional elements to consider. These include data collection and storage (especially of customer's personal information), sharing of information (medical, health, and fitness information is highly controlled), the Children's Online Privacy Protection Act (COPPA) and any international equivalents impact a business that allows minors to use their app, and anything that might be construed as gambling comes under strict regulations. These issues are heightened as the firm's app may be employed in domains other than where they are developed. Thus, it is possible that you may not violate the law in a state such as California but will in Alabama. The result is a need for solid legal insight as you move forward in this domain.

Our view is that new businesspeople need to acknowledge the central role and importance of the legal system, recognize how it will impact their

KOSHER HOME

Kosher Home founders had determined the industry, type of business, mission, fundamental positioning, and basic operations of their new business. However, they began to realize after talking with several local bank managers and loan officers regarding their initial financing that there were concerns over their "type of business." Initially the entrepreneurs thought this question referred to their positioning or plan for success, but they quickly found out that the financiers were asking about legal form of the business.

The two entrepreneurs wanted everything to be fair and even between them so with very little thought they had chosen a "partnership." They mistakenly believed that this form of business would indicate their commitment to the business and their desire to have investors involved in the business. After all, in law firms and accounting firms, being made a partner is considered the highest honor and confers upon the partner rights to the profits of the firm. The founders had made great progress in developing their business. However, when they talked to a potential investor to help them expand the business even further, they realized their business form was a problem.

The founders met with this investor and made a presentation of their business idea. It had taken two weeks to get on his calendar, and the meeting was going to be quite brief. He was intrigued by the business idea and by their "numbers." He then asked them what type of business entity they had formed, and Jack and Toby responded that they had formed a "partnership." The potential investor fell silent. After what seemed like an eternity to the founders, he responded that he would not invest in a partnership because of the personal liability and problems associated with the lack of liquidity. He finished up with a few polite comments, wished them the best of luck, and said goodbye.

Jack and Toby were shocked, but in analyzing the meeting afterward, they realized that the type of business was of significant interest to potential investors, bankers, and perhaps themselves. They realized they needed to reconsider the legal foundation for their business, as it was a more central issue than they originally believed. The opportunity to obtain any investment from the ideal investor with whom they had just met was probably lost forever owing to the lack of an adequate legal foundation. They were now determined to investigate the legal issues in more detail before they went forward any further.

QUESTIONS

1. How would you describe the liability issues that concerned the potential investor?
2. Do these concerns seem relevant? How would you address them?

business lives, and be prepared to compete in that arena. The businessperson cannot ignore legal issues. As a result, entrepreneurs need to recognize that it is likely they will at some time go to court to resolve disputes. If, on the other hand, a supplier or customer did not live up to an agreement in China, the entrepreneur might go see a powerful person who would mediate the dispute between the two parties using his personal judgment and experience as a guide. If the entrepreneur's relationship with that mediator was poor or if the other party had very strong ties to the mediator, the entrepreneur would likely lose. In the United States, the entrepreneur has the ability to use the court system for a legal remedy that is bound by precedent and the Uniform Commercial Code. The nature of business is that there will be disagreements, and as a result, you as an entrepreneur are likely at some point to be in court. Although this may not be the ideal path to arbitration, it is better than the alternative of having no legal system, or a weak one.

An important part of operating a business is having a fundamental understanding of the basics of commercial law and the potential remedies when there is a dispute. The establishment of a basic legal foundation will help the entrepreneur navigate the legal environment much more easily.

Significant time and effort can be saved in the long run with some careful thought at the founding of a new venture about legal issues. This chapter will examine a number of legal issues that impact the founding of the new business, including:

- The forms of business
- Contracts
- Leases
- Regulations, including licensing requirements
- Copyrights, trademarks, and patents
- Insurance
- Board of advisors or directors

LO9-1

Discuss the various legal forms of business to determine the best design for a proposed new business.

Various Legal Forms of Business to Determine the Best Design for a Proposed New Business

There are three basic types of legal business organization: sole proprietorship, partnership (including both general and limited liability), and corporation (C, S, and limited liability company). Each of these will be examined below.

Sole Proprietorship

sole proprietorship

The simplest form of business organization, characterized by the fact that the person who owns the business and the business itself are treated as the same entity.

A **sole proprietorship** is the simplest form of business to establish, as the person who owns it and the business itself are treated as the same entity. Driven by the belief that new business is good for the economy and should be encouraged, most communities have made the process for obtaining a sole proprietorship license quite simple although there can be distinct differences between communities that will affect the rate of sole proprietorships formation.[3] A quick trip to the local courthouse or public administration building, filling out a simple form, and paying a small fee is usually all that is required to establish a sole proprietorship. More and more communities are making this process even simpler with a complete online process. All of the business income and losses for a sole proprietorship are treated as part of the individual's overall income and are reportable on schedule C of your 1040 tax form. Absent other licenses that may be required to operate your business (a topic we will cover in more detail later in this chapter), the establishment of a sole proprietorship allows an individual to legally transact business.

Many single-person businesses are set up as sole proprietorships.
©LWA/Dann Tardif/Blend Images RF

The major benefit of this form of business is that it is very easy to form and easy to dissolve. There is virtually no separation between the founder and the business. There are strict rules regarding record keeping, and it is important that the founder maintain a firewall between personal and business expenses since the government does not want to pay for the daily living costs of the entrepreneur. However, the entrepreneur may be able to deduct relevant business expenses from the business income.

The drawbacks to this type of business are numerous, and for businesspeople who develop a substantial business, these drawbacks will outweigh the ease of establishment. The first disadvantage is that a business that involves more than a single founder cannot be a sole proprietorship. Kosher Home, by its very nature of having been founded by two individuals, could not be a sole proprietorship unless the founders placed 100 percent of the authority with a single individual, and the other founder was considered an employee (not a very attractive prospect to the founder treated as an employee). The law does not recognize other equity investors in this type of business. This limitation is a significant drawback for the growth potential of a new business, not only from an initial investment perspective but also because as the business develops it may need additional outside investment, which a founder may get in exchange for part ownership of the business. Such investment would be virtually impossible in this legal form. This inability to have additional owners also means that equity incentives to attract top employees and executives are not possible as you could not give them any ownership as part of their compensation. This leaves the founder with two options: either obtain all new monies as personal debt or go through the process of changing the legal form to a more robust one as the firm grows.

A second significant disadvantage of a sole proprietorship is the liability for the owners associated with it. In the sole proprietorship all of the liabilities of the sole proprietorship are the direct responsibility of the owner of the business. Thus, a debt for the firm is a personal debt for the business owner. The result is that if the business does something relatively risky, such as trading commodities, or even something mundane, like taking delivery of a substantial level of inventory that ultimately cannot be sold, then those debts of the business are treated as debts of the owner.

A third issue is one of legitimacy with suppliers and customers. Owing to the fact that this legal form is so easy to dissolve, suppliers typically require personal guarantees for the debts of the firm from the founder of the business. The result is that the value of the business is limited since it is so tightly tied to the founder. If the founder should seek to sell the business, it can be difficult to accomplish.

Thus, a sole proprietorship is very popular among individuals who:

1. Are unsure of their business idea and just want to see what might happen (if the business proves successful these individuals often re-form the business later, using another business form).
2. Have a very small business where the time limitations of the founder will keep the business from growing significantly.
3. Have a business where the costs of equipment are low and, therefore, so are the risks. For example, a new business that embroiders names on shirts and hats can have relatively low costs and low risks.

Partnerships

partnership
A type of business formed between individuals directly. It includes both general and limited varieties.

A more complex business form is a **partnership**. There are two broad categories of partnerships: general and limited. The two differ significantly from each other and will be reviewed separately.

General Partnership. If two or more people are involved in the founding of an organization, they can form a partnership. Similar to the founding of a sole proprietorship, the means of forming a basic partnership is relatively simple; however, it does involve an extra step beyond that of a sole proprietorship. When filing for a partnership, most local communities require a partnership agreement. Although there are no set requirements that such an agreement must take, these agreements generally specify who is involved; what each party is expected to contribute to the founding of the firm (whether it be cash, services, or property); how profits, losses, and **draws** by the partners are to be treated; how one partner can buy out the other(s) if that individual decides to leave; how new partners are brought into the partnership; and how disputes are to be settled.

draws
Distribution of funds from the business. It is usually in the form of a cash dispersion in advance of salary, bonus, expected year-end distribution, and the like.

We periodically hear from potential partners that they simply do not need such items to be specified. These individuals may have known each other for years and feel very comfortable with each other, so that they trust each other and are ready to tie up their combined financial wealth. As a consequence these individuals do not take the time to develop a rich and full partnership agreement. However, recall what we stressed at the beginning of this chapter. This is a legalistic society, and a business is fundamentally a financial transaction, which should be treated as such. The time to prevent problems is early in the relationship, prior to any conflict (which, by the way, is inevitable in any interaction between two or more people). We recommend the early establishment of clear and legally binding dimensions of the partnership. Thus, our advice is to get assistance from your accountant or lawyer in drawing up such an agreement. The time spent up front on an agreement will save hours and hours of frustration and conflict later.

To illustrate the importance of this process, we will describe a partnership we worked with that had been formed to develop a landscaping business. The business developed quite well for several years and grew to where the firm had more than 50 employees and annual revenues in excess of several million dollars. When the partners began, both were married, had known each other for years both personally and professionally, and attended the same church. One partner worked in the field operations while the other handled new business development for the company and managed the office operations. The wife of the partner who worked in the field was the in-house accountant for the business. Unfortunately, after several years it became clear that there was an affair between the partner working in the office and the wife of the other partner who was also working in the office. During the next few months, both partners filed for divorce and the pair having the affair moved in together. The rift in the business became obvious to customers, suppliers, and the employees of the business to the point that the business was on the verge of collapse.

The two partners had developed a short partnership agreement when they formed the business, but it was based on one they found online for free, and they had simply deleted passages that they did not want to address. At the time the two were best friends and believed that they did not need an extensive agreement. The document the two partners had generated was not clear on how they would split the business if either partner wished to terminate the agreement without the agreement of the other partner. The result was that the case ended up in court, connected to two messy divorces. Of course, the business continued to suffer. Employees left, customers chose other landscaping companies, and suppliers changed their credit terms for the business because they were concerned about the dissolution of the business. The result was a costly battle for both parties, with the field partner retaining the business and the office partner receiving a cash payment. Unfortunately for the partner who got the business, there was not a noncompete clause in the partnership or termination agreement. Once the legal case was over, the partner that left with the cash payment set up a new business in the same area and sought out customers from the previous partnership.

In general, breaking the partnership among partners has a negative impact on new businesses.[4] However, in the case of the landscaping business, a better-constructed partnership agreement could have allowed for a fair and less costly dissolution of the partnership. Plus it could have protected the existing company from the partner who left and set up a competing business.

If a partnership agreement is not developed and signed, the partnership will be governed by either the Uniform Partnership Act or the Revised Uniform Partnership Act. These partnership laws were developed as suggested formats and adopted by each state. Thus, although there is some variation among the states, they are nonetheless a relatively effective means to handle the basics of partnership. Although the laws vary somewhat from state to state, certain standards are in place in the absence of a preformation agreement. The rules in the acts are reasonable, but they rarely match exactly what most individuals would prefer for their business. For example, in these acts all assets are treated as equal for the partners. However, we find that rarely is there a true 50–50 partnership. Inevitably, one or more partners contribute more capital or take more of a role in running the business than the other(s). Given this situation, new-business owners would likely want to write a partnership agreement that recognized the larger contribution and perhaps provided a larger ownership stake. Similarly, issues like noncompete agreements are not covered in these acts.[5]

A general partnership shares some of the characteristics of the sole proprietorship. The owners report their shares of losses or profits on their own personal income tax returns in proportion to their interest in the firm. Business expenses have some flow-through to personal tax forms, but the restrictions are significant. General partnerships require little more in the way of formal paperwork than sole proprietorships and dissolution can be quite easy, although it does require a formal record with the local authorities.

Some of the drawbacks of general partnerships are the same as they are for sole proprietorships. The issue of liability is usually a bit more of an issue than it is for a sole proprietorship. Partners are generally held to be jointly liable for all debts incurred by the partnership. This means that a debt agreed to by your partner for the business becomes your total responsibility if the partner fails to meet her obligations. Each partner is assumed to be involved with all decisions, which translates into a fiduciary relationship between partners. In other words, partners have the responsibility to watch out for the best interests of the other partners.

Whereas a sole proprietorship virtually eliminates the firm's ability to bring in new equity investment, a general partnership opens this door just a bit. To accept new equity investment in a partnership, each established partner must surrender a portion of her ownership position. This is usually a process in which the new "partner" buys out a portion of each of the existing partners in a transaction that also adds some financial muscle to the organization. A new partnership agreement is required each time this process occurs, and there are limits in some communities as to the number of partners a business may have.

LLP
A limited liability partnership.

general partner
In an LLP, the individual considered the manager of the firm, who, as such, has unlimited liability for any debts or judgments against the firm.

Limited Liability Partnership. Some of the drawbacks to a general partnership encouraged the development of another type of partnership: a limited liability partnership (**LLP**). An LLP still has at least two individuals who are partners in a venture (although technically, one person can form an LLP and declare a full pass-through of all income on his or her federal taxes); however, there are two classes of partners in such a venture. The first is a **general partner**. The general partner is considered the manager of the firm and, as such, has unlimited liability for any debts or judgments against the firm. In contrast, the other partners are considered to be passive investors, and as such, their liability is limited to their investment in the business. The other partners are called *limited partners* and can work for the firm but may not be active in the management of the organization. The only requirement of an LLP is that at least one partner is considered to be a general partner. Otherwise, the positives and negatives discussed in the previous section for general partnerships also apply to LLPs.

Corporations

Subchapter S Corporation
An organizational form that treats the firm as an entity separate from the individuals. This allows the owners to treat the income as they would if the firm were a sole proprietorship or a partnership. It has limitations in the number and type of shareholders.

The result of forming a sole proprietorship or a general partnership is that the business debts flow directly to the owner(s), meaning that all owners are responsible for any debts of the firm that arise. Thus, owners can have their life savings disappear if the business goes bankrupt. The critical issues of personal liability and the desire to limit exposure to the original equity investment led to the development of other forms of organization. A corporation addresses both drawbacks by viewing the business not as synonymous with the individual but as a separate entity.[6] If a corporation suffers substantial losses, the founder(s) will lose only his investment in the business.

There are a variety of corporations that the U.S. legal system has developed, and we will address the three most common forms. Historically, a new business formed a simple protected corporate form known as a **Subchapter S Corporation**, while a business that was larger, or one that was developing into a large business, formed as a Subchapter C Corporation. These corporation types take their names from subchapters in the Internal Revenue Code. However, today another form of corporation, the Limited Liability Corporation (LLC), has become a predominant business form in the United States. We discuss S, C, and LLC corporations in greater depth next.

Levi Strauss & Co's corporate headquarters in San Francisco, CA. What are the advantages of working for a corporation?
©McGraw-Hill Education/Christopher Kerrigan, photographer

Subchapter S Corporation. As with all corporate forms, the Subchapter S has the benefit of protecting the owners by treating the firm as a separate entity. Thus, the liability is generally limited to any investment the owners might have in the organization. However, a Subchapter S allows the owners to treat the income of the firm as they would if the firm were a sole proprietorship or a partnership. Thus, the owners report their income or losses on their own personal income tax returns. The business must file informational tax returns that report each shareholder's portion of the business that allows the IRS to ensure the owners of the corporation are reporting their income.

The benefits of a Subchapter S can be summarized as follows:

1. Limited liability for owners of the corporation.
2. The potential to consolidate financial statements of business and personal income for the tax benefit of the owners.
3. Relatively easy formation compared with a Subchapter C Corporation.
4. Legitimacy in the market as a more established form of business (the right to put "Inc." after your business name).

However, there are negatives to this form of business as well. Although the effort to form this type of organization is substantially easier than that involved in forming a Subchapter C Corporation, it is nonetheless quite cumbersome and expensive when compared to either a sole proprietorship or a general partnership form. We strongly recommend that an entrepreneur who wishes to form a Subchapter S Corporation get an experienced professional (lawyer or accountant) to process the paperwork. A second consideration is the limitation to the number of shareholders in this type of organization. Historically, a Subchapter S Corporation has had a numerical limit to the number of shareholders. Currently that limit is set at a maximum of 75 shareholders. This limitation is fine for a closely held or family corporation but is a significant limitation to a rapidly growing organization or one that has any thought of going public in the future.

Subchapter C Corporation. Subchapter C solves some of the issues raised regarding Subchapter S Corporations, while creating others. Subchapter C Corporations also have limited liability for the owners, but the corporation pays an income tax.[7] This leads to the situation where the corporation pays a tax on its profits. Then those profits after taxes can be paid as dividends to the owners. However, the owners will have to pay taxes on their personal tax returns for the income distributed as dividends by the **Subchapter C Corporation**. This is the double taxation situation that is often discussed in the United States.

Subchapter C Corporation
An organizational form that treats the firm as a unique entity responsible for its own taxes. There are no limitations to shareholder participation and the "owners" are protected beyond their equity investment.

It is possible for the developing new-business owners to mitigate the double taxation cost. The owners are also considered employees of the Subchapter C Corporation and as such are paid salaries and bonuses. The costs of these salaries and bonuses can be viewed as costs to the business. Thus, the owners can pay themselves virtually all of the profits each year so that little actual profit is reported by the corporation, and therefore, little corporate tax is owed. Profits that are not paid out for such items as salaries, bonuses, and/or dividends are then retained by the corporation for future expansion. A Subchapter C Corporation also has the advantage that fringe benefits that are paid out are not treated as income for employees. Thus, owners can have their health insurance and other benefits paid by the corporation, which then expenses each of these as a cost of business.

An important feature of a Subchapter C Corporation is that there are no limits to the number of shareholders that the organization may obtain. The only real limit is the number of authorized and distributed shares in the organization. Shares in the firm must have an initial value at which they are offered, a "par" value. Thus, the corporation has a floor value that is equal to

New York Stock Exchange
©vichie81/Getty Images RF

the par value times the number of shares distributed, and this translates into the shareholder equity of the firm. We recommend that the par value be set very low so that the new company can authorize a very large number of shares (millions or even tens of millions). In both Subchapter C and S Corporations, authorizing more shares, holding annual board meetings, and reporting standards to local, state, and federal authorities are among the issues that must be formally addressed by the corporation. The result is that a corporation has higher administrative costs than is typically seen in a sole proprietorship or a general partnership. For example, a Subchapter C Corporation requires a rather detailed corporate charter; software packages are available to guide the new businessperson through the process.

The entrepreneur forming either a Subchapter S or a Subchapter C Corporation will have to have the following:

1. *A corporate name*—the new organization cannot choose a name that is considered a replication of another company's name. Patent and trademark attorneys offer services that include detailed searches of company names (and allow business owners some level of comfort with their choice) all the way to obtaining a nationwide trademark on the name.
2. *Location of the corporate headquarters*—for a new business this is generally the same as the business address.
3. *General nature of the business*—specified for the filing.
4. *Names, addresses, and titles*—of all corporate founders and initial investors.
5. *A so-called time horizon for the firm's existence*—for all intents, this is usually "in perpetuity."
6. *Authorized stock and capital*—the par value times the number of shares issued is considered the initial capital of the organization. Some states require the company to have that amount on deposit in a business account with a bank.
7. *By-laws of the organization*—the basic rules that will govern activity in the new company.

LLC
A limited liability corporation (LLC).

Limited Liability Corporation. In recent years the **LLC** has become one of the most popular forms of incorporation for new businesses.[8] This business form is still relatively new; for example, it was only in 1994 that California passed a law to allow such entities. The limited liability corporation has many similarities with the Subchapter S Corporation. There is the limited liability feature, which exposes each shareholder only to the amount of their investment. However, the LLC allows the new venture to have more investors, and it allows other corporations to hold stock in the company (a feature not available to Subchapter S Corporations).[9] An LLC may have as few as one individual listed as an officer of the company, referred to as a "member" of the corporation. The LLC is similar to a Subchapter C Corporation in that all of the information required is the same but is unlike a Subchapter C Corporation in that profits from the organization can be handled flexibly. The owners are allowed to flow the profits through to their personal returns to avoid double taxation, which occurs with a Subchapter C Corporation. Furthermore, there is substantial flexibility (unlike with a partnership) regarding the amount of income that is designated for each individual. It does not have to be in proportion to that owner's holdings.

The cost of formation of the LLC is very low as this type of organization is formed by simply submitting the paperwork to the state government and having a charter issued prior to beginning operations. State governments establish how this business entity is formed and a few states, such as New York, also require that the founder of the new business publish notice of forming the LLC in the local newspaper. Some states limit their use and will not allow professionals such as accountants and lawyers to form such business entities. As we have stated before, professional advice in regard to what is appropriate within your state is money well spent.

EXERCISE 1

1. What form of business do you believe will be the best for your new venture? Why?
2. Looking five years down the road, what form of business will be best if your business goes as you hope? If there is a difference in your conclusion, why would that be so?

Basics of Contracts

LO9-2

Explain the basics of contracts.

Beyond the legal form of the new organization, there are a number of other legal issues that entrepreneurs should consider prior to beginning operations. A **contract** is an agreement between two parties to perform certain activities for some consideration. A contract does not have to be written, but it should be consistent with the theme presented in this chapter; we strongly recommend that the entrepreneur employ formal written contracts whenever there is an agreement with another party.

contract
An agreement between two parties to perform certain activities for some consideration.

As with our other recommendations, we strongly suggest the use of an attorney in the creation of any legal agreement. In general, a contract

ETHICAL CHALLENGE

As you build your business, there are legal and ethical challenges that affect how you decide to price a product. Martin Shkreli saw an opportunity to buy drug rights from big pharmaceutical companies and then raise the prices significantly. He formed a company called Turing Pharmaceuticals and without developing a single drug bought three drugs from another company and then pursued windfall profits by dramatically increasing the price of the drugs. He was unapologetic about the increases believing that medical plans and patients would pay whatever price he charged because their lives depended on the drug.

Shkreli quickly became famous as the "most hated CEO in the world" when he bought a decades-old drug, which treats a rare infection in HIV/AIDS patients, and increased the price per pill from $13.50 to $750. He claimed that he was only doing what his investors wanted and that what he was doing was perfectly legal. While legal, the ethics of the decision were roundly criticized.

Shkreli is not alone in his behavior. The very next year, drug giant Mylan was caught in a firestorm of bad press when it was brought to light that they had raised the price of the life-saving EpiPen by over 500 percent during the previous seven years even though costs had not increased. Again, the Mylan CEO Heather Bresch claimed that what was done was perfectly legal. The firm ultimately changed its pricing but not back to the original level that was charged.

QUESTIONS

1. How much do you plan to charge for your product/service and why?
2. Are there ethical limitations on how much you should charge?

should include several items that are reasonably straightforward this discussion:

1. Who the parties are in the contract. This preamble describes briefly who the parties are so that it is clear who is involved and in what manner.
2. What each party agrees to do and for what consideration (i.e., their cost, pay, product received, etc.).
3. When the transaction is to take place.
4. The timing of payment, if other than immediately.
5. When the activity is to take place and how long the contract is in place.
6. Warranties.
7. How the contract can be terminated. There may be damages specified.
8. Whether the contract can be transferred.
9. If the firms are in different states, which state's law applies?

LO9-3

Define the role of leases in the legal formation of the new business.

Role of Leases in the Legal Formation of the New Business

One of the most significant contracts that a new business is initially involved in is the lease where the business will operate. Lease contracts may be of any term length that is agreeable between the parties. Whatever the length of the lease, there are several issues that the new business owner should consider:

1. What exactly is the new business owner leasing? Beyond the basic address and exclusive access to the premises, leases should address utilities; access to parking (either exclusive or shared); responsibility for the external premises (including lawn care, painting, etc.); structural repairs/improvements; approval of leasehold improvements; and responsibility for permanently installed equipment (heating/air conditioning, plumbing, electrical, etc.).
2. Can the business owner renew the lease? The lease should specify how long it is in effect and if there is the opportunity to renew the lease. Such renewability is not critical in all leases, but the entrepreneur needs to evaluate such details in light of their business. The initial space that is leased may not be critical for some types of businesses, such as an Internet-based business where no customers will be coming in on a daily basis. For these businesses, the website and telephone are far more important issues. However, if you have a bakery that makes specialty cakes, your customers grow accustomed to where you are located. If you have to move such a retail-based business, there are significant limitations to maintaining a customer base.
3. Who is responsible for improvements? Who has responsibility and authority for physical plant improvements? A lease that includes the responsibility for making improvements to the facility should be accompanied by a lower lease payment. One entrepreneur bought an existing hair salon and negotiated what she believed was a reasonable lease with the landlord. During the first summer that she occupied the building, the air conditioner stopped working, and the lessee found out that she was responsible for replacing the air-conditioning unit; however, the landlord had the exclusive right to approve the unit. The landlord wanted a top-of-the-line unit to replace the old unit, while the lessee just wanted to install a functional mid-priced unit. The decision

had to be made quickly, as it was midsummer in the southwest United States, with temperatures over 100 degrees. The owner of the business had no choice but to put in the unit the landlord wanted. The unit and the related improvements cost more than $25,000.

4. Who has responsibility for maintenance and other facilities issues? Who has responsibility for issues such as the utilities, landscaping, janitorial costs, trash removal, parking lot maintenance and security, window washing, and real estate taxes? Can you place the signage you want, or are there restrictions?
5. Who has to carry the liability insurance and at what level? Many leases require the tenants to carry insurance not only for themselves but also to cover any liability of the landlord. Insurance can be expensive, and it merits particular attention to be clear who has what responsibility for insurance.
6. Can your landlord enter your place of business? Most leases give the landlord some rights to enter your business to inspect it. The landlord wants to make sure you are taking care of the rental location and that nothing illegal is occurring. However, it can feel like an invasion if the landlord can come into your business whenever he or she desires.
7. If there are problems, what are the procedures for addressing and resolving them? If you cannot use all of your space and have a financial need, can you sublet some of your leased space to others? Many leases prohibit such subleasing. Most leases also do not allow you to cancel the lease unless you meet the specified conditions in the lease. To illustrate, recently a developing business was looking for a location for a new retail store. There appeared to be a number of good opportunities in the area where there were multiple buildings with empty space. Unfortunately, the business owners found that one space they really liked was already leased by a business that no longer existed. The lease had been written with the personal guarantee of the business founder[10]. Most states do not allow a landlord to charge two individuals for rent on the same space. Interestingly, the landlords chose to leave the space empty and collect full rent for the remainder of the old lease rather than rent the space to the new start-up at a lower rate. The individual who had personally guaranteed the lease before going out of business could only get out of the lease by filing personal bankruptcy, which he was not willing to do. If there are other problems and disagreements between the landlord and the business owner, how will these be solved—mediation, arbitration, or other means? If there are problems, can you withhold your rent?

Leases help protect long-term businesses.

©David Shwatal/Alamy RF

Hopefully you can see that a lease is multidimensional and should be carefully crafted before signing. Consistent with our belief stressed in this chapter, new business owners can prevent many problems by ensuring that legal issues are thoroughly investigated and that they employ experts where needed.

EXERCISE 2

1. Put together a list of all the items you think are critical to discuss with your potential landlord.
2. What are the three or four most important items? Write down your minimal acceptable negotiation position for each.

LO9-4

List how laws, rules, and regulations benefit new businesses.

How Laws, Rules, and Regulations Benefit New Businesses

New businesses generally deal with fewer regulations than do established larger businesses. Many regulations enacted by the federal government do not apply to businesses with fewer than 50 employees (this number varies with the regulation). Some industries are highly regulated regardless of size, whereas others are only loosely regulated even for the large, well-established organizations. If a new business deals with toxic waste such as asbestos, it can expect to have to file extensive registration documentation and be subject to significant regulation immediately, regardless of the size of the firm. Thus, regulation-related issues need to be carefully considered as the business is developed. This same issue will also apply in industries involving alcohol, medical-related industries, and military-related businesses. However, at the other extreme, an Internet business that sells retail goods faces only minimal regulation.

There are some basic regulations that cut across the spectrum of businesses. Virtually all businesses must have an Employer Identification Number for tax purposes. Additionally, a business with employees will be required to calculate and deduct various taxes for federal, state, and, in some cases, local authorities. The payroll requirements are specific and well developed. Fortunately, an entrepreneur can simply purchase a canned package for doing payroll and should be able to meet all of these various requirements.

Some states, such as California, have far more expansive laws governing business practices. Although environmental regulations at the federal level are typically designated for large businesses, in some areas the states will also apply those laws to all businesses. Similarly, specific cities may have unique sets of special regulations. A city such as New York has extensive additional regulations for all businesses. A restaurant in New York City has to post information on the calories and fat content in all of its products, and any food that is deep fried must use very specific types of oil.

ADA
Americans with Disabilities Act—specifies protections in business for those with disabilities.

Obviously, the special rules and regulations for your industry and location should be explored before you start your business to ensure that you are meeting all requirements. Excellent sources of information regarding regulatory requirements are the Small Business Assistance Center (run by the Small Business Administration) in your area, the state or local department of economic development, and the local chamber of commerce. More and more government agencies are developing websites to provide all this information and, in some cases, even allow for online submission of materials. All states and cities are critically aware of the role new businesses play in their economic viability. The result has been the establishment of offices to help new businesses to navigate these laws and regulations.

Do you think the food regulations including health inspections, display of health code grades, liquor licensing, calorie information, and ADA certifications are fair to new business owners?

©Erik Isakson/Blend Images LLC RF

One set of regulations that bears particular mention is the Americans with Disabilities Act (**ADA**). This law applies fully to any firm with more than 15 employees and in some communities has been applied to all businesses.[11] The law requires that there be no discrimination in the hiring, management, or dismissal of employees with disabilities. If the firm has someone with a covered disability, the business must make reasonable accommodation for that individual. Additionally, virtually all retail and most office businesses must make their places of business accessible to people with physical disabilities. The requirements of the ADA have spawned lawsuits in every region of the country. So many aspects of the law are still being litigated that specific requirements associated with the law can be hard for a business to pin down. The requirements of the law can also change after the new business has opened.[12] The result is that this area of the law must be constantly monitored by the new business owner.

Licensing

Related to the topic of regulation are the licenses that the business must obtain to operate. A license can be as simple as a business license that is used by communities to track business performance (and thereby tax income), or it may be specifically related to the fundamental operations of the business. Examples of licenses and permits include the following:

1. Business license
2. Local ABC (Alcoholic Beverage Control) liquor license
3. Occupancy permits
4. Federal liquor license (Bureau of Alcohol, Tobacco, Firearms, and Explosives)
5. Business license (from the local city and county authorities)
6. Sign permits
7. OSHA permits for food handling
8. Fire safety permit

The above list is illustrative and does not represent all the licenses that a business will likely need. However, looking at this list a few things should be noted. At a minimum, most businesses must acquire a license to do business in the county or city in which they will be operating. This type of license is quite simple to obtain, as it normally requires only that one of the principals of the business fill out a form (more and more often online), pay a set fee (usually less than $100 and often quite a bit less), and agree to report basic information about the business's performance on a set schedule. The business will be required to pay a business license tax each year; the tax is often based on company sales. While completing this procedure, we suggest that the new businessperson search for other licenses that might be required for the operation. Because lack of knowledge is no excuse for failing to have the proper licenses, we always recommend talking with current business owners and/or local authorities concerning the procedures and licenses required in each locale. For those firms who are facing more challenging licensing, such as one that involves disposing of hazardous waste or serving alcohol, it is best to visit with a lawyer.

copyright
The legal means to protect intellectual property. It grants ownership on creative materials generated, such as books, magazines, advertising copy, music, artwork, or virtually any other creative product, whether published or unpublished.

Importance of Copyrights, Trademarks, and Patents to a New Business

LO9-5
Explain the importance of copyrights, trademarks, and patents to a new business.

A topic that merits brief mention is intellectual property protection through copyrights, trademarks, and patents. A **copyright** can be claimed on creative materials generated, such as books, magazines, advertising copy, music, artwork, or virtually any other creative product, whether published or unpublished. In the United States, a copyright is assumed to apply to anything that is your own original work (whether that original work itself is filed with the U.S. government or not). The copyright is valid for the life of the author plus 70 years.

trademark
Claim of intellectual property that is associated with a specific business. This may be the name of the firm, a symbol representing the firm, or the names of its products.

patent
Claim of intellectual property that covers a specific innovation.

A **trademark** is legal protection of the intellectual property that is associated with a specific business. This may be the name of the firm, a symbol representing the firm, or the names of its products. Most large companies have trademarked their company name, symbols, and tag lines.

You may not use a product's name such as Sprite, as it is the trademark of a specific product for the Coca-Cola Company. Although not as universally recognized as a copyright, a trademark is assumed in place once a firm begins to use the symbol or name. However, a firm can and probably should register its use to ensure the protection of the trademark. A new business is well served to perform a search to ensure that it is not violating a trademark. A firm that is violating a trademark can be sued and is required not only to pay damages, but also may be forced to change its name. A trademark is valid for 10 years and can be renewed as long as the firm or product is active.

The Coca-Cola trademark is recognized around the world.
©McGraw-Hill Education/Mark Dierker, photographer

The last intellectual property protection is the most complex and expensive. A **patent** covers a specific innovation. A patent is good for 20 years from the point that it is filed, fees are paid, and it is accepted by the U.S. Patent and Trademark Office for processing. Recent changes to the patent regulations have meant that patent protection is being granted on a "first to file" basis rather than a "first to invent" basis. This might have significant impacts on the timing of efforts by new businesses.[13] Patents are expensive to obtain and expensive to maintain, so they should be used only in the case where obtaining the patent is part of the sustainable competitive advantage of the organization.

There are three types of patents: Utility, Design, and Plant. A Utility patent is for a new process, machine, article of manufacture, or composition of matter, or any new and useful improvement of those. A Design patent is for a new, original, and ornamental design for an article of manufacture. Finally, a Plant patent is for someone who invents or discovers and asexually reproduces any distinct and new variety of plant.[14]

A patent can be a potent entry barrier for a business, as it prevents direct imitation for that period of time. Unfortunately, close copies may skirt the patent laws, so a patent should be but one avenue of competitive protection.

For businesses that founders hope will expand internationally, one issue to recognize is that copyright, trademarks, and patents filed in the United States only apply in the United States. If the firm moves to expand abroad, the entrepreneur will have to file each of those documents in each of the markets in which they plan to sell.

LO9-6

Define the role that insurance plays in the risk portfolio of the new business.

Role That Insurance Plays in the Risk Portfolio of the New Business

A topic related to the legal concerns of all types of business is insurance. One of the key concerns that should have been clear in the discussion of the form of organization is that the new business chooses the level of liability it is willing to risk. One means to limit liability concerns is through the effective application of insurance.

There are several basic types of insurance, but a key one is a firm's property insurance. Property insurance covers the building, fixtures, and inventory in all of the buildings in which the business has a function. One key concern is whether the insurance covers replacement cost or only current value. Much like owning an older car, you may have equipment that has only limited value in a resale market but is very expensive to replace if you have to buy it new. The firm must decide what types of risks it will accept and cover itself versus those that it will purchase insurance to cover. It is fairly standard to obtain coverage for fire, windstorms, hail, and smoke. However, the firm may also wish to obtain a special form of insurance that covers issues such as floods and earthquakes. The greater the insurance coverage obtained by the new business, the greater the cost. Thus, each firm needs to take some care to balance risk and cost.

The other forms of insurance an entrepreneurial business might obtain include liability insurance, bonding insurance, and workers' compensation.

- A new business can also obtain liability insurance, which helps to protect the business against lawsuit judgments. Such insurance does not cover intentional acts of malice; however, it does cover the business for accidents. Product liability insurance is expensive, but it can also be obtained to provide a legal defense fund in the case of a negligence lawsuit.

YrFURN—AN APP FOR FURNITURE

As the team was building the business, they really felt that getting the contractors in place, setting up all the equipment and supplies would be the biggest time holdup to starting the new business. Several weeks into the process, one of the team's mentors asked the group if they had all their licenses and insurance in place. In all the effort to start up the business they had simply had not taken the time to consider what legal requirements might be needed.* They were stunned to find out that there were a number of licenses that they were going to have to acquire, and that insurance was a significant consideration. These included:

1. A local business license just like that for any new business that was required by the city where they operated.
2. They had not formed any type of legal company structure with the state.
3. The leasing company had required them to get minimal hazard insurance, but a mentor told them that they needed general liability insurance and that they should have some type of umbrella policy to protect the company. Their mentor further recommended that they should talk to an agent who worked in this area to determine what else they might need.
4. A license for a sign. (A recently passed city ordinance required each business owner to apply for a license to put a sign on the building and/or the street. The restrictions on new signs were substantial.) These licenses were not particularly expensive to obtain; however, the time and effort it took to address these licenses was not a small matter.

The decision about how to structure the company and deal with state authorities was a bigger one. After investigating the cost of creating a Subchapter C corporation, they decided on an LLC as the fastest and cheapest means to bring the business into existence. However, after they had filed all the paperwork, they were by several of their investors that an LLC would not work for them. They wanted stock issued commiserate to the amount of money they invested, and they wanted the company to have a formal board of directors. More importantly, they wanted the protections that a C corporation provided them. The team realized that they needed a lawyer and sought one out to get all of this arranged and to advise them on all licenses and regulations. It was not as simple as they thought to start a new business. The team then also began to work on developing a board of directors.

QUESTIONS

1. What licenses do you believe will be required for your business idea? Check with the local Small Business Assistance Center to see if you are right.
2. If you are dealing with a product or issue that is politically sensitive, how will that affect your licensing effort?

*Recall as we noted at the first of chapter that while we present things sequentially often things happen simultaneously. Thus, legal issues like those here may occur at the same time as some of the financial issues.

- Bonding is a type of insurance in which the business is covered in case the workers cause any damage in the performance of their work. To illustrate, a plumber may hire an assistant who makes some of the calls on customers. The assistant may make a mistake that leads to a pipe breaking, which floods the house or apartment. The damage done can be very costly and perhaps even cause bankruptcy. However, through bonding, the insurance company agrees to pay for such damages. In an office setting the owner can also purchase bonding to cover losses from employee embezzlement.
- Workers' compensation insurance covers liability for workers who are injured on the job. In many states, workers' compensation insurance is required and can represent a major expense for a business.

Insurance is such a critical issue that it merits spending time with an insurance agent, or multiple agents, to discuss the needs of the new business. Discussion with multiple agents will allow the new businessperson to obtain different viewpoints on the issue. The new business owner should seek out agents who have expertise in the industry in which the business operates.

LO9-7

Discuss how to develop an effective board of advisors or board of directors.

How to Develop an Effective Board of Advisors and Board of Directors

Two related entities that can help the new business owner foresee potential legal liabilities are boards of advisors and boards of directors. These boards are composed of people who have both insight and experience with which to advise the founders. An effective group of advisors will not only help the new business owner foresee if legal problems might arise but also help the new business wind its way through a full range of other issues and opportunities where experience is the best teacher. The new business should have at least one of these entities that will advise the founder. A business that chooses to form a corporation must have a board of directors. These are individuals who have a fiduciary responsibility to the shareholders of the organization. In new corporations, the shareholders and board of directors are often the same individuals. In contrast, a **board of advisors** may be formed at the discretion of the founders (regardless of the legal form chosen); it is composed of individuals outside the new business who will advise the firm.[15]

board of advisors

A group formed at the discretion of the founders (regardless of the legal form chosen) and composed of individuals outside the business who advise the founders.

Although the size of the board of advisors is a matter of choice, as a practical matter, it is better to have a few, well-placed individuals who are motivated to help the firm through the start-up process rather than enlist a large number who serve as a means of false showmanship. There is a set of basic needs for most new businesses; thus, we suggest choosing individuals who have experience navigating the following:

1. Licensing requirements for your type of industry in your locality (if such licensing is relatively complex or difficult).
2. Regulations for your specific industry.
3. New start-up experience and success.
4. Financial and accounting background with new start-ups.
5. Human resources experience, especially establishing basic personnel criteria.

This board can formally meet on whatever schedule seems appropriate. Many boards of advisor meetings are held virtually using applications such as Skype. The reality is for a new firm to obtain highly knowledgeable people willing to help, the new firm cannot ask the potential advisors to commit too much time. Often these highly knowledgeable individuals may be happy to have the entrepreneur contact them as issues arise without the formality of calling for a meeting to resolve the problems. Asking busy people to travel and spend a half day or more in a formal meeting may be too much of a commitment of their time.

In keeping with the efficient operation of a new business, we suggest that the board size be maintained at fewer than six individuals. Some advisors may be investors or else are involved in a professional capacity working with the firm. However, many expert advisors get involved with start-ups because of their love of seeing a business flourish. As the firm develops, formality and compensation can be considered.

SUMMARY

This chapter covered a wide variety of legal issues related directly to the starting of a new business. The legal form that the founders choose has implications from an operational, tax, and legal perspective. The new venture owners must be aware of and deal with regulations imposed by local, state, and federal authorities; obtain all relevant licenses; and be sufficiently savvy regarding the evaluation of contracts, leases, and insurance. All of these areas can be quite complex, and throughout the chapter we suggest that awareness of the issues is the first step, but getting some professional advice is the most prudent long-term move.

KEY TERMS

ADA 176
board of advisors 180
contract 173
copyright 177
draws 168
general partner 170
LLC 172
LLP 170
partnership 168
patent 178
sole proprietorship 166
Subchapter C Corporation 171
Subchapter S Corporation 170
trademark 178

REVIEW QUESTIONS

1. Why is a legal system so critical to a new business?
2. Do you think such legal protections are more or less important to a new business than to an established business?
3. What are the impacts on a business that chooses to form as a sole proprietorship?
4. What are the impacts on a business that chooses to form as a partnership?
5. What are the impacts on a business that chooses to form as a Subchapter S Corporation?
6. What are the impacts on a business that chooses to form as a Subchapter C Corporation?
7. What are the impacts on a business that chooses to form as an LLC?
8. What are the major differences between a board of directors and a board of advisors?

BUSINESS PLAN DEVELOPMENT QUESTIONS

1. What licenses or permits will be required for your new business?
2. Develop a spreadsheet with all the licenses or permits that must be obtained. Provide columns for Entity Administering License or Permit, Process Started, Application Complete, License or Permit Obtained, Fee, and Renewal Period.
3. What insurance products seem to make the most sense for your new business? What will this cost the company?

INDIVIDUAL EXERCISES

1. List the attorneys in your area who are recognized experts in new business start-ups.
2. Do an Internet search for contracts that can be used by new businesses. What did you find out?
3. What licensing requirements affect Web-based businesses?

GROUP EXERCISES

Break into teams of three or four people. Develop the following information and then present it to the individuals in your group, discussing why you made those choices.

1. Create a small chart outlining the varied types of people you would want to sit on your board of advisors, and explain why you would choose them.
2. Make a contact list of seven to nine people to invite onto your board of advisors, include their names, telephone numbers, e-mail addresses, positions, and what you believe they would bring to your new business.

ENDNOTES

1. W. Scott, *Institutions and Organizations* (Thousand Oaks, CA: Sage Publications, 1995).
2. Q. Huang, R. Davidson, and J. Gu, "Impact of Personal and Cultural Factors on Knowledge Sharing in China," *Asia Pacific Journal of Management* 25 (2008), pp. 451–71.
3. P. Coomes, J. Fernandez, and S. Gohmann, "The Rate of Proprietorship among Metropolitan Areas: The Impact of the Local Economic Environment and Capital Resources," *Entrepreneurship: Theory & Practice* 37, no. 4 (July 2013), pp. 745–70.
4. C. Galbraith, "Divorce and the Financial Performance of Small Family Businesses: An Exploratory Study," *Journal of Small Business Management* 41 (2003), pp. 296–310.
5. Linda Stevens, "Drafting Noncompetes in a Tough Enforcement Climate," *Corporate Counsel*, February 22, 2017, http://www.corpcounsel.com/home/id=1202779699925/Drafting-Noncompetes-in-a-Tough-Enforcement-Climate?mcode=1202614998157&curindex=0&slreturn=20170123072010.
6. R. Lewis, "Why Incorporate a Small Business?" *National Public Accountant* 39, no. 11 (1994), p. 14.
7. L. Hodder, M. McAnally, and C. Weaver, "The Influence of Tax and Nontax Factors on a Bank's Choice of Organizational Form," *Accounting Review* 78 (2003), pp. 297–326.
8. J. Freedman, "Limited Liability: Large Company Theory and Small Firms," *Modern Law Review* 63 (2000), pp. 317–55.
9. T. Taulli, "The Right Number of Shareholders for Your Company," *Bloomberg Businessweek*, December 12, 2008, www.businessweek.com/stories/2008-12-12/the-right-number-of-shareholders-for-your-companybusinessweek-business-news-stock-market-and-financial-advice.
10. Allen Buchanan, "How to Avoid a Personal Guarantee in Leasing Commercial Space," The Orange County Register, June 9, 2016, http://www.ocregister.com/articles/rent-699008-lease-owner.html.
11. ADA website, "Information and Technical Assistance ADA," www.ada.gov/2010_regs.htm.
12. Sun Sentinel Editorial Board, "Rein in Runaway Lawsuits on Small Businesses," *Sun Sentinel*, January 26, 2014, http://articles.sun-sentinel.com/2014-01-26/news/fl-editorial-disability-lawsuits-dv-20140126_1_small-businesses-ada-federal-lawsuits.
13. U.S. Patent and Trademark Office website, http://www.uspto.gov/inventors/patents.jsp. Accessed July 20, 2014.
14. Ibid.
15. N. Upton, E. Teal, and J. Felan, "Strategic and Business Planning Practices of Fast Growth Family Firms," *Journal of Small Business Management* 39, no. 1 (2001), pp. 60–74.

chapter

10

Human Resources Management

learning objectives

After studying this chapter, you will be able to:

LO10-1 Explain the elements of human resources.

LO10-2 Discuss the process of hiring employees.

LO10-3 Analyze the means for retaining employees.

LO10-4 Determine the pertinent aspects of employee probation and firing.

LO10-5 Understand Broad Coverage Regulations and Laws.

LO10-6 Distinguish the unique aspects of human resources within a family business.

OLGA KAY—MOOSH WALKS

MOOSH · WALKS™
BY OLGA KAY

Olga Kay is a YouTube star with more than a million followers. She was born and raised in a poor, rural town in Russia. When she was 14 her entire family ran away with the circus. She decided to learn juggling, and by the time she was 16 she was invited to the United States to tour with the Ringling Brothers and Barnum & Bailey Circus. She appeared in commercials, for instance juggling Smirnoff Vodka glasses. By 2002 she had moved to Hollywood to have a career in show business.

Olga started posting videos of her life on YouTube and quickly had a large following of mostly young girls. She began creating channels based on her interests, and today she has five channels. By 2014 she was posting 20 videos a week, had more than a million followers, and was emotionally and physically exhausted. Due to the royalty structure and fee payments of running advertisements through YouTube, even with all this effort, Ms. Kay was making just over U.S. $100K.

She really wanted to create a more sustainable business model based on a product. As a child Olga was unable to afford new clothes. But drawing on her creativity and individuality she created a line of socks. Each sock is a character with a story and most have ears. She featured her sock characters on a video and had calls immediately from girls who wanted to purchase them. From this initial demand, she set up an Amazon account and began Moosh Walks.

She wanted to turn Moosh Walks into a business that would free her from her constant demand to feed new material to YouTube. That meant that she had to move from making the socks herself. She had to try six different manufacturers before one would make the socks with ears. She invested $20,000 and designed a website with no product, no pictures, just drawings of the socks for young girls. She ran a preorder campaign on her website and YouTube channels to see who was interested. There were so many orders that when she actually got the socks in, she had already recouped her money.

With no formal education, she has an intuition for business that accurately lined up with a lean start-up approach. She wanted to learn more about customer reactions to the actual socks, so she opened a pop-up shop in Los Angeles to see how potential customers reacted to the socks. As she talked to them she realized that the market was much bigger than young girls. She decided to add new lines of socks for dad, mom, and babies.

She still sells online via Amazon but now has her socks available in 14 stores. She says that every business must have a reason for existence beyond making money. For her it is to give girls (and now everyone) the ability to stand out and be unique. The business was totally self-funded, and she reinvests a lot back into the business. She still maintains her video presence but has cut it back dramatically to focus on Moosh Walks. At last check Moosh Walks is selling tens of thousands of socks a year.

Questions

1. Into what other areas do you think she can take this business?
2. As she grows she will have to hire employees. What advice would you provide her?

Sources: https://mooshwalks.com/pages/about; Jonathan Small, "Sock Entrepreneur Olga Kay's 10 Easy Steps to Success," *Entrepreneur*, June 16, 2016 (https://www.entrepreneur.com/article/277593); Leslie Kaufman, "Chasing Their Star, on YouTube," *New York Times*, February 1, 2014, https://www.nytimes.com/2014/02/02/business/chasing-their-star-on-youtube.html?smid=pl-share; Murray Newlands, "YouTube Star Olga Kay Can Juggle What It Takes to be an Entrepreneur," *Forbes*, November 1, 2015, https://www.forbes.com/sites/mnewlands/2015/11/01/youtube-star-olga-kay-can-juggle-what-it-takes-to-be-an-entrepreneur/#6d1c58d03f4f.

KOSHER HOME

Kosher Home had started with the two founders but now had up to six additional employees including a part-time mashgiach who certified that everything was kosher. The founders wanted their employees to be courteous, friendly, professional, and highly knowledgeable about procedures that were important to the firm, heath rules, and the rules associated with observing kosher; to sell kosher food the employees would have to be Jewish although knowledge about kosher could vary widely among any observant Jews. The founder's nightmare scenario was that they might violate kosher in some manner, in that case the social media backlash would be significant.

The rules for kosher food can be extensive. For example, the only types of meat permitted are cattle and game that have "cloven hooves" and "chew the cud." If an animal species fulfills only one of these conditions (e.g., the pig, which has split hooves but does not chew the cud, or the camel, which chews the cud but does not have split hooves), then its meat may not be eaten. Following the slaughter of animals, a trained expert removes certain forbidden fats and veins after which the meat is soaked in a bath in room temperature water for a half hour. Next, to draw out the blood, the meat is placed on salting tables where it is salted with coarse salt on both sides for one hour.

All kosher milk products must derive from kosher animals. In addition, the milk of impure cattle and game (e.g., donkey milk) is prohibited. Dairy products may not contain non-kosher additives, and they may not include meat products or derivatives (e.g., many types of cheese are manufactured with animal fats). Additionally, a number of preprocessed foods contain small portions of milk products, such as whey. According to food product regulations, such tiny additives do not have to be declared on the packaging but may render the product non-kosher. This applies especially to bread.

Milk and meat products are not to be mixed together. This means that meat and milk products may not be cooked together, but also they may not be served together on the same table and not eaten at the same time. Different utensils must be used for meat and milk products. Finally, there must be trained individuals (rabbis) who approve the process in order for the firm's food to be certified as Kosher.

The founders found that the problem with their employees was not in their commitment, technical knowledge, or food knowledge. The greatest difficulty was ensuring all employees meet not just the rules but the spirit of kosher. Particularly one employee Jacob was very committed to the firm, but he kept making sloppy mistakes in the preparation and packaging of the food. Clearly, Kosher Home bought kosher items to package in certain quantities and did not do things such as slaughter animals. Nonetheless, the maintenance of separate utensils and ensuring products were packaged so that no mixing would occur was critical.

Ultimately, the founders decided Jacob had to be let go. Even though letting the employee go was difficult and resulted in the firm being understaffed, it was a blessing in disguise: The fact that Jack and Toby had stood firm on the rules became a model for all the employees. The two entrepreneurs also realized then that they needed to be very clear about the rules and procedures for their employees if they were going to have to fire some of them over these issues. As a result, the entrepreneurs developed more detailed rules and policies tailored specifically for their firm.

QUESTIONS

1. What other standards do you think Kosher Home will need for employees?
2. In your proposed business what would be the key human resources issues you might need to consider?
3. If you have two employees who cannot get along and it is disrupting the delivery of your product or service, how would you work out a solution?
4. If there is no solution, how would you determine whom to let go?

[*] Recall as noted earlier that the activities in each chapter are laid out to imply sequential behaviors.

Human resources management includes the hiring, inspiring, and managing of personnel, which is one of the toughest and yet most important functions for an entrepreneurial firm to develop.[1] For example, hiring personnel who are consistent with your business strategy and style is critical to business success, since without them it is unlikely that you will be able to implement your strategy. Similarly, managing the firm's personnel so that you increase employee skill development allows the firm to develop a key resource. This type of resource is one that other firms cannot easily copy and one that may, in turn, lead to better firm performance.[2] The business of simply meeting the basic legal requirements of your human resources function can be daunting—yet is insufficient for the firm to be successful. This chapter will explore the rich set of issues, both legal and nonlegal, that a start-up business must consider.

The Elements of Human Resources

LO10-1

Explain the elements of human resources.

Human resources has been defined in economics as the quantity and quality of human effort directed toward producing goods and services. What this means to an entrepreneur is far more than simply having the right number of people with the right skills for a particular job. The success of entrepreneurial firms pursuing new opportunities requires a number of deliberate actions by the business founder concerning human resources issues.[3]

human resources
As defined in economics, the quantity and quality of human effort directed toward producing goods and services.

The elements that this chapter will explore include hiring employees (job descriptions, job advertisements, discrimination, job interviews, testing, job offers); retaining employees (compensation and benefit systems, wages and hours requirements, performance reviews); and dealing with difficult employees (probation, firing). After dealing with these issues, the chapter will also examine several other issues specifically relevant to dealing with family in a business. We specifically address family business in this chapter. One of the most important differences between a typical entrepreneurial start-up and one that is a family business are issues related to human resources as some of the employees are family.

The Process of Hiring Employees

LO10-2

Discuss the process of hiring employees.

To visualize how important hiring is to an entrepreneurial firm, compare the impact of one person in a large organization to that of one person in a small organization. If a large organization has 1,000 employees, one problematic employee represents only 0.1 percent of its workforce. In a small entrepreneurial firm with five employees, one employee causing problems represents 20 percent of the workforce. An unhappy person not working at full capacity will result in the entrepreneur spending an inordinate amount of time dealing with the problems caused by the troublesome employee. Thus, a poor employee has a triple impact on the entrepreneurial firm: (1) the owner's time is lost; (2) the organization does not fully benefit from the employee; and (3) the problems may bleed over to other employees. Where larger firms can absorb the resulting difficulties due to their built-in slack (excess resources), an entrepreneurial firm can be devastated by a bad hiring decision. The process of finding and hiring new employees is critical and should involve a series of deliberate steps.

Job Description

A **job description** describes the job that is to be filled. In an entrepreneurial business, this document is not meant to be a formal, highly structured document as it might be in a large corporation.[4] Nonetheless, we highly recommend that all positions that are hired into the business have a written job description. Too often entrepreneurs say they know what they want in an employee, but they never write it down. The reason is probably multifold, including a lack of time, an unclear picture of the new position, or a desire to remain flexible for the right individual. However, the process of generating a job description will assist the founder immensely as he carefully considers

job description
Document that describes the job that is to be filled.

the skills, background, and ability of a potential new hire. All too often, the entrepreneur who fails to develop a job description ends up hiring someone because he "likes" the person.

Taking the time to write down those skills and capabilities will go a long way toward ensuring that all dimensions of the job are considered. The operation of a computer and the ability to do word processing is widespread. However, if you do not ask the job applicant if she has those skills, you may be unpleasantly surprised after hiring the person. You may even need to be more specific than simply saying you want those general skills. For example, you may need someone who can work particularly fast at typing or entering data into and using an Excel spreadsheet. However, the skills that the average person may have in these areas may not reach the level you need for the specific software program you are using. You will need to determine what skills are critical at the stage of hiring and those that you are willing to help develop after you hire someone.

In a similar vein, there is information you need to share with the potential employee. If you require uniforms, will they be provided or are they an employee's responsibility? This kind of information may be seen by the founder as a small matter, but it may be enough to impact whether or not an employee will be happy in the job. Imagine the impact if an employee arrived on the first day only to be told that he was responsible for bringing in his own tools, but no one had mentioned that to the employee. When making a hiring decision, the new businessperson needs to consider whether there are skills not required today but which may be needed in the near future. Putting the job description in writing helps in this process by ensuring that all the elements of the job are considered, as well as forcing the business owner to consider changes as the firm grows. A brief example of a job description is shown below:

Job Title: Furniture Refinisher

Salary: $37,900–$57,200 per year

Benefits: Medical for employee is provided at no cost to the employee. Medical for family is provided whereby the employee pays a premium equal to the difference between the family-policy premium and the employee-only premium.

Vacation: Two weeks of vacation will be earned after six months of employment.

Sick Days: The individual will accrue one sick day for every two months of employment.

Description: This individual will be responsible for evaluating, repairing, and refinishing a variety of office furniture, including desks, cabinets, file cabinets, bookcases, and chairs.

Skills: Skills needed in woodworking, metal fabrication, upholstery, as well as general carpentry skills. Having completed a carpenter apprenticeship program is a plus.

EXERCISE 1

1. What jobs will be necessary in your new business during the first year?
2. Briefly outline the skills needed to handle each job.
3. Given the reality of the market where you are located, how much do you expect to invest in salaries and benefits during the first year?

Many businesses today are virtual, whereby the employees all work remotely and stay connected via the Internet. There can be a tendency in the fast-paced, Internet-based society to not take the time to write up such items as job descriptions. In that setting, however, it is critical that the entrepreneur be even clearer on expectations and sharing information since the direct interpersonal connection is reduced.

Job Advertising

Once the entrepreneur has generated the job description, she needs to try to attract the largest pool of applicants possible for the job. Although word of mouth is a means to advertise for a job, we suggest that it is but one of many possible methods for attracting a wider audience. There are a variety of ways to advertise and a large number of organizations that can help promote information on your job opening at little or no cost. These include:

- College placement offices
- Trade associations
- Employment agencies
- Online job posting

Similarly, if the business is in a very visible location, then a sign can be posted outside the office. If the business is a virtual business, then placing a notice on LinkedIn or specific discussion boards where people with the specific skill set you desire visit.

A more expensive means to locate potential employees is to use some type of job-placement website with a classic help-wanted ad. These include the many sites available such as Monster, Indeed, Ziprecruiter, and more localized sites. These advertisements vary widely in cost and ability to reach the audience you desire. Information from the advertising location on readership or viewership, statistics on reply rates, and rates charged are all important pieces of information for the entrepreneur seeking to place an advertisement.

Finally, for very unique skill requirements, there are companies that do an extremely good job recruiting and placing people. These companies traditionally charge the company seeking to hire the employee, and that fee can range from a set fee to a significant percentage of the placed employee's first-year salary. This can be very expensive, so the new business owner needs to clearly think through the benefits of casting a more professional net.

In writing the advertisement for the new hire, the entrepreneur should keep it concise and oriented toward the basic information needed for a potential applicant to evaluate his qualifications for the position. However, there are thousands of generic advertisements placed every week that look identical to one another. You will want your advertisement to be distinct enough to stand apart, so it will draw the attention of potential applicants. If possible, your ad should communicate the culture of the firm and your desire to have the right person join your organization. The advertisement should also express excitement about the business. Overall, remember to write the ad to sell the job and the business honestly to the potential employee. Even though many people who read the advertisement may decide that they are not qualified, you would like them to walk away with a positive view of the business from their reading of the advertisement.

The advertisement should ask applicants to submit a résumé and a short list of references. Virtually all potential candidates will have résumés prepared unless they are applying for jobs at the very lowest skill levels. A deadline should be established for applying in order to fairly evaluate the applicants in comparison to each other. A typical wording might state, "The application deadline is January 15, 201X, or until the position is filled." This allows a comparison across candidates after January 15 and also allows for the possibility that no one will meet all of your requirements by the deadline.

Discrimination. It is important in designing the advertisement that the firm use nondiscriminatory language. Title VII of the Civil Rights Act prohibits **discrimination** in hiring, dismissal, level of pay, or promotions on the basis of

discrimination
In the workplace, hiring, dismissal, level of pay, or promotions based on race, color, gender, religious beliefs, or national origin of the employee. Such actions are prohibited by federal and state laws.

Supreme Court rulings have played a huge part in how human relations function in modern business.

race, color, gender, religious beliefs, or national origin. This law currently applies to all firms with more than 25 employees. However, there are also state laws that may apply to firms with fewer than 25 employees, plus other federal laws that put the entrepreneur at risk even if the firm has fewer than 15 employees. Therefore, the entrepreneur should avoid any discrimination or even the appearance of discrimination. The adherence to a nondiscrimination posture takes effort by the entrepreneurial business.[5]

The entrepreneur should write job descriptions and advertisements in a nondiscriminatory manner. Terms such as *salesman*, *handyman*, *young*, or *counter girl* should be avoided. Antidiscrimination laws do not require that you hire any one particular person; however, you must give everyone an equal opportunity to be considered. The wide advertising of a job and the establishment of a job description will help the entrepreneur establish that he or she acted in a nondiscriminatory manner. If you advertise widely, you have not prevented anyone from applying. The job description helps to ensure that all individuals are judged on the same basis.

EXERCISE 2

1. Pick a key position in your new business and list the specific deliverables you expect from the person in that position.
2. Write an ad for this position in your new business.
3. Have your fellow classmates evaluate it for effectiveness and proper language.

Interview

Regardless of whether the candidate has or does not have a résumé, you should ask each one to fill out an application for employment. It is important to establish set criteria for every applicant and to have the ability to track exactly who applied for each position. A variety of generic forms are available at any office supply store or via any one of several software packages. We believe that at a minimum, the following information should be obtained in the application and interview process:

- Name, address, telephone numbers (home, cell), e-mail address (if applicable)
- Other addresses for the past three years
- Social Security number (SSN)
- Driver's license number and state of issue
- Work history
- Date available for work
- Position for which the candidate is applying
- How the candidate heard about the job
- Education and training
- Professional organization memberships
- Any record of conviction and, if so, details of that conviction
- If not a U.S. citizen, the appropriate documentation authorizing the candidate to work. (Note that sometimes very good people will come

and apply for a job and ask you to sponsor them for a work visa. This typically requires several thousand dollars, which the applicant may be willing to pay. You as a business owner will have to be willing to take the time to act as a sponsor. You will also have to verify that this job requires some unique set of skills that only this person has.)

- References

Once the candidate pool has been set, the founder must winnow the candidate list down to a group to be interviewed. If possible, we recommend that you sit with the applications and the job description at one set time period, so that a direct comparison of the applications and job needs can be completed. Many businesses use some type of video feed program (e.g., Facetime or Skype) to interview candidates without having to incur travel costs. Those candidates who do not have the minimum requirements for the position should be rejected immediately. Those who closely match your job description should be the ones where you focus your next effort. Those that appear to be the best fit in that group should be considered for an interview.

During the interview process (whether it is in person or done electronically), it is important that the entrepreneur not discriminate against any given individual. There is a short list of topics that should not be asked about in any interview.[6] You should not ask questions about, nor can you consider in the hiring decision, any of the following:

- Age
- Race
- Disability
- Gender
- National origin
- Religion or creed
- Marital or family status
- If English is your first language
- If you drink alcohol
- Arrest record
- Pregnancy or if you have children
- Military discharge status

Note that you can ask about prior convictions, but you may not ask about the candidate's arrest record. An arrest is not the same as a conviction. In summary, the discussion during the interview should be based on the needs of the job.

The interviewer should also use the interview to provide a realistic preview of the job and the company to the interviewee. You should not overpromise what the job will be or the relevant job security present in the firm. Too often firms try to sell the employee on the job by overpromising what the job is or underselling the expectations the firm has of the employee. Instead, you should provide a valid and realistic perspective that promotes the firm and also sets appropriate expectations for the potential employee.

Although it is a tedious process, the founder needs to check as many references as possible. However, the entrepreneur should balance the checking of references with the nature of the job. If the job requires very low skills, then perhaps the need for references might be a bit less important. However, if the job is more central to the organization and has higher required skill levels, then the importance of the references increases. The entrepreneur should also closely check references if the employee might be in a position to put either the business or its customers at risk. Thus, someone mowing lawns for you in a lawn mowing business might require only a simple employment check. In contrast, a new plumber, who will have access to clients' homes and must be covered under your liability policies, requires a more rigorous background check. The references proposed by the interviewee and any others that the founder believes would have knowledge of the person should be contacted. If the job requires driving, as it does for many salespeople, then the entrepreneur should inform the job candidate that he will be checking the candidate's driving records. In order to make these contacts and receive information, the person hiring must have signed permission from the candidate.

The interview process and the checking of references is a time-consuming process. It is for this reason that the screening of résumés or applications prior to beginning this course of action is important. However, the entrepreneur does not want to shortchange the interview and reference process. As a result, you should keep your mind open about which candidate to hire after an initial interview and background check, and then conduct a second round of interviews.

Some organizations go even further in making sure that the person is right for the firm and the firm is right for the person. For example, several organizations that we have worked with over the years require the candidates to spend a full day at the company. During the day the applicant will work with other members of the team, have lunch with the other workers, and get to see and be seen in the day-to-day environment. An evaluation by the employees of the company and the candidate at the end of the day provides the needed feedback to management prior to a hire decision. The entrepreneur should keep continuous records of all advertisements that have been run whether a physical publication or on Internet, who responded, and the criteria for the job. If there are ever questions and/or if discrimination is charged, this type of record keeping will be quite helpful in defending your actions.

Testing

Ultimately, the entrepreneur should choose the employee that best meets her needs. Testing can be a part of that decision process, and testing comes in many forms and in response to many concerns. Some business owners wish to assure a drug-free workplace, and the founder has the right to insist on testing.[7] In fact, some states, such as Florida, offer a reduction in the rates of workers' compensation insurance if the business has a drug-free workplace program. This can be encouraged by requiring all new employees to submit to a drug test as well as requiring all employees to periodically submit to random drug testing. Most entrepreneurial businesses choose not to have drug testing, and they face risks in conducting such tests. The privacy rights of employees can come into conflict with the desire to have a drug-free workplace. Entrepreneurs are encouraged to consult a local lawyer before beginning such a program. An interesting question that faces many entrepreneurial firms in a state like Colorado or Washington is how to deal with a drug-free workplace when marijuana is legal in the state.

Another level of testing consists of testing candidates on the basic requirements of a position. For example, we know of one business that requires all of its potential employees to pass a 10-question, multiple-choice basic mathematics test to be eligible for an interview. The founder's explanation for this is that every employee is handling cash, and basic mathematics is a fundamental need of the organization. A number of companies extend this testing to include personality testing or work behavior testing. All of this is perfectly acceptable if a direct link between performance on the test and the skill set necessary for success on the job is made.

EXERCISE 3

1. Prepare a set of questions for an interview of the potential employees you identified in Exercise 2.
2. What types of testing might be appropriate for your business?

The Offer

Once you have selected your top candidate, you need to extend an offer. We suggest that all of the details of the offer be developed prior to any conversation with the candidate. Consideration should be given to the possibility that the candidate might wish to negotiate the deal. You should decide on your negotiation position and how much you are willing to offer for this particular candidate. While this negotiation is primarily an art, we do recommend that once an offer is made, you allow the candidate the opportunity to accept the offer or return to you very quickly with a counter position (establish the amount of time that the offer will remain in effect before you withdraw it and offer the position to another candidate).[8] At that point, you can make whatever concessions you think are appropriate and then respond to the candidate. Once an offer is agreed upon between the parties, it should be put in writing by the founder, signed, and sent to the candidate. Only when the candidate returns a signed original of the offer letter should you consider the position closed. We don't wish to be too formal with this process, but we have watched many entrepreneurs be frustrated by employees who thought their agreement differed from that actually offered by the firm.

The Means for Retaining Employees

LO10-3

Analyze the means for retaining employees.

Once you have actually hired each new employee, you'll want to retain the employees that perform well. The above process takes a lot of time and effort. If it is done poorly and you don't retain the employee, then this process can simply be a waste of valuable time and money, not to mention the loss of productivity as each new employee has to be brought up to an acceptable level of performance. Therefore, the entrepreneurial business needs to retain those employees that add value. The key issues here are the compensation and benefits offered as well as the method and means of reviewing performance.

Compensation is going to be a hot topic among employees, which makes equitable treatment in an employer's best interest. Are there ever instances in which paying two employees a different amount for the same job and experience might be a good idea?
©James Brey/Getty Images RF

Compensation

The compensation system chosen by the firm is the aspect that is often highest in the minds of employees. In building the compensation system, the entrepreneur needs to maintain a fair and equitable system for all employees, both now and as the firm progresses into the future. Salary and benefits may appear to be a private matter between you and your employees; however, history would suggest that all information quickly becomes public knowledge among fellow employees. Even if the firm is a virtual one and no one works in the same office, the employees will easily communicate with each other on issues of compensation.

equity theory
The theory that we all judge how we are treated relative to how we see others being treated.

Equity theory is helpful to understand how to avoid problems with compensation. This theory argues that we all judge how we are treated relative to how we see others being treated. Employees have a powerful need to feel that their compensation given their level and performance is equitable relative to that of other employees in their firm or other individuals in similar situations.[9] As a result, all employees need a clear rationale for how their compensation stacks up against that of others in the organization. Employees can accept that someone who has been in the organization longer has a better overall package; however, they will have difficulty accepting it if they are hired at the same time as another employee and do the same job but receive less pay. The owner might have a reason for that difference, but the presence of the difference would be difficult for the employee to understand.

Owing to the level of complication within the workforce of most large firms, these firms require a systematic program that evaluates comparable employees both in the region and around the country. This systematic review of the employees will often include the following: (1) how they performed relative to their objectives; (2) plans for future employee growth through experience and training; (3) defined objectives for the next year; and (4) pay raise being awarded.

An entrepreneurial business needs a significantly less developed system than does a Fortune 500 company. The entrepreneur should decide on a basic form of compensation. The options might include the following:

- Hourly wage
- Salary
- Commission
- Hybrid/profit-sharing system

hourly wage
The amount paid per hour for work performed.

salary
A set amount of compensation for a given time period.

commission
Payment by the entrepreneur of some percentage of sales, typically associated with the compensation of sales representatives.

An **hourly wage** is simply the amount paid per hour for work performed. A **salary** is similarly straightforward, as it is a set amount of money for a given time period. A **commission** is involved when the entrepreneur pays an individual a percentage of sales and is typically associated with the compensation of sales representatives.

A commission compensation system can be abused and may be a source of frustration for employees and the entrepreneur. Abuse of the system can occur when the salespeople are so focused on their commission that they fail to watch for the overall good of the firm. For example, a commission can be based on sales made, and those sales could involve financing instead of immediate payment. A difficulty might occur with a particular salesperson who books a large number of clients who are financially weak and who later default. The salesperson got the commission, but the firm is stuck with bad accounts.

hybrid compensation system
A compensation system where there is a salary along with commission.

profit sharing
An example of a hybrid compensation system. The firm may set some relatively low level of salary but offer to share a percentage of the profits at the end of the year or some other period of time with the employees.

bonus
Similar to profit sharing, a reward offered to the employees based on their performance. Typically, bonus systems are not as well defined as profit sharing; instead, the level of reward is left to the discretion of the entrepreneur.

Another potential for frustration with commissions comes when the firm either does, or does not, change the commission program to reflect the growth of the firm. To illustrate, when the company is young, the first salesperson may be paid a commission of 20 percent on sales. As the firm expands and hires more salespeople, the business would suffer if the owner attempted to continue paying a 20 percent commission. At this stage the firm is more established, with customers contacting the firm directly. Yet, the founder would have difficulty telling the new salespeople that he would be making less per sale than the existing salesperson. Similarly, the founder would have difficulty in cutting the existing salesperson's commission. Therefore, when you set the first salesperson's commission, realize that you may be establishing the standard for a long time in the organization. Any change that lowers compensation will be viewed by those employees already in place as a negative.

The entrepreneur can also build a **hybrid compensation system**, where a sales commission can be paid in addition to a basic salary. **Profit sharing** is another example of a hybrid system. The firm may set some relatively low level of salary but offer to share a percentage of the profits at the end of the year or some other period of time with the employees. A **bonus** system is similar to profit sharing; a bonus is offered to the employees based on their performance. Typically, bonus systems are not as well defined as profit sharing; instead, the level of reward is left to the discretion of the entrepreneur. The time period for which such profit sharing or bonuses are given should be relevant to the individuals in the firm and within the realities and constraints of the business. It is important that the entrepreneur provide bonuses in a timely manner. An entrepreneur may visualize a year as a relevant time frame, whereas workers may be looking for monthly or quarterly feedback on their performance through a bonus. It is very useful for the entrepreneur to consider the industry standards in developing her compensation system. Those in your industry who have developed a compensation system that works have the potential to provide information not only on the level of total compensation but also on how to structure it.

Legal Issues with Pay. The **Fair Labor Standards Act (FLSA)** establishes a minimum wage for workers. Virtually all workers (other than workers on small farms and administrative employees) are covered by the act. This law requires that employees be paid a minimum wage, which in 2017 was $7.25 per hour. However, states or cities may have higher minimum wages. For example, in 2014 the minimum wage in Seattle was $15.00 per hour. It is even possible for local governments to pass their own minimum-wage requirements as long as they exceed the federal requirement. Many major cities have what they call "living wages"; a living wage is an index wage that requires the minimum wage to be at least what someone who works 40 hours a week needs to stay out of poverty. If your business is covered by the FLSA, it is also covered by the Equal Pay Act, which requires that an employer not discriminate in pay to men and women who do the same job.

Fair Labor Standards Act (FLSA)
The act that established a minimum wage for workers.

The FLSA requires that all nonexempt employees who work over 40 hours a week be paid at the rate of time and a half. Compensatory time is not typically allowed from one pay period to the next. Therefore, if the pay period is only one week and you have employees work overtime this week, then you must pay the overtime rate for those hours. You cannot give them time off next week as compensation. If, however, the pay period is two weeks, then time off in one week can be used as compensation for time worked in the previous week. Thus, the firm needs to be very clear on its time frame for issues such as pay. Another legal issue related to pay is child labor. The government closely regulates the use of children under age 16. The entrepreneur would be well advised to seek out legal advice if he plans to employ children, even his own, in the business if they are younger than 16 years of age.

Benefits

There are a wide variety of benefits that any business can choose to offer. For example, benefits can include the following:

- Paid vacations
- 401(k) plan
- Paid holidays
- Medical care
- Retirement plans
- Sick leave
- Life insurance

The package of benefits the firm chooses to offer can have as much impact on the success of the entrepreneurial business's human resources efforts as the compensation offered.[10] Some benefits represent costs to the entrepreneurial business but are relatively easy for the entrepreneurial business to provide. For example, a two-week vacation after an individual has worked at a firm for a year can be provided by most firms. There is an expense since you are paying an employee that is not working; however, calculating when the benefit is due and managing the process is relatively easy. The same may be said of paid holidays and sick days; the sick days build up over time as the employee is working with the entrepreneurial business.

Benefits that are more difficult to effectively manage include medical care and retirement plans. Medical care is one of the most expensive costs for any business, and yet it is also one of the most desired benefits by employees. The latest figures from the Bureau of Labor Statistics found that benefits cost 31.4% of total compensation costs for an employee.[11] However, historically, the plans most entrepreneurial businesses provide are not the full-coverage plans provided by large businesses. In fact, at one time many small businesses did not offer any insurance to employees. While changes are always being made, currently under the Affordable Care Act, firms with more than 50 employees are required to offer their employees insurance. Federal and state governments have established exchanges grouping individuals and small firms together in an effort to seek to lower the health care insurance expense. There are also tax incentives for small entrepreneurial firms to encourage them to offer health insurance to their employees, even if it is not required. One of the biggest beneficiaries of this act, in fact, are the entrepreneurs in a business that employs only themselves and their family. Now under the exchanges these individuals can obtain a more reasonably priced health care product.

The impact of such costs to the entrepreneurial business compared to the large business cannot be overestimated. One of the biggest differences in the cost of auto plants for such large American auto manufacturers as General Motors versus those from Japan, such as Toyota, who have plants in the United States, is health insurance. The Japanese-owned plants' pay is equivalent to that of GM, but the Japanese auto plants are all new, and they have hired young, healthy workers. The American auto plants, on the other hand, are staffed by older workers, a trend that only gets more severe with every layoff, since workers with seniority get laid off last. The result is that the health benefits cost GM far more than they cost Toyota. Health insurance can be a competitive disadvantage when U.S. companies have to compete against companies from countries where health care is provided by the government.

If the entrepreneurial business does offer insurance, the cost of health insurance per employee will be more than that for a large firm. Large firms have the advantage of spreading losses across a large number of people,

ETHICAL CHALLENGE

You were part of a two-person team that was assigned to interview candidates for a new sales position. The new employee will be on the road several days a week and will need to be able to work with a wide variety of people. The main client companies that the salesperson will have to work with are manufacturing companies in rural areas.

During the interview, your partner starts asking a series of questions that make both you and the candidate very uncomfortable. After the first interview you talk to your partner about the questions that he asked. They included these: (1) Are you married? (2) Do you own a car? (3) How do you feel about dealing with people who have no formal education? (4) Do you have any children? (5) Do you attend church?

Your partner explains that knowing these answers will really improve the chances of choosing the right candidate and will make it more likely that you will keep that person. He tells you that if the candidate is bothered by the questions, then he or she doesn't have to answer, and that will tell you all you need to know.

QUESTIONS

1. What should you do? Is there any justification for asking these questions?
2. What if the candidate doesn't mind answering the questions?
3. What if the candidate does mind answering the questions—how should you respond?

whereas the entrepreneurial business can be dramatically impacted by a single significant claim. To illustrate, out of 100,000 employees you may expect 23 heart bypass operations and can budget for that with insurance. In an entrepreneurial firm, you may have only 10 employees—but what if one employee needs a bypass? The insurance company has likely not charged you enough to cover the costs of the bypass, no matter what it has charged you in the past. The result is that the entrepreneurial firm is a much greater risk than the large firm. This leads to higher deductibles, user copayments, and out-of-pocket costs for employees of an entrepreneurial business. The entrepreneurial businessperson will need to investigate the costs and packages offered by a variety of insurance companies. The sources for such insurance can be located through other entrepreneurial businesses in the area, the chamber of commerce, national trade associations, and the Internet. The entrepreneurial businessperson would be well served to investigate and compare various medical programs closely before choosing one.

Although traditional retirement plans have fallen out of favor, some types of personal retirement plans have become quite popular. Referred to generally as 401(k) and Roth 401(k) programs, they are usually offered by an employer so that employees can contribute to their retirement on a tax-free basis. Most entrepreneurial firms do not provide any matching, although many larger firms offer matching funds for these accounts.

Performance Reviews

No matter the size of an organization, whether the business is brick and mortar or virtual, performance reviews should be a part of the management system.[12] In a **performance review**, the entrepreneurial business owner reviews the employee's goals and outcomes on those goals over some given period. Workers are motivated by more than salary. The formal conversation with a worker who is doing a good job, showing that her work is appreciated, is another form of compensation. If the worker is not performing as expected, then the employer should also be very clear about that fact. Although we recommend that all performance reviews be done in writing, we do not suggest that a complex form need be used. Providing effective feedback can be handled in a number of ways but should cover each of the areas of the employee's responsibility. Entrepreneurs should provide formal feedback on a frequent basis. Not only does the new firm operate in a manner that does not lend itself to waiting a year, but newer generations of employees are looking for more frequent and specific feedback.

performance review
Review by the entrepreneurial business owner of the employees' goals and outcomes on those goals over some given period.

During this feedback, the founder is well advised to provide praise where it is warranted and detail any deficiencies and areas that need to be developed. As will be discussed in the next section, it is critical that the employee know exactly how his performance is compared to expectations. Too often the entrepreneur does not want the confrontation, so will give only positive feedback but then later fire the person. The result is a surprised employee who may seek legal representation to get compensation for being unfairly fired. As will be discussed in the next section of this chapter, if you have not provided accurate performance reviews, the individual may win if the parties do go to court.

Central to being able to do any review is the setting of goals for the employee. The setting of such goals allows the entrepreneur to judge how well the employee is performing. These goals should be realistic, tied to the performance of the company, based upon some measurable outcome, and reset periodically. Again, the time frame for these goals should be one that is relevant for the employee. Thus, for some jobs it may be weekly or biweekly, a time period that relates to the pay period. For most jobs, the relevant time frame will be quarterly or perhaps longer.

LO10-4

Determine the pertinent aspects of employee probation and firing.

The Pertinent Aspects of Employee Probation and Firing

Despite your best efforts, you will at some point hire the wrong person. At times you may find it necessary to fire that person. The entrepreneur has the right to hire and fire employees. However, you still must have legitimate, well-documented reasons for the firing. If you do not, you are opening yourself up to a lawsuit by the dismissed employee. Furthermore, you should provide all employees (short of their having done something illegal) the opportunity to rectify their performance.

Struggling employees are a reality that most entrepreneurs will have to deal with at some point.

Thus, you must develop a paper trail regarding all employees and must be particularly diligent in your efforts to assist a poorly performing employee. Recall that in discussing reviews, we argued that an employer needs to be honest about an employee's performance and document those times when she is not performing as desired. This can form part of your paper trail. You specify over time what is expected of the employee and then document how she is or is not performing to expectations. Firing someone for poor performance that has been documented over a time and in which you have offered a means to correct the problem will go a long way toward providing a defense in any legal proceeding and a proper justification for the employee. If there are concerns about firing an employee, the entrepreneur should not hesitate to contact a lawyer for advice.

When hiring an employee, an entrepreneur typically does not consider issues such as a noncompete agreement or a secrecy agreement (one designed to protect the competitive advantage of the business). However, when you dismiss an employee these issues may become critical. If you are a restaurant owner and have several secret recipes that are central to your success, then you do not want a disgruntled kitchen worker to post that information on the Internet. If the business is based on computer coding, then key employees might remove documentation when they leave. This can render the code almost useless as it cannot be easily modified. In both cases the employee signing proper documents can help to mitigate the issue. At the initial hiring, you can limit later problems if you consider having your employees sign the appropriate documents. These documents are available via many software packages and are relatively easy to understand.

LO10-5

Understand Broad Coverage Regulations and Laws.

Broad Coverage Regulations and Laws

There are a series of issues related to employees that all entrepreneurs must be concerned about, although not all companies may be directly impacted by each in the same way.

workers' compensation
Laws designed so that employees who are disabled or injured while on the job are provided with some type of compensation.

Workers' Compensation. **Workers' compensation** laws are designed so that employees who are disabled or injured while on the job are provided with some type of compensation. Workers' compensation insurance is regulated by each state, with some states running their own insurance funds, whereas others use private firms. The rates of the insurance can differ widely in the various states, depending on the regulations and generosity of the state legislature. However, the rates for individual firms within that state are fairly

YrFURN—AN APP FOR FURNITURE

Now that the business was up and running, Brad, Kyle, and Brandy had a number of close friends and family members who wanted to help them and who had skills related not only to a SaaS business but also to the running of an entrepreneurial business. The team was burning the candle on both ends starting early every day and working 18 hour days, seven days a week trying to handle all the issues that were arising. The firm has started to hire employees to handle customer service calls and e-mails. The team soon discovered that rather than improving the situation, these new employees often did not have the skills necessary to effectively deal with their customers.

However, there were other hires that did help the founding team significantly. Brad and his sister had always been close. She was within a month of earning a degree in accounting from a national career school and wanted to work with her brother. The team agreed to hire her to maintain all of the books, which included keeping track of every item that came into and out of the business. Unfortunately, Brad had no idea how much they should pay her or how he would interact with her in the business.

Brad and his sister had sat down together at a local coffee shop one morning to talk about her joining the company. He shared with her that he desperately needed someone to help him since he was struggling to keep track of the expenses, with so many vendors to work with and with his attention on developing customers. He asked her how much she wanted to make and what she thought would be reasonable. She told him that she was willing to take a minimal salary and virtually no benefits if she could participate in the profits of the business. She suggested that if she really did her job well, then the whole company would do well. The team had held out stock for just this type of thing. The debate among the founding team was whether the position in accounting for Brad's sister was critical enough that it deserved an equity stake. The founders did like the fact that she would be taking very little from the business unless it did very well. They wanted to minimize cash outflow early on, and they wanted to reward early employees of the business.

The team agreed that she would start the next day and that she would work whenever she was not in class. They would pay her the going rate for a bookkeeper, and she would be entitled to any benefits the business had available. The team decided that she would be awarded 1 percent of the business; however, she would only get this if she stayed with the company for three years (or until they were bought-out by another firm). If she left before that, she would not have any equity stake in the business.

The relationship between Brad and his sister worked very well. Since his sister was such a big help, the team started to think about other relatives to bring into the business to allow the founders more time to focus on customer development.

The pressure to hire others close to the founders proved more problematic. The firm needed someone with extensive customer service experience. They originally thought that the business would be self-running with little interaction with customers; they were very wrong. They could not keep up with the calls, e-mails, texts, or postings from retail customers and even furniture salespeople. Furthermore, they were stunned to find so many great suggestions for improvements embedded in the complaints. They were hiring numerous customer service agents. Kyle's father really wanted them to hire one of his cousins. Kyle's father had invested $100,000 into the business and was quite vocal about his thoughts.

This cousin had almost 20 years of experience in customer service, but he had been in some legal trouble. His personality was a bit rough and while he was talented, he did not seem very motivated. This suggestion proved very troubling. While the team was open to hiring family, as shown by hiring Brad's sister, they were not sure if they should hire Kyle's cousin.

QUESTIONS

1. How would you handle the situation facing the team regarding Kyle's cousin?
2. What alternatives would you suggest in staffing?

standard and are generally based on the industry and size of the firm. The payments are typically given to the employee if he qualifies, whether or not the entrepreneurial business owner was at fault for the injury from an unsafe workplace. However, the payments to the employee are limited to partial wage replacement and medical bills. The employee cannot receive workers' compensation for pain and suffering. The employee usually cannot sue the entrepreneur for his injury if he accepts workers' compensation payments.

OSHA
The Occupational Safety and Health Administration, which is charged with protecting the health of workers.

The Occupational Safety and Health Administration. The Occupational Safety and Health Administration (**OSHA**) is charged with protecting the health of workers. OSHA has attempted to shape its regulations to be more lenient toward small business. For example, whereas all employees of any size firm are covered by OSHA, firms with fewer than 10 employees do not have the record-keeping regulations that apply to larger businesses. Additionally, any fines are lower for entrepreneurial businesses with fewer than 25 employees than they are for large businesses. Effectively, OSHA will not impact many new entrepreneurial businesses, such as small retailers. However, other entrepreneurial businesses, such as manufacturing firms, need to pay specific attention to OSHA requirements regardless of their size. We would advise an entrepreneur to consult with industry associations and your local chamber of commerce to judge the potential impact on your firm. If the impact looks to be significant, then a visit with your attorney is merited.

Falls from ladders are a leading cause of injuries on construction sites. One OSHA requirement is that employers must provide fall protection and the right equipment for the job.
©Huntstock/Getty Images RF

unemployment compensation
Financial assistance for some period of time to those people who lose their jobs through no fault of their own; provided in every state by law.

Unemployment Compensation. Every state has an **unemployment compensation** law, which was put into place to provide financial assistance for some period of time to those people who lose their jobs through no fault of their own. Unemployment compensation pays to the former employee some set amount of money for a given period after she loses her job. During the time she receives these payments, she is required to look for a job. The entrepreneur is required to pay an unemployment tax to help fund this system. That tax will vary by state depending on the unemployment benefits that state provides, as well as the experience rating (the history of unemployment) of the company.

The Americans with Disabilities Act. The Americans with Disabilities Act (ADA) generally covers those firms with 15 or more employees and provides that each and every business must provide unfettered access to all disabled people. This means at a minimum that ramps or elevators and Braille signs must be provided in the business. The entrepreneurial business may also be required to offer special accommodation to employees who need physical adaptations to work at the firm. Some states and cities have additional requirements beyond the ADA that may impact the entrepreneurial business in this regard.

LO10-6

Distinguish the unique aspects of human resources within a family business.

The Unique Aspects of Human Resources Within a Family Business

A special category of human resources management is encountered when the business is a family business.[13] A family business is one that is generally run by and for the benefit of a particular family. Human resources in such businesses are still critical, but since family members make up many of the significant employees in the company, everything becomes more delicate.[14] The combination of father, mother, uncles, aunts, and children all in the business has impacts well beyond the standard human resources practice. The introduction of family brings new issues into the business that must be considered. One difference that arises in such businesses is that hiring does not always occur in the manner described previously in this chapter. Instead, the family member is simply hired without interviews, clear understanding of their skills, or explicit mutual understanding of expectations. You should recognize that this does not eliminate issues of discrimination if the firm is large; placement of family members because they are family members into positions in a large business can still result in charges of discrimination. The key issue in discrimination is that everyone is not given a fair chance at a job.

Managing family members can be difficult, as these individuals know all of the "hot buttons" that make a fellow family member angry. However, there is no effective way to fire or truly discipline the person without causing major ruptures in the family structure. The result is that family businesses and the human resources in them have more in common with family counseling than they do with the legalistic methods described in the earlier part of this chapter.

One especially tricky human resources issue that occurs in family business is succession.[15] The business may have been founded by the father or mother. He or she is ready to retire and has a son and daughter in the business. Who in the next generation becomes the leader of the business? Too often the parent will put off the tough choices. The parent dies and a battle results in the family. To avoid this situation, the parent needs to choose a successor and prepare that person for the position by ensuring that he or she has all the contacts and understanding necessary to be successful. If the parent then decides to leave the business early, that parent needs to step back and let the designated son or daughter lead the business as he or she sees fit. Firms struggle to survive with two leaders of the business. The fact that the other child is not selected can result in difficulties in the family. Again, part of the means to overcome these difficulties is to work with professionals who act almost as family counselors to help the family see the rationales for the choices and how to deal with them positively.

SUMMARY

This chapter examined the wide range of issues involved in the human resources aspects of hiring, rewarding, and compensating employees. Many legal issues are involved in this arena, which explains why there are books devoted exclusively to the topic. We have endeavored to develop a basic checklist for the new entrepreneur to use in the process of developing the firm's human resources requirements.

The chapter examined a number of complex issues related to human resources and the hiring process, including the following:

1. Hiring
2. Job descriptions
3. Job advertising
4. Discrimination
5. Interviewing
6. Testing
7. Making an offer

The chapter also examined the means by which companies retain employees, including the following:

1. Compensation
2. Legal issues
3. Benefits
4. Performance reviews

Human resources is intimately tied to keeping businesses within the legal structures that affect all companies. These include the following:

1. Workers' compensation
2. OSHA standards
3. Unemployment compensation
4. ADA—the Americans with Disabilities Act

The chapter finished with a short discussion about how human resources actions are changed by being in a family business.

KEY TERMS

bonus 194
commission 194
discrimination 189
equity theory 193
Fair Labor Standards Act (FLSA) 195
hourly wage 194
human resources 187
hybrid compensation system 194
job description 187
OSHA 200
performance review 197
profit sharing 194
salary 194
unemployment compensation 200
workers' compensation 198

REVIEW QUESTIONS

1. What means would you suggest to improve the process of hiring the right people for a new business?
2. What elements should a good job description contain?
3. What are the various ways to advertise a job opening?
4. What means would you suggest to help avoid job discrimination?
5. What techniques improve the interviewing process?
6. How can testing be used to improve the hiring decision?
7. What is the best method for making an offer to a candidate?
8. How does compensation impact the ability to retain an employee?
9. What legal issues are related to the retaining and firing of employees?
10. What benefits might be offered to new employees?
11. How are performance reviews related to employee retention?
12. Describe the impact that OSHA could have on a new restaurant operation.
13. How does ADA affect retail organizations?
14. What is the impact on hiring decisions when the business is family owned and run?

BUSINESS PLAN DEVELOPMENT QUESTIONS

Develop a human resources plan for your new business that consists of the following items:

1. Pay scale plan
2. Benefit plan
3. Advertising plan
4. Interviewing and hiring plan

INDIVIDUAL EXERCISES

Identify an entrepreneurial business in your area and ask the entrepreneur the following questions:

1. How do you recruit new employees?
2. What is your turnover among employees?
3. How do you compensate individuals to try to retain them at the firm a long time?
4. Do you employ family members? Why or why not?

GROUP EXERCISES

Rewrite the following poorly worded job descriptions

1. JOB TITLE: Coffee Room Lady

She has to do everything to keep the four coffee or snack rooms running smoothly: ordering and stocking merchandise, as well as collecting money and controlling credit. She is told what to do by verbal instructions from the supervisor. If she has any problems she tells him about it and he tells her what to do.

One of the things she does is to order the merchandise from various vendors. When it arrives she puts it on the shelves for the employees. When they buy the stuff she collects the money or IOUs using a calculator or paper and pencil. Every day she has to clean the coffee room. This includes the coffeepot.

2. JOB TITLE: Break Room Attendant
Perform duties to order and stock merchandise, maintain cash and credit control, and clean the four break rooms. Work from instructions. Buy merchandise from vendors. Stock merchandise for purchase by employees. Maintain bookwork for cash and credit transactions. Clean break room and equipment daily. Notify supervisor of problems. Use cleaning equipment, coffeepot, calculator, paper, and pencil. Follow safety rules and keep work area in a clean and orderly condition. Perform other related duties as assigned.

ENDNOTES

1. S. Haber and A. Reichek, "The Cumulative Nature of the Entrepreneurial Process: The Contribution of Human Capital, Planning and Environment," *Journal of Business Venturing* 22 (2007), pp. 119–45; B. Marint, J. McNally, and M. Kay, "Examining the Formation of Human Capital in Entrepreneurship: A Meta Analysis of Entrepreneurship Education Outcomes," *Journal of Business Venturing* 28:2 (2013), pp. 211–24.
2. J. Hayton, "Strategic Human Capital Management in SMEs: An Empirical Study of Entrepreneurial Performance," *Human Resource Management* 42 (2003), pp. 375–92.
3. R. Baptista and M. Karaoz, "The Impact of Human Capital on the Early Success of Necessity Versus Opportunity-Based Entrepreneurs," *Journal of Small Business Economies* 42, no. 4 (2014), pp. 831–47.
4. M. Carroll and M. Marchington, "Recruitment in Small Firms," *Employee Relations* 21 (1999), pp. 236–51.
5. R. Carlson, "The Small Firm Exemption and Single Employer Doctrine in Employment Discrimination Law," *St. John's Law Review* 80 (2006), pp. 1197–273.
6. Vivian Giang, "11 Common Interview Questions That Are Actually Illegal," *Business Insider*, July 5, 2013, http://www.businessinsider.com/11-illegal-interview-questions-2013-7.
7. E. War, "Employee Drug Testing: Aalberts and Walker Revisited," *Journal of Small Business Management* 29 (1991), pp. 77–84.
8. Liz Ryan, "Ten Things Never to Say While Negotiating a Job Offer," *Forbes*, May 30, 2016, https://www.forbes.com/sites/lizryan/2016/05/30/ten-things-never-to-say-while-negotiating-a-job-offer/#370d924a5fd0.
9. Sarah Carmichael and David Burkus, "Your Coworkers Should Know Your Salary," *Harvard Business Review*, March 10, 2016, https://hbr.org/ideacast/2016/03/your-coworkers-should-know-your-salary.
10. S. H. Appelbaum and R. Kamal, "An Analysis of the Utilization and Effectiveness of Non-Financial Incentives in Small Business," *Journal of Management Development* 19 (2000), pp. 733–64.
11. Bureau of Labor Statistics. December 8, 2016, https://www.bls.gov/news.release/ecec.nr0.htm.
12. Heather Clancy, "Why Your Next Performance Review May Be More Useful," *Fortune*, February 22, 2017, http://fortune.com/2017/02/22/performance-reviews-employee-feedback-frequency/; Tom Gimbel, "Why Your Younger Employees Hate Performance Reviews," *Fortune*, February 13, 2017, http://fortune.com/2017/02/13/millennial-employees-performance-reviews/.
13. K. Eddleston, F. Kellermann, and T. Zellweger, "Exploring the Entrepreneurial Behavior of Family Firms: Does the Stewardship Perspective Explain Differences?" *Entrepreneurship Theory and Practice* 36 (2012), pp. 347–67.
14. S. King and G. Solomon, "Issues in Growing a Family Business: A Strategic Human Resources Model," *Journal of Small Business Management* 39 (2001), pp. 3–14.
15. "Business Succession Planning 101," *National Law Review*, February 23, 2017, http://www.natlawreview.com/article/business-succession-planning-101.

chapter 11

learning objectives

After studying this chapter, you will be able to:

LO11-1 Discuss the basics of a marketing plan.

LO11-2 Explain how to develop a pricing model.

LO11-3 Differentiate between the various types of promotion available to a new business.

LO11-4 Identify the methods for sales management.

Marketing

MIKE RADENBAUGH—RAD POWER BIKES

Mike Radenbaugh started his business when he was in high school. Attending a rural high school, 15 miles from his home, and owning an unreliable car, Mike looked for alternative ways to get to school. While Mike was an avid bike rider, he found that riding his bike was a problem not only because he was often late due to traffic or the weather but also sweaty when he arrived. The result was he started to work on a means to motorize his bike with an electric battery.

Mike's first efforts were clunky with old parts and big lead-acid battery. Eventually, he was able to refine his prototypes to the point where he had a bike that looked good and worked well for getting him to school. The response of those who lived in the community led him to realize that there may be others who would like a similar bike. Therefore, in the summer of 2007 he founded his company modifying existing bikes to be electric bikes.

Mike was joined by two friends in the business effort who were passionate about bike transportation and had unique skills. Tyler Collins focus was online sales and marketing, while Marimar White-Espin was an expert in operations and systems and as result focused on production. Mike spent his efforts on product development and manufacturing. For the next 7 years, the founders ran a conversion and installation company that refitted existing bikes to be electric bikes while they worked their way through college. The business grew mostly by word of mouth and people finding them on the Internet.

All that changed in 2014 when they decided to build their own bikes from scratch and sell them in a direct to consumer model. Rad Power Bikes value proposition centered on offering premium electric bikes for almost half the cost that a consumer could buy a comparable bike for in traditional bike shop or online through distributors and dealers. The entrepreneurs aimed to run a very lean operation, and going direct to consumer meant that they bypassed a dealer distribution system that added a lot of cost to the bike.

In May 2015 the entrepreneurs introduced a new electric bike, RadRover, which had a Samsung lithium battery and an in-wheel electric motor all on an aluminum frame. The more powerful battery and lighter frame meant the bike had a range of 50 miles and could hit speeds of 20 mph. That distance and speed could be easily extended if the customer added some pedaling power. It took only three to five hours to fully recharge the battery from an ordinary outlet.

The entrepreneurs used crowdfunding to finance the development of the RadRover with an Indiegogo campaign that brought in over $200,000. Since then they have launched the RadCity (an electric commuter bike), RadMini (a folding bike), and RadWagon (a cargo bike capable of carrying up to 350 lbs.).

The company is under pressure from cheaper foreign-made bikes and high-end bike companies in the United States. However, the entrepreneurs believe they continue to have a competitive advantage by offering a very high-quality bike at a lower price point than the market. They have hired 13 people with several of them focused strictly on customer service—providing advice, parts, and accessories.

In 2017 Forbes named all three co-founders to its 30 under 30 listing in the Manufacturing & Industry category.

Questions

1. Do you believe product enhancements should be the focus of the entrepreneurial venture or expand the existing products into a broader market?
2. What marketing advice would you provide them for expanding their market?
3. Who do you believe their perfect customer is?

Sources: https://www.radpowerbikes.com/pages/about-us; "Rad Power Bikes Founders Make Forbes 30 under 30 list," *Bicycle Retailer*, January 5, 2017, http://www.bicycleretailer.com/north-america/2017/01/05/rad-power-bikes-founders-make-forbes-30-under-30-list#.WLct4oWcHug; Derek Markham, "RadWagon Electric Cargo Bike Could be the Ticket to Low-Car Living," TreeHugger, August 26, 2015, http://www.treehugger.com/bikes/radwagon-electric-cargo-bike-could-be-ticket-low-car-living.html; Murray Newlands, "Is There an Electric Bike Revolution? Seattle's Rad Power Bikes Thinks So," *Forbes*, November 15, 2016, https://www.forbes.com/sites/mnewlands/2016/11/15/is-there-an-electric-bike-revolution-seattles-rad-power-bikes-thinks-so/#5182cf603746; Derek Markham, "Roll Over Everything with the RadRover Electric Fat Bike," TreeHugger, May 8, 2015, http://www.treehugger.com/bikes/roll-over-everything-radrover-electric-fat-bike.html.

At this point in the process of building a new business, you should have developed a unique product or service to offer and established its business operations so that it is physically able to offer that product or service to the public. However, if the public does not know about the product or service, regardless of how much effort has been put into the business to date, all of that prior work will accomplish very little. The old axiom "if you build it they will come" works fine in the movies, but the reality of business is that you must do quite a bit to make potential customers aware of your business. People are creatures of habit, and in order to get some form of change in their behavior, marketers must stir the target customers to action.[1] Thus, a new business must aggressively seek to make its target customers aware that they have a product or service that offers a solution to a problem of those customers. A central part of this is that the business needs to build a credible case as to why individuals need to use their product or service, either because it is better, cheaper, higher quality, or reparable, or has some other characteristic that other existing products or services do not offer.

LO11-1

Discuss the basics of a marketing plan.

Basics of a Marketing Plan

Creating the business and the means to operate it is a necessary but not sufficient condition for business success. An underlying theme throughout this book is that planning and preparation are critical to the success of an entrepreneurial business. This does not mean plans do not change. Rather, with a plan a firm is better able to evaluate its past actions, changes in the environment, and what actions need to occur in the future. The same is true of marketing. There is little to manage, record, or evaluate without having customers. Therefore, to be successful, the entrepreneurial business also needs a specific plan for its marketing effort. Then when faced with changes, the firm can adapt that plan rather than begin anew with each small problem faced.

marketing plan
The plan developed by the entrepreneurial business to specify who the customers are and how they will be attracted to the company.

The **marketing plan** is developed by the business to specify who the best customers are and how they might be attracted to the company. Developing a marketing plan can be a complex undertaking. Furthermore, marketing is a complete discipline whose level of complexity can be daunting. There are many consulting companies and business courses available to aid you in developing your marketing plan. As the new business grows, it may be advantageous to employ an outside firm to help focus on its marketing efforts. However, hiring experts or consulting firms at start-up will cost you resources at a time when it would seem that the business could least afford the expenditure. Because such expenses can be very high in some cases, they can be hard to justify when you have limited cash despite the additional knowledge gained. The information garnered in the process of researching and evaluating the market that you are operating within will return substantial benefits to the owners.

The focus of this chapter is the establishment of a workable marketing plan that can be developed by any entrepreneur. This plan should, at a minimum, include identifying your market, specifying the ideal and general target customer, determining a pricing policy that is in line with the strategy of the firm, developing promotion, determining sales management procedures, and finally, forecasting sales. After developing each of these areas for a marketing plan, we will spend some time discussing unique distribution channels.

Identifying Your Market

In Chapter 4 we outlined a means for the entrepreneur to identify her target market and identify the "industry" in which she will be competing. This was done in the context of developing the idea for the business. The new business

KOSHER HOME

Jack and Toby had tested their idea and adapted it by starting small in their local area working with synagogue. To build their business Jack and Toby needed to expand their business. One issue that became clear quickly was where to sell; there are approximately 12 million individuals in the United States who keep kosher. But many people in the United States eat kosher food simply because they believe it is healthier. The result is that an estimated 21 percent of Americans either regularly or occasionally eat kosher products. The firm could not target all of these people even if they wanted to do so.

Jack and Toby decided to purchase data from a large national firm on individuals who meet the general criteria of potentially observing kosher at home. The firm would identify people who likely keep kosher by mining big data on issues such as who had donated to specific charities, purchasing characteristics, and activity in specific organizations. Even with all that, looking for 12 million people would again be expensive; therefore, they needed to determine where to focus. Kosher Home is in the Western United States, and in looking there they determined the three cities with the highest Jewish populations are Los Angeles (4.1 percent of population is Jewish and it has 90 kosher restaurants), Las Vegas (4.1 percent of population is Jewish and 14 kosher restaurants), and San Francisco (3.1 percent of population is Jewish and 17 kosher restaurants). Focusing in these concentrated cities also meant that they could ensure that kosher-certified trucks would deliver the products to the customer.

The entrepreneurs decided on a multiple prong approach to using this data. They would do the following:

- Initial mailing of a brochure to each person on the list.
- Follow-up phone call to the home of the person.
- Follow-up e-mails to the person.

The key they felt was to build that personal relationship. The goal being that once they had a customer they would communicate with their friends and family promoting the product.

QUESTIONS

1. Do you think that Kosher Home original target market (isolated communities) should still be its target market?
2. What is the benefit of focusing the firm on urban concentrated locations?
3. Out of all of the marketing outlets available, which will be the most productive for Kosher Home? Why?

now needs to use that information as a foundation to develop a practical and actionable plan for attracting those customers.

An initial point needs to be made about the marketing effort for a new business. These marketing efforts need to be as clearly stated as the business's mission statement.[2] The use of such a mission and/or strategy statement helps to ensure that the firm is focused and will not seek to be all things to all people. The same focused approach needs to be used by the new business to market the firm's products/services to those customers that are most likely to buy its products or services at the price desired. As appealing as it may sound, an entrepreneur is not trying to get every person to buy from the business. Instead, the entrepreneur is trying to reach those individuals most likely to actually buy from the business.

You will recall from our prior discussions that for a fixed location, business customers will travel only a given distance to buy from that business. This distance grows shorter as the number of competitors in the area increases. Therefore, a sandwich shop, hair stylist, dry cleaner, or similar business could reasonably expect to have large numbers of competitors and should expect customers to drive only a very short distance to shop at their location. If you market to too broad an area, the costs can be financially draining. A newspaper advertisement in a paper that serves a large city has virtually no targeting to specific consumers—it is a shotgun trying to hit a small target for the

Geography and marketing can work hand in hand for business success.

©Blend Images/Alamy RF

entrepreneur. A new business would simply hope that someone who had a need for its product or service would happen to see the advertisement, live close by, and respond to the advertisement. The entrepreneur needs to target their advertising very specifically to the market they are pursuing.[3]

Recall the exercise from Chapter 4 where we asked you to develop a reasonable geographic estimate of the radius your business might draw customers from if you are not starting an app or Internet-based business (we will discuss how this analysis changes for Internet businesses below). As we stated in an earlier chapter, if you open a sandwich shop in the downtown area of a city, the shop most likely competes with other sandwich or fast-food shops in a one- to two-mile radius, and perhaps less, if walking is the primary means of transportation for downtown lunching workers. There are limits to how far someone will travel for a sandwich. Drawing a practical radius around your potential new business location will help the business target the customers who are most likely to patronize your business.

In considering the geographic area, the entrepreneur should also consider how he will reach the potential customers in the area. Every contact outside his market area is really wasted money. There is a wide variety of potential marketing activities that can be pursued, including flyers, sponsoring events within the area, using social media, advertising on location specific apps, and affiliating with complementary businesses. As you look to define your geographic area, there will be several methods that fit naturally with part of your geographic area but which may not be consistent with another geographic region. Thus, the new business must target the right geographic area and do so with the right marketing tool to be successful.

To illustrate, consider a business that plans on using direct mail to contact potential customers. You may find that a given zip code covers 85 percent of the market you planned to target. The other 15 percent of your target geographic area is split between two other zip codes. The cost of addressing those two zip codes, owing to the smaller size and special attention, may exceed the addressing costs for the other 85 percent of your market. Therefore, the reasonable thing to do at this stage would be to limit your target market to the one zip code. Defining a geographic market served should be a more complex analysis than simply drawing a circle around your potential business. The drawing of a circle is only a start. Building on that, the entrepreneur should make a reasonable estimate of what she can do with the least resources to reach the most people as efficiently as possible. Once the geographic area is defined, then the business owner should remember that the money invested in her marketing effort should be primarily, if not exclusively, aimed at her target market area.

Target Customer

Once the geographic area is defined, the entrepreneur needs to define the particular segment of the market that he is seeking to serve. For example, if the entrepreneur is establishing a children's consignment and resale store, it is not likely that parents who send their kids to an exclusive private school in the area will shop there. Even though the private schools may ask you to advertise in the programs for their school events, spending your scarce advertising dollars in that venue would be a wasted effort if you expected these parents to buy there (although seeking their clothes to sell might be useful).

As part of the basic market/customer identification performed in Chapter 4, you have identified broad customer groups that the new business would serve. Now your operational marketing plan needs to go deeper and specifically identify potential customers. Most new businesses have restricted resources, and this is one of the things that differentiate an entrepreneurial business from a large business. It is this lack of funds that pushes the entrepreneurial firm to direct all of its marketing resources toward reaching the ideal customer. Therefore, once the entrepreneur has identified the target market, she needs to identify the specific customers who meet those criteria in the market area chosen.[4]

Consider a new athletic club that was opening in an upper-income area of a large city. Most gyms in the region charged $100 to $150 per month for someone to belong to the club. That represents a cost of $1,200 to $1,800 per year, not including any initial membership fees. An individual would need a reasonable income to support that expense. The owners of the gym also believed that the distance that individuals would drive to a gym was slightly farther than the distance they would drive to a sandwich shop. A brief survey of members enrolled at a friend's gym in a nearby city found that most customers drove approximately two and a half miles or less.

The owners drew a circle of two and a half miles around their location and found that a relatively high population lived in the area. However, this region of the city had a mixture of individual homes and apartments. The newer apartments typically had their own small gyms. Additionally, many of the older apartment complexes were relatively inexpensive and populated by individuals who worked service jobs in the restaurants and retail outlets in the area. The owners came to realize that their perfect customers were the individuals who lived in the houses in the target area. This helped the owners pinpoint their customers very specifically. Those individuals they needed to reach were homeowners in their area who had a high enough income to join the gym and renters who did not have the service already in their apartment complexes. Advertising could now be targeted using real estate records. The methods used could be direct mail or phone calls (to those not on the national do-not-call list).

This is not to suggest that the gym would turn away potential customers who did not meet their ideal profile. There might be some customers who joined the gym because they heard about it from another source. There might be others who would join with a friend. However, these customers would not be a direct result of the firm's marketing, so the cost of obtaining those customers would be much lower.

Once the target population is identified, the entrepreneurial business should try to answer questions such as these: (1) How many of these individuals exist within your market area? (2) What percentage of these individuals do you believe is reasonable for you to attract as customers? (3) What is the percentage in the general population of people that belong to a gym? (4) Do these numbers match your cash flow projections? (5) What do you need to change if they do not?

Of course, the analysis above changes for a business that is operated exclusively or primarily on the Internet. This type of business serves a wide geographic footprint that must be accounted for in the design of the business. The company's Web presence may be a significant factor in a purchase or inquiry.

The definition of a customer for businesses that primarily use the Internet is the same as for all other firms. However, these firms are clearly not limited by geographic limits in the same manner. A firm has to be clear about its reach whether that is local, regional, national, or international. As always, a key issue becomes how to cut through the clutter on the Internet such that the target customer can locate the business.

For example, a simple term such as Kosher Home can generate thousands of responses on a search engine such as Google. Designing the site appropriately

EXERCISE 1

1. Identify your ideal customer. Describe in short bullet points what characteristics this customer has that makes your product or service attractive.
2. How will you make the ideal customer aware of your business?

and even paying for placement will allow your business to appear in the first page of views when a search is executed. This all falls under the category of Search Engine Optimization. Search Engine Optimization is the application of techniques for improving your chances of being "seen." All search engine programs (Google, Bing, Yahoo, etc.) offer companies the opportunity to pay for special placement at the top of particular word searches.[5]

LO11-2

Explain how to develop a pricing model.

How to Develop a Pricing Model

Pricing of your product or service is a critical consideration for the new business. One approach is to value your products for what you believe they are worth to the market. Most entrepreneurial businesses charge a premium for their products or services. However, the higher the profit appears to be, the faster competitors will challenge the business.

One method for an entrepreneurial business with specific products that are comparable to other products in the market is a cost-plus pricing method, where the firm determines its cost and then adds onto that cost some level of profit it determines to be appropriate. This method can be difficult to implement effectively.[6] The method requires that the entrepreneurial business initially determine what the total cost is for a particular product. This break-even point is referred to as the **pricing floor**, since the entrepreneur will not want to price a product at a loss. In calculating the floor cost of your product, you will need to include your estimated cost of marketing and an administrative overhead allocation. The cost of your estimated marketing might change as you develop your marketing plan. As a result, you would need to go through the pricing process several times as you refine the marketing plan.

pricing floor
The break-even point, or the lowest amount that can be charged for a product or service while still making a minimal profit.

loss leader
A product or service that is sold at a nonoperating loss (i.e., the price only accounts for the actual cost of the product) to simply get customers in the store.

Occasionally, the new business owner may choose to have a product that is referred to as a **loss leader**. In other words, a business may sell something at a nonoperating loss (i.e., the price only accounts for the actual cost of the product) to simply get customers to patronize the business. A new business may also chose to price products/services in a variety of low profit or no profit ways to spur sales overall. Our advice is that the new business owner not employ loss leaders until the business has developed some substantial momentum. The entrepreneurial business owner needs to get the firm on solid ground before employing such actions, which take considerable skill and have high risk associated with them. A loss leader can become quite a burden if customers buy the leader without buying the other services or products of the company. A loss leader approach is actually the main one used by many Web-based businesses. They seek to grow the number of unique users by providing something for free. The hope is that the numbers will rise to a point where the company can either sell advertising or ancillary products or product add-ons in order to earn revenues.

In determining the cost of a product or service, we also suggest that the new business owner avoid the time-consuming nature of making detailed calculations for every product, especially if there is a wide product selection. Instead, the entrepreneur should place products in reasonable categories that balance the need for detailed pricing, as compared to managing an ever-expanding database of information. The major airlines are large enough to have the resources and the technological ability to manage a system where every person on the plane may pay a different price, depending on when the ticket was bought and on predicted occupancy of the plane when it takes off. As an entrepreneur, you will not have that level of sophistication, nor is it necessary for an effective pricing policy. Therefore, having a data system that generates information that is useful and manageable should be the focus.

Information on the costs of the business is the foundation for determining **cost-plus pricing**. Although the "plus" aspect can be determined in a variety of ways, the most common approach is simply adding a given percentage to the cost basis for the business.[7] A new business can seek a profit of 10 percent, 15 percent, 20 percent, 25 percent, or 100 percent or more on product categories. Part of the desired profit margin will be determined by how competitors price their products and how much overhead the business has. There will be a comparison effect as consumers evaluate different firms' products and make decisions based on an internal cost–benefit calculation. For example, you may have a retail clothing store. Your prices may be higher than those at a large mall store, but your personalized service may be evaluated by consumers to be worth that premium. Alternatively, you may be able to charge a premium if you have an image that consumers believe to be valuable. If another clothing store opens up down the street and has clothing lines similar to yours that are priced at 15 percent less, then your business might start seeing a real loss of customers. Significant deviation between your prices and those of your competitors will have to be justified and will have to have merit with customers. The entrepreneur needs to keep abreast of his competitors and their pricing to be able to make such judgments.

cost-plus pricing
Pricing in which the entrepreneur initially determines her cost structure and then determines what profit margin is desired and adds that to the cost.

Pricing a service is a bit more complex. With a product, you have a potential price floor based on costs, whereas a service such as counseling, a web-based game, an online store, financial advising, or interior decorating has time as the primary operational cost. There will still be overhead expenses (rent, computers, utilities, etc.); however, the principal value inputs are your education and experience, which are difficult to establish as a cost. In the case of services, we encourage the entrepreneur to more closely examine the pricing of competitors. These prices can be critical information in determining how to value your service. We would suggest that you do not underestimate the value of experience. A consultant with extensive experience delivering expert testimony in courts will be able to charge far more than a consultant just starting out. A business built on a **SaaS (Software as a Service)** model or even a business built exclusively on an app should be priced based on the goals of the organization. If that is building up users, the model might include a low price while a value-based model will be priced significantly higher.

SaaS (software as a service)
This business model is based on providing all or most of the business value electronically and remotely.

The entrepreneur providing a service should also recognize that pricing is a valuable tool to balance customer flow with the time he has available. There are price-sensitive customers who will make decisions based solely upon price; therefore, for those customers, as the price goes down customer flow goes up, and vice versa. Entrepreneurs who have been in business for a while may find they have too many low-margin customers and cannot provide the level of service they would like to provide. Thus, as their customer base increases, they might need to raise prices to limit the customers coming in at an unprofitable level so that they can serve them and profit from their business adequately.

In establishing pricing, there are several caveats that the entrepreneur should remember. Typically, a business starting out will need to offer an even greater value for the money charged to build a customer base. Once the business has developed a positive reputation, the value offered to the consumer can be changed to provide a bit more financial benefit to the company. Recall that individual consumers are generally unwilling to change the suppliers of their goods and services. As the business grows, the entrepreneur can shift from a cost-plus type of pricing to one that is based more upon what the market will allow.

A second caveat applies to the actual price charged. Small increments of money should be avoided regardless of the exact percentage of margin desired. Thus, rather than charge $1.01 for a low-cost item, a more attractive pricing

EXERCISE 2

1. How will you price your product or service? Why?
2. How will you validate your pricing plan with customers?
3. What do your competitors charge? Why should your price vary from that industry standard?

would be $0.99. The $0.02 difference makes a reasonably large difference in appeal to consumers. Similarly, when prices are over $1,000, the entrepreneur should avoid using cents in the price.

Finally, the new business owner will have to determine if she wants to offer a quantity discount. Much of this decision is based on the nature of the business that the entrepreneur establishes. For example, a retailer typically does not sell in large enough quantity to be concerned with such issues.

LO11-3

Differentiate between the various types of promotion available to a new business.

The Various Types of Promotion Available to a New Business

promotion
The means by which a business advances its product or service.

Although it is only one part of marketing, people often think of marketing as the promotion of the product or service. **Promotion** is the means by which we make our product or service known to potential customers. The most readily seen versions of such promotion are visual advertisements, viewed on the Internet, station, or seen on television. However, there are many means of promoting the business and each has varying costs and impacts. Promotion must be targeted to the market and customer groups within the industry, as we discussed previously in this chapter. Furthermore, you will want your promotional efforts to reach the specific target consumers in the most efficient manner possible.

pure promotions
Promotions that are strictly financial arrangements in which you pay for some outputs, such as radio advertisements.

mixed-model promotions
Promotions that cost something but also have an element of community support.

virtually free promotions
Promotions that have very limited financial cost but have time-commitment requirements from individuals in the firm.

Although most promotional efforts involve some type of financial commitment, there are some promotions that are strictly financial arrangements in which you pay for some outputs. These are referred to as **pure promotions**. There are other promotions that cost something but also have an element of community support and are referred to as **mixed-model promotions**. Lastly, there are promotions that have a very limited financial cost but have a time-commitment requirement from someone in the firm; these are referred to as **virtually free promotions**. We will briefly discuss each of these ways to promote the business.

Pure Promotions

This category encompasses the majority of promotional efforts targeted by the firm. Any form of advertising that is purely designed to promote the products or services of the company falls into this category. This type includes use of signs, flyers, Web pages, newspapers, radio, trade shows, and television. Each of these will be reviewed briefly.

Signs. An oft-overlooked means of advertising the company comes in the form of a sign on the building or on the street, and on the letterhead/checks/business cards of the firm. A catchy name, a well-designed logo, and some substantial efforts to get the logo and name out can pay significant benefits in recognition and impression management. For most customers, there are myriad businesses with which they can spend their money. Why a customer spends that money with your business is at least partially a result of what that customer thinks of your business when that purchase decision comes about. Most sign firms will be willing to aid you in the development of whatever signage you purchase, although the quality of that advice may vary widely. The key thing to remember as you design your signage is that "simple but distinctive" is the goal.

Flyers. As we mentioned earlier in this chapter, if you can target a very specific geographic area and perhaps identify a likely customer profile, then using something as simple as a flyer might be very effective. Flyers can be delivered directly to the potential customers' businesses or homes, or they can be posted at appropriately visible spots. Flyers can be changed frequently, printed cheaply, and delivered with low-cost labor. Unfortunately, these very characteristics also mean that they have a smaller impact upon customers.

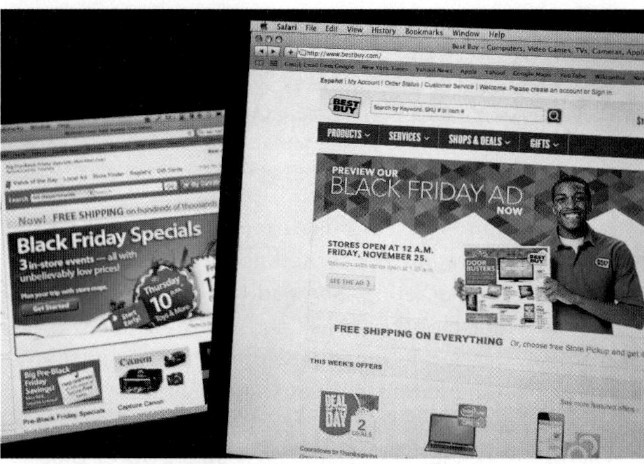

Black Friday, the day after Thanksgiving, is the busiest shopping day of the year. It has often been considered the unofficial start to the holiday shopping season.

©Andrew Harrer/Bloomberg/Getty Images

Social Media. All companies must have a well-designed Web page. Although a Web presence was considered a unique competitive advantage just 15 years ago, today it is an expectation. Customers look to Web pages for detailed company information, information about products and services, and the ability to purchase online. The sophistication of your Web page is dependent on the goals of your organization, but particularly for a business that sells a unique product with a wider target market, this may be one of the primary means to reach clients who live outside your region. The first step, acquiring a domain name, is an easy process available from a number of third-party providers on the Web. The second and third steps include purchasing space on a server (almost always a service provided by the same acquisition provider, as well as a number of Web design firms) and having a company design a Web page for your business or developing yourself if you have the skill set. For any Web design beyond the most basic, we suggest that you hire a professional website developer.

In addition, the Internet provides a ripe and growing means for promoting your company through social media. There is a wide variety of banner ads, pop-up ads, and promotional placements available for purchase. Companies can use the search engine companies (Google, Yahoo!, Bing, Firefox, Chrome, etc.) and/or can also work directly with other companies to advertise complementary items on their sites. **Search Engine Optimization (SEO)** is a term for all the efforts made to increase the visibility and placement of business information and is one of the best promotional approaches available. The cost of SEO advice is relatively inexpensive since there are so many companies providing these services. However, their knowledge and expertise can be critical to an entrepreneur's success.

Search Engine Optimization (SEO)
A term for all the efforts made to increase the visibility and placement of business information.

Newspapers. A standard but rapidly declining method for promoting your business is through a newspaper advertisement. This process involves two steps: One is designing the ad, and the second is placing it in the newspaper. Your local paper will work with you on both parts, or you can hire an advertising agency to design and place the ad for you. Either method is effective; however, newspaper advertisements mean that you will be paying for "views" by many individuals who will never be your customers. This a broad-based "shotgun" type of advertising. It should also be recognized that in many large cities there are specialized newspapers that may be better suited to your business.

Radio and Television. As with newspapers, a radio/television advertisement can be designed and aired by the station, or you can employ an advertising agency to develop and place an ad. Although there may be only one major newspaper in a market, it is likely that you will have a number of radio and

ETHICAL CHALLENGE

An entrepreneur was carefully examining her expenditures and was highly concerned about all the money being spent on marketing. She had hired a director of marketing eight months earlier and charged her with dramatically increasing the in-flow of customers for the business. The marketing budget was set at $200,000 exclusive of salary and benefits for the director.

The entrepreneur saw that almost $170,000 of that money had been spent in the last six months, and yet sales had only incrementally increased. When she met with the marketing director, she was told that it takes a long time and a lot of money to really see a difference in new customer acquisition. The marketing director has spent heavily to ensure their firm was well placed when someone did a search on a search engine. She let the entrepreneur know that she had some real insight into this because her brother and her boyfriend both worked for the company she had hired. In fact, she had placed virtually all of the media buys with her brother and boyfriend.

The entrepreneur was shocked by this and by the fact that virtually the whole budget had already been spent. Being on the first page of any internet search results that come up are vital. The shifting of the firm's web page and other techniques to meet the algorithm of the search engine seemed useful. But now there would be only $30,000 for the next six months of marketing. The entrepreneur was also very troubled by the fact the company the director was using employed both her brother and boyfriend.

QUESTIONS

1. Do you believe there is a conflict of interest here?
2. Should the entrepreneur expect results already?
3. What do you think of the fact that so much of the total budget has been spent?
4. What would you do and why?

television stations reaching your target group. This fact encourages us to recommend the use of an advertising agency whose loyalty is to you and which will place the ads regardless of the desires of a particular station. Radio and television advertisements are qualitatively more difficult and financially more draining than the other approaches. A radio or television advertisement must be designed to make your points, not upset anyone, and be sufficiently creative to draw customers to your business.

Trade Shows. Trade shows are events established around a particular theme where individuals are allowed to set up booths to promote their goods or services. In an industry such as toy manufacturing, there is an annual trade show (as well as numerous regional shows) in which all toy manufacturers display their products to sell to retailers. Similarly, for services, there are often trade shows in which an entrepreneur may wish to participate. If you have a wedding planning service, you will likely want to participate in bridal shows that happen in a number of cities. Trade shows can be expensive to participate in. However, a business can successfully participate by strategically focusing its efforts and ensuring that pre–trade show promotion makes potential customers aware of the presence of the firm at the trade show.[8]

Mixed Promotions/Community Support

There are a number of opportunities to promote your business and help out the community in a way that targets your customer base. Schools are in constant need of sponsors. Angling your sponsorship to those activities that will provide maximum exposure to your potential client base is an effective and relatively inexpensive means of keeping your name in front of them. Depending on the business, sponsoring sports activities, clubs in the school, events (dances and fundraising activities), and the like allows you to put your stamp on positive activities and hopefully reach the parents/children in your target customer group. For example, if you have a sports store in a city suburb, then sponsoring sports teams in the immediate area will allow you to be viewed as the official outfitter of those teams. The members of those sports teams, their families, and their friends will more than likely buy what they need from you in the future because of that relationship.

A second group of mixed promotions/community support are churches within your target area. Church groups look for sponsors to help in various activities for the community or for their youth. Carefully targeted efforts can help the new business reach an audience that is not normally as targetable.

Virtually Free Promotion

Virtually free promotions are also widely referred to as **bootstrap marketing**, because they require little investment. There are many opportunities to speak with groups about your business or even a specific area of expertise. To illustrate, the individuals that started the athletic club we discussed earlier in this chapter sought out speaking opportunities to groups in their area. The age of the typical Lions, Optimist, or Kiwanis Club member was within the range of the target market for the club. Additionally, those individuals that have time to commit to such organizations typically have sufficient income to belong to a health club. Therefore, the owners actively sought out opportunities to talk about health programs and how to start exercising to a variety of groups. To arrange such talks, they contacted leaders of the groups and offered their services, particularly at the beginning of a new year, which is when many people start off each year with fresh resolutions about their weight. Incidentally, that is when gyms have their greatest increase in membership.

bootstrap marketing
Marketing efforts that require little capital.

There are speaking opportunities with schools, clubs, and religious groups throughout the year. If the group is relevant to your business, you should take advantage of talking to it. The presentation should be more generic than a simple promotion for your business. For example, an owner of a garden supply store may visit with a club such as the Optimists about what flowers to plant in the spring or how to maintain lawns. After you make these presentations, it will hopefully be your business that the consumer considers when she seeks out a business in your field. There are other free opportunities that an entrepreneur should seek out including if an opening arises with the local news to comment on current events. There are many local morning talk shows for which you could put together something interesting for a show spot. For instance, if you have a restaurant, then you may be able to prepare a favorite dish on the local morning show.

In any case, it is important to remember that no single advertisement will be sufficient for the business. The attention of your target market is pulled in many different directions. It can take numerous "impressions" for an individual consumer to take notice of your firm or product.[9] When the firm develops its promotional program, it is important that a systematic effort take place that will commit the time and effort needed to be sure that the firm obtains the recognition of the consumers.

EXERCISE 3

1. Think of the promotional activities that are relevant for your business.
2. Which of these would be most economical for a new business?

LO11-4

Identify the methods for sales management.

sales management
The methods employed to, and the individuals who build and maintain relationships with customers.

The Methods for Sales Management

Sales management refers to the individuals who build and maintain relationships with customers, as well as to the methods and means by which they do this. To a certain extent everyone in an organization is involved in sales; however, sales management refers to how that whole sales process is managed. Issues that need to be considered include the following:

1. How many contact points will the business have with each customer?
2. How will each customer be greeted?
3. What is the process for managing a customer once an order has been placed?

YrFURN—AN APP FOR FURNITURE

The business had been operating for a short while and the team felt that most of the bugs had been worked out of the operation. Employees were handling everything quite well, but the growth in the app being downloaded had plunged to just a few dozen a day. Initially, YrFurn had received some very favorable free press from online blogs and even a short online article in one of the furniture industry magazines. That along with all the prerelease visits the team had made to various furniture stores led to a high initial download. The firm still had the issue of immediacy. Fewer than 20 percent of those downloading the app used it within the next few weeks after download. The team knew they had to do something significant to ramp up sales and uses.

They first considered as many free methods to publicize the business as they could. They contacted virtually every furniture-related magazine, outlet, and association offering to write articles for their readers. Several took them up on the offer as long as the article was not a blatant pitch for their product. It was obvious that free advertising was going to be a slow way to grow.

The group had done some rudimentary work in Search Engine Optimization (SEO) aimed at having their app and/or website come up early in the search whenever someone typed in "view furniture." The process had not been very expensive, but that word was not particularly popular. The more popular terms like "furniture" resulted in the firm rarely being on the first or even second page of searches and as a result few hits. The founders contacted several SEO consulting companies who promised that they could get them on the first page of searches for terms like "furniture," but it was going to be expensive.

The founders were also advised to run ads on a variety of sites including Facebook, eBay, and even Yahoo! They would have to pay for every click (i.e., every time someone clicked on their ad), and it could run up the price quite quickly.

While they were debating the best approach or approaches, Brandy suggested that they approach some of the really big furniture stores within a hundred miles of their location and try something different. She suggested that they work with the salespeople to get their app into the hands of any customer who did not buy something that day. YrFurn would set up near the front entrance and suggest to these customers that they download their app and try it out with all the furniture that store (and others) had to offer. They did not have to return to that store but hoped that the customer would do so. These customers would be offered the app for 99 cents instead of the standard $3.99.

She envisioned that the salespeople would guide these potential customers over as they had already shown a propensity to use that store, and this might get them back in the store. If the program worked well, these customers would use the app virtually immediately, and they could roll it out nationwide by partnering with stores and hiring local people to "man" the locations every Saturday and Sunday. It would be expensive at first but might lead to a lot of word of mouth.

QUESTIONS

1. Which of these approaches do you think the team should pursue?
2. If the team only had limited funds for this, what order would you suggest they pursue each idea?
3. What other ideas would you recommend to the team?

4. What look will the sales force present?
5. What controls are in place to ensure the quality of the product delivery?
6. How much information will be collected on each customer?
7. What will the business do with the information collected?

Designing and maintaining a sales management system is certainly part art and part tedious coding; however, a consistent approach and image that is designed around your mission statement will pay off tremendously as your business develops. The process starts with the hiring of a sales force.* One of the real keys to entrepreneurial business success is the development of a relationship with the customer. A popular television show (*Cheers*) was set in a bar and every time one of the regulars came into the bar, the employees in the bar would loudly greet him. That is the level of recognition that many customers desire from a business, whether they are being provided a haircut, buying clothes, or being advised on their investments. Indeed, one of the reasons for patronizing a new business could well be this expectation for exceptional recognition of loyal customers.

Beyond that level of recognition, returning customers are looking for an understanding of their needs, not just a fixation upon making a sale. A client of ours loves good wine and while he could go to any of a dozen stores that sell a wide selection of wine, he chooses a business run by a small group of wine enthusiasts. Every time he walks into the store, they greet him and make suggestions to him based upon their personal knowledge of his tastes. If he chooses a wine, even an expensive wine, that they believe he will not enjoy, they are quick to point this out to him and try to steer him to wines that he will enjoy. They are not fixed on the label, the price, or the fact that they have 30 cases of another wine back in storage. Relationship management is a process and a practice.

Forecasting Sales

Estimating sales without any history is an act of guesswork that is dependent on the founder's ability to narrowly focus on a customer group as well as to attract that customer group to purchase. There are many ways to estimate sales, all of which should be modified as real sales data become available. The two methods we will examine are market potential and customer demand.

Market potential methods take a macro look at the market and estimate potential sales for the firm based on the number of potential consumers in the target area. This data is then modified by a likely percentage of those potential consumers that will be attracted to the specific business. This can be estimated by looking at the direct competitors in the area or looking at close competitors in another, similar area. As we pointed out in Chapter 4, your direct knowledge of the market and your competitors will be essential to your sales forecast. To illustrate, the founders of the gym we have been discussing believed that their customer base would exist within a two and a half mile radius of the business and that those customers would own houses. Data from the census bureau and the local government helped identify the number of homes that met the criteria. The individuals starting the gym estimated there were one and a half potential consumers per house and limited their analysis to those individuals who had full-time employment. The result

*The role of the sales force considered here in Chapter 11 and the role of human resources considered in Chapter 10 illustrate an issue that the authors have highlighted several times. The chapters here present the material in a sequential manner, but many of the issues that the entrepreneur must decide occur simultaneously. The entrepreneur cannot know whom to hire for the sales force until she knows how she wants to market the product or service. Therefore, while the two issues are separated here, it is actually difficult to makes such splits easily.

was a potential population of almost 50,000 customers in their geographic area of interest.

The entrepreneurs must then estimate what percentage of their total market potential might use a business in a given area. For some companies, there will be industry information from industry associations. However, even without this it is relatively easy to estimate. For example, several of the fitness websites estimate the number of people who are members of a gym. Armed with that information and a quick search to find out how many gyms there are in the United States, our founders estimated the size of their likely customer base. They then talked to a gym owner in another state to find out how long it took that gym to ramp up to its current level of customer traffic. They made a logical estimate of monthly growth and then modified it as customers actually signed up for memberships.

The second method is customer demand. This method takes a micro look at the market and estimates how many customers the business can handle given its location, staffing, and other details. The founder then estimates how many individuals it will take to break even, make X profit, and so on. For example, one business made the following estimate:

1. The business had parking for no more than six cars at one time.
2. It was estimated that each customer would be in the storefront for an average of 30 minutes (two-thirds of the time browsing—20 minutes; one-third of the time purchasing—10 minutes).
3. Staffing meant that most of the time they could handle only four customers actually making a purchase.
4. The average sale was expected to be $850.
5. It was estimated that during a typical day, only twice per day would the storefront be full of customers.

With this information, the business was able to establish a sales forecast and staff the business appropriately. The owners modified their forecasts based on the experience of the firm once it was actually in business.

Distribution Channels

The prior discussion focused on entrepreneurial businesses that establish a fixed location and serve customers from that location in retail or wholesale. However, there are other methods of distributing one's products and services. These methods do not require an extensive understanding of geographic location, since, for example, they may be selling an industrial product that has the potential for a nationwide distribution, or they involve situations, such as Internet services or sales, where there is no limit due to geography. These methods include the following:

1. Independent sales agents
2. Contract sales force
3. Web
4. Mail-order catalogs

Each of these will be discussed in turn.

independent representatives

Representatives for a variety of products for a number of companies in a given domain who try to sell those products.

Independent Sales Agents. **Independent representatives** can be used to sell industrial products.[10] The independent distributor is the representative for a variety of products for a number of companies in a given domain. The independent representative agrees to sell or distribute each of the products for a percentage of the sales price. The percentage that the representative will receive depends on the demand for the product and how much effort the manufacturer wishes that representative to invest in promoting its product. A new business starting out needs to negotiate carefully the price paid to such representatives. Clearly, these representatives will promote those products for which they make the most money. Securing the right representatives for the right price can be crucial to achieving success when using this distribution channel.

Sales and marketing depend on each other for success.

©Yuri Arcurs/Getty Images RF

A new medical device company that we worked with for some time used distributors to sell its products. These distributors already had the necessary relationships with specific doctors, and these relationships are critical in the sales of any new medical product. Some doctors will actually allow representatives from certain sales agents into the operating room to help demonstrate the use of a new product. For this to occur, the distributor has to have salespeople with the proper training and relationships with the doctors. In this setting, choosing the right independent distributor was probably more critical than any other hire in the firm.

Contract Sales Force. A second distribution channel is a **contract sales force**. Contract sales companies provide independent salespeople with a wide variety of experiences and contacts on a contract basis. Thus, you can hire a sales force for your firm for a given period of time. Even though it is a relatively expensive means of jump-starting sales, it can be the difference between success and failure. We worked with a company whose entire business plan was dependent on quickly locking up venues in long-term contracts. Then, armed with those contracts, the company could market its service to potential clients. The process envisioned in the plan required more than 20 experienced salespeople for a period of nine months. After that time, all sales could be handled by four inside salespeople who were to be hired during this process. A contract firm provided more than 80 résumés, from which the founders selected 21 salespeople to initiate the business.

contract sales force
Independent salespeople with a wide variety of experiences and contacts, provided by a company on a contract basis.

Web. We have previously discussed the value of a Web presence as a means of promotion, and it can also be used as a distribution channel.[11] Internet-based marketing employs the Web in much the same way that a fixed-site store uses its physical location as an advantage. A company Web page displays the products, provides the means to ask questions about those products, and in many cases allows the customer to buy the products. The list of Web page capabilities and its uses for marketing is expanding daily. Such sites can be used by businesses that focus purely on Internet sales or by those that use it as a supplement to the other marketing efforts of the firms. Web-based businesses rely on the designs of their Web pages to present the information about the products and their benefits. Web design is a crucial part of the company process. However, it is important to remember that the Web page is there to sell products, not to show off some technical prowess in Web page design.

To illustrate, consider the wonderful graphics and animations that are capable of being included in a business website. These graphics take time to load, however, and that delay can be frustrating for your customers, especially if you are loading videos as a part of the Web page. Similarly, if you walked into a local store and no one offered to help you within five minutes, you would likely leave the store with no intention to return. That time frame is compressed when it comes to navigating a website, as customer patience is very short. Similarly, in designing the website, the entrepreneur should ensure that they do not design a site that works only with a particular browser type. The site must be usable, with the minimum number of clicks necessary for the clients to achieve what they wish to accomplish. Individuals will not roll endlessly through a series of screens to reach what they desire. Lastly, the content of the Web page must be timely. Time and effort must be dedicated to maintaining the Web page so that the information is accurate. A Web page is not something that can be created and forgotten.

The classic example that individuals can look to for a Web-based business that started small, although it is now huge, is Amazon.com. Amazon's website is accessible and easy to use. The site not only provides information but also allows customers to browse, purchase, pay for, and arrange shipping for any of millions of products. Businesses of most any product can also sell through Amazon or one of the many other sites including Etsy, eBay, etc.

Developing a system to the level of Amazon is prohibitively expensive for a new business. Every firm needs to determine if the Web will be its only outlet or if it will use the Web to supplement the business's fixed location. Web sales reach well beyond any physical boundaries and generally reach low-cost customers for the business. However, the business must offer very unique items that cannot be easily obtained elsewhere for there to be sufficient demand to warrant the time and effort involved with the mixed model. The end result may be that the time and effort to develop the Web page correctly may be more than the new business is willing to invest. If this is the case, the new business should still consider a basic Web page that provides information and directs customers to call to place their order. Such a site is relatively easy to prepare and maintain. The level of complexity increases dramatically as the business attempts to increase the capability to include the ability to order and pay for products.

Mail-Order Catalogs. The last type of distribution method is mail-order catalogs. While it might appear to be out of date, the reality is that catalogs remain a powerful force for driving sales.[12] Many businesses do not have a fixed retail location but instead reach customers through the mail. These individuals will mail a catalog to customers at their homes. The catalogs will display a consistent set of products and provide a means to order those products—typically over the phone but increasingly via the Web with an offer to talk to a person if needed. A professional company can be hired to receive the calls and send the orders to your business. Mailing out the goods themselves is typically not difficult, unless it is the Christmas season, where time sensitivity is critical and the standard delivery systems are overloaded.

As could be predicted, identifying which customers to mail the catalog to is a critical part of the process. A new firm cannot afford to mail a catalog to every person in the country. Thus, understanding and targeting your customer once again becomes critical. One useful means to do this is to buy a mailing list from a group that may have an interest in products that you wish to sell. For example, if you wished to establish a mail-order business for historical guns such as flintlock rifles, you could consider buying the mailing list of the National Rifle Association. Similarly, if you wished to sell environmentally sound cosmetics, you could seek to buy the mailing list of the Sierra Club and send the catalog to women on the mailing list.

In virtually all businesses you must be able to handle credit card sales and returns. Credit card fraud has been particularly troublesome for some time with various approaches employed to reduce its negative impact. The new business needs to estimate the number of potential credit card transactions as transaction fees need to be accounted for in the pricing of products.

SUMMARY

Marketing is a critical function in the entrepreneurial business. Too often the new business focuses strictly on the technological aspects of the product produced and not the customers.[13] To be successful, the new business must know which customers would be ideal targets for its products or service. It is clear as we examine this chapter that marketing of the product and the strategy of the firm share a great similarity. The new business must use its developed mission and/or strategy to narrowly target the perfect customers. If the new business does not understand these issues, it is easy to spend the firm's scarce resources in a manner that produces no tangible benefit.

KEY TERMS

bootstrap marketing 215
contract sales force 219
cost-plus pricing 211
independent representatives 218
loss leader 210
marketing plan 206
mixed-model promotions 212
pricing floor 210
promotion 212
pure promotions 212
SaaS (software as a service) 211
sales management 216
Search Engine Optimization (SEO) 213
virtually free promotions 212

REVIEW QUESTIONS

1. Describe the basics of a marketing plan.
2. What advice would you provide to a potential new business owner about establishing a marketing plan?
3. What elements are necessary for a target customer profile?
4. How is a target customer profile used in the operation of a new business?
5. What are the means by which products or services may be priced?
6. How can a new business leverage free promotions?
7. What promotions might a new business use and why?
8. In what context might independent sales agents be used?
9. How is a contract sales force used in new businesses?
10. Explain how the Web is used by businesses for advertising.

BUSINESS PLAN DEVELOPMENT QUESTIONS

1. What are some of the ways that you can identify competitors in your market area?
2. How will you create sales for your business?
3. How will the Web be used in your business? How do you ensure that your site becomes known to your potential clients as they search the Web?

INDIVIDUAL EXERCISES

1. What channels do you intend to use to market your product or service?
2. What are the costs for each?
3. Develop an overall marketing plan that encompasses a defined customer target area, the methods of promotion, the pricing, and the distribution channels.

GROUP EXERCISES

Throughout history, well-known companies have lowered prices to increase sales. History suggests, however, that this technique simply reduces profitability and leads to a decline in the overall business. The business then has a harder time justifying its place in the market. Customers generally associate a lowered price with lowered quality. First individually and then in your group, answer the following questions:

1. Can you think of examples of products that would suffer if their prices were lowered?
2. Why can some businesses easily lower prices and gain customers whereas others cannot?
3. Can you think of any products or services where lowering prices could result in enough of an increase in sales to justify the lower prices?

ENDNOTES

1. R. Grewal, R. Mehta, and F. Kardes, "The Timing of Repeat Purchases of Consumer Durable Goods," *Journal of Marketing Research* 41 (2004), pp. 101–16.
2. M. Gruber, "Research on Marketing in Emerging Firms: Key Issues and Open Questions," *Journal of Technology Management* 26 (2003), pp. 600–21.
3. Romaniuk, Jenni, "Five Steps to Smarter Targeting," *Journal of Advertising Research* 52, no. 3 (2012), pp. 288–290.
4. T. McCollum, "High Tech Marketing Hits the Target," *Nation's Business* 85, no. 6 (1997), pp. 39–42.
5. Matthew Toren, "How to Optimize Ad Placement and Maximize Revenue," *Entrepreneur*, February 2, 2017, https://www.entrepreneur.com/article/288570.
6. Ira Kalb, "Price Wrong and Lower Your Profits," *The Huffington Post*, February 12, 2017, http://www.huffingtonpost.com/ira-kalb/price-wrong-and-lower-you_b_14697472.html; T. Nagle and R. Holden, *The Strategy and Tactics of Pricing* (New York: Prentice Hall, 1995).
7. R. Guerreiro, E. Cornachione Jr., and C. Dassai, "Determining the 'Plus' in Cost-Plus Pricing: A Time-Based Management Approach," *Journal of Applied Management Accounting Research* 10, no. 1 (2012), pp. 1–15.
8. J. Tanner, "Leveling the Playing Field: Factors Influencing Trade Show Success for Small Firms," *Industrial Marketing Management* 31 (2002), pp. 229–40.
9. J. Gregan-Paxton, J. Hibbard, F. Brunel, and P. Azar, "So That Is What That Is: Examining the Impact of Analogy on Consumers' Knowledge Development for Really New Products," *Psychology & Marketing* 19 (2002), pp. 533–51.
10. K. Blois and S. Albers, "Sales Force Management," *Oxford Textbook of Marketing* (Oxford, UK: Oxford University Press, 2000), pp. 292–318.
11. T. Chitura, S. Mupenhi, T. Dube, and J. Bolongkikit, "Barriers to Electronic Commerce Adoption in Small and Medium Enterprises: A Critical Review," *Journal of Internet Banking & Commerce* 13, no. 2 (2008), pp. 1–13.
12. Tim Parry, "The Catalog Is Far from Dead," *Multi-Channel Merchant*, March 15, 2016, http://multichannelmerchant.com/marketing/the-catalog-is-far-from-dead-15032016/.
13. D. Stokes, "Entrepreneurial Marketing: A Conceptualization from Qualitative Research," *Qualitative Market Research* 3, no. 1 (2000), pp. 47ff.

chapter 12

learning objectives

After studying this chapter, you will be able to:

LO12-1 Discuss the use of a critical path chart.

LO12-2 Describe how location can be used as a competitive advantage.

LO12-3 Discuss the important issues in the financing considerations of new firms.

LO12-4 Distinguish between the various methods with which a new firm establishes legitimacy in the market.

LO12-5 Explain the importance of production management in start-up ventures.

LO12-6 Explain how production charting is accomplished.

LO12-7 Describe the importance of quality as a competitive tool.

LO12-8 Discuss the type and condition of equipment needed at start-up.

LO12-9 Explain how timing is a competitive advantage.

LO12-10 Recognize the issues related to time management in the starting of a new business.

Establishing Operations

WEEDMAPS—THE YELP OF MARIJUANA BUYING

How do you take something that is considered illegal in much of the United States and make a legal business out of it. Regardless of one's opinion on the subject, legal marijuana sales exist in the United States. As of 2017, 28 states as well as Washington, DC, allowed for the purchase of medical marijuana, whereas two states, Colorado and Washington, allowed for any adult to purchase marijuana for recreational use. Six other states and Washington, DC, now allow people to possess marijuana without a medical prescription. Despite being legal in these settings, running a business in this industry is still a legal minefield.

According to the federal government, marijuana is a Schedule 1 narcotic with no accepted medial value. In addition, there are thousands of people in jail for past possession of the product. Add to that, it is still highly regulated even in states where it has some form of legality. The Marijuana Enforcement Division in Colorado issued a 230-page document prescribing how it must be advertised, sold, and distributed in the state. At this point, the federal government has decided not to pursue their established enforcement actions in those states where it is legal; however, it is undecided how long that will last. Any business enabling the sale of an illegal substance is subject to seizure and jail time for the owners.

The industry is projected to be a $20 billion a year business by 2021. There are more marijuana dispensaries in Colorado than Starbucks and McDonalds combined. Both residents and tourists can buy up to one ounce of marijuana at a time. However, these dispensaries cannot generally open bank accounts as most banks do not want to cross the federal government ban. This means the business is almost exclusively cash based, not only for customers but for paying suppliers, paying employees, and even paying taxes.

Founded by Justin Hartfield and Keith Hoerling in 2008, WeedMaps is a firm navigating this legal minefield. The firm provides a website that provides the menus and pricing of legal marijuana dispensaries across the United States. The firm makes money not by charging visitors to the website but charging those business owners who list there. WeedMaps helps customers find legal marijuana suppliers in addition to helping the firms that list with them manage their products. Hartfield says the site is tracking half a million products in real time, "not just strains but also edibles, lotions, tinctures, salves, balms, clothing, bongs, and vaporizers. Anything a dispensary sells is on our weed menu." Today, the firm has grown to over 200 employees and is considered by many to be the Yelp of marijuana.

They continue to hold a unique position in the market. Google and Facebook don't allow ads that promote drugs, while Yelp will allow listings but not all the extra advertising features these outlets want to share with their customers. As a result, WeedMaps is the largest in the market.

There are legal constraints on every business. Some are just more intense than others.

Questions

1. What are the operational issues of an all cash business?
2. What controls do you think WeedMaps needs to have in place? Why?
3. What insurance issues concern you about this business?

Sources: Melia Robinson, "It's 2017: Here's Where You Can Legally Smoke Weed Now," *BusinessInsider*, January 8, 2017, http://www.businessinsider.com/where-can-you-legally-smoke-weed-2017-1; Paresh Dave, "Weedmaps—a Yelp for Pot—Is Riddled with Suspicious Reviews," *LA Times*, August 24, 2016, http://www.latimes.com/business/technology/la-fi-tn-weedmaps-data-breach-20160817-snap-story.html; Jeremy Berke, "This Could be the No. 1 Problem Facing Legal Weed Businesses in America," *BusinessInsider*, April 20, 2016, http://www.businessinsider.com/no-1-problem-facing-legal-weed-businesses-2016-4; B. Eha, "High Hopes and Blunt Truths for the $2.3 Billion Legal Marijuana Market," *Entrepreneur*, January 13, 2014, www.entrepreneur.com/article/230772-1; T. Hughes, "Legal Pot Becomes a Touchy Workplace Issue," *USA Today*, April 7, 2014, www.usatoday.com/story/news/nation/2014/04/07/marijuana-pot-workplace-employers-hiringjobs/7272467/; B. Weiss, "Thank You for Smoking Marijuana," *Wall Street Journal*, March 14, 2014, http://online.wsj.com/news/articles/sb10001424052702303630904579419033028056534; http://medicalmarijuana.procon.org/view.resource.php?resourceID=000881.

Planning is the first step in the entrepreneurial development process. A great many individuals do little more than this initial investigation. During this initial process, the individuals that stop may find a fatal flaw, decide that the business is not nearly as lucrative as they had originally thought, or simply determine that they do not want to take the risk. The decision to not pursue the business is completely legitimate, and it is better to make it early if you believe that the business does not present the right opportunity for success. The process provided in this book, in fact, is designed to encourage the student to fully examine the business opportunity prior to actually starting a business. Our expectation is that the specific plan you develop in this class may not be one you open, but you will learn a process that will allow you to keep examining potential businesses until there is one you do want to open.

However, at some stage, if the business is one that is viable, the entrepreneur must decide that she has investigated the idea sufficiently and that it is time to actually begin operations. While we would advocate good research and examination of your idea, the critical point of difference between an entrepreneur and someone with an idea is *action*. This chapter examines the practical, process-based actions that must occur to actually begin operations.

During the initial start-up period, the expenses of the firm are often higher than expected, and the time to reach the break-even point takes longer than expected. A root cause of many of the problems for a new business can be traced to the lack of development of an operational plan.[1] It is this lack of operational plans that can lead to a cash crunch in the organization as the new firm stumbles while trying to actually put its ideas into action. As a result,

KOSHER HOME

Jack and Toby had picked a clear industry (prepared meals) and a unique niche (kosher food) to compete, used trial and error to generate unique products, dealt with operating and legal problems, staffed the firm, and selected a marketing strategy. Thus, the two entrepreneurs had developed a successful venture. However, one of the issues they were not prepared for was an issue of their legitimacy.

The firm had started experimenting with various products in a single synagogue. They had now picked three major cities to focus on for their expansion. However, one of the local publications focused on Jewish readers in Las Vegas had written a small article profiling the firm. While the two founders were happy that they were profiled, the publication suggested that while Kosher Home was a great idea it did not appear that the firm would be in a position to survive beyond the end of the year. The two entrepreneurs were not sure from where the reporter got that idea, but it became very clear that they needed to address this issue quickly. Eventually, the firm would need more investors to become as big as they hoped. If consumers did not believe that the firm would survive, then it might be impossible to obtain those critical new customers who would establish the viability of the business as they expanded into these major population centers.

Jack and Toby realized that one issue was how they presented the firm. At the time of the interview, the two entrepreneurs did not have simple things like business cards as they tried to conserve funds. Similarly, the two met the reporter in a very low-cost diner seeking to save every penny for the firm. The two realized that they needed to establish their legitimacy in the market place. However, legitimacy as an Internet firm requires more than business cards. The two realized that they needed to establish their legitimacy in the virtual world of the Internet both in terms of serving the Jewish community and in terms of their prepackaged food.

QUESTIONS

1. How would you establish the legitimacy of the firm on the internet for their prepackaged food?
2. How would you establish the legitimacy of the firm in the Jewish community as a kosher food company?
3. Would these efforts be complimentary or separate?

the firm may have a great idea and be on a clear path to breakeven but run out of cash before it has the opportunity to achieve that success. The firm should have a solid understanding of the specific operational issues related to that business prior to starting the new venture.

There are a number of distinct actions that must be taken in order for a new business to begin operations. Although there may be some crossover among these actions, we separate them into the following categories:

1. Critical path chart
2. Location
3. Financing considerations
4. Legitimacy
5. Production management
6. Production charting
7. Quality
8. Equipment
9. Timing
10. Time management

Each of these will be examined in turn.

The Use of a Critical Path Chart

LO12-1

Discuss the use of a critical path chart.

The first operations-related concept we want to introduce in this section is also one of the most popular for organizing a wide range of activities in a firm. An absolute imperative for any organization, but most especially for a new business, is the efficient use of time. Many tasks can be handled concurrently, but others must be performed sequentially. Identifying the actions that must occur, in what order they should occur, and what order will be most efficient is one of the first operational steps for a new business. Although it is often not possible to identify every action item that will be required prior to the start of a new business, the effort to develop a complete list will allow the new business to have a faster, more thorough, less expensive start-up. Failing to plan may leave the new business waiting weeks for some small step that could have been completed earlier, concurrently with other actions taken by the firm. For example, items such as obtaining a state tax ID or a city license are not difficult but may take some time, depending on the requirements. However, the firm may not be able to buy equipment for the business or rent facilities until these licenses are obtained.

Although there are a number of methods and formats for completing a critical path analysis, we present a relatively common, easily understood format that we have used with a number of new start-ups.[2] Initially, the entrepreneur must identify the most likely amount of time it will take for each of the key tasks to be completed, the actual time one of the owners will be involved, any prerequisite tasks, and who is responsible for the task. The chart of critical activities might look something like the one in Table 12.1 for a small manufacturer. This process could be the same for many different types of manufacturing. However, it should be noted that the initial efforts of the entrepreneur concern so much more than the actual manufacturing. It should also be noted that while we have specified the tasks for a manufacturer, the tasks will be different for different types of businesses.[3]

Note that the assigning of responsibilities and estimated times is more than an intellectual activity. When you specify who will do a task and how long it will take to be completed, you set for yourself a control mechanism to ensure that you are going to be ready when you intend to open. If you do not set

STEP	TASK	TIME TO COMPLETE	ACTUAL TIME INVOLVED	PREVIOUS TASK REQUIRED	RESPONSIBILITY
1	Establish business bank accounts	1 week	3 hours		James and Margaret
2	Obtain bank loan	2 weeks	4 hours		James and Margaret
3	Establish accounting system	3 weeks	1 week		Margaret
4	Lease Facility	2 weeks	20 hours	2	James and Margaret
5	Obtain equipment (office and manufacturing)	4 weeks	8 hours	2 & 4	James (manufacturing) and Margaret (office)
6	Acquire raw materials	4 weeks	30 hours	2 & 4	James
7	Make initial sales calls	8 weeks	90 hours	2 & 4	James and Margaret
8	Produce initial inventory	4 weeks	150 hours	4, 5, 6, & 7	James and Margaret

Table 12.1
Critical Path Table

timetables and responsibilities, it is possible for the founding of the business to drag on, using up precious financial and emotional resources. The founders setting the schedule allows them to get a solid handle on how soon they can begin operations. The owners understand that while they must wait on some tasks, they can complete other tasks so that their time is used efficiently. The owners also can set some priorities on where their time should be focused. Note that it would be difficult to acquire raw materials and have them delivered prior to the leasing of the facility, then that should take priority. If leasing of the facility took more time than estimated, then the entire process would be delayed and then that should again be addressed early in the critical path analysis.

Underestimating the amount of time it will take to begin operations is a mistake that harms many new businesses. You should estimate the times very generously, since many critical steps may take significantly longer than originally planned. New businesspeople often do not recognize a given step they will need to accomplish in order to successfully develop their business. It is for this reason that you will hear many new entrepreneurs say getting the business to the state it could generate revenue often takes two or three times what they first thought. The listing of critical tasks and the resulting critical path chart can help to overcome this problem.

From the lists of critical tasks identified in Table 12.1, the new business can then develop a chart that demonstrates how the activities fit together. The chart of how your actions fit together is your **critical path chart** that shows the set of activities that are dependent on each other and that take the longest time. The chart listing the critical tasks provided in Table 12.1 will produce the critical path chart shown in Figure 12.1.

critical path chart
Chart that demonstrates how the activities necessary to start the firm fit together and build on each other. This chart allows you to understand which activities can occur concurrently and which must already be in place before the next activity can occur.

As you can see from the critical path in Figure 12.1, it will take a minimum of 12 weeks to open the business in this case. There are some things the firm can do at the same time, such as setting up the firm's bank accounts and starting to work on bank loans. However, the new business will likely not be able to start to lease a facility until it has its financing in place. Potential landlords will initially screen out those individuals they do not think are serious as they seek to lease a property.

The businessperson can make the critical path as detailed as is necessary. The chart for the small manufacturing firm in Figure 12.1 is actually quite simple. The new businessperson should be guided by developing a chart that provides the most assistance and information. The purpose of the chart is not

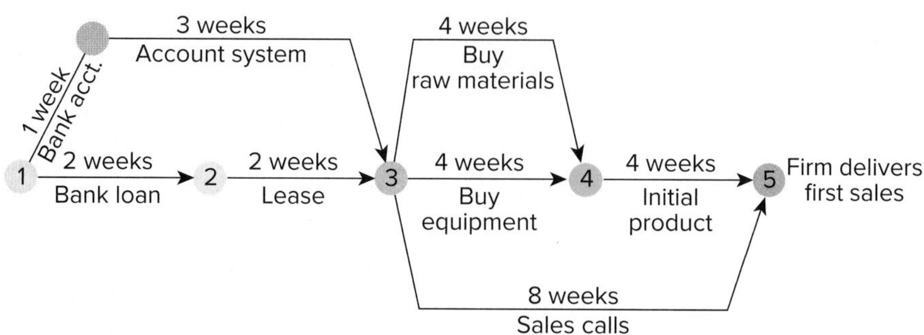

Figure 12.1
The Critical Path Chart

to be a formal document for a business plan. Instead, it is designed to help focus the founders' efforts so they are not slowed down by some simple activity that was not visualized. Therefore, it may be useful for the founders to create a more complex form of a critical path chart that can be developed by estimating three different time needs for each task: minimum, most likely, and maximum. For complex start-up operations, there are several project management software packages that will assist you in developing a task chart and producing a critical path chart. They are available online and at most office supply stores. The new businessperson must judge the level of detail that he desires in a critical path chart and whether purchasing such a program will aid him or not. The process for an Internet-based business is somewhat simpler than for a manufacturing business. However, there are critical steps that can delay the start of any business such as obtaining the required licenses.

To further illustrate the importance of such planning, consider one of the entrepreneurial businesses that students in one of our classes wished to start. The students wanted to start a Study Café that would be open from 4 P.M. to 8 A.M., seven days a week. The business design was simple but elegant and potentially quite lucrative. The café would provide a well-lit, open-forum, safe space to study individually or meet with groups. It would make a majority of its money by selling basic food and drinks and leasing out the conference rooms in the facility. There was cheap space available close to the campus where a restaurant had gone out of business. (The prior restaurant had appealed to students but closed every night at 9 P.M. and strongly discouraged students from "hanging out.") The students' original intent was to open just prior to the start of classes in the fall semester. However, after completing the critical path chart, they realized that they would complete everything necessary to open their doors in April. This would mean the business would open for operation at the end of the spring semester. The city in which the Study Café wanted to open was a college town where only the resident college students would be interested in staying up until the early hours of the morning. As a result, the business would have to suffer through the summer months of limited business while the expenses just piled up.

As a result of their critical path analysis, they approached their opening from a completely different perspective. Rather than starting the process immediately and seeing when they could open, they went to the end of the chart and set the opening date as August 1. They then calculated the critical path chart in reverse, with the date they were to open being the starting (and therefore missing) element. Estimating the longest path for opening the Study Café, they were able to establish a date to begin the process of putting together the

Is the Study Café a lucrative business idea? Why or why not?

EXERCISE 1

1. Develop a list of all activities necessary to start your business.
2. Assign timing to complete each step by validating each element.
3. Develop a critical path table of activities. Think very carefully about what activities can be completed concurrently.

operations of the business so as to minimize wasted effort and money while still opening for operations by August 1.

Entrepreneurs should constantly update their critical path analysis as they develop the plan for a business. Entrepreneurs should also share that critical path analysis with potential suppliers, friends, and industry experts—with anyone who will look it over for you and add, modify, or delete activities. The critical path analysis is a living document that should be modified during the process of actually accomplishing the tasks. We have worked with a number of new businesspeople who take large flip chart sheets of paper and post a critical path chart on the wall of their home, office, or wherever it can be easily viewed. As tasks are accomplished, delayed, added, or changed, the chart is continually updated.

LO12-2

Describe how location can be used as a competitive advantage.

How Location Can Be Used as a Competitive Advantage

One of the most important steps in the critical path chart will be the identification and purchase or lease of a location for the new business. The old axiom from marketing is that the three keys to business success are location, location, and location. Although this might be a bit overblown, we certainly agree that location is a critical factor in the successful operation of a new non-Internet business.[4] How do you decide upon the best location for the money? The method that we use involves breaking the business down into the critical design features of the business. You may recall from Chapter 5 that you should develop a list consisting of all of the resources or capabilities of the organization.

It is very easy to simply fall into the trap of trying to locate a business based on the capital available or some convenience factor that has little to do with the actual strategy of the business. This is a mistake that can, by itself, send all of the other planning down the drain. For example, one of the authors met a young couple for dinner both of whom had been students in his classes. They were very excited because they had decided to open a restaurant and wanted us to come by once it was open. It was a reasonable restaurant idea, but its location constituted a fatal flaw. They were opening the business near their home because they knew the area "so very well." This decision also allowed them to return to the area where they had both grown up.

However, the area the couple located the business was more than 60 miles from any major city and, worse than that, they had selected as their location a run-down **strip shopping center** with very cheap rent. A strip center is a small, one-story retail center typically located parallel to a well-traveled road. This type of center is referred to as a strip center since it is often developed on a strip of land irrespective of the development in the area; a strip center generally has no major **anchor stores** to draw in customers. The fact that the entrepreneurial couple were locating in the strip center itself was not the problem. Instead, it was the specific strip center that they had selected. The reason the rent was so cheap was that the shopping center was virtually empty. It was empty not because the center was too new to have tenants; instead, the customer base in the area was too small and poor to support any of the businesses that had previously operated there. Their proposed location was more than two miles from the interstate. Therefore, they would not be getting the interstate travel traffic that would be passing through this isolated location. Despite our

strip shopping center

A small retail center located typically along a major road. The center has only small businesses and the center itself occupies only a small strip of land along the major street.

anchor stores

Major retail stores, such as department stores in a mall. They serve as the anchor for the retail establishment.

warnings and suggestions, they went ahead with the business with their father's seed money (almost $150,000) only to see the small restaurant collapse within six months. Even the best idea can be killed by a bad location.

Although there are many very sophisticated methods for performing a location analysis, in simple terms, locations can be graded by the type and amount of traffic that the particular location draws. If you are setting up a warehouse, then you neither need nor want an "A" location in a mall, on a busy street, or in a tourist-heavy downtown area. Match the type of business and the amount of money that you wish to invest in the first years of operation. Take the time to analyze the long term as well. If you will need to move within a short period of time because you achieve all of your targets and outgrow your space, then you may want to consider a location that includes an option to allow for expansion.[5]

What businesses are best suited for a strip shopping center? What businesses might not work in such a space?

©McGraw-Hill Education/Andrew Resek, photographer

To illustrate the rich options that a firm can pursue, we helped a small group of founders of a real estate firm that started out as three people renting space from a travel agency (literally, three desks in the back of the building). As luck would have it (for the new business at least), the travel agency was struggling, which allowed the new business owners to rent more and more of the building as their business expanded. Within 18 months the team was

ETHICAL CHALLENGE

Ralph had decided that after he retired what he really wanted to do was open a restaurant. He had always wanted to do this but was concerned about doing so when he had a good corporate job. About a year prior to his retirement date, he went on the hunt to find the perfect location for his new restaurant. Ideally, he wanted a location that had previously been a restaurant that had gone out of business. He wanted the equipment and set-up to be as cheap as possible.

He quickly found three locations that met his criteria, and all three were in areas with good visibility. They had ample parking and good foot and car traffic because of strong anchor stores that ranged from a grocery store to a big-box pet store. Unfortunately, only one would lease to a truly new business. The others required a business that had been in operation for at least two years.

There was a big difference in the monthly rent between the one that would rent to him and the others. In addition, the one that would rent to him required a personal guarantee and a five-year lease commitment. Ralph did not want to be held back by this, so he sought out a good friend of his and someone who had mentored him in the past. This person had a side business selling imported items that he had been doing for over 10 years. He was registered on Dun & Bradstreet, had a C-corporation, and a website.

Ralph convinced him to be the lead in renting a business location. He would pay this friend the rent payment, but the friend would be the lease holder. Ralph's business would be listed as a subsidiary of the C-corporation. This allowed him to get around the requirements and allowed him to open in one of the two other locations that only leased to established businesses. If Ralph did this he would obtain a cheaper location with fewer restrictions.

QUESTIONS

1. Do you feel that what Ralph did with the lease is ethical?
2. Why would lessees require a business to be an established one?
3. Are the penalties being demanded by the first lessee reasonable?

renting 80 percent of the building and approached the travel agency owner about taking over the entire building and setting up a lease-purchase agreement. The travel agency finally closed, and the entrepreneurial team was able to acquire the building location. Having established a client base, they really wanted to hold onto their location. As will be discussed later in this chapter, location is one of the things that provide a business with legitimacy. If you have a location and maintain it for some period of time, then you are more accepted and acceptable with potential clients and suppliers, because your business appears to be more stable.

Commercial real estate firms are a source of unparalleled information for the new business owners trying to locate their business. Building owners pay agents in a leasing agreement that is usually based on a percentage of the first year's lease. Although commercial real estate agent income can be quite substantial, the commercial real estate market is relatively small and an individual's reputation is critical to future bookings. Therefore, agents focus extensively on ensuring that the new business signing the lease is successful. The fact is that the cost for all this expertise is paid by the building owner, and a successful business that pays its bills is very desirable. Thus, commercial agents can be a valuable asset to new business owners as they seek to locate properties that match their needs.

LO12-3

Discuss the important issues in the financing considerations of new firms.

The Important Issues in the Financing Considerations of New Firms

While not addressing the details of financing operations here (we have covered those issues in depth earlier), we nonetheless want to acknowledge the gamut of financial issues related to the operational start-up of a new business. Financing the initial operations begins with the variety of initial payments and the process of setting up the business and ends with the first completed sale. The new organization has to be in a position to make initial payments for:

1. Security deposits.
2. Utility setup fees.
3. Purchase or lease of initial equipment and installation.
4. All licenses and inspections.
5. All initial supplies (this is a significant and often overlooked expense).
6. Hiring and training of initial staff.
7. Initial advertising expenses.
8. Bank set-up fees.

These costs can be substantial, and the new business must ensure that it has the proper resources to conduct these activities. (For an interesting discussion of start-up costs in the artesian cheese industry, see the 2014 article by Bouma, Durham, and Meunier-Goddik).[6] Recalling our critical path analysis, if one element, such as purchasing of some key inputs, must be delayed because of a lack of resources, the impact can be to place the entire development of the new business's operations behind schedule.

It was highlighted earlier that the issue of establishing a bank relationship is critical. The new business is well served to establish a variety of financial relationships with its bank. Some of these key issues include establishing a revolving line of credit (working capital), acquiring a business credit card account, and setting up a basic business checking account. These accounts should have a primary signatory and a confirmation signatory as an audit safety condition. No one individual should be able to write checks for the business in excess of a specified amount (usually $500) without a countersignature. Using confirmatory signatures ensures both parties know where major expenses occur and that the bill is accurate.

Picking which bank to work with is more than a choice of which branch is closest to you. Working with small businesses is a specialized skill that all banks will say they possess, but which, in fact, may be very limited at a given institution. Some banks develop expertise in large commercial accounts such as Fortune 500 customers. Other banks have an expertise in retail banking, primarily serving individuals. Still other banks have their principal focus on small and medium-sized businesses. A bank may have a range of customers, but you want to ensure that it has an expertise in your type of business and understands issues such as timing of payments from customers. If you have a small retail firm, you may need large draws on your lines of credit to get the Christmas merchandise onto your shelves. If you are a small oil and gas exploration firm, you will have other specialized needs, such as determining the value of given leases that you include in your assets. Whether your bank can work with such issues is an important question for a new business owner. The expertise of other successful entrepreneurs in your area provides valuable insight into these issues.

The Various Methods with Which a New Firm Establishes Legitimacy in the Market

LO12-4

Distinguish between the various methods with which a new firm establishes legitimacy in the market.

A topic rarely discussed in the establishment of a new business is the issue of legitimacy. **Legitimacy** is the term we use to discuss acceptance by key stakeholders, such as customers and suppliers, who believe the firm is a genuine business that will still be in operation next year. Developing the perception of legitimacy for both customers and suppliers can be difficult, although it is critical to the long-term survival of the business.[7]

legitimacy
The acceptance by key stakeholders such as customers and suppliers that you are a genuine business that will still be in operation next year.

The new business will need to look like and act as an operation that will be in business for the long run in order to achieve some level of legitimacy. If a customer buys a product and the company is no longer in business, who does she turn to when she has a problem? When a supplier sells goods on terms of 90 days, where will that firm get its payment if the firm that bought the goods goes out of business before the 90 days? Thus, both customers and suppliers want to ensure your business will be operating for the long term before they do business with you.

You will recall from our discussion of community supports in Chapter 2 that business incubators were discussed. These institutions are a potential setting for new businesses (especially nonfood service businesses) to locate their initial operations. They offer new businesses office space at reduced rates, as well as providing services such as a receptionist who answers the phone with the business name, conference room facilities, and basic office equipment (copying, fax, Internet, telephones). The effect of these supports is that it helps to build the perceived legitimacy of the business with the look of a more professional presentation as well as the endorsement provided by the incubator operator. Incubators are usually swamped with new businesses that would like to be considered. The incubator operators try to pick those businesses that have the best chance for success.

EXERCISE 2

1. What do you look for in a business before you patronize it?
2. If you were going to sell equipment and supplies to a new entrepreneurial business on credit, what would you want to see from the new business before selling to them?
3. What are you going to do that will increase the legitimacy of your new business?

Regardless of the business location, the entrepreneur needs to consider the potential means with which to establish the legitimacy of the business in the eyes of the customers and suppliers. Below is a list of classic items that may help establish more legitimacy for your new business:

1. A business checking account with the firm's name printed on the checks; start the check numbering higher than 001 or even 101.
2. A business credit card.
3. A bank line of credit.
4. Professional business cards.
5. Professional letterhead, billing slips, envelopes, and so on.
6. Professional advertising material.
7. The prestige of the business address.
8. Job titles—titles cost you very little, use them liberally.
9. Telephone answering support.
10. A high-quality Web page.
11. A board of advisors and/or directors with excellent community visibility.
12. Endorsements from well-recognized and respected individuals.

You may have noticed that some items in the list above are quite inexpensive, whereas others are both time consuming and expensive. We suggest that all new businesses develop a plan to establish and continually enhance their legitimacy. While you may not choose to do them all, and appearances are not everything, the business's legitimacy is critical at the outset of the business.[8] Thus, every reasonable way to improve the firm's legitimacy should be taken.

Purely online businesses and especially a business based on an app have an even tougher challenge with establishing legitimacy. Whereas many of our previous elements of advice are oriented toward appearing professional attaining a large number of downloads/users goes a long way to establishing this credibility with an app. To attain this type of "buzz" a purely online or app based business should consider:

1. Attaining Free Reviews from Bloggers who your potential customers follow.
2. Invest in high quality visuals for the app store.
3. Add a Social element to the app.
4. Engage with anyone who visits your site on the app store in order to quickly adapt the app.

LO12-5

Explain the importance of production management in start-up ventures.

The Importance of Production Management in Start-Up Ventures

Another important element in the success of a new business is the establishment of a production management system.[9] A *production management system* defines the steps that are involved in moving from your product or service offering to the point where you actually receive money. This importance is exaggerated in the early stages of a new business, as the firm has only limited resources, as well as strong time pressures to perform well at the outset. To illustrate, many years ago when inkjet printers were fairly new, we worked with a small group of individuals' rather simple but interesting plan to refurbish printer cartridges. This was targeted at college students. Their original plan had them handling the vast variety of cartridges on an individual basis. They would simply deal with each cartridge as it came in and depend upon their individual knowledge and experience to punch the hole in the cartridge, refill the ink, plug the hole, and finally seal up the cartridge for resale. They accepted the fact that they would develop procedures for each type of cartridge but thought that this would develop over time. The process of discovery would allow them to handle a wide variety of cartridges early in the life of the company.

We pointed out to the entrepreneurs that their projections depended upon their handling more than 10,000 cartridges a month by the sixth month of operation, and that an ad hoc system being handled directly by the owners would likely not lead to success. The time wasted as each cartridge was treated as a unique order would simply be unwieldy in a very short time period. As a result, they employed a mechanical engineer who developed a very simple set of procedures with fixed equipment to handle the most common types of cartridges. For these stations with fixed equipment, they employed individuals to process the most common cartridges. For all other cartridges they maintained a job shop section to develop procedures and process those cartridges. Over the next eight months, they developed a production management system and methodology that allowed them to dramatically cut costs. On more than one occasion the entrepreneurs commented to us that more time spent prior to start-up in developing a process would have resulted in enormous financial dividends to the owners. The production system developed post-hoc was expensive and resulted in many lost opportunities.

It is important to emphasize that all businesses have production systems, whether or not they are codified. All service and Internet businesses have preferred ways of dealing with items such as customers, paperwork, orders, and services. These constitute the foundation of a production system. Putting together a production management system to handle the most common and expected routines will ensure consistent handling and enable the employees to focus their energy on the other, unusual aspects of the job.

While this topic is quite complex and is its own field of study, we discuss the two most important elements to production management as they relate to entrepreneurial business. These are production charting and quality.

How Production Charting Is Accomplished

LO12-6

Explain how production charting is accomplished.

There are many established software programs available for new business owners to help them establish the production processes they will use in their firms. To emphasize the importance of such methods, entrepreneurs need only look to franchises. The text will discuss franchises in greater detail in Chapter 14. Here we simply point out that one of the reasons that franchises are so successful is that they have well-established methods of operation. The franchisors have prepared these methods for the franchisees in a plan detailing each step that occurs in the production process and when each step is to occur. This type of exercise is enormously helpful for all new entrepreneurial businesses.

This level of detailed understanding about a firm's production typically comes from a **production chart.** You will recall that at the beginning of this chapter, we discussed a critical path chart. A production chart is similar; however, rather than focusing on the founding of the business, this chart details each step that must occur within the production process. It takes the reader step by step through the processes necessary to provide the customer with the finished product. It starts with the order being received and finishes with the final delivery to the customer. The production chart is similar to the critical path chart in that some steps in the production process can occur simultaneously while others must occur concurrently. In presenting this chart, we have chosen a slightly different format from the traditional one used in most

production chart
A chart that provides a detailed understanding of a firm's production process.

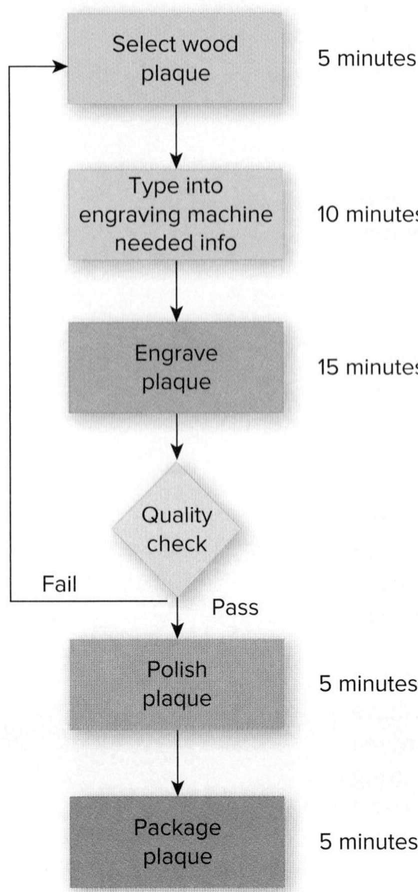

Figure 12.2
Production Chart

textbooks. Most textbooks focus on established company production processes and have many items occurring concurrently; however, we have found that new firms have limited personnel and the processes are more sequential. The process detailed in the production chart in Figure 12.2 is very simple: production of a plaque from a trophy shop.

Even for early-stage ventures, the production chart can become complex quite quickly. Imagine the difficulty in producing meals from a menu that may have 25 different entrées with different vegetable selections. How does the restaurant assure that all of the items are produced so that those that take longer are started sooner, those that take less time are started later, and all items are finalized at approximately the same time and are delivered to the table when they are at their peak? Now add in complexities such as appearance, appetizers, salads, and drinks. The production chart for a business that appears quite simple can, in fact, be quite complex.

As noted, all businesses have a production process. It is easy to recognize the processes in a manufacturing setting. However, even a retail firm has a production process. Goods come into the store and then are counted, tagged, stocked, sold, detagged, and bagged, or if not sold moved to the discount area. If firms do not have a detailed understanding of the methods needed for these basic processes, it is quite easy to end up creating bottlenecks and procedures that negatively impact both customers and employees. One business that we got to know was in a tourist area and catered to the tourist trade. To save money the owner decided to use a dial-up telephone line for credit card transactions. As compared to a dedicated high-speed line, this choice meant an additional 45 seconds per transaction with dialing delays and busy signals as a common problem. Complaints continued to rise, and the owner noticed more and more people either walking out of the store or deciding, upon looking at the checkout line, to go elsewhere. As a result, the entrepreneur chose to move to a dedicated line for credit card transactions. At the same time, he changed his required procedure that each item purchased be recorded in a ledger by the cash register, as that process was slow and cumbersome. At some expense he moved to a bar code system to improve the throughput of customers. The dedicated high-speed Internet line and the bar code system were both more expensive, but once the owner realized the negative impact on his production process of not having them, the rationale for each became quite obvious. If the entrepreneur had thought through their retailing business as a production process, they likely could have avoided the problems. They would have been able to put in place the changes as they built the stores, since they would have seen the impact on time and sales more clearly early.

In a similar vein, we once dealt with a clothing retailer who did not have a clear understanding of the store's current process, nor what processes should be in place. The owner would bring all goods in at cost and continue to carry all unsold items in inventory at their original cost. The predictable result was an ever-growing percentage of the store being consumed by obsolete stock, and this eventually led to failure, as the firm ended up with a storeroom and retail space full of goods that appeared on paper to be quite valuable, but were in fact items that had little or no market value. The firm's bank eventually figured out that there was ever growing stock of valueless materials. They employed the clauses in the line of credit that allowed the bank to cut the credit line of the firm to virtually nothing. This cash crunch resulted in an inability to place orders for goods the store needed in the upcoming year, and the store eventually closed. There is no universally "correct" way to deal with the issue of obsolete stock; however, it is necessary to establish a procedure for handling such stock.

The procedure should be aggressive and recognize that there is little to no value in holding onto obsolete inventory, even if its cost was significant.

There are many established production management systems that operate on any computer available to new business owners. If you are starting a business that is part of an established industry, then you should talk to others in the industry regarding the popular packages for the management of your business processes. Starting one from scratch is a waste of time and money. A little effort investigating the industry should provide tremendous positives for the organization.

The Importance of Quality as a Competitive Tool

LO12-7

Describe the importance of quality as a competitive tool.

Another important consideration in all aspects of a business venture is the investment in quality. In the recent past, designing quality into your product or service was a means to differentiate an entrepreneurial business from the larger mass-market businesses. Increasingly, however, quality is an assumed standard whether the entrepreneurial business is in manufacturing or is a service business. Individuals have to look no farther than fast-food restaurants. For illustration purposes, look at a franchise such as McDonald's. It sells a number of products for $1.00, has playgrounds for kids, maintains clean tables and restrooms, and even puts a toy in a meal for children. The playgrounds are expansive and expensive, while the food quality is guaranteed across the spectrum of all McDonald's restaurants. It is a tremendous value for a very small price, and each store opens with the full complement of offerings. For a new business to compete with McDonald's, it will need to have an equivalent offering to be considered by customers. Therefore, new businesses need to be clear about the expectations for quality in whatever business they pursue.[10]

One of the keys to successfully delivering quality is the monitoring and measuring systems put into place by the founders. Dr. W. Edwards Deming is considered the father of the quality movement in the United States. One of his arguments is that quality needs to be constantly and consistently improved. Thus, there needs to be a continuous set of measures for each of the various processes of the organization. Without recorded data, it is impossible to judge the performance of the processes that have been put in place by the owners.

Deming went much further and argued that while the organization should set goals for quality in the organization, these goals are not to drive every action. If a firm focuses only on those goals, the firm might make short-term decisions that were detrimental to the overall direction of the company. To illustrate, a firm may have a target for on-time delivery that it is striving to improve upon. Although this is an admirable goal, and perhaps even a point of differentiation in the industry, if the firm gets so wrapped up in on-time delivery that this becomes the only focus of the organization, the firm can easily miss other critical issues, such as delivering the correct item. Delivering the wrong item on time would result in great statistical success (concerning timing, at least) but would destroy value in the firm.[11]

Deming strongly suggests that the firm be guided by what he calls the "scientific method." In this method, rather than changing lots of things at the same time, the firm should change only one thing at a time, measuring the impact of that change. It is through this systematic method that a firm knows if it is moving in the right direction and also knows the true impact of each change.

Additionally, Deming suggests that rather than focusing strictly on obtaining the lowest prices for supplies, firms should focus on the quality of the inputs. He argues that without quality inputs, the output has no chance to be high quality. To illustrate, there was a large privately held, relatively large bakery in Oklahoma that used 12 different types of flour. The owners shopped by price, so there were actually as many as 15 different suppliers they used at different points in time. The result was that the firm would use inputs that met the formal requirements for the flour, but each had slight differences in their characteristics, such as moisture content. These differences were very small, but they still led inexorably to differences in the baking processes. Thus, each time a new supplier's product was employed, the owner of the firm found that her workers had to test and adjust the production process. After years of handling this situation, the owner followed the advice of a close friend who simply recommended that the bakery employ one supplier who would guarantee the quality standard. Saving the constant testing and product waste would more than make up for any additional expense. It is this type of realization that has moved firms to focus on forming **strategic alliances**, where firms join together to form long-term, mutually beneficial relationships. Firms, both large and small, now seek to establish a reasonable price for their inputs and then seek out a long-term relationship with a supplier that can meet that price and supply a consistent, high-quality product. A consistent input helps the firm produce a consistent output.

strategic alliances
The joining together of firms to form long-term, mutually beneficial relationships.

LO12-8

Discuss the type and condition of equipment needed at start-up.

The Type and Condition of Equipment Needed at Start-Up

Acquiring the initial equipment for a business can be a daunting task. The basic equipment can easily be one of the most expensive elements for a new business. Clearly, a small manufacturer that needs to purchase specialized

YrFURN—AN APP FOR FURNITURE

The team found out early in their efforts that many suppliers did not want to work with YrFurn unless they were sure it was going to be around for a while. The team knew that the first six months were critical to developing their reputation.

The team set out to show that they were an established organization. As mentioned previously, (1) they rented an office, (2) established the business as a C-corporation, and (3) recruited a board of directors. The team spent a lot of effort designing a very professional website, and they hired a marketing firm to ensure that their app presentation materials (online and in print) were of very high quality.

The team established their customer service team as a feeder to the app development team. As calls came in, all complaints and recommended changes were packaged for the use of the app development team to make changes in the app. The customer service team kept records of who asked for what, and as those changes were made, the customer was called back to let them know that their recommendation had been included in the app.

Following the concepts of a lean start-up as well as the agile approach being used, YrFurn was making up to 20 changes a day to the code that ran the app. Immediacy is a big issue in the arena of app legitimacy.

Even with all those elements in place, the team felt that their number one issue with endorsement by furniture retailers remained the issue of legitimacy. The team decided to consider something more radical. They felt that if one of the CEOs of a major furniture retailer or manufacturer would join the company as either an investor or board of directors member; that they would be able to leverage that connection to spread the word of the firm. The team went to work researching who the best candidates might be.

QUESTIONS

1. What other board members would you suggest for the business?
2. What other critical operations issues should the firm be focusing on to ensure that it can scale up as it gains market share.

equipment will have a higher initial outlay when compared to a service business. Yet even an entrepreneurial business such as an Internet business can incur significant expenses for equipment as computers and related items are purchased. Businesses with even greater equipment needs, such as a restaurant, need to accurately evaluate the equipment needs while at the same time recognize that there is a wide flexibility in the types, ages, methods of acquisition, and availability of all equipment obtained for the new organization. Purchasing new equipment may guarantee that it is the most current available and that it will be delivered directly to the new business; however, it is usually the most expensive method, and delays may be significant if the items are not in stock. Purchasing older equipment has its own risks with quality and availability but should always be investigated. It is relatively common for new equipment to depreciate 50 percent or more in the first year. Similarly, it is possible to lease equipment. The ability to lease the equipment is particularly attractive to new firms as it has the lowest initial costs. However, over the long run, such leasing can prove expensive.

Therefore, the new business owner needs to clearly understand what equipment is needed, how long it will be before it will need to be replaced, and what are the long-term impacts of the decision. This understanding should also include both what equipment is needed to begin operations and how quickly the company might need more or even bigger equipment. The new business owner should then prepare a chart comparing the price and the positives and negatives of buying new, buying used, or leasing that equipment. The positives and negatives should include not only the immediate cost and the ability to overcome the cash flow crunch that impacts all new businesses but also the impact on the firm's quality and the long-term impact if the entrepreneurial business grows.

How Timing Is a Competitive Advantage

LO12-9

Explain how timing is a competitive advantage.

It is interesting to note that choosing when to start a business is an important operational element. The temptation for most new businesses is to start their operations as soon as possible. This is rarely an effective strategy. Instead, the potential entrepreneur should select the time to enter the market based on when it provides the greatest competitive advantage.[12] The timing of your start is a function of several factors: (1) the general environment, (2) competitor moves, (3) cycles in purchasing/supply patterns, and (4) lifestyle issues.

The general economy moves in cycles of boom, slowdown, recession (or the many other terms that are used as euphemisms for this term), growth, and boom. Although the general rule might be that you should open your business during or at the beginning of a boom, the reality is that different businesses depend on different conditions. A foreclosure business depends on poor economic times, and storage facilities do best when the economy is heading downward, among others.

Competitor moves may also dictate the opening of a new business. If your business plan is dependent on having no direct competitors within a specified radius of your operation, a move by another business may accelerate or dramatically alter your plans. Alternatively, the failure of several similar businesses may suggest an alteration of your opening or strategic positioning prior to your actually opening the business.

Some (we might suggest most) businesses have cycles for their purchasing. Some suppliers have production runs that are scheduled a year or more in advance. Your ability to obtain critical supplies may dictate your lead time and opening time. It can be difficult, for example, to obtain significant Christmas inventory in September. The shipping time for these goods and other factors typically requires that a retailer make decisions much earlier.

An entrepreneur that we advised some years ago had a significant issue with the supply of wooden tubes that were needed for its production. The sole supplier of this particular size and quality of wooden tubes had a production run of eight weeks in March/April of each year for that particular product. All orders had to be in place by January. This new business reoriented its entire opening and operation around the acquisition of these wooden tubes. The owners placed an order in January, took delivery in three batches between April and June (storing all of the tubes in a warehouse that they leased), and began production of their product in November. Their first sale was in February of the following year, by which time they had placed yet another order for the following year. The ability of the new business to understand these timing issues required extensive planning and forecasting, without which it would have failed.

LO12-10

Recognize the issues related to time management in the starting of a new business.

The Issues Related to Time Management in the Starting of a New Business

The last item is one that is meant to help the new business owners as they seek to manage this wide variety of operations. It is clear from the discussion provided here that the business owners will need to manage their own time efficiently if they are to be successful.[13] There are several steps that are helpful in this process.

1. Write down what has to be accomplished in all parts of the business formation.
2. Prioritize which tasks are critical and which would be helpful. Those that are critical must be done and should be the priority.
3. Segment items in terms of the time frame they need to be accomplished—short term and long term. The short-term items that are critical have to take priority. The fires that are burning have to be put out before the longer-term issues approach.
4. Allocate time that is strictly for dealing with operational issues. The more you become involved in establishing the business and its operations, the more individuals will wish to visit with you about the business. Even though some of these individuals will be helpful, many simply wish to sell you something you do not need or to find out what you are doing. As your agenda becomes filled you must ensure that your attention is not diverted to nonproductive activities. This does not mean you should not be flexible when opportunities arise, but it does mean that you must have a clear vision of your work goals.
5. Write tasks down and mark them off when you accomplish them. As your agenda becomes more complex, you will gain satisfaction from seeing things being removed from it. However, this method also ensures that you will not forget key items (there should be a strong tie back to your critical path chart). In writing these things down, it is best if you can do this in a systematic, organized manner. Keep a notebook, whether it is electronic or written down, every day to see what you must accomplish and take notes about it. This approach can also be a valuable resource for keeping notes about meetings, issues that arise you as you think about the business, and issues that others raise with you. From these items and other information, you can keep track of issues to do today, this week, this month, and so forth.

SUMMARY

There is a wide variety of operational issues that must be considered as the new business begins operations. These include (1) developing a critical path chart; (2) establishing a location; (3) financing considerations; (4) legitimacy; (5) production management; (6) production charting; (7) quality; (8) equipment; (9) timing; and finally, (10) time management. Each is important to the start-up of a new business, and with proper planning and implementation, these various activities can substantially improve the opportunity for success.

KEY TERMS

anchor stores 230
critical path chart 228
legitimacy 233
production chart 235
strategic alliances 238
strip shopping center 230

REVIEW QUESTIONS

1. Why is a critical path chart useful to potential investors?
2. Are all locations equal?
3. What elements should be considered when leasing a new business location?
4. What would you recommend that a new business do to improve its acceptance and legitimacy in the market?
5. Why is a detailed chart of how business operations are conducted important to the new business?
6. How can quality be built into any product or service?
7. Should all new companies open as soon as they are physically ready? Why or why not?
8. Explain some key time management techniques that will benefit any new entrepreneur.

BUSINESS PLAN DEVELOPMENT QUESTIONS

1. What elements would you include in a critical path chart for your proposed business? How would you ensure that your estimates were accurate?
2. What is the potential locations for your business? Evaluate the different locations and pick one that is the most attractive.
3. What criteria are critical for the location decision of your new business?
4. What are the specific ways you plan to build legitimacy for your business?

INDIVIDUAL EXERCISES

1. What are the "lease or buy" equipment issues you will face in your business?
2. Can you employ used, or will you need new equipment in your business?
3. What is the difference in price of new and used equipment in your proposed business?
4. What are the critical timing issues involved in your business?

GROUP EXERCISES

1. Establish a plan to address each of the critical issues related to the starting of operations for a new organization.
2. Imagine that your team has decided to franchise the business idea. Develop a set of processes/procedures that would allow a third party to become a franchise of your operation.
3. Present your operational plan to the class and ask for feedback.

ENDNOTES

1. A. Gunasekaran, L. Forker, and B. Kobu,"Improving Operations Performance in a Small Company: A Case Study," *International Journal of Operations & Production Management* 20, no. 3/4 (2000), pp. 316–36.
2. F. Levy, G. Thompson, and J. Weist, "The ABCs of the Critical Path Method," *Harvard Business Review* 41, no. 5 (1963) pp. 98–109.
3. Simon Parkin, "Game Writers Must be Multi-Disciplinary Masters, Says Veteran Panel," *Gameasutra*, February 27, 2017, http://www.gamasutra.com/view/news/292542/Game_writers_must_be_multidisciplinary_masters_says_veteran_panel.php.
4. K. Jensen and G. Pompelli, "Manufacturing Site Location Preference of Small Agribusiness Firms," *Journal of Small Business Management* 40 (2002), pp. 204–19.
5. Scott Huntington, "What to Do When It's Time to Expand Your Business," *ChicagoNow*, February 9, 2017, http://www.chicagonow.com/small-biz-blog/2017/02/what-to-do-when-its-time-to-expand-your-business/.
6. A. Bouma, C. Durham, and L. Meunier-Goddik, "Start-Up and Operating Costs for Artisan Cheese Companies," *Journal of Dairy Science* 97 (2014), pp. 3964–72.
7. D. Shepard and A. Zacharakis, "A New Venture's Cognitive Legitimacy: An Assessment by Customers," *Journal of Small Business Management* 41 (2003), pp. 148–68.
8. B. Nagy, J. Pollack, M. Rutherford, and F. Lohrke, "The Influence of Entrepreneurs Credentials and Impression Management Behaviors on Perceptions of New Venture Legitimacy," *Entrepreneurship Theory & Practice* 36 (2012), pp. 941–55.
9. K. Papke-Shields, M. Malhotra, and V. Grover, "Strategic Manufacturing Planning Systems and Their Linkage to Planning System Success," *Decision Sciences* 33 (2002), pp. 1–30.
10. Parker Davis, "7 Simple Strategies for Improving Your Customer Service Quality," *Business2Community*, March 1, 2017, http://www.business2community.com/customer-experience/7-simple-strategies-improving-customer-service-quality-01789314#sw9RogmP6jbOt4uL.97.
11. W. Deming, *Out of the Crisis* (Cambridge, MA: Massachusetts Institute of Technology,1992).
12. K. Brouther and G. Nakos, "SME Entry Mode Choice and Performance: A Transaction Cost Perspective," *Entrepreneurship Theory & Practice* 28 (2004), pp. 229–48; J. Liao and W. Gartner, "The Effects of Pre-Venture Plan Timing and Perceived Environmental Uncertainty on the Persistence of Emerging Firms," *Small Business Economics* 27 (2006), pp. 23–40.
13. S. Covey, A. Merrill, and R. Merrill, *First Things First* (New York: Simon & Schuster, 1994).

part 5

chapter 13

©WendellandCarolyn/Getty Images RF

learning objectives

After studying this chapter, you will be able to:

LO13-1 Explain the need for developing an exit or harvest plan and ideal timing for that plan.

LO13-2 Outline the steps for selling a business.

LO13-3 Discuss the concept of turnaround and business in decline.

LO13-4 Recognize the implications and issues involved in closing a business.

Exit/Harvest/ Turnaround

EVERNOTE

Evernote was founded in 2008 by Phil Libin. The firm provides a note taking app that works on multiple platforms such as Windows or Mac, iOS or Android. Once the material is entered, the system links what is generated to cloud storage. The user can utilize the system for text, audio, or images. The user can then search that material with optical character recognition (OCR) reader. The firm is still private and valued at over a billion dollars.

However, in 2008 this young small firm was preparing to shut down. As has been noted in the text, cash is king in small firms. The economy of all major nations in 2008 struggled as the housing crisis came into full force. The result for Evernote was a rapid loss of customers and increasing number of accounts payable that the firm could not collect. In turn as is the case with most small businesses, the terms that creditors put on Evernote got stricter. The result was a cash crisis.

With less than two weeks of cash in the bank, Libin began to start the process of shutting the firm down. He noted that you do not want to just hit a wall and then close the next day. Instead it has to be a rational, systematic process. What saved the firm was a happy customer who reached out at that critical moment. The customer was inquiring about using the product but after a set of discussions decided to make a substantial investment in the firm that allowed it to continue.

After the firm's success in attracting more customers, it was able to attract more outside investment. One of the points made clear by Evernote is that apps often follow a "smile graph." That is the shape seen when you graft the percentage of sign-ups on the *Y*-axis while months form the time factor on the *X*-axis. Users initially flock to a new app using it heavily; however, over time many of those individuals drop off. They return to the firm when they realize the value you were offering and finding nothing similar—thus driving the signups again up. This creates the smile shape. Another key insight Libin has learned is that every time the firm triples in size, you need to break everything and change all the systems. He has found that as the firm grows, there is a constant need to create completely new systems that fit with where you are at that time.

In 2017 the firm announced that it was cash-flow positive and would no longer take any additional outside capital. The firm now focuses on paid subscriptions and a very lean structure to ensure profitability.

Questions

1. Would you have chosen to shut the firm down over a two-week period or pushed the business to the very last dollar trying to save the firm?
2. Where are you going to cut expenses in your proposed business if you have to save the business from closing?

Sources: Jordan Novet, "Never Say Never: Evernote Says It Has No Plans to Take on More VC Money," *Venture Beat*, February 13, 2017, http://venturebeat.com/2017/02/13/never-say-never-evernote-says-it-has-no-plans-to-take-on-more-vc-money/; A. Vilpponen, "From Brink of Bankruptcy Towards an IPO—The Evernote Story," *ArcticStartup*, May 4, 2012, http://arcticstartup.com/article/from-brink-of-bankruptcy-towards-an-ipo-the-evernote-story/; J. DeMers, "5 Businesses That Almost Failed and Showed Us Why It Pays to Keep Going," *Entrepreneur*, April 11, 2016, https://www.entrepreneur.com/article/272710; R. Feloni, "The Cofounder of Evernote Shares the Best Advice He's Ever Received as a CEO," *Business Insider*, August 7, 2015, http://www.businessinsider.com/evernote-founder-shares-his-best-management-advice-2015-8.

Eventually there will come a time when the founder(s) needs to, or wants to, exit business. This decision may be based on a variety of factors. One may be that the business has done very well and the founder(s) has decided to cash out of the venture. On paper the founder(s) may appear to be very wealthy, but if all of the assets are in the business, then the individual's assets are not liquid and are subject to rapid changes in wealth as the value of the business changes. Selling the business turns some of the hard earned sweat equity into cash. The ability to turn some or all of the business value into cash at some point allows the business owners a flexibility in their choice of actions and businesses as they go forward.

Alternatively, it may be that things have not gone well and the founder(s) needs to either turn the venture around or close down the business. A wide set of issues must be addressed in all of these cases, including such issues as a plan for establishing the value of the business, attracting buyers, negotiating a sale, meeting all of the legal requirements for the sale, consummating the deal, and paying off the investors. These issues can become even more complex if you have to look at turning a business around. While difficult, the ability to turn a business around is a valuable skill for an entrepreneur. This chapter will explore these areas.

LO13-1

Explain the need for developing an exit or harvest plan and ideal timing for that plan.

Need for Developing an Exit or Harvest Plan and Ideal Timing for That Plan

The entrepreneurs benefit from considering several dimensions of what is required to sell the business, both at the founding and when they begin the selling process.

Why Consider Exit or Harvest Now?

It may appear odd to consider the topic of exit and harvest while you are only beginning the process of getting the new business up and running. However, early stage entrepreneurs must consider a well-defined exit plan before personality clashes arise. A business is an investment of both time and money. In addition, developing a practical exit plan can provide some peace of mind to the family and the investors, so they know what to expect if things do not go as planned. The key starting point for any decision to exit or harvest the firm is establishing the valuation of the firm. Developing an accurate valuation as the firm begins to have cash flow also helps the entrepreneur in other other ways:

1. Provide insight for the founders as to the amount of future capital and labor that they should invest in the effort.
2. The business obtain loans (either direct or working capital) by demonstrating the value of the firm to potential creditors.
3. Convince outside equity investors of the potential long-term returns associated with the harvesting of the business.
4. The owners field potential offers to buy out the business (a relatively common occurrence in the life of a business).
5. Benchmark the growth of the firm by establishing a true starting point.

Why Consider Exit or Harvest Later?

Having laid at least some initial groundwork will help the entrepreneurs if they later decide to exit the business. As discussed in Chapter 2, the entrepreneur must determine what he wants to accomplish in the business. If the business

KOSHER HOME

Starting and running the business had proven harder than Jack and Toby had thought. The two entrepreneurs were thus pleasantly surprised when in a surprise call, one of their customers called them and offered to buy the firm outright for $400,000 cash. Even better, the potential buyer wanted the founders to stay on with the business and would pay them a salary to manage the business. The buyer would provide the founders a guaranteed two-year management contract at $90,000 per year per person, plus 15 percent of the yearly profits during those two years.

The buyer presented this deal to the founders of Kosher Home claiming that the total package was worth approximately $800,000 (assuming that profits grew respectably), which he claimed was the value of the business right now. The resulting conversation among the two partners focused on three critical issues.

First, should they even consider selling the business at this point? Second, if they did consider selling, what would be a reasonable price for the business? Third, what were their personal long-term goals, and did this offer get them closer to those goals? To consider these questions, Jack and Toby had to figure out how much the business was worth. For advice, they approached a friend who had worked in mergers and acquisitions (M&A) as a consultant to manufacturers, and he suggested that the real value of a business was simply the market value of the assets of the firm plus a premium (which he referred to as goodwill), which represented the future value of the firm. He suggested that many M&A deals pay a 20 percent premium above the market value of an established public business. Using this calculation, the founders estimated that the business was worth $180,000 ($150,000 in equity capital and equipment plus 20 percent). However, this number did not seem to account for the potential of the business, and in any case, this was substantially less than what the buyer had offered.

The founders contacted two members of their board of advisors and asked for their advice. They quickly discounted the friend's advice regarding M&A as not applicable to a services business. The advisory board members told the founders to forecast net cash flow for the next five years (five years was chosen as a reasonable return period) and then discount that number back to the present time using a reasonable discount rate for risky newer ventures (say, 20 percent). So, the founders estimated net cash flow for the next five years as follows:

Year 1 $94,296	5-Year Total Earnings $322,159
Year 2 $15,075	Discount Rate @ 20% 2.488
Year 3 $102,305	322,159/2.488 = $129,485
Year 4 $132,066	
Year 5 $167,009	

Neither of these valuations seemed to be even close to what the buyer was offering.

QUESTIONS

1. What do you think is a fair value for this firm?
2. How do you believe the founders have miscalculated the real value of the business as it stands today?
3. Assuming that a fair value can be calculated, should the founders sell the firm at this point? Why or why not?
4. What does your answer to Question 2 say about your risk propensity?

is very successful but is no longer interesting or enjoyable, it is probably a good time to exit. A business takes too much time and personal commitment to be something that is not enjoyable. Similarly, there may be other opportunities available. The entrepreneur may not have time to run the existing business and pursue these new opportunities at the same time, so it becomes necessary to exit the first business. Alternatively, the founder may sense that whereas the business is strong now, the future does not hold the same potential for similar success, so it might be a good time to exit.

One example is an entrepreneur we knew who set up a number of sports shoe stores. Several years after founding, the owner began to realize that there were major chains entering the market, which was leading to market saturation in his area. He would have to completely reset the strategy of the business in order to compete in the future. This individual decided to harvest the venture and sell it to someone else. He reaped the value of the business that he had grown without having to go through the painful process of resetting the strategic position of the firm.

LO13-2

Outline the steps for selling a business.

Steps for Selling a Business

When a business owner decides to sell or harvest the business, there is a series of steps that need to occur. The first is to develop some sense of the true value of the business. The second is to prepare the business to be sold. The last step is the negotiation and actual selling of the business.

Valuation

There are several standard valuation models and rules of thumb for established, publicly traded businesses. For example, public companies have an established market capitalization that is technically the value of the business as it exists at the present time. Following the standard on Wall Street, this market capitalization already accounts for future earnings and all future prospects of the business that are known today. If you wished to acquire one of these organizations, the general assumption would be that the market capitalization is the floor from which all negotiations begin. Calculating the premium that will be offered above the market capitalization is more a matter of art than one of science.* Issues such as how much cash will be paid versus stock transferred and the future investment in the newly combined organization are a matter of negotiation, not to mention the overwhelming concern regarding what will happen to the executives of the acquired firm. These issues are substantially different when we consider the valuation and acquisition of a privately held venture.

Virtually all new businesses are private firms that do not report their earnings to the public. In addition, new businesses often adjust their annual company "earnings" with the payment of large year-end bonuses to the founders in order to limit the profit and, therefore, the taxes on the business. The new business may also have creative company **perquisites** ("perks") for the owners to minimize the tax owed by the organization. The owners of a new business may also have other individual personal expenses paid for by the firm. The result is that the firm pays fewer taxes, but the firm also may appear to be worth less than it is really worth to the entrepreneur.

perquisites

Benefits paid for by the company. Examples include vacations, vehicles, loans, gifts, financial contributions to retirement plans, and so on.

For example, a firm such as Kosher Home that is owned by two individuals allows the founders to use "profits" for the benefit of the firm as well as themselves in a perfectly legal and ethical manner. If sales were particularly good in one year, the founders may decide to provide luxury cars as a perk for themselves. This expense dramatically reduces the "profit" of the venture, whereas the reality is that the business is quite profitable. Similar expenses also occur in public companies; however, they are required to disclose such items in an audited annual report, whereas a new business venture rarely goes to the expense of having audited financial records. Thus, it should be clear that different methods of valuation are needed when considering the purchase of a private company.

There are a large number of unique systems used for the valuation of a private business. Most accounting groups and many private companies provide business valuation services. We would suggest that you work with these organizations when you are really ready to sell the business. They will use commonly accepted practices to refine the value of the ongoing business. However, in general, we

*There are a number of other quick methods for calculating a purchase price, including a multiple of sales, discounted future earnings, discounted projected free cash flow, and so on. We provide all of this by way of comparison.

encourage the entrepreneur to use only a few of the most common methods to get a rough estimate of the value of the business as the business begins and grows. Valuing a business is as much art as it is science. Ultimately, the true "value" of the business is the amount of money that a willing seller and a willing buyer agree upon for the sale of the business. Thus, you want to be well prepared for the range of prices that may be offered and understand why you might agree or not agree with those prices. An investor, lender, or potential purchaser may take issue with several of the assumptions in your projections or might want to reduce the numbers more severely than the founders believe is realistic. To maximize the selling price of the firm, the founders must intimately understand the numbers to be able to discuss such issues intelligently with those individuals. These methods include (1) discounted future net cash flow, (2) price/earnings valuation, (3) asset-based valuation, (4) capitalization of earnings valuation, and (5) market estimation valuation.

Discounted Future Net Cash Flow. By far the most widely accepted method of valuation, and the most insightful, involves some form of discounting the estimated future net cash flows of the business. As you might recall from Chapter 6, cash flow tracks the actual cash inflows and outflows of the business. For estimation purposes, a potential buyer can subtract any perks that have affected the net cash position of the venture. The detail available in a well-designed cash flow statement and the understanding that it is not profit, but free cash flow that is the key to entrepreneurial success, makes this the ideal document to use in the valuation of a business.

The cash flow method of valuation requires that the net cash flow of the business be projected for some period of time into the future. Our experience has suggested that estimating cash flows five years into the future and adding a salvage value for the firm is a good ballpark floor valuation for a business. For an Internet business, the cash flow method works very well although there is typically no salvage value for any of the assets since even used computers normally have minimal value. The information for this example appears in Figure 13.1.

In this example, the net cash flow for each year is as follows:

Year 1 $101,885

Year 2 $30,575

Year 3 $143,725

Year 4 $161,000

Year 5 $446,100

Those most interested in a good estimation of firm value (potential buyers, lenders, equity investors, and founders) will recognize that these numbers are simply estimates that are based on a set of assumptions. To understand and accept the cash flow predictions, it is important that each interested party accept the underlying assumptions. Therefore, a critical addition to any business plan, and certainly a necessity for any valuation analysis, is a complete set of assumptions used by the founders. An example from a group of entrepreneurs that were proposing a specialty transport company appears in Figures 13.2 and 13.3. Individuals could rent the bus to go to special events or hire it to go to different bars in a city or just to drive around and party. The plan was to sell alcohol and limited food on the bus. We will use this firm as an example to evaluate the different valuations that the firm could expect.

Discounting the Cash Flow. The example above illustrates that to understand a cash flow statement, an entrepreneur needs to have an in-depth knowledge of the assumptions that went into the statement. Given the nature of predictions and assumptions in general, there is a need for these values to be discounted by some rate that not only represents the return expected by an investor but also accounts for the riskiness of the venture. We have seen discount rates range

RECEIPTS:	YEAR 1, $	YEAR 2, $	YEAR 3, $	YEAR 4, $	YEAR 5, $	TOTALS, $
Sales	$ 25,000	$325,000	$ 675,000	$880,000	$1,560,000	$3,465,000
Consulting	20,000	20,000	60,000	80,000	100,000	280,000
Total Receipts	45,000	345,000	735,000	960,000	1,660,000	3,745,000
Disbursements:						
Salaries	$ 45,000	$ 95,000	$ 210,000	$305,000	$ 450,000	$ 1,105,000
Travel	4,050	31,050	66,150	86,400	149,400	337,050
Car Leases	4,000	6,000	7,500	11,000	13,800	42,300
Rent	900	6,900	14,700	19,200	33,200	74,900
Payroll Taxes	2,700	5,700	12,600	18,300	27,000	66,300
Insurance	5,500	6,000	7,500	9,000	13,000	41,000
Fuel/Maint.	960	4,500	8,000	13,000	21,000	47,460
Executive Comp.	64,000	72,000	78,000	84,000	89,000	387,000
Benefits	13,500	28,500	63,000	91,500	135,000	331,500
Advertising	2,000	26,000	54,000	70,400	124,800	277,200
Supplies	225	1,725	3,675	4,800	8,300	18,725
Utilities	3,150	24,150	51,450	67,200	116,200	262,150
Misc.	900	6,900	14,700	19,200	33,200	74,900
Total Disbursements	$ 146,885	$ 314,425	$ 591,275	$ 799,000	$ 1,213,900	$ 3,065,485
Beginning Balance	0	98,115	128,690	272,415	433,415	
Equity Investment	200,000					
Net Cash Flow	**($ 101,885)**	**$ 30,575**	**$ 143,725**	**$ 161,000**	**$ 446,100**	**$ 679,515**
Ending Balance	$ 98,115	$ 128,690	$ 272,415	$ 433,415	$ 879,515	$ 1,812,150

Figure 13.1
Example Cash Flow Statement

from a ridiculously low 10 percent to an almost absurd 90 percent. However, a rule of thumb for new businesses being operated by owner-managers is to use 30 percent as a discount factor. This should not only account for a generous annualized rate of return but also build in a reasonable factor for risk. While we are in favor of simplicity in these calculations, we recognize that some interested parties prefer to separate return from risk. There are a variety of sophisticated financial models available to those who wish to be more precise in their analysis.

Cash Flow categories will vary with the type of business being analyzed.

©Alan Schein/Alamy RF

Using this rule of thumb, the entrepreneur should take the net cash flow figure generated for each year and discount that cash flow back to today's dollars. The discount rate remains the same, while the factor increases as you move farther away from today. Thus, in year 2, the discount rate is squared (1.3 * 1.3), in year 3 it is cubed (1.3 * 1.3 * 1.3), and so on. To illustrate with our previous example, we calculate the present value of the net cash flow below.

Illustration of Present Value of the Net Cash Flow. Using the information in Figure 13.1 and assuming a 30 percent discount rate, we can calculate the present value of the net cash flows as follows:

Figure 13.2
General Cash Flow Assumptions for Specialty Bus Company

Recall we are employing a specialty bus company under different valuation lenses. The assumptions that go into the cash flow, which allow us to make the valuation, include the following:

- Liquor sales are not included in the cash flow statement and are determined on a per trip basis, depending on how much alcohol the group orders. We will charge a 10 percent markup rate for each order.
- We applied an 8 percent payroll tax to salaries.
- The growth predications vary widely since the first year will require a ramping up of sales.
- However, our first year there will be extensive growth as the product becomes better known.
- The fourth year the growth is slowed as the firm does not expect to enter a new territory in the metropolitan area.
- The fifth year the firm again moves into a neighboring city in the metropolitan area and offers the service there.
- Gas costs were based on an assumption that the price is $3.60 per gallon for diesel fuel. According to the Energy Information Administration, this has been the average price for the last two years in the Midwest region.
- We assume there will be no significant economic recessions within the next five years.
- We have researched laws pertaining to continuous operation for a commercial driver and will assure that all itineraries are planned accordingly.

$$(101{,}885)/1.3 + 30{,}575/1.3^2 + 143{,}725/1.3^3 + 161{,}000/1.3^4 + 446{,}100/1.3^5 = \text{PV(NCF)}$$

$$(101{,}885)/1.3 + 30{,}575/1.69 + 143{,}725/2.19 + 161{,}000/2.85 + 446{,}100/3.71 = \text{PV(NCF)}$$

$$(78{,}373) + 18{,}091 + 65{,}959 + 56{,}372 + 120{,}145 = \mathbf{\$182{,}194}$$

Without accounting for the sale price of the business, this calculation would suggest that the current value of the business is approximately $180,000.

Price/Earnings Valuation. Another method of estimating the value of a business is to use the industry **price/earnings (P/E) ratio**. This is a relatively straightforward approach that uses the industry in which the start-up operates. The founder should locate the P/E ratio for public companies in the same industry via the many sources of this information (the Internet, *The Wall Street Journal,* the library, etc.). That average should be multiplied by the net cash flow for year 5 and discounted back as a potential sales price in year 6 of the venture. Therefore, for our specialty bus company we employ 1 + the discount rate raised to the sixth power. In our example that would be 1.3^6 (4.826).

price/earnings (P/E) ratio
A value derived from public companies that divides the current earnings per share into the price per share.

Illustration of P/E Ratio Valuation. This example illustrates how to calculate your P/E ratio valuation:

P/E for Industry	10 (obtained from industry sources)
Net Cash Flow for Year 5	$446,100
Discount Rate	30%
Sale/Residual Value	446,100 * 10 = $4,460,000
	$4{,}460{,}000/1.3^6$ = Discounted Sales Price
	4,460,000/4.826 = $ 924,005

Figure 13.3
Example of Specific Cash Flow Assumptions

Although there are general assumptions that go into the cash flow calculation, an individual will also need to make assumptions for the very specific firm setting before the cash flow can be discounted. The specific cash flow assumptions we make include the following:

- Sales tax for each state and the surrounding municipality is 7 percent, applicable to the rental price.
- Income will be consistent throughout all of the centers in the different states. This is because we have hand-picked each school and have taken great efforts to make sure that they are all similar in population, athletic activity, demographic makeup, and geographic locations.
- Maintenance overhaul will occur in the first quarter for each bus at a cost of $1,000 per bus.
- All acquisitions and expansions will be financed internally; there will be no need for second- and third-round financing.
- Salaries are set at $30,000 for each officer, with an increase to $35,000 in year 3.
- Insurance is a once-a-year payment, including $10,000 for base coverage with each additional bus adding $1,000 plus tax, stamping, and processing fees.
- Waste removal is billed by volume plus service fees, estimating $75 to $100 per visit.
- Credit card charges account for 30 percent of all sales with a processing fee of 2.1 percent.
- Transportation costs are associated with moving buses within the state.
- Accounting/legal fees will occur periodically throughout the year, with a concentration of accounting fees during tax season and legal fees during periods of expansion or acquisition.
- Fees and permits include registration costs, inspection fees, and other associated costs with each bus, as well as the costs of providing commercial drivers' licenses (CDL) and training to officers at the inception of the company.

Using these calculations, we would suggest that the value of the firm today would be the addition of the present value of the future cash flows plus the discounted sales price of the firm. For this example, that would be the following:

Discounted Cash Flow	+	Discounted Sales Price	=	Current Value
$182,194	+	$924,005	=	**$1,106,199**

There are two other relatively popular methods for valuing a business: asset-based valuation and earnings valuation.

asset valuation
A method of business valuation that simply totals all of the hard assets of the organization and adds in a goodwill value.

Asset-Based Valuation. **Asset valuation** involves accounting for all of the hard assets of the organization: buildings (if owned), equipment (if owned), furniture, cash, and marketable securities held in the name of the company, as well as (in most cases) the value of any signed and executable contracts. Once all of the assets of the organization are tallied, the value of the business is typically calculated by taking that total number and adding an acquisition, or goodwill, value to it. This acquisition/goodwill value is determined by examining similar companies that have been acquired or more often by simply looking at the percentage premium being offered in general on all new public acquisitions. If the business were performing poorly, there would be virtually no goodwill value. Asset valuation is typically the lowest business valuation number that you will calculate, unless you are an asset-intensive business. This valuation method works best for firms with hard assets and not an Internet business.

Illustration of Asset Valuation. Following is an illustration of asset valuation for a restaurant rather than our bus company since it allows a richer set of assets. The bus company leased its buses, so there were very limited assets. In a case such as that for the bus company, asset valuation method is of limited use:

Building (Market Value Minus Mortgage)		=	$108,755
Equipment			
1.	1 grill	=	$ 8,450
2.	3 cook counters	=	$ 950
3.	2 fryers	=	$ 1,300
4.	1 walk-in freezer	=	$ 1,850
5.	3 refrigerators	=	$ 4,600
6.	2 computers/accessories	=	$ 1,300
7.	Various cooking utensils	=	$ 3,904
8.	Bar equipment	=	$ 3,700
			$ 26,054
Furniture			
1.	41 (2-top) tables	=	$ 10,900
2.	17 (4-top) tables	=	$ 6,050
3.	6 (6-top) tables	=	$ 2,800
4.	197 chairs	=	$ 13,902
5.	4 counters	=	$ 980
6.	1 complete bar	=	$ 3,700
			$ 38,332
	Cash/marketable securities	=	$ 26,800
	Total asset value	=	$ 199,941

Total Asset Value * Acquisition Premium = Value of the Business

$199,941 * 4.3 = $859,746

In this particular instance, a quick analysis of the industry revealed that an average asset-acquisition premium for this particular industry was running at approximately 4.3 times assets. Each industry will be unique and the appropriate multiple will vary over time with changing market conditions and industry M&A activity. Therefore, the business as it currently stands (via this method) would be worth approximately $860,000. This method tends to depress the true future value of a growing business, so some investors and lenders will factor in a growth premium to "bulk up" the total valuation. "Art" intrudes once again.

Capitalization of Earnings Valuation. Very similar to asset valuation, **capitalization of earnings valuation** is performed by taking the earnings (net profit) of the organization; subtracting or adding any unusual items that the lender or investor believes are not customary, normal, or usual items; and dividing that figure by a capitalization rate. The capitalization rate is determined (rather loosely) by the nature of business, including longevity, business risk, consistency of earning, quality of management, and general economic conditions. The capitalization rate is generally an agreed upon number rather than something that can be "looked up."

capitalization of earnings valuation
A method of valuation achieved by taking the earnings (net profit) of the organization; subtracting or adding any unusual items that the lender or investor feels are not customary, normal, or usual items; and dividing that figure by a capitalization rate.

Illustration of Capitalization of Earnings Valuation. This illustrates capitalization of earnings valuation using our example of a specialty bus firm:

Net Profit (Earnings) of the Company = \$32,900
Capitalization Rate = 0.2

$$\$32{,}900/0.2 = \$164{,}500$$

Using this system involves much more than simply accepting a final net profit figure. As was stated in Chapter 6, the net profit of a new business is an easily manipulated figure that is wholly dependent on the needs and desires of the founders. Therefore, lenders and investors adjust this figure to account for the individual actions of the founders. Would-be buyers readjust the net profit of the company to account for these nuances of a new business and then apply a capitalization rate that is a combination of the buyers' risk propensity and the current situation in the business acquisition marketplace.

market estimation
A method of business valuation that involves taking the earnings of the business and multiplying that figure by the market premium of companies in its industry.

Market Estimation Valuation. A valuation via **market estimation** is by far the simplest of the techniques. Fundamentally, it involves taking the earnings (or projected earnings) of the business and multiplying that figure by the market premium of companies in their industry. A popular method is to take the EBITDA (earnings before interest, taxes, depreciation, and amortization), reworking the figure based on an analysis of the cash flow statement, and multiplying the remaining figure by a market multiple. An examination of the NASDAQ or NYSE provides a group of companies in virtually every industry classification. Taking the group as a whole or attempting to find companies that are similar to your business yields an estimated market premium, also called an industry multiple, that can be used to calculate the value of the business. Once again, lenders and investors will attempt to adjust the earnings of the organization to reflect a more balanced picture.

Market Estimation Illustration. The following illustrates market estimation valuation using our sample specialty bus firm:

Net Profit (Earnings) of the Company = \$32,900
Industry Multiple = 13

$$\$32{,}900 * 13 = \$427{,}700$$

Valuation Overview. As can be seen, there are wide variations in the potential valuations of this business, from several hundred thousand dollars to one and a half million dollars. Every company has unique features that provide it with some type of competitive advantage. In Chapter 5, we developed a strong argument for the development of a sustainable competitive advantage that enabled the new business to gain true economic rents relative to the competition. These "art" characteristics of an organization are important considerations in the valuation of a business and should be part of the equation when determining the true value of your business. To illustrate the art involved in valuing a firm, consider how to value an app. The entrepreneur should consider there may be three ways to do it. If the app has been available for less than six months and has a consistent source of revenue for at least three months, you can expect an acquisition price of between eight and ten months of revenue. When an app has been available for more than six months and has a consistent source of revenue for at least three months, you can expect an acquisition price of

EXERCISE 1

1. Using your projected cash flow statement, develop a business valuation for your proposed company. This will mean forecasting cash flow five years into the future.
2. Use your annual net cash flow as an estimate of earnings. Use the earnings valuation method and the market valuation method to estimate the value of your organization five years from now. Assume that the P/E for your industry is 7 and the acquisition premium is (P/E ratio plus 3).
3. Using the same cash flow statement, estimate your total assets and compute an asset-based valuation for the business.
4. Looking at the range of figures that you have just developed, explain why one particular figure is more representative of the value of the business.

between 12 and 14 months of revenue. When an app has a high number of consistent downloads for three months or more without necessarily monetizing, you can expect to an acquisition price of approximately $0.05 per download for a six to eight month return of investment.[1]

Preparing the Business for Sale

When the determination has been made to sell the business, the entrepreneur must begin a process that is somewhat akin to selling a home. There is a need for the entrepreneur to make sure the business looks its best in order to obtain the highest premium possible.

One of the key issues for the survival of the business after the sale is the change in leadership that will occur. Consider for a moment a business we knew that sold equipment to research laboratories. The founder of the business had all the key contacts for the business. When he first tried to sell the business, there were very few individuals interested in the firm. This was despite the firm's having received the Outstanding Small Business of the Year award from the local government the prior year. The key problem was that there was little value in the business beyond the founder himself. Buyers bought the company's products because of the founder's reputation and his unique ability to install the products. Potential buyers did not want to buy a firm whose contacts and relationships walked out the door when the founder sold the business. This story raises important questions for any seller. How will the business run after the founder leaves? How do you transfer the founder's contacts and reputation to the new owners? There should be a transition plan in place for this transfer in order for any purchase to be viable. (See the cases at the back of this text to see several firms facing these same challenges today.)

This difficulty is compounded by the reality that most entrepreneurial businesses run a very tight operation where every individual has specific functions and there is little slack available for cross-training. The company founder might handle all of the marketing and sales for the organization. This may include meeting clients, handling contract negotiations, and being the point person for each customer, while the company has another individual handle all of the operational details. Replacing this personal contact person would require that the founder begin to incorporate others in the handling of customers and/or include a new individual to join her in the process of client meetings. All of this requires a significant investment in the future without obvious payoffs in the present. Most entrepreneurs find this quite difficult. These and other types of human resource issues unique to an entrepreneurial business were covered in Chapter 10.

The firm also needs to examine its operations to ensure that the procedures of the business are codified and simplified for easy handover to a new owner. It is a reality in entrepreneurial businesses that the operational procedures develop as the business grows. The effort to put these procedures in writing will go a long way toward making for a more seamless transition. Another operational issue is the accounting of the firm. A system where the founder keeps the books herself is perfectly acceptable and perhaps even desirable when starting up and running the new business. However, a potential buyer wants to assure himself of the accuracy of the financial information. Our advice for ventures considering a sale is to contract with a CPA firm to have it do the following when looking to exit the firm:

1. Audit last year's financial statements.
2. Put all of the statements into a standardized format.
3. Develop procedures for the accounting of all activities.
4. Provide an audit of this year's financial statements and render an accounting opinion.

ETHICAL CHALLENGE

In the process of preparing his firm to be sold, one entrepreneur sought to make the business look as attractive as possible to prospective buyers. He had the opportunity to make a large sale right before the business would be inspected, which would make his financials look much better. However, the entrepreneur was well aware that the buyer who would make this large purchase from him/her was in bankruptcy proceedings and that he might or might not actually be paid for the large sell. The entrepreneur also had a large manufacturing equipment base that he had poor maintenance records for. Due to the poor records, the entrepreneur realized that he could just clean the equipment and positively impact the asset valuation without really changing what the assets were, so the value of the equipment might lie in its appearance.

QUESTIONS

1. What are the entrepreneur's legal requirements in presenting the business to a buyer?
2. Do the ethical requirements differ from the legal requirements in what must be presented? Isn't it simply "buyer beware"?
3. How do you as a business owner make sure that the firm looks attractive to purchase but at the same time provide realistic information?

This effort provides a level of legitimacy to the business and assures the buyer of the accuracy of the financial statements of the organization.

Maintaining an estimate of the value of a business as it grows and develops is the responsibility of the business owner. However, the entrepreneur should obtain a professional valuation of the business before attempting to actually sell the business. The valuation may turn out to be much less than the owner feels that the firm is worth, and therefore, there would be little need to pursue the attempt to sell the firm.

Specialization within a business, like hospital auditing, can make the process of selling a business more complicated. What are some things to consider?
©peterspiro/Getty Images RF

The methods that will be used by the professional valuation experts will likely be very similar to those detailed earlier in this chapter. The entrepreneur would be well served to conduct one's own estimate and then compare that to what the professional advises. The entrepreneur should actively challenge the analysis and discuss it with the valuation professional. The knowledge that the entrepreneur develops regarding the valuation of the business will help as they negotiate the sale of the business.

Another important aspect in preparing the business for sale is the recording of all the informal practices of the organization. Policies and procedures developed in the life of a new venture should be recorded and available to a new buyer. Issues such as when to order certain supplies, what time to begin closing each day, the process of closing each day, the methods for dealing with customers, payment practices, human resource benefits and policies, and the like must all be codified. Anyone who wants to purchase an entire company should have all of these practices in writing—both for ease of analysis and for clarity of understanding that this provides regarding the inner working of the business.

The business founders also need to plan for the type of sale that will maximize their returns. The best method to use to actually exit the firm will very much depend on the type of business. Businesses that have moved well beyond the founder's personality will be simpler to sell than those that are intimately tied to the active participation of the founder. Although there are literally thousands of possible ways to construct a sales agreement, it might take some careful forethought and years of preparation work to make the business valuable to an outside investor.

One of the authors recently worked with an established accounting business where the two founders were both in their early 70s. Although they were looking to exit the business, they really wanted a continuing revenue stream. One of the founder's sons was also an accountant who wanted to take over the company. Unfortunately, neither partner believed the son had the ability to carry on the work of the business in a managing role. Therefore, the two partners began to ponder how they would sell the firm. In the accounting business, as in many other companies, relationships are critical to the success of the business. Rather than make a quick sale that would lead to both founders leaving the firm immediately, they envisioned an opportunity in which they would leave gradually. They also had a specialized customer base that consisted primarily of hospitals. Hospital audits are usually completed on a schedule that differs from that of traditional corporate audits, which could allow a larger accounting business to better rationalize its accounting work flow. At a conference during the prior year, a larger firm had expressed an interest in an association with the partners' smaller firm. The two partners later approached the head of the larger firm and worked out a deal that included the following:

1. A small up-front cash payment.
2. A five-year management agreement with the two founding partners.
3. A gradual handover to executives from the larger firm.
4. An annuity payment to the founders for 10 years, based upon bookings.

The result was a smooth sale of the business in which both the acquiring and the acquired firms' owners were pleased with the results.

Actually Seeking to Sell the Business

Once the decision has been made to sell the business to an outside party, a number of choices are available to the entrepreneur. The most common is to sell the business intact to a third party with the aid of a broker or lawyer. A second very common option is to sell the business to a competitor or to a larger business interested in your location, your position in the market, your product, and so on. A third option is to divest portions of the business that will maximize the value of the business. It is not uncommon for the total value of the firm to be higher if the business is split into separate entities especially if there is real estate owned by the firm or the firm has become highly diversified over time. A fourth option, which is rarely used but is certainly the option most idealized by the business press, is an **initial public offering (IPO)**. The reality is that only a very small number of start-up businesses that end up being very high growth actually seek to conduct an IPO. In fact, for the entrepreneur, an IPO may not be the most profitable means to exit the business. Given the rarity of this type of event, we only mention the possibility of an IPO.

initial public offering (IPO)
The initial listing of a firm as a public entity in the public equities market.

Not surprisingly, actually putting a business up for sale is a bit more art than it is science. The process of getting the word out that a business is for sale can occur through a variety of avenues:

1. Hiring a business broker who will market the business for a percentage of the sale price.
2. Contacting competitors or businesses that have expressed an interest in your business.
3. Letting your accountant and your lawyer know that you are interested in selling your business. Individuals in both of these professions have numerous business contacts and may be aware of individuals seeking to buy a business.
4. Contacting your suppliers and perhaps (if appropriate) your significant clients to let them know about your interest in selling the business.

Negotiation Strategies

Although it may be obvious to state this, negotiating a sale is the art of trying to reach an agreed price between a willing buyer and a willing seller. Thus, a sale is based in the needs and wants of both parties. For example, if the buyer has other similar businesses in the city and the acquisition of your firm will provide coverage in the final section of the city where they currently are not located or will provide the buyer an outlet in the fastest-growing part of the city, then perhaps a higher price will be offered. Similarly, if the buyer is only interested in the business if he can get a bargain, he might try to pay less. The entrepreneur should not believe there is some absolute price that the buyer will not go above or below. Negotiating to sell the business is a process that the entrepreneur must actively engage in if she is to be successful.

Negotiation is a completely separate field of study, and texts exist for understanding the nuances and techniques that are available. Several important points to keep in mind regarding the negotiation of a sale include the following:

1. Use a professional mediator for anything but the most basic level of discussions. Your lawyer can play this role provided she has the experience. As we discussed in Chapter 9 (the legal aspects of the business), you will want all issues to be clear and specific. Do not make assumptions. Your lawyer can make sure that what you think the contract says is what is actually put in writing.
2. Know the buyer. Ask for as much information about the company that is making an inquiry as they ask from you, or more. If they agree to pay you over a period of years but they default after a year, the result may be that you have a failed business returned to you, with only part of the former value of the firm having actually been paid to you.
3. Retain your own advisors. It is very tempting to save money at this point and allow the buyer to provide the services; however, you are well served by having your own independent advisors.
4. Recognize that there are a myriad of options for selling the business. You may sell the company as a whole, or you can break up the business for maximum value. For example, you can sell the equipment to one company, the location to another, the name to yet another, among other scenarios. The goal upon exit is to maximize your own value.
5. Get cash for the firm. Frequently buyers may want to combine your firm with their firm to create a new business. As a result, the purchasing firm will offer you part cash and part stock in the new venture. If you take stock in the new venture, you are dependent on their success, and your liquidity is often reduced.

YrFURN—AN APP FOR FURNITURE

YrFurn had not been in business six months before one of the investors in the business approached the team with a question that shocked them. Would they be interested in selling the business and continuing with it as the management team? They had always thought that the best outcome would be to sell the business, but they were sure it would take two to three years of growth to be able to make real money on the deal.

The team had built out a full business that was growing modestly. They were expanding nationally at a somewhat spotty but consistent pace. The firm was gaining market share as word of mouth expanded, and they now had an IT director with a two person coding team that worked with their external contractors and a full customer service group that consisted of seven full-time employees.

Flabbergasted at the offer, the team asked the investor how much she thought the business was worth. The investor told them that she did not know right then but knew a good operation when she saw one. She wanted to have a chance to go through everything in detail as well as spend a week or so interviewing everyone at the business. She asked the team to think about a few things in the meantime.

How much did they think the business was worth? Would they want to maintain an ownership interest in the business? How long might each of them be willing to commit to running the business if the investor purchased it from them? Would they sign a noncompete agreement, and if so, how long did they think was reasonable?

Brandy, Brad, and Kyle quickly got their bearings and told the investor that before they could commit to pursuing this that the team needed to discuss it among themselves and the rest of the board of directors. They assured the investor that they would get back with her within a week.

QUESTIONS

1. What would you recommend that the team do during the next week? Why?
2. The business is so new, why should the team even consider an offer at this point in time?
3. What would you advise them to do to determine the value of the business right now?

6. Look to the details. For example, new owners frequently want a noncompete agreement from you once you sell. This will prevent you from directly competing with the new owners for *X* number of years. However, if your buyout is not substantial, how will you make a living? Be sure you know all the details and ramifications of the negotiations.

Turnaround and Business in Decline

LO13-3

Discuss the concept of turnaround and business in decline.

Another related issue that faces entrepreneurial businesses is turning around a firm that is in a decline. It is possible that you have developed a solid business that prospered for a number of years. However, after some time and for a variety of factors, both internal and external to the firm, the business starts a period of decline. The effort to reverse that decline is referred to as **turnaround**.[2]

turnaround
The effort to reverse the decline of a business.

It is very difficult to turn around an entrepreneurial business successfully once it starts into a decline. The fact that these businesses have limited slack* or excess resources results in the businesses' having a very small leeway to respond to a decline. This is in contrast to large firms with massive resources, which the firms can rely on for years in the face of poor performance.

*"Slack" in this case includes the time available per individual that is not dedicated to day-to-day work.

Remodeling is just one way to help turnaround. What are some other options?

©Jason Homa/Blend Images LLC

The firm must first seek to retrench.[3] This activity is analogous to medical situations where doctors must quickly seek to stabilize the patient before they can do more substantive actions. If they do not stabilize the patient first, the patient might die and there will be no value in trying other activities. For an entrepreneurial business, such retrenchment efforts focus on the firm's gaining control of its cash flow quickly, regardless of the impact to the long-term effort. This can be accomplished by bringing in accounts receivable more quickly, delaying the payment of accounts payable, renegotiating with suppliers so that supplies do not have to be paid for in cash, eliminating staff, and working with employees to cut costs. Once the bleeding of cash flow has been slowed, the firm can move on to more substantive actions.

While it is obvious that a huge environmental shift in the economy can cause a serious decline in virtually all businesses, the root internal causes of decline are usually based in either operating or strategic problems. To place it in straightforward terms, operating problems relate to either not selling enough of the product or not being sufficiently efficient in producing the product. Strategic problems are most often related to poor positioning choices. Strategic problems often include diversifying into unrelated domains and not being able to successfully manage the business.

Unfortunately, businesspeople tend to focus on the easiest problems to solve first. These are most often simply symptoms that take significant time to correct and yield very little in overall business results. Therefore, we advise businesspeople to pick the one key reason that the business is suffering. Identify it as either operating or strategic and dedicate the resources of the firm to solving that one immediately.

If it is an operating problem, then the solution should be an operating solution. These solutions include increasing marketing or marketing effectiveness to sell more products if the problem is that sales are down. Alternatively, if the problem is production inefficiency, then the focus should be oriented toward reengineering, simplifying, and measuring. Recall that we discussed quality management in Chapter 12. This is most often the focus of operating solutions and is certainly one of the best places to start the effort to turn around the business.

Strategic solutions rely on exiting those poor strategic choices that have been made over the years. We watched a wonderfully successful firm that installed in-ground pools diversify into backyard furniture and toys (such as swing sets). The business had solid positive cash flow and was looking to find a positive outlet for all the cash it was generating. Within a year the owners realized that not only were they losing money on their new business, but they were also installing fewer swimming pools because their corporate officers were distracted by trying to get the new business up and running. They quickly exited the nonpool installation businesses and redoubled their efforts on their core operations. It took almost two years to return the firm to the point where it had been before the foray into the seemingly related business. Recall that we discussed in Chapter 2 the need for entrepreneurs to evaluate the skills they personally possess before going into a business. In this situation, the entrepreneurs may be quite good at managing a pool installation business, but that does not mean that they will be successful with businesses that appear on the surface to be related. The key to success is not seeking to learn the backyard furniture business (one that involves a wide inventory with no need for installation), but instead, focusing exclusively on the pool installation business. When bad strategic choices are made, exit them quickly.

The business press suggests for a large, established business that the CEO of the organization and its top management team be changed in a turnaround situation. The argument suggests that these individuals have paradigms, or ways they view the world, that created the decline in the first place. It is, therefore, supposed to be difficult for such individuals to see the problems and be creative in developing solutions to solve those problems. Entrepreneurial businesses do not have this option since the entrepreneur is running the business. We have found few business founders that are looking to fire themselves. Therefore, it is necessary that the entrepreneur in a decline situation actively seek creative solutions. While not easy to do, this means that they must question themselves and others to a much greater extent than they have done before.[4] A well-developed board of advisors, which we have discussed previously, can be a critical aid in this regard. A board of advisors that will provide honest and insightful advice that challenges the entrepreneur can be very helpful in viewing new ways to compete and new ways to overcome the problems faced by the firm.

EXERCISE 2

1. Imagine Kosher Home is not successful. What do you think they should do to determine the turnaround actions they should follow?
2. What is the greatest barrier such a small service firm faces in such a turnaround?

Implications and Issues Involved in Closing a Business

LO13-4

Recognize the implications and issues involved in closing a business.

It is unfortunate, but bankruptcy may need to be filed by the entrepreneur if the turnaround effort does not succeed quickly enough. The processes/procedures for bankruptcy are arduous and have lasting impact upon the founder(s), and yet there are circumstances where this is the only viable route. There are several types of bankruptcy that can be filed.[5]

Chapter 11 bankruptcy allows the firm to be reorganized. When you file a Chapter 11 bankruptcy, the firm receives immediate protection against all lawsuits and other efforts to collect from the firm.[6] At this stage the firm has 90 days to propose a reorganization plan. This plan needs to show how the business will pay off its past-due debts and stay current with its other debts. The company's banker and other creditors will commonly refer to your account as a "workout." They will be willing to meet with you and seek a resolution regarding the money that is owed to them. Most creditors will be willing to take less than their full payment with the hope that the strength of the firm will return in the future and they will then be in a position to receive more of their debt repayment. If they do not work with the failing business, they face the potential of the business simply liquidating and the lender receiving only a small percentage of the proceeds from the sale of the assets. This reduction in the amount of money that the creditors ultimately accept is referred to as a "haircut."

If the firm's debts are less than $2 million, there is a fast-track version of Chapter 11 that gives creditors far less control than in a larger organization Chapter 11 filing. The fast-track plan must show how back taxes will be brought current over a five-year period. It must also show how those creditors who have pledged collateral behind their debt will be brought current. The unsecured creditors are those who do not have collateral pledged behind their debt, and their debt is the lowest priority. It is generally not necessary to show how unsecured creditors will be paid in this type of Chapter 11 reorganization. During the reorganization process it is possible to terminate leases, contracts, and union agreements that are too burdensome. The bankruptcy judge has the ability to force creditors to accept a plan for reorganization if it appears equitable and fair but the creditors are still unwilling to accept it.

Unfortunately, there are instances where the business must simply be closed. In this case, a Chapter 7 bankruptcy is invoked. In these cases, selling the business consists of selling the "assets" of the business. The assets of the organization include all of the physical assets (equipment, signs, furniture, fixtures, etc.) as well as any valuable intangibles, such as the corporate name or patents held. The process is similar to that of selling the business, but the owner can add a liquidator to the scenario, as well as the possibility of an auction, as a quick means to clear out of the business.

Two other types of bankruptcy are Chapter 12, used by family farming businesses, and Chapter 13, which is used by sole proprietorships. In each of these cases, the individual files for bankruptcy and includes the firm in his or her personal assets and liabilities. Chapter 13 is intended for entrepreneurial firms with limited debts and assets. The effect of a Chapter 13 filing is similar to that of a Chapter 11. However, since it is for a smaller firm, the process is even easier. For example, the time to approval is typically quicker, and no creditor committee is required.

A final point to be made regarding the turnaround or closing of a business is the protection of personal assets. As was discussed in Chapter 9 (legal), the form of business chosen has many impacts upon the operation of the business as well as the ending of the business. One of those is the extent to which the individuals involved in founding a firm are personally liable for its debts. Incorporating a business (using the Subchapter S, Subchapter C, or LLC forms that were discussed in Chapter 9) goes a long way toward providing limited liability to the entrepreneur. However, many entrepreneurs personally guarantee loans that are made to the company. Doing this negates the limited liability nature of a corporation and exposes the entrepreneur to a major loss of personal assets.[7] While no one starts a business with the intent of failure, the reality is that many do fail. Effectively preparing for that possibility at the beginning of the venture can be a great blessing in the event that the business does not develop as the founder(s) had hoped.

SUMMARY

This chapter focused on the exit, harvest, turnaround, and closing of the entrepreneurial business. These are tough but important issues that should be considered when designing a new business. What should be clear is that these activities are as much art as science. Even something that appears as straightforward as business valuation is actually a process that leads to a set of results as opposed to a unique answer. The entrepreneur who chooses to pursue starting a new venture is well advised to develop a plan for harvesting a business as well as handling situations that might require a major turnaround or closure.

KEY TERMS

asset valuation 252
capitalization of earnings valuation 253
initial public offering (IPO) 257
market estimation 254
perquisites 248
price/earnings (P/E) ratio 252
turnaround 259

REVIEW QUESTIONS

1. Why would an entrepreneur seek to exit a business?
2. How can an entrepreneur be a millionaire on paper yet have no money in the bank?

3. What are the steps in valuing a business?
4. Explain the difference in the following valuation methods.
   a. Present value discounted cash flow
   b. Price/earnings ratio
   c. Asset value
   d. Capitalization of earnings
   e. Market estimation
5. What steps should a business owner go through to prepare the business to be sold?
6. What four options does a business owner have to sell the business?
7. Which of these is the least likely to be pursued by the business owner?
8. What are six things a business owner should keep in mind as he enters negotiations to sell a business?
9. What is a turnaround?
10. What are the different types of bankruptcy and when are they each appropriate?

BUSINESS PLAN DEVELOPMENT QUESTIONS

1. As you think about your potential business, what would be the most likely valuation method you can use?
2. Thinking toward the future, if you ever had to turn around your business, what would likely be the key issue that drives that problem? Is there some means to ensure that you address that problem before your business is up and running?

INDIVIDUAL EXERCISES

1. Develop a harvest plan for your planned business. Have several fellow classmates review the plan for completeness.
2. What are the two or three things that you would want most out of a sale or succession negotiation?
3. Imagine a worst-case scenario. Explain how you have protected your personal assets.

GROUP EXERCISES

Form into groups in the class. Go to your favorite search engine and put in the term "small business for sale" and your city name.

1. What website did you identify with firms for sale in your area?
2. How many firms are listed?
3. Pick one business. What is the asking price for that business?
4. What is the basis for that asking price? Can you see one method that they appeared to use from the types of valuation methods discussed in this chapter?
5. Tell your group about your evaluation of the business that is for sale and whether you think it is a good business opportunity or not.

ENDNOTES

1. https://www.fliptopia.com/valuation.
2. H. A. Ndofor, C. Wesley, R. L. Priem, *Strategic Management Journal* 34, no. 9 (September 2013), pp. 1123–33.
3. A. Schmitt and S. Raisch, *Journal of Management Studies* 50, no. 7 (November 2013), pp. 1216–44.
4. R. Quinn, *Deep Change: Discovering the Leader Within* (San Francisco, CA: Jossey-Bass Publishers, 1996).
5. R. A. Anderson, I. Fox, and D. P. Twomey, *Business Law: Principles, Cases, Legal Environment* (Cincinnati, OH: South-Western Publishing, 1999).
6. H. Loizos and K. Werres, "On the Road to Disaster: Strategic Misalignments and Corporate Failure," *Long Range Planning* 49, no.4 (August 2016), pp. 491–506.
7. U. Lilienfeld-Toal and D. Mookherjee, "A General Equilibrium Analysis of Personal Bankruptcy Law," *Economica*, 83, no.329 (January 2016), pp. 31–58.

chapter

14

Franchising and Purchasing an Existing Business

learning objectives

After studying this chapter, you will be able to:

LO14-1 Describe the elements of franchising.

LO14-2 Explain the process of buying a franchise.

LO14-3 Discuss the process for buying an existing business.

CHOCOLATE WORKS

Many small businesses find that they have developed a very successful model for a business. That said these entrepreneurs do not necessarily want to take the great risk to expand the business to a national or international level. Instead, the entrepreneurs pursue a lower risk strategy of taking their idea and franchising it for others to pursue. With this the entrepreneurs can cash-in on their business model.

In 1973, Joe Whaley's father founded Chocolate Works in New York on Fifth Avenue in Manhattan. The store sells chocolates but is unique in that it not only makes the chocolates it sells but also organizes chocolate parties so that individuals can host events on the site of the retail or manufacturing operation. Additionally, the firm makes custom chocolates for corporate gift giving. With this the firm has developed three different sources of revenue from chocolate. The firm was very successful but found there was far more demand than the one store could serve. Joe decided to start franchising the business in 2012. The initial focus for franchises was on the New York and bordering states, but ultimately the goal was to be a national player.

There are now 15 franchisees in three states with many other stores in the planning process. The cost of the units can range from $300,000 to $450,000 to set up. This cost includes the initial fee to the franchisor of $50,000. The other costs are for equipment and the facilities. The entrepreneur must have liquid assets of at least $200,000 to buy the franchise and then total assets of at least $300,000 since Joe wants to ensure the entrepreneur has the resources to be successful. The franchisee pays 5 percent of its gross sales revenue to Joe as the franchisor and a $300 month marketing fee. As a franchisor Joe will make his revenue not only from the percentage of gross revenue but also the selling of the inputs to the entrepreneurs that buy a franchise.

Questions

1. Could the business you are planning be franchised?
2. If it can be franchised, what would be the decision process you would pursue to determine if you should franchise the idea or seek to own all the expansion yourself?

Sources: S. Wescoe, "New Ventures: Custom, Do-It-Yourself Chocolate Shop Debuts in Madison Farms," LVB.com (April 11, 2016), http://www.lvb.com/article/20160411/LVB01/304079995/new-ventures-custom-doityourself-chocolate-shop-debuts-in-madison-farms; http://www.franchisingusamagazine.com/latest/chocolate-works-now-franchising; https://www.entrepreneur.com/franchises/chocolateworks/334268; http://www.chocolateworks.com/about-us.html.

KOSHER HOME

A good friend of Jack and Toby's was Matt Jerrod. Matt observed the hard work and risk that the two founders of Kosher Home took on and was impressed. However, the risk of the business seemed too great to Matt given his conservative nature. Additionally, he did not have any readily identifiable skills that he thought seemed relevant; recall that Jack and Toby had specific skills related to the product. In discussing this situation with Jack and Toby, the two entrepreneurs suggested Matt look at doing a franchise.

Matt found through his research that the opportunity for success is much higher with a franchise than it is with an untested start-up, if for no other reason than the business model of the franchise is tested and documented by the firm selling the franchise. In addition, the franchise has some level of support (although it can vary considerably) from the business that sells the franchise.

Thus, franchising seemed to offer a calculated risk he could tolerate. He also knew that franchises typically come with operational systems already in place. These preexisting operational systems would help Matt overcome his shortcomings in any skills that are missing.

However, the realization that a franchise might offer the best opportunity for Matt was just the first step in his business start-up process. Which franchise should Matt choose was the next step? An initial investigation found that there were thousands of franchisors, with wide variations in the availability, price, resource requirements, level of support, and success rate of those various franchises. Matt knew that he wanted to be in a service industry with lots of customer contact even though his experience in sales was not deep. However, he fundamentally liked people and wanted to work with them.

Matt started looking in his community for potential needs while at the same time looking for franchises that were available. He found resources on the Internet that were very helpful to read about franchises in both *Entrepreneur* and *Forbes* magazines. Matt's capital was limited, so he narrowed his attention to franchises that were lower in initial cost.

Two specific opportunities drew his attention as he reviewed lists of franchises. The first was in fast food. The second opportunity was a cleaning service. He was interested in fast food since he thought there was always a need for food in a city. The cleaning business intrigued him as he had worked as a janitor in college to pay expenses and also thought there was always a need in business to use such services, especially if they were of high quality and trustworthy.

Matt's found numerous types of fast food. He ultimately decided that rather than something such as ethnic food, for which he did not have the background, he would focus on a very simple food—sandwich shops. The cost for these franchises could be as low as $50,000 and rarely would exceed $250,000. In each of the franchises he investigated, he would not have to own the building but could lease the space, which would significantly lower his costs. His investigation found the range of services offered by the franchisor to the franchisee also varied greatly. Looking deeper, he found three franchises of interest. Each of these had an initial cost of approximately $150,000, had very strong operational plans, and had well-developed support services. For example, each of these franchises helped the franchisee locate the store in the best location available and had managers on staff that worked onsite during the pre-start-up and start-up phases of the business.

Examining cleaning franchises, he found far more franchises than he initially expected. The start-up cost of such a franchise was very low with some at approximately $10,000. Additionally, the number of employees could be as low as one to two and the initial total cost of start-up was far less than $50,000. In particular, two franchises were appealing with his total initial investment of less than $50,000.

Looking deeper, while the cost of the fast food franchise was higher, the payoff could also be higher. A cleaning business seemed to be very hard to differentiate, so it would be driven by cost decisions by the customers. This concern for the cleaning business became greater when he looked online and found there were a large number of operations already in the city.

Matt's next move was to have initial conversations with each of the three potential fast-food franchisors. However, Matt went deeper and contacted several franchisees from each of the franchisors. He chose the franchisees by looking online at different cities in his state. The sample he selected may not have been ideal since it was not a random selection, but it avoided using the franchisors' lists of who he might call which he feared would result in one-sided information.

Interestingly, even within his limited sample, Matt found that franchisees for two of the franchisors he was

(continued)

interested in had significant complaints about support and value for their dollar. Only one franchisor had no franchisees that were unhappy. Looking at the success statistics (profit levels, sales growth, number of franchisees that go out of business, and increasing sales price of franchisees wishing to sell), Matt found that this one franchisor ranked the highest in the industry.

This franchisor offered a relatively unique concept for a sandwich operation, utilizing grilled meat. While not the only firm to offer this concept nationwide it was unique for where Matt lived. Further, the franchisor used a three-mile radius as its competitive density, meaning that no other franchisee of that particular brand would be allowed to open a shop within three miles of Matt's. The strategy of the firm, its product, and its operations all seemed to be a good fit for Matt. The next step was to proceed to start negotiations to buy a franchise from this franchisor.

QUESTIONS

1. What are the questions and concerns Matt should focus on as he begins his communication with the franchisor?
2. Franchisors do not sell a franchise to just anyone that wants one. What could Matt do to become an attractive candidate as a franchisee for the franchisor?

This book has focused principally on the process of starting a new entrepreneurial business from scratch. Two other common options exist for individuals interested in starting their own businesses. The first is purchasing a franchise. The other is purchasing an existing business. Both of these activities have opportunities and drawbacks in comparison to starting a new business and we will examine these, beginning with the opportunities and drawbacks with franchising.

The Elements of Franchising

LO14-1

Describe the elements of franchising.

The purchase of a well-honed, thoughtfully positioned franchise can dramatically decrease the downside risk inherent in the process of starting a business. Franchising can be viewed as the new business entrepreneur's creation of a business from a well-established formula. Thus, the franchise is essentially a prepackaged business, where there are policies, procedures, and buying patterns in place prior to beginning operations.

The **franchisor** is the firm that originates the idea for the business and develops the operational methods. The entrepreneur is the franchisee. The **franchisee** pays a fee to obtain a franchise from the franchisor. This fee entitles the franchisee the right to open a branch of the business in a given area, use the franchisor's name, and operate a business within the guidelines of the agreement. The franchisee also receives operational advice on how to run the business and typically some level of marketing support to promote the firm. Responsibility for the business location, establishment of the business, and build-out is the franchisee's and must usually be fulfilled in accordance with the specifications of the franchisor.

The franchisor, in turn, establishes minimum standards regarding the operation of the business. For example, the **franchise agreement** is the basic contract generated by the franchisor for all franchisees and it usually contains clauses requiring the purchase of supplies, the displaying of marketing material, and the payment of fees that are based upon the sales of the branch operation. The requirements, however, may be more extensive. For example,

franchisor
The firm that originates the idea for the business and develops the operational methods, then sells them to franchisees.

franchisee
The entrepreneur who buys the franchise from the franchisor.

franchise agreement
The basic contract generated by the franchisor for all franchisees; it usually contains clauses requiring the purchase of supplies, the displaying of marketing material, and the payment of fees that are based upon the sales of the branch operation.

McDonald's requires that its franchisees clean not only their own property but also the territory that borders their franchise unit.

In 2016 the International Franchise Association reported that franchises made up almost 900,000 establishments in the United States, providing almost 9 million direct jobs.[1] The range of franchises you use every day would likely surprise you. For example, most hotels, most restaurants, and many daily service providers are locally owned franchise operations.

In part, the reason franchising is so widespread is that the franchisor can offer a standard, well-known product, that is produced by a consistent, well-tested process. The group purchasing power for supplies, supported with specific regional and perhaps more generic brand-building national advertising, furthers the success of the franchise. The franchisor will also continue research and development on the products and processes that a small single business simply could not afford to pursue. This all occurs with the entrepreneur spending less of her resources than if she had had to found such a firm by herself. The franchisor benefits by enabling a rapid expansion while minimizing the funds invested in that expansion.[2]

Going into business with a Dunkin' Donuts franchise, for instance, allows you the freedom of ownership while also providing built-in support. How might ownership differ for franchisees versus traditional business owners?

©McGraw-Hill Education/Jill Braaten, photographer

The success of franchising is dependent on the hard work of the franchisee and the value added by the franchisor.[3] You will recall that we discussed agency theory in Chapter 2. There are factors that mitigate alignment of goals between a manager and an owner. In a franchise operation, businesspeople work for themselves, not for some large corporation and, as a result, all the decisions that the entrepreneur makes are to maximize the value of their own business. The success of franchising is also a result of the fact that the franchisee will act in ways to maximize the profit of the business where a corporate employee might not do so, a prediction consistent with agency theory.[4]

The franchisor makes money in a variety of ways, including these: (1) selling the franchise to the franchisee; (2) selling supplies to the franchisee; (3) collecting a percentage of sales; and (4) in some cases, providing company-specific training courses/materials. For example, a very successful franchisor such as Dunkin' Donuts, which sells donuts, muffins, coffee, and baked goods in more than 40 states, charges a fee to obtain a franchise, but the significant income comes from royalties and being able to sell the franchisee items that range from Dunkin' Donuts-labeled donut boxes to coffee cups and napkins. The franchisor typically argues that it can obtain the supplies cheaper through its bulk buying; plus, it wants to ensure that the output continues to be a consistently high-quality, name-enhancing experience, since it is sold under the Dunkin' Donuts brand. A franchisee that has inconsistent quality or service not only hurts her own business but impacts the brand image of all franchisees.

The continuing revenue stream to the franchisor from royalties and selling of inputs to the franchisee is a more important revenue source than the initial fees for selling the franchise. Thus, the franchisor and the franchisee are successful by helping each other. The franchisor makes money when the franchisee stays in business, needs lots of inputs, and pays continuing royalties. On the other hand, the franchisee is successful if the franchisor puts a program in place for all of the franchisees to be successful, such as high-quality marketing, good site selection, high-quality products, and continuous research into both product/process development and brand management.

The Process of Buying a Franchise

LO14-2

Explain the process of buying a franchise.

As we have emphasized throughout this text, the entrepreneur that is best prepared will be the most likely to succeed, whether her focus is starting a business from scratch, buying a franchise, or purchasing an existing business. Thus, many of the issues in choosing a franchise are similar to the issues already examined in this text.

General Franchise Questions

Some issues can be viewed as broad, generic issues rather than issues specific to that particular franchisor. These general issues include the following:

1. The potential franchisee should carefully evaluate her individual interests and skills to determine a potential fit with running a franchise and to identify an industry or multiple industries in which she wishes to attempt to purchase a franchise.
2. When determining the industry to enter, each potential franchisee should examine that industry, the potential competitors in the industry, and their position relative to other new franchisees that are entering the industry.
3. The potential franchisee should carefully examine the competitive strength of various franchises in the industry. For instance, what are the various sustainable competitive advantages in the market?
4. The individual looking to buy a franchise should identify a franchisor that is the best potential match for him or her in terms of support, history, expansion plans, and so on.
5. The person considering a franchise should examine that franchisor as though the potential franchisee were buying the whole business. This includes contacting other franchisees to discuss their experience as well as comparing the franchisor to other franchise opportunities.

Specific Franchise Questions

Each franchisor will have a different package it will try to sell a franchisee. The franchisee needs to examine the exact package that is offered and balance the cost and the benefits offered. The issues to consider in examining which franchise to purchase include these: what a franchise includes; franchisor and franchisee obligations, as stipulated in the United Franchise Offering Circular (UFOC); and steps in the process of obtaining a franchise.

Each of the issues to consider in purchasing a specific franchise will be examined in turn.

What Does a Franchise Include? An extraordinary range of support can be provided by a franchisor to the franchisee. This ranges from simply buying into a name and general plan for operation to what almost amounts to a full partner for your business. There is no universal standard regarding what is provided by a franchisor; instead, as in any market system, different franchisors offer distinct sets of supports at varying prices. The entrepreneur must choose which package of benefits she wishes to pursue, at what price, and with what level of control by the franchisor. The discussion below lists some of the issues that a new businessperson buying a franchise should consider to ensure the franchise has the right mix of supports and costs for him.

Both the franchisor and the franchisee have an alignment of interest in their mutual desire to produce a quality product and successfully expand the business. However, they can have honest disagreements about what is best for the organization. Franchisors make decisions based on what is best for the total business; franchisees want to have the ability to cater to their local market. Thus, can you as a local franchisee of a sandwich shop in Texas add hot peppers to the standard sandwich—or if you are in Wisconsin, can you add sauerkraut to the same sandwich? The franchisor may want uniformity and thus consistency, but the franchisee will want the flexibility to meet local needs. The individual buying a franchise needs to examine if the franchise will have the level of flexibility she feels is necessary for success.

When you purchase a franchise, you typically are buying some consistent items, although the specifics of what you are buying in each individual case should be examined. These include the right to:

1. An established name, branded products, and service.
2. Operate under that name for a period of time. The time period is usually some standard, such as 5, 10, or 20 years.
3. A single store or the right to have multiple units.[5]
4. A commitment from the franchisor to limit the number of franchises within a specific radius of the new franchise. This is one of the most important issues involved in the purchase. One of the key competitive advantages is having the name-brand operation without having to compete against fellow franchisees. In the best situations, franchisees work with each other in local geographic areas.

The franchisor typically provides both the operational systems and the monitoring techniques to run the business in a manner that matches the rest of the organization. The specificity of this operational information varies widely from franchisor to franchisor. You will recall from Chapter 12 that an in-depth understanding of operations is necessary to be successful in an entrepreneurial business. Although most of the operational management systems will have been designed by the experience of the franchisor, the franchisee must intimately understand both why and how these systems work. To illustrate, if you purchase a franchise for a shop that makes photocopies, the franchisor will have established procedures for the design of the internal layout of the shop, plus the look and feel of the physical storefront. It will have established processes for virtually every type of service that could be requested by a customer. If you do not have at least a minimal understanding of copy shops, it will be difficult to judge the operating system the franchisor is providing. Buying a franchise does not eliminate the need for the entrepreneur to have a deep understanding of the business. If you do not have that understanding, you cannot judge the quality of the operational support provided by the franchisor.

True understanding of those processes comes from experience. In many cases, potential franchisees are required to work in an established operation of the business for some period of time prior to their being allowed to purchase a franchise. This time period allows the potential franchisee the opportunity to learn the business from the ground up, learning the procedures not from a manual, but from experience with an established operation. This fact is particularly important since some franchisors have very specific limits on how many changes you can make to their operational systems. The franchisor wants a franchisee in Oklahoma City, Oklahoma, and another in Utica, New York, to operate in essentially the same manner in order to develop and preserve the brand. A careful examination of the amount of regional or local customization available can be an important part of the business acquisition process.

A number of specific support areas that the potential franchisee should use to evaluate the franchisor's operations include the following:

1. *Accounting Support.* As part of the operational aspects of the business, the franchisor will often provide an accounting system that is custom tailored to the dual needs of the franchisor and the franchisee.

2. *Marketing Support.* This is a broad area that encompasses such things as brochures, signs, logos, television advertisements, newspaper advertisements, sales techniques, and internal business design. The quality, quantity, and overall value of each of these items can vary widely from franchisor to franchisor. There are also some significant downside risks to this apparent positive. First of all, advertising support comes at a price. Most franchisors charge each franchisee a fee that becomes part of a larger common advertising budget. The franchisor develops the advertising and buys the spots or spaces in the newspapers. Doing this centrally allows for volume discounts as well as expertise in ad development and placement. Second, if you are the only franchisee in Colorado while most of the other franchisees are in Minnesota, Iowa, and Wisconsin, you are likely to see a smaller relative share of the advertising budget being targeted to your area. Thus, you would want to know what the franchisor's marketing plans are if you are the isolated franchise in Colorado.
3. *Training.* Franchisors offer a variety of training opportunities for the new franchisee and their employees. These include classroom training, training at other locations, having an experienced manager work at your location for a period of time, or, as we have mentioned, working at a current establishment. The more that is offered as part of the franchise fee the better it is for the franchisee. In addition, the availability of continued training opportunities should be an important criterion to help ensure franchisee success.
4. *Real Estate Services.* Some franchisors operate a large and profitable real estate brokering service. Others offer a more basic site selection service, or nothing at all. The assistance in real estate selection, acquisition, building construction, and the like can be invaluable if done professionally.
5. *Other Services.* Human resources support to develop performance management programs, quality control methods, forecasting, and purchasing of equipment are all very valuable services that act as guidelines rather than mandates in deciding on a franchise.

As this discussion indicates, there is a wide range of potential activities that the franchisor may provide to the franchisee. The range of those activities, the quality of those activities, and the cost should be judged by the entrepreneur.

EXERCISE 1

1. Rather than starting a business from scratch, you have decided to look into franchises. What industry and what franchise opportunities might you consider?
2. What special skills do you bring to the franchise?
3. What market conditions exist that suggest to you that this franchise might be successful?

Government Requirements for the Franchisor-Franchisee Relationship. The principal governing mechanism of the franchisor–franchisee relationship is the **Uniform Franchise Offering Circular (UFOC)**. As with many business domains, at one time there were excessive abuses in the industry. Individuals thinking they were buying a franchise that gave them an opportunity for success found that they had paid for what amounted to little more than a name, which often had a terrible reputation. The result was the passage of the UFOC, which specifies what information must be provided to the franchisee prior to her investment.

Uniform Franchise Offering Circular (UFOC)
The principal governing mechanism of the franchisor/franchisee.

This document must be provided to the franchisee early in the process of her buying a franchise. In effect, the UFOC is a franchisor disclosure document with 23 specified items:

1. **The Franchisor, Its Predecessors, and Affiliates.** Full disclosure on any predecessors to the current business and other businesses affiliated with the business must be disclosed.

2. **Business Experience.** The background of the principals must be detailed. Issues such as how long they have been in the business and their experience in the industry must also be detailed. You want to make sure those running the franchisor have experience in the industry.
3. **Litigation.** Any pending litigation must be noted. Such litigation can destroy the value of your franchise if it concerns issues such as who developed the idea for the product and your franchisor loses.
4. **Bankruptcy.** Any prior or current filings by firm or key management must be disclosed.
5. **Initial Franchise Fee.** Under items 5 and 6, the franchisor must disclose all fees that are charged.
6. **Other Fees.** The "other fees" category is an area that entrepreneurs should clearly understand. The cost of the initial purchase of the franchise may appear low, but if there are extensive fees that the franchisor can charge the franchisee for services that are offered, the value of the franchise may be very different than initially thought. The supports provided may appear to be desirable; however, there may be separate costs for those supports that are independent of the initiation fee to buy the franchise.
7. **Initial Investment.** This is more than the initial fee paid by the franchisee; it includes a reasonable estimate of the total investment needed to begin operations.
8. **Restrictions on Sources of Products and Services.** This is one of the critical parts of the document, where franchisor sourcing is detailed. The potential franchisee needs to be clear about what must be purchased directly from the franchisor and what may be sourced independently.
9. **Franchisee's Obligations.** Specific obligations must be listed. For example, the franchisor may require that the product be produced by certain equipment and that equipment be replaced on a certain time schedule. These restrictions can extend into domains that the entrepreneur may not initially consider to be the purview of the franchisor. Thus, once again questions such as what flexibility the entrepreneur will have in operating the franchise need to be examined. For example, upon opening, you as the franchisee may be happy with some balloons, having the local mayor cut a ribbon, and a story that goes into the local paper. But the franchisor may have an extensive program that it requires of all new franchise openings. The franchisee may be required to fund these activities through various fees, whether or not he agrees with the program.
10. **Financing.** Many franchisors make significant financing available to potential franchisees. The financing available and terms are outlined in this section of the document.
11. **Franchisor's Obligations.** In this section, all of the ancillary services are detailed. As outlined above, this may include site selection, training, placing experienced managers on-site for a period of time, and so on.
12. **Territory.** This section details the amount of exclusivity your franchise will have relative to other operations of the franchisor.
13. **Trademarks.** Items 13 and 14 detail the exact status of all trademarks, patents, copyrights, and trade secrets that are part of the business.
14. **Patents, Copyrights, and Proprietary Information.**

15. **Obligation to Participate in the Actual Operation of the Franchise Business.** The franchisee can be required to take an active role in the daily management of the business, as opposed to simply hiring managers.
16. **Restrictions on What the Franchisee May Sell.** This section lists limits placed on the franchisee by the franchisor. The franchisor may put extensive restrictions on the franchisee as to what she can do with the product and its production.
17. **Renewal, Termination, Transfer, and Dispute Resolution.** The exact method of dispute resolution is detailed, along with which party will have the financial responsibility.
18. **Public Figures.** This details any public figures or celebrities involved in the business and what they are paid.
19. **Earnings Claims.** This section contains a description along with some specific detail regarding the financial performance of typical franchisees.
20. **List of Outlets.**
21. **Financial Statements.**
22. **Contracts.** This section contains sample contracts you will be asked to sign later.
23. **Receipt.** You will be asked to sign a page to acknowledge that you received this information.

The entrepreneur is well served to study the document carefully to understand all of the details of the business arrangement. It is a long document, and should be read through several times and reviewed with an attorney prior to agreeing to the stipulations. A clear understanding of the document now will prevent significant problems in the future.

Franchise Process. The founding of a franchise is quite similar in form and method to creating a new business from scratch. A significant up-front cash payment is necessary, and the ability to leave the venture if the entrepreneur does not enjoy the business is severely limited. Similarly, an assessment of the skills of the individual should be a mandatory beginning of any new business investigation. If the individual has no skills in styling hair and he buys a hairstyling franchise, the odds of success are not particularly good, regardless of what supports are present in the franchise.

A successful franchisee has taken steps to understand the new market, such as location, longevity of demand, and skills needed.

Depending on the franchisor for market analysis is a poor move under any circumstances. The market must also be thoroughly and independently understood by the potential franchisee. As we pointed out earlier, sometimes there is a very good reason that no similar businesses are in a particular area. We knew an individual who was searching out a franchise to buy. She hit upon the idea of buying a franchise that supplies temporary employees to local businesses. Unfortunately, all of the local businesses (and there were only a few) used only full-time employees. The market for temporary workers was severely constrained. We would also caution against purchasing a franchise that is part of a fad. Cereal Cafe's were all the rage, but owning one of those franchises turned out to be a disaster for the franchisees. Fads die as quickly as they are born, but the franchise agreements last anywhere from 5 to 20 years. It does little good to invest money in a franchise that will see demand for the product disappear quickly. In the case of a fad, we have very simple advice. Get in, make as much money as you can as an independent, and GET OUT!

The International Franchise Association is a good source for quickly locating potential franchisor firms; its Web page can be found at www.franchise.org. Each of the franchisor firms typically has a Web page where you can request information from that firm. They will gladly send you a packet of information that details the firm's operations, its business, and the costs of the franchise. At this stage, there will be a very short application form that the entrepreneur must fill out. With this information the franchisor will call the entrepreneur and have a phone interview to ensure that the individual is at least a potential match for the firm. The entrepreneur needs to note that it is a mutual selection process. The franchisee can select among one of the 1,400 or more franchise opportunities. The franchisor also gets to decide to whom it will sell a franchise. Given the geographic restrictions imposed by many franchisors and encouraged by the franchisees, it is in the best interest of the franchisor to pursue only the most motivated, best capitalized, and most skilled individuals. A poorly performing or disruptive franchisee detracts from the overall operation as well as taking time and effort of the franchisor away from the business of growing the brand. Because of this, it is simply easier to make sure that there is a match between the two parties from the beginning.

Once the potential franchisee has been vetted (a credit and personal background check has been completed), the entrepreneur will be sent the complete UFOC and asked to fill out a more complete application. A series of meetings ensues between the franchisor and other franchisees in the area, between the franchisor and the potential franchisee, and between the potential franchisee and the other franchisees in the area. The ability to meet other franchisees is critical in the evaluation process. Although the UFOC does not require that specific information on profitability of individual franchises be provided, it is quite simple to back into such information by calculating the total profits of the group and then dividing by the total number of franchises. Unfortunately, there may be a bimodal distribution, with some great performers and some that perform poorly. The ability to interact with franchisees in your geographic area, with similar profiles to what you can expect from your operation, helps provide great insights into the reality of the franchise life. You will gain tremendous insights from these individuals regarding their relationship with the franchisor. The relationship between franchisor and franchisee is somewhat like a marriage; they are both dependent on each other for success. If the relationship is an unhappy one, there can be nothing quite as miserable. Existing franchisees can also provide insight regarding the value of the franchisor's staff. Many of the services that the franchisor provides are dependent on the quality of the people providing the service. Marketing advice is a qualitative area that can be either very helpful or of limited value, depending on who is developing and delivering the research.

Assuming that both parties are pleased with their findings, negotiating the deal is the next step. Although the franchise fee tends to be set in stone, most franchisors are willing to negotiate on a wide range of items. For example, if there are few franchises in an area, the franchisor may be willing to finance a greater portion of the start-up expenses, provide additional marketing support, or even pick up some of the initial expenses of a franchise in order to get a foothold in a new geographic area. Similarly, if you have had prior success in business and the franchisor is new, it might negotiate a completely different deal with you in order to get started with a self-sufficient operator. Also, very high-profile individuals frequently can negotiate unique deals. For example, in a region of the country where there is a professional athletic team, high-profile players on that team often obtain preferential opportunities. This

ETHICAL CHALLENGE

CANNABIS FRANCHISE

There has been a rapid decriminalization of cannabis around the United States. States such as Colorado and Washington have largely legalized the sale of the drug. Other states have moved to allow medical marijuana such that obtaining the prescription is often a mere formality. The result has been a rapid expansion of small businesses, who grow and refine the drug into various consumables, and retailers. There are already firms that are starting to explore the franchising of the models they are developing. This movement to create cannabis franchises has led to a reality television show *High Profits* which is about the development of such a franchisor.

While there has been wide acceptance of marijuana, such a franchise reflects many of the challenges that face any domain where there is rapidly changing acceptance. There are clearly high profits available in a cash only business meaning no issues with delinquent payments. The biggest issue is that it still remains a U.S. government violation to grow or distribute marijuana. Buying into or selling a franchise in this turbulent environment is fraught with problems.

QUESTIONS

1. What are your thoughts on the ethics of operating a marijuana franchise in this environment?
2. What are the real profit margins when you are dealing with a product that is a controlled substance?
3. Will the franchise still be worth anything if the U.S. government decides to enforce federal statutes?
4. There is a firm that is licensing (not franchising yet) called Café Serendipity—http://cafeserendipity.wixsite.com/cafeserendipity/franchiseopportunity. Is this a viable opportunity?

allows the franchisor to publicize that that person is one of its franchisees. The entrepreneur should explore what aspects of the contract are negotiable by making a list of wants and desires.

Some areas that such negotiations should explore include up-front capital requirements, financing arrangements, and continuing fees. Does the ability exist to purchase other franchises or build out the existing franchise? The time frame of the franchise (5, 10, 20 years) may be negotiable, as well as a first right to renew your franchise. An important consideration is not only the territory of the initial franchise but also first rights on adjacent or fast-growing territories. Some franchisors will have performance quotas to maintain the franchise; if your business faces performance requirements be sure to ask what those quotas are and what percentage of franchisees meet the quota. If you fail at those quotas, or some other aspects of the franchise, can you negotiate the remedies to solve that problem? Does the franchisor require a personal guarantee? The personal guarantee is something many successful entrepreneurs seek to avoid, because it places their personal assets at risk. Are there operational constraints that you feel would put you at a disadvantage relative to your competition that you wish to have the franchisor waive? The entrepreneur is well served to take the time to work with a lawyer and develop a solid contract that meets the needs of the franchisor and still gives the franchisee the best opportunity for success.

EXERCISE 2

1. What specific concerns do you have regarding a potential franchise that you may buy?
2. Put together a list of three items that you must have in place prior to accepting a contract to purchase a franchise.
3. Do you believe that franchises are more or less risky as compared to beginning a new business from scratch?

LO14-3

Discuss the process for buying an existing business.

The Process for Buying an Existing Business

We covered the process of obtaining a franchise first because this process is well defined and well regulated, and there is a wealth of information available to anyone who would like assistance. Another very popular means of going into business for oneself is the purchase of an existing business.

How to Buy an Existing Business

Similar to a franchise, an existing business has the benefit of having an established set of processes; although unlike a franchise, a continuing business has an established cash flow that you are purchasing. As such, the operation has a higher likelihood of success when compared to starting a business from scratch, and yet that does not mean that buying a business does not take as much planning and thought as starting a business from scratch. There are still significant risks involved in buying a business.[7]

YrFURN—AN APP FOR FURNITURE

Bill Chen was a good friend of Brandy, and as Bill observed how YrFurn prospered, he become more convinced he should follow his desire to go into business for himself. He had a good job working for an engineering firm where he was able to use his computer and technology skills, but he felt that his prospects for rising any further in the organization were limited. Bill was increasingly concerned with the strategic direction that the firm was pursuing and believed that the advice of long-time employees was being routinely ignored. This led Bill to begin to investigate new business opportunities.

Bill knew he wanted to do something that took advantage of his computer and technological skills. Therefore, Bill began to look at new businesses tied to the Internet. He knew that phone apps were a market that was exploding in size; however, he also knew that getting noticed among all of the apps was very hard to do. Bill also knew that social networking was a high-growth area for technology. One study found that people under the age of 30 were spending over 30 percent of their time on social networks. Outside of the biggest players in each market, the rest of the field tended to be very fragmented.

In each area the issue came down to how to structure his venture so that it was unique in the marketplace and attracted sufficient attention to make a business. He thought of potentially focusing on some specific niche but soon found that there were already a large number of players in each niche he considered.

Bill explored virtual data rooms. He knew that increasingly, firms were moving out paper copies from their offices to load documents on "the cloud." One aspect of this transition is that firms needed secure locations to place the documents for their far-flung teams when conducting sensitive activities, such as due diligence for a merger and acquisition. Virtual data rooms are established to hold the data securely.

Unfortunately, Bill found that it takes a large staff to do this work requiring an initial investment of more than $500,000 by the time basic start-up costs were considered.

While the two largest firms had relatively small market shares, Bill was still concerned that these firms would be very aggressive in their pricing and hard to beat.

This led Bill to look at Internet-based franchises. He found that these franchises ran from an initial cost of $99 to $25,000. He believed the actual costs would be double or triple the cost of the franchise by that time he included other start-up costs. However, with total costs at less than $100,000, Bill thought these franchises were potentially a great option and there were a great many of them to choose from.

QUESTIONS

1. What factors should Bill focus on when evaluating an Internet-related franchise?
2. The key success factors of franchises typically are the operating systems they provide the entrepreneur, which help the entrepreneur ensure that he can run the business effectively from day one. Would such a benefit also be present in an Internet franchise?

Because a business you may buy is an ongoing entity, there is a greater premium attached to the business than if you started it from scratch. The primary exception to this is if you buy a troubled business at a discount. If that is the case, you will need to quickly restructure that business. Turnaround is a special topic and requires very specific skills for you to be able to act quickly to reverse that decline.[8] Our typical advice to entrepreneurs is to not attempt such activities unless they have specific skills and a plan to turn around a business that is in significant decline.

For the purchase of a reasonably stable or healthy firm, all of the same processes that have been discussed in this text should be the foundation of your effort. Therefore, you first need to understand your own skills and abilities and the nature of the current market. Assuming that you have completed all of the preliminary analysis effort, there are still several unique aspects to purchasing an existing business. These include (1) locating a business to purchase, (2) developing a plan for the business, (3) negotiating a deal to acquire exactly what you want from the operation, and (4) organizing the process of change within the organization.

Locating a Business to Purchase. Locating a business for sale is a job that takes lots of patience and effort. There are **business brokers** in virtually every city in the United States that specialize in selling businesses. Additionally, businesses are listed for sale in newspapers, in local magazines, and on websites. All of these are fine places to start your search process; however, we recommend several other means for finding a business that meets your needs:

business brokers
Businesses that specialize in selling businesses.

1. Attorney and CPA firms may have clients who have expressed their desire to sell their business. Contacting local firms and asking about businesses they might know that are for sale usually yields some interesting possibilities.
2. Our personal favorite way to find a business to buy is to identify a particular business that you believe is not maximizing its opportunity, one to which you believe you could bring unique skills and advantages that could propel the business. We recommend that you put together a short e-mail to the owner indicating your interest in the business and follow that up with a request to take the owner to lunch to discuss the opportunity. Most (if not all) owners of an ongoing business are willing to listen to an offer to buy their business.
3. The trade association for an industry usually maintains a listing of all member companies and is a wealth of information regarding the status of various organizations within the industry.
4. The local Small Business Administration Office and/or the Small Business Development Center in your area has significant contact with businesspeople and both are geared toward supporting and encouraging the growth of entrepreneurial business.
5. Another favorite of ours is to look at the bankruptcy filings in your local community. Many companies file for bankruptcy due to lack of financial resources or poor management practices. The opportunity to contact these individuals and buy the operation before the bankruptcy procedure is completed can be the source of a business at a bargain price. However, remember that this effort would be a turnaround project that would require unique skills and abilities.

Plan of Operation. Once you have located a business for sale, but prior to beginning the negotiations to purchase the business, you as the potential entrepreneur should develop a plan of operation for the business. The cost of the business should include any premium for its current performance. What will you do differently from what is currently being done? If you are paying a premium for a business but have no plans to change the business operations, then how do you hope to achieve success?

Will you bring a new mission to the business? Will you position the firm or its product differently? Do you have some unique talent or skill that will make the business that you are considering buying a success, or make it more successful? An understanding of what you have to offer and what the current business is missing will provide the basis for your negotiations. What is important to the current owner may or may not be important to the potential owner, given the new direction for the company. Adding value to a business is a critical step in the process of deciding to purchase a business. We would recommend that the entrepreneur take the same approach as was outlined in Chapter 5 to develop a new mission for the organization. What are the resource-based advantages of the new organization under the new leadership?

Having developed a new plan for the business, the potential entrepreneur is prepared to negotiate the deal. In Chapter 13 we outlined procedures that a seller should use to put her business in the best position for sale, as well as negotiation strategies. We would recommend that a potential buyer do the same and demand this from any seller.

Finally, there is the complex issue of organizing the process of change from the former business to the new business. Although there are a number of ways in which this can be accomplished, the tasks are relatively the same. We must point out that there is a lot of nuance and "art" in the handling of these processes. Once negotiations are complete and all contracts are signed, there will be a transition period that should be spelled out in the contract for sale. During that transition time period, a number of tasks should be completed. The new owner should accomplish the following:

1. Meet and discuss the transition with every member of the current staff. If there is a layoff plan, then that should be enacted immediately.
2. Spend significant time being visible in the new operation, talking with employees, making suggestions, and doing some of the more menial work.
3. Make all significant changes in one day so as to alleviate any lingering concerns by the employees.
4. Implement new metrics and standards as soon as possible.
5. Ask that the former owner(s) not to be at the business for several weeks while the transition is taking place. Loyalties and work processes get confused when the former owner is around every day.
6. If appropriate for the type of business that has been purchased, send out a letter or e-mail to every customer and supplier informing each one of the ownership change. Ideally this letter should be signed by both the former owner and the new owner.

SUMMARY

This chapter examined two common methods for becoming an entrepreneur. Both techniques fundamentally rely upon all of the same analysis and development techniques that have been developed in this text. Franchises are a well-developed and expansively available method for starting a business. There are more than 750,000 franchises in the United States, and franchises are rapidly expanding in many parts of the world.[9] Franchise operations run the gamut from those that are fully developed complete partners in business to others that are little more than a name. Franchises significantly improve the chance of survival for an entrepreneur but do not eliminate the potential for failure.[10] We reviewed the UFOC as well as those areas that are unique to a franchise operation. We finished the chapter with a discussion of the unique considerations involved in buying an existing business.

KEY TERMS

business brokers 277
franchise agreement 267
franchisee 267
franchisor 267
Uniform Franchise Offering Circular (UFOC) 271

REVIEW QUESTIONS

1. How does a franchise work?
2. How do the franchisee and the franchisor differ?
3. What is the benefit of buying a franchise versus starting your own business? Are there any drawbacks?
4. What are the questions a person should ask herself before she starts a franchise?
5. What is typically included in a franchise?
6. What is the UFOC? What are its major provisions?
7. Why would someone buy an existing business?
8. How do you locate a business that you would like to purchase?
9. Once you actually buy the business, how do you make sure that you are successful?

INDIVIDUAL EXERCISES

1. Starting with the Independent Franchise Association Web page, www.franchise.org, put together a plan for purchasing a franchise.
2. For the industry that you chose in Exercise 1 of this chapter, how many franchise opportunities exist?
3. What resources exist to help you in your effort to acquire a franchise?

GROUP EXERCISES

1. Form small groups in the class. As a class, pick one industry, such as retail restaurants. Have every team then select a franchise to buy in that industry independently.
   a. What is the range of franchises picked?
   b. What is the range of costs and services offered?
   c. Why did each team pick the franchise that it did? List your top five reasons for picking that franchise.
   d. Each team should make a five-minute presentation on the franchise it picked as if it were selling the idea to an investor.
   e. Then vote as a class for the best franchise idea.

ENDNOTES

1. Matthew Haller and Jenna Weisbord, "Franchise Businesses to Continue Growth Trend in 2016, Outpacing Economy—Wide Pace," *International Franchise Association*, http://www.franchise.org/franchise-businesses-to-continue-growth-trend-in-2016-outpacing-economy-wide-pace.
2. R. Dant and P. Kaufmann, "Structural and Strategic Dynamics in Franchising," *Journal of Retailing* 79 (2003), pp. 63–76.
3. M. Grunhagen and M. Dorsch, "Does the Franchisor Provide Value to the Franchisee? Past, Current, and Future Value Assessments of Two Franchisee Types," *Journal of Small Business Management* 41(2003), pp. 366–85.
4. J. Combs and D. Ketchen Jr., "Why Do Firms Use Franchising as an Entrepreneurial Strategy? A Meta Analysis," *Journal of Management* 29 (2003), pp. 443–66.
5. J. Bercovitz, "The Option to Expand: The Use of Multi-Unit Opportunities to Support Self-Enforcing Agreements in Franchise Relationships," *Academy of Management Proceedings* (2002), pp. Y1–Y7.
6. J. Quittner, "Thinking of Starting a Business? Lock Down Profits in Virtual Data Rooms," 2013, www.inc.com/best-industries-2013/jeremy-quittner/virtual-data-rooms.html.
7. K. Sadgrove, *The Complete Guide to Business Risk Management* (UK: Routledge, 2015).

8. V. M. Desai, "The Behavioral Theory of the (Governed) Firm: Corporate Board Influences on Organizations' Responses to Performance Shortfalls," *Academy of Management Journal* 59, no. 3 (2016), pp. 860–79.
9. M. Haller, "Slow Steady Growth to Continue for Franchises in 2013," *International Franchise Association*, 2013, www.franchise.org/Franchise-News-Detail.aspx?id=58916
10. S. Holmberg and K. Morgan, "Franchise Turnover and Failure: New Research and Perspective," *Journal of Business Venturing* 18 (2003), pp. 403–19.

part 6

MiniCases

MiniCase 1
Thinking Critically: Collin Laverty—Cuba Educational Travel

MiniCase 2
Thinking Critically: Scott Dixon—Great Clips

MiniCase 3
Thinking Critically: Cassmer Ward—The Clear Collar

MiniCase 4
Thinking Critically: Sandra & Steve Moore-Moore A/C & Heating Services, Inc.

MiniCase 5
Thinking Critically: Jeffrey Offutt—JITA Printing

MiniCase 6
Thinking Critically: Kevin Callahan—PeerPoint

MiniCase 7
Thinking Critically: Bill Zeuch—ComicLock, LLC

MiniCase 8
Thinking Critically: Chris Bisson—Value Connect

MiniCase 9
Thinking Critically: Ricardo Baldi—Baldi Gardens

MiniCase 10
Thinking Critically: Kyle Mittendorf—Brilliant Medical Boutique

MiniCase 11
Thinking Critically: Cliff and Jo Ellen Silverman—GaGa Ball Pits

MiniCase 12
Thinking Critically: Jeff Barry—RavioliOli

MiniCase 13
Thinking Critically: Paul Inserra—American Meltdown

MiniCase 14
Thinking Critically: Carlo Capua—Z's Cafe

MiniCase 1

THINKING CRITICALLY

Collin Laverty—Cuba Educational Travel

Collin Laverty studied international business in college, traveled to Cuba in college, and worked for a think tank associated with Cuban/U.S. relations after graduation. Building on that foundation in 2012, at age 28, Collin moved to Cuba and set up Cuba Educational Travel. The firm was designed to help students and others come to Cuba based on new openings in travel that President Obama had allowed to the country. Starting with less than $5,000 in capital, numerous contacts that he had built up over the years in Cuba and among U.S. regulators, and a strong entrepreneurial drive, he started the business. Today, four and a half years later the firm has approximately $12 million in revenue and 14 employees.

President Obama began to allow individuals to obtain a license to travel to Cuba in 2011. Obtaining his license that year allowed Collin to begin to help student groups to come to Cuba in 2012. Since that initial opening of travel, there has been an ever decreasing level of control of individuals going to Cuba. The result has been that where relatively few Americans came to the island initially, the number of American tourist in Cuba was estimated at over 250,000 in 2016; the nation had over 3.5 million visitors to that year with Canadians being the largest group of visitors.

The rules of travel have now changed to the point that there is no longer the need for U.S. citizens to travel in organized groups that characterized the initial start of Collin's firm; today individuals can show up at a U.S. airport, certify by they want to go to Cuba for an approved purpose such as education by simply saying so, board a U.S. airline, and go to the island on their own. The result of the rapid changes in the rules and regulations has meant that Collin is constantly changing and adapting his business model. Many universities still employ his services to organize student groups to the island since he can ensure transportation for the group, English speaking guides, class speakers, and other items necessary for the university students' experience. However, the changing travel environment has pushed Collin to diversify into other Cuba travel activities.

Collin now offers a "white glove" experience for very high net worth travelers. These individuals might arrive in private yachts or private jets. Collin needs to arrange not only entry but a level of experience that is far greater than those typically expected by students. Food, housing, transportation, and experiences all must be consistent with the much higher prices Collin charges for this service.

Other services Collin now offers include arranging only part of the travel experience an individual may need. Airbnb's fastest growing market in the world is Cuba. An individual may be able to arrange their own housing but need other help with other elements of their visit. Collin is willing to arrange those needs for an individual. He now also provides service for entities such as cruise ships, which are beginning to visit Cuba. The company organizes shore excursions that include local activities and sightseeing.

As the market has opened, there are an ever increasing number of firms that are hosting corporate retreats in the island. Prior to the loosening of travel constraints, a firm doing business in Cuba could be liable for fines if they transacted any business in the United States. For most firms around the world, it was a choice of doing business in Cuba or the United States. Now many firms both in the United States and abroad are looking to host their annual meetings in Cuba since they no longer will be prosecuted for violating U.S. laws on doing business with Cuba. For example, Collin recently organized the annual retreat for over 300 employees for a large Scandinavian Internet business that had significant sales in the United States.

Finally, outside of travel Collin has also established a separate business that advises corporations wishing to enter the Cuban market. As the Cuban government continues to reform and the U.S. government is less stringent in its enforcement of business transactions in Cuba, large numbers of firms are looking to enter the Cuban market. Collin's expertise and relationships in the island have proved vital to help companies better understand this market as they begin to enter.

Collin has always had to be very creative in the operation of the business. For example, the Cuban banking system is not connected to the U.S. banking system because of legal restrictions in the United States. Because of this Collin must carry large amounts of cash to pay for things in Cuba. However, while he is use to change and adaption, the recent U.S. election has introduced a new stress into Collin's firm since it is not clear how the new administration will respond to the openings that the President Obama introduced. Many of the changes made thus far were done by executive order, and as a result the new president can reverse the changes in rules on doing business with Cuba very easily. Consistent with his adaptations to prior changes, Collin is not allowing this current challenge to stop him. His goal is to capture as much market and profit as he can in case negative changes in the rules are introduced. If there is not a major change, then he hopes to ensure his business is in a position to continue to grow. This coming year he is specifically seeking to be in a position to adapt quickly if any one segment of travel business decreases or increases. He hopes to separate the student travel, white glove travel, and event planning into separate groups that will allow not only greater expertise in each area but also the ability to better respond and adapt as changes occur in each type of travel. This way any given unit could be shut down quickly if one type of travel is prohibited by the new administration. Additionally, he hopes to move his current advising of firm entry to Cuba from one of where he is paid a consulting fee to one in which he takes an equity stake in the business. His hope is to become the local partner for some of the firms entering the market so that the business becomes a continuing stream of revenue.

Collin's experience in Cuba in constantly adapting and changing to meet the current need demonstrates the value to the entrepreneur in understanding their environment and adapting as it does.

Two key suggestions from Collin's experience for entrepreneurs include:

1. relationships in business key
2. change and adaptation is always needed

President Trump in 2017 again changed the rules for travel to Cuba which re-introduced a number of barriers for Americans to go to Cuba. Collin has adapted once again and the firm continues to expand.

THINKING CRITICALLY

Scott Dixon—Great Clips

There are so many franchise opportunities available that it is crucial to narrow down your goals to find a business opportunity to match. The International Franchise Association (http://franchise.org/) lists more than 1,200 franchisors with widely varying buy-ins, support, and expectations.

Scott Dixon was very clear on his interest in purchasing a franchise. He wanted (1) to minimize the up-front capital investment, (2) a relatively recession-proof business, and (3) a manager-run business, so he could continue in his current career. Scott is a finance graduate from the University of Georgia and earned his MBA at Georgia State University. For the past 20+ years, he has been a management consultant with a variety of firms from start-ups to Booz, Allen Hamilton. He enjoyed his work but was looking for something that had the long-term potential to provide a consistent income that was totally within his control.

The investigation of which franchise to buy into began with his outdoor hobby interest, moved to after-school programs aimed at helping students with STEM, health clubs, and even a quick look at quick-service restaurants. All required the owner to be the manager and did not seem fully recession proof. Scott was more than willing to sacrifice his weekends and evenings to work on the business but did not want something that required his day-to-day attention.

After going to a Great Clips location to get his hair cut, he narrowed his investigation to hair salons. For more than a year, he investigated all the hair salon franchise operations including visiting with many owners in and out of his home area of Tampa, Florida. He particularly liked the very clean model that Great Clips had put together and their focus on a repeatable process designed to get customers to want to come back. The company was well ahead of the competitors in technology, and it could all be operated with a manager model.

Great Clips provided support that Scott was really looking for in a franchisor. Each business market has a market manager, a real estate manager, and a business operations manager. These individuals are constantly available to help out or work with the franchisers like Scott. In general each Great Clips is given a 1.75-mile radius within which another Great Clips cannot open. This may be adjusted a bit depending upon population density. Start-up costs per store include a royalty agreement, buildout construction, equipment, furnishings, and a grand opening range from $100K to $150K (buildout being biggest variable).

It is important to note that a key aspect of buying into a franchise is the opportunity to buy into one that has inherent competitive advantages. The businesses are all tied together in image, operations, technology, and marketing. The owner is expected to be able to run the business at the median level of sales or profits. While great owners in great locations can and do exceed those levels, in general the competitive advantages lie with the franchise not the franchise owner or operator.

Scott opened his first location in February 2012, his second location in December 2014, and his third was planned for Summer 2017. He is actively looking to open three more locations in the next two years and hopes to run six-to-eight stores in and around his area. He has carefully used the earnings from one store to provide the cash to develop the next store. Each store has about eight-to-ten staff, including the manager and generally a mix of about 75 percent full time to 25 percent part time.

As an owner of multiple locations who works a full-time job, he has had to make some concessions that probably impact the speed with which he can grow his businesses. He really doesn't have the time to scout for new locations. Working his full-time job has also meant that he has not paid enough attention at times to ensure new stores get into a consistent rhythm as soon as they should be. That rhythm requires being in the store and making incremental changes to how staff interact with customers and ensure that strict processes are followed. For his Grand Opening weeks, he takes off work to help execute a smooth opening.

Scott has some solid advice for folks considering a franchise opportunity:

1. Nothing makes the business run more smoothly than hiring an experienced manager who also has experience in this industry. The manager runs all the day-to-day operations of the business, ensures that all the Great Clips policies are followed, and sets the store culture. Scott can only visit each location once per week or two. He is dependent upon excellent management. Finding, hiring, and retaining these folks is crucial to the whole operation.
2. Unlike a lot of new entrepreneurs, Scott has a high preference for having new locations rather than refurbishing an older location. He believes that nothing is more important than getting an "A" location that looks modern and clean and has excellent anchor stores.
3. He has figured out the demographic sweet spot for his store fronts to exceed the median of Great Clips stores. He looks at three things: (1) population density; (2) number of family members in each household; and, most importantly, (3) median income for the area. He tells the story of his first location in which he did not hold to these key demographics. He was excited to open the first location and let his sweet spot slip. The result is that regardless of what he does with the store, he realistically believes it will never be better than the average Great Clips store.
4. Finally, like so many entrepreneurs, he feels that he is just too slow to let go folks who are not effective employees. He tried and tried to bring one manager up to speed on the processes, culture, and approach he wanted for a specific store. The manager was almost solely concerned about her own advancement and working norms, with almost no concern for the broader team and changing team behaviors. Scott worked with her for three months while employees quit and the operation flatlined. He finally fired her and wished he had acted more swiftly.

Scott's area in Tampa, Florida, built up quickly, so in order to grow he is being forced to look toward Orlando and Sarasota. This will mean more travel to visit each store but also gives him some risk mitigation as each area has its own market fluctuations.

MiniCase 3

THINKING CRITICALLY

Cassmer Ward—The Clear Collar

Cassmer (Cass) Ward had been in an entrepreneurial situation before he helped found the Clear Collar (www.theclearcollar.com). He joined a struggling engineering firm as the CEO. The engineering firm was losing money on revenues of less than $1 million. Over the next six years Cass was able to move the firm to profitability with revenues in excess of $25 million.

In 2008, Cass found an opportunity that was too obvious and too good to ignore. Cass was in one of the EMBA entrepreneurship courses and pitched an idea that had been crafted by his father-in-law years before but never developed into a business. In the early 1990s, Alan Donaldson who was an emergency-room nurse with more than 20 years of experience was frustrated with the classic cervical collar that must be repeatedly removed from a person's neck to be checked following a neck injury. The new product was clear, allowing the emergency-service professional the ability to continuously assess the patient's neck without having to frequently remove the collar.

One evening, using everyday household plastics, Alan created the prototype of what would become the world's first fully transparent cervical immobilization collar. A man ahead of his time, he found that the technology and process to manufacture a comfortable, transparent cervical collar simply didn't exist.

In 2008, Cass formed a team of EMBA students, and with the blessing of Alan Donaldson, they developed a business plan that won the EMBA Business Plan Competition. The team then decided to turn the plan into a real business. Cass said, "It ended up being a perfect storm for success, the technology in TPE (plastic) technology was there, survey research indicating that the market was eager for this kind of product was there, and, of course, the patent was there. Now all we needed were start-up funds."

Cass and two other classmates dedicated themselves full time to the effort for the next 12 months. The new Clear Collar team promoted the concept to angel groups, medical professionals, and medical investors across the nation. The new company formed a board of directors and a board of advisors. The group felt that they needed at least $1.2 million to bring the idea to life. The founding team contributed $50,000 to get things started and went out and raised the rest of the capital over the course of a year. They ultimately raised $2 million.

For the Clear Collar team, getting molds cast, lining up manufacturers, working with distributors, and fighting an entrenched powerful set of competitors all proved to be substantial barriers to success.

The biggest impediment to early success, however, was the ability to make the product accessible. While the company had built a sales model based on sales representative-based distributors, they found that those distributors were very slow to react. The distributors wanted to see customers asking for the Clear Collar. Once customers asked about the Clear Collar, then the distributors became interested. This created an issue, as the company had to market to both direct consumers and to the distributors. Once the product began to gain acceptance in the medical community, the team was challenged by the sales scope related to volume and margin. The company continued to market to end users and distributors but then had to focus on the individual reps within the distributors.

While the distributors would agree to offer the Clear Collar, incentive plans and sales campaigns had to be delivered to the reps. However, this became a challenge due to the volume and margin limitation of the product offering. Sales reps were looking at an incentive to sell a $10 product to receive a $1 commission. While the 5 million cervical collars were sold in the United States every year, sales reps were forced to make a decision on whether to sell 500 collars to several different agencies to make $500 or 1 gurney to one agency to make $500. Time and effort played a bigger role in the sales rep's decisions/motivations.

Another issue was the adoption time lag to change to a new technology in the emergency service response. No one wanted to be an early adopter from the purchasing side. Although all of the direct users loved the Clear Collar, they didn't make the purchasing decisions. The purchasing decisions were made by a number of different sources (e.g., the municipality, the hospital, a third-party owner, etc.) This made it an uphill battle. Even with some of what became Cass's biggest accounts, it took 12-to-18 months to close the deal.

The Clear Collar team never planned on the sales cycle taking that long and did not have the resources to deal with this issue. At the same time, response/capacity from the manufacturing partner created issues. New versions with improvements were delayed, and shipping to customers on time became a big issue. This all became a huge demotivating factor for the sales team.

The result was, despite early strong interest in the product, the firm has shut down. While there is still interest in the intellectual property, the value of the IP is diminishing every day considering the main patent expires in 2020. The board was arduous in the process of deciding whether to sell the company (which would be at a low valuation); bring in more capital (ditto); or sell/license all of the intellectual property (IP). While the company dissolved in 2015, there are still numerous agencies that adopted the Clear Collar looking to place more orders. Additionally, several companies continue to circle the concept with intentions of purchasing the IP, yet there have been no transactions to date.

Cass has some advice for individuals interested in starting a new business:

1. You need to have great internal operations to fulfill orders, support sales/customers, and manage inventory. You will get offers from a lot of people/partners who can help or have advice on how to do so effectively. Be cautious. Be sure to listen but only do what is best for your business model, not what makes sense for them.
2. Everyone thinks sales come from a good marketing plan. *Wrong.* It is from an excellent sales plan. What does this mean? Not only know how to make your product accessible, but what are the hoops you need to jump through to make it accessible? Who does the purchasing? What is most important to the decision maker? Is the decision maker the user? If not, who does the product benefit and how can that benefit the decision maker? Understand what it takes (and how long) to complete the sale. The decision-making process when you buy a pack of gum is completely different from when you buy a car. What type of decision-making process is used when buying your product?
3. Make sure you are accountable and/or hold any vendors, partners, suppliers to the terms and conditions of your business. As a business owner, you want to provide your product as easily as possible to your customer. In order to do so, you are responsible for all factors from raw materials to delivery. Whoever you partner with to assist in the sales cycle must be a party that buys into and delivers the same message/service that is representative of your company.
4. Make sure you know the value of your product and commit to it. Once you try to compete with competitors that do not offer the value your product offers, you automatically devalue your own product. The effect of this results in you competing with price, which again diminishes your value. At that point you have turned your extraordinary advantages into ordinary attributes.

MiniCase 4

THINKING CRITICALLY

Sandra & Steve Moore—Moore A/C & Heating Services, Inc.

Starting a business is often a family affair with the entire family joining to support the start of the business and later running it. This family effort is the case for Sandra and Steve Moore. The couple started Moore A/C and Heating Services in Rowlett, Texas, in 1987. Steve had worked for others prior to 1987, but when his employer would not allow him to see his dying aunt in the hospital, Moore decided he needed more control and flexibility over his work life. Thus, he went out on his own.

The start of the business required not only Steve's expertise in heating, ventilation, and air conditioning (HVAC) but Sandra's knowledge in running an office. Additionally working as a nurse, Sandra was able to add her income to support the business with initial cash flow; the initial start-up period was hard and lean. While many of Steve's customers followed him from his prior employer, there were new expenses for equipment that had to be purchased. With initial capital of less than $15,000 from savings, the couple was able to survive. Throughout the life of the business, Steve's expertise in HVAC has been in high demand. For the next 10 years, Sandra continued to work full-time as a nurse and part-time working in the office.

As a result of their joint efforts, the firm continued to expand. Today, Moore A/C & Heating Services has a database of over 10,000 customers; although in any given year, they may service only several thousand. The growth of the business has allowed the Moores to employ their two grown sons (Nate and Scott) full time and one son's wife on a part-time basis. While Steve continues to be the principal technician in the field, Scott is the general manager and Nate manages the equipment. Their daughter-in-law helps with marketing of the firm, particularly through social media.

The challenges they face today are the future of the firm as Steve begins to look forward to less time in the field, if not retirement. The company employs six full-time and two part-time people who all draw a salary from the firm. However, the staff working in the field servicing A/C and heating units consists of only Steve and one other employee. Having two sons in the office reflects some of the changing nature of business in A/C and heating. Much of the firm's revenue now comes from contracts for services where a customer pays a set fee each year to ensure that their units are inspected and serviced to ensure optimal function, and then a discount is provided on service for any problems. The use of such contracts ensures a more consistent cash flow and helps rationalize when service calls are made since they can be scheduled in advance. Thus today, much of the business revenue comes from selling the contracts to the customers and then arranging the resulting services. The greater office support also reflects the fact that much of the profit for a business now comes from sales of equipment and not servicing the equipment.

The challenges going forward include how Sandra and Steve can build the firm to the point it can be sold if they desire. Now the firm receives significant benefit from a strong community relationship. It is a top rated firm on Angie's List for A/C and heating in Rowlett and Wylie, Texas, small cities of about 100,000 people. The Moores also have strong relationships across the community from their activities in the chamber of commerce and their church. However, these are all very personal connections. To an outside buyer they do not necessarily represent value since they are not transferable. Thus, the family is starting to examine how to build the business so that the relationships are not so personal that they cannot be transferred. This is particularly true since Steve, as the owner, does the principal servicing of units. The Moores may choose to allow their sons to take over the business in the future, but if so the issue that arises is how to structure the business so that it will be successful to the point that

Steve and Sandra can still draw some part of the stream of revenue for their retirement.

To help achieve this restructuring, the Moores have begun attending seminars on how to structure the business. These seminars have reinforced the challenge of bringing the entire family into the hard discussions on the future of the firm. While the Moores sons are involved with the business, they do have differing commitments. Nate is very active in a popular regional band; his wife is employed outside the business. Scott's wife works part time for the firm, and they have a small child. For Steve and Sandra, who have devoted so much of their lives to building the business, their biggest challenge now is balancing business growth, the business's future, and maintaining their close family's ties.

The Moores have three pieces of advice for anyone starting a family business.

1. The family needs to be fully supportive of the business. While Steve started the business, the business could not have reached success it has without the income from Sandra work's at different points and time.
2. Succession is a key issue in a family business (one the Moores are struggling with now). In setting up the business and bringing family into the business, there is a time when one hopes to either exit or reduce their time in the firm. But decisions made today will affect that exit or reduction of time.
4. Managing a family business requires extensive communication as keeping equity among children in the firm and also rewarding effort and time is hard to manage.

MiniCase 5

THINKING CRITICALLY

Jeffrey Offutt—JITA Printing

Jeff Offutt spent 28 years building an expertise that today allows him to compete in the highly competitive printing industry. Starting out in his uncle's print shop in 1989 while still a teenager provided Jeff a rich background in printing. Beyond working on the printing press, Jeff has worked in most of the aspects of the industry including the following:

- Prepress—the creation of a print layout and final printing that involves the manufacturing of a printing plate for mounting on a printing press
- Mechanical stripping—arranging and joining film negatives as part of the process of preparing printing plates
- Color house—scanning of transparencies into digital system allowing for color corrections
- Computer systems—developing computer systems as printing changed to allow for high speed access to the desktop
- Photoshop—making color alterations to digital images to take out imperfections

That combined background gave Jeff the confidence and expertise to start his own business in 2009. Individuals who knew Jeff saw an opportunity for Jeff to open a printing shop plus be able to provide the printing they needed. Jeff was convinced, and initially using the equipment of this group, he would pay them for clicks of what he printed for his customers. He would then bill his customers for whatever was generated. The group supported Jeff by paying the lease on the printing machine, but with Jeff running it, they were able to obtain their printing cheaper and in a timelier manner. This approach allowed Jeff to start his business with only $5,000. He focused on any type of printing including business cards, brochures, pamphlets, and high-end promotional materials. His only requirement was that the order be over $75 to ensure it was at the volume necessary to be cost effective for him. The customers were obtained through lots of long hours of knocking on doors in the area around the shop where he was located, which is in a business district of Houston. The key selling point for the business was that he could do the work faster than his competitors at a reasonable cost. He often got business others said would take weeks because he was willing to work longer hours to ensure the work was done quickly and accurately. The result was that once he served a customer and did an excellent job he retained them. A year and half later Jeff was paying the lease on the printer himself but was still able to provide his original supporters their printing needs at a reasonable price and timely manner.

Today Jeff relies on word of mouth for his customers. The business has expanded and now has seven employees including him. The business leases four large printers for the work—two color and two black and white—each of which costs $72,000 a year. Jeff's technical ability has allowed him to focus on digital printing that allows a much faster turnaround than offset printing. The offset printing industry is shrinking while the digital industry is growing. However, without the extensive years in the industry Jeff would not have had the expertise to pursue this successful business.

While experience was a key factor that allowed Jeff to succeed, one shortcoming that Jeff was very clear about was his lack of business knowledge. He was an expert in the printing industry. However, beyond understanding simple computer-driven accounting, he did not have the business background to deal with issues such as pricing, profit margins, and employee pay. The initial years were hard for Jeff as he learned the fundamentals of the business side to compliment his printing expertise.

While Jeff is a clear entrepreneurial success story, one of the interesting background issues that you should know is that Jeff is a convicted felon. From 2002 to 2008 he was in prison (twice) for robbery. Entrepreneurial passion can be motivated by much more than money and freedom—for Jeff it is the activity that has allowed him to change his life. Jeff was part of the Prison Entrepreneurship Program in

Texas. This program uses entrepreneurship to help reduce recidivism in prison from over 50 percent to less than 7 percent. The opportunities afforded by pursuing entrepreneurship is not only changing lives but also helping to move people from costing over $25,000 a year to house them in prisons to helping them become productive citizens of the nation. You can read more about the PEP program at http://www.pep.org/. Entrepreneurship impact on people and society can be so great.

Jeff's advice to new entrepreneurs includes the following:

1. Get a mentor to help you learn from their experiences. Jeff has had many mentors since his release from prison, and they have helped him grow into the person he is today.
2. Find industry reports that tell you what the profit margins, cost, and other industry benchmarks should be for the type of business. Otherwise you do not have a measure on how to structure what you do and judge if it is a success. Today, Jeff targets the industry average of 10 percent net profit. This is a target level he acquired early on in his business because his mentor coached him in this area.
3. Hire good people. You cannot do it all yourself and you need people to rely on. Today the employee team that Jeff has put together has a total of 85 years of printing experience among them. The result is that his team can act quickly and decisively when any problems arise.
4. Life throws you many challenges, but those challenges do not determine your life forever. Individuals can change their lives through hard work and focus. For Jeff his faith and entrepreneurship are key elements of that change.

MiniCase 6

THINKING CRITICALLY

Kevin Callahan—PeerPoint

Kevin Callahan started out as French teacher and a lay Catholic Chaplain, but most of his life's work led to the entrepreneurial venture he now runs. Kevin studied French in school and earned a master's in French as a student in Paris. He moved to Quebec and became a public high-school teacher where he remained for 15 years. Not being a citizen of Canada cost him his position during a severe downturn in the economy.

Married and with children, Kevin wanted to stay in Quebec, so he took his skills dealing with classrooms full of children (organization, discipline, an ability to handle all personality types) and moved into real estate with a nationally known firm. Over the next few years, he became one of the top 10 percent of his company's agents in Canada. The real estate firm moved him into management and asked him to turnaround problem offices. He became quite talented at developing agents, creating processes, and quickly turning unprofitable locations into profitable operations. Unfortunately, the 1990 recession in Canada led the business to rationalize, and Kevin was caught up in the reduction of retail locations.

After being laid off Kevin took the next 6 months off to earn a programming certificate and consider his next business move. He combined his teaching and training development skills to engage with small software companies, developing and delivering training that their "geeks" could not. He was hired by one of the largest computer integrators in Canada to develop procedures and technical training of corporate staffs in prep for Y2K.

It was the mid-1990s and the whole business world was starting to panic about the so-called Y2K bug. For those who don't know, most programs at the time had been written in an environment where we only had 80 characters of input for any single record. Names were shortened and a coding scheme developed over the decades. Most programs had an error code to test records and that error was either 12/31/99 or 9/9/99 meaning that many programs would stop running as the new century began. Virtually all business programs written had to be scoured to clear out 1999 as an error. It was referred to as the Year 2000 bug or Y2K. Thus, there was a boom in computer-related businesses like the one that hired Kevin.

Kevin later moved to Chicago and continued the same type of work while he pursued an MBA degree. His MBA efforts led to a desire to lead business turnarounds. He had done that work in the real-estate offices years earlier and was now armed with significant financial acumen that he wanted to put to work.

He worked on a contract basis as an interim COO for a number of firms in different industries. He was able to use his skills to help small growing companies transition from an "entrepreneurial" to a "management" structure, providing the staff and operations processes that enable rapid growth.

Kevin was working as the interim COO for a medical training company. The company provided a wide variety of required annual training for the medical profession. His efforts there put him in direct contact with the company that accredited the training. Accrediting medical training is a complex effort that involves vetting every doctor doing training and certifying that they have no unique conflicts of interest. The process was cumbersome and very paper oriented. It might take 90 days to clear a single doctor as paperwork went back and forth.

Kevin's wide background put him a position where he felt he had all the skills necessary to run his own business. Kevin approached the owner of the business he was working for as a COO about buying out the accreditation company. The company was not profitable and barely holding on to its operation. Kevin negotiated an extraordinary deal and along with his (now) partner bought the business, PeerPoint Medical Education Institute.

Kevin allowed the business to run on autopilot while he worked out his time as the COO of the other company and eventually took over PeerPoint full time. His first move was to craft a means of automating the whole accreditation effort. He first developed a framework for how the whole process works and how it could be automated. He hired an outside IT firm and had the whole platform attached to SalesForce.com for scalability and ease of use. With the new approach literally everything was online, and he was able to not only cut down the processing time by a factor of four but also significantly drop the price of the effort.

There are several competitors in the market; however, they are rapidly falling behind PeerPoint. Kevin sees the business growing quickly over the next few years as he gets the word out about the efficiency and ease of doing business with PeerPoint.

Kevin has some advice for folks considering a new business:

1. To do well in a business you need to be an expert. He recommends talking with everyone you can in the industry. Research the market and learn as much as you can before you enter a new business. He also hires experts for aspects of the business that he does not know well. He is not a marketing expert but quickly moved to hire someone who is results oriented.
2. "Get out of your seat and knock on doors." Kevin believes that it takes guts to run a business and that running it is not done from a desk. It is about getting out and knowing what is happening with customers. He relates a story about wanting to find every home in his territory that was listed as "For Sale by Owner (FSBO)." He hired school kids to ride around their neighborhoods after school each day looking for new FSBO signs and paid them $10 each for a new one that they found. He then knocked on their door to convince the home owner to sign with him.
3. You need to have a year's worth of day-to-day living expenses in the bank before you open for business. He advises not taking out a business loan unless it is strictly for the business. Taking out a loan for the entrepreneur to pay him or herself is a mistake.
4. Finances are important. A deep knowledge of how the business operates and how it makes money is something that every entrepreneur should know. Kevin sought his MBA in order to gain this deep understanding of the financial side of business, and it has helped him uncover opportunities for himself and for his client companies.

MiniCase 7

THINKING CRITICALLY

Bill Zeuch—ComicLock, LLC

Many of us collect “things” that can range from shot glasses, commemorative spoons, baseball cards, hats, typewriters, stamps, coins, travel tags, ceramic things, to glass door knobs. There are also collecting societies for virtually everything as people have a desire to socialize with those with similar interests and a real desire to display their prize collections. How to do so when the items you have collected are not just interesting but very valuable is a real challenge. The collector does not want to impact the value of their items in the process. Just such an issue drove Bill Zeuch (an avid comic book collector) to create ComicLock, LLC and his products Comic Lock (a $399 metal and museum-quality locking glass case) and ComicMount and AlbumMount ($5.99 plastic two-in-one mounting display system for mounting symmetrically on walls or any flat surface).

Bill was an art major who graduated from Kent State University and immediately went to work in the math analytics/point of sale (POS)/supply chain field, ultimately running the sales analytics team for a company whose main customer was WalMart. A real desire to get into retail led Bill to accept a position as the VP of category management/customer insights at OfficeMax. At the time, Bill and his team managed over 34,000 unique items (SKUs), deciding what to buy, how to price, and where to place every item. While working for OfficeMax, Bill had an idea about selling inventory items to other noncompetitor retailers at a sharp markup for OfficeMax, but a much better deal for the retailer. He and his team successfully grew the business to over $40 million in sales. He clearly had an entrepreneurial orientation while working for a large company. After OfficeMax Bill went on to work for several other companies including the Nebraska Book Co. and Sears. He is currently the chief merchandising officer for Party City based in New Jersey, but the entrepreneurial desire is still in his soul.

As a result of that entrepreneurial desire, Bill started ComicLock, LLC four years ago. The goal was to develop a well-designed product to display his very expensive collection of comic books. He wanted to craft a business that he could run with his family and still keep his job. He saw the process as a way for his children to really appreciate the effort and impact a business could bring.

He and his wife made all of the investment to get the business started. They hired an attorney to set up the business, hired a web designer to craft together their Internet presence, and shopped around for a metal fabricator who would work with them to design and build his first product, ComicLock. Samples of his products appear below.

ComicLock

ComicMount

AlbumMount

The products developed initially sold exclusively on Amazon and eBay; this first product was not only a good product but also a great learning experience. At $399, it was generally sold to very high net-worth people who bought it to protect and display their most valuable comics. Learning from their Amazon experience, Bill and his wife began to call on trade shows. After a year they had sold $100,000 worth of the product. Bill found after all their expenses were accounted for that it was only a barely profitable product.

Bill realized that the big money was going to be in an inexpensive way for average collectors to display their passion. That was going to have to be plastic and a completely different approach. In a bold move, he ended all sales of the ComicLock and went to work on designing and packaging a plastic display that could easily be hung up on walls in symmetrical rows and columns, as well as giving his guests the option to be able to also use it as a shelf stand on any flat surface.

He designed two products—one for comic books and one for album covers. Each was crafted for simplicity of use and packaged for easy mailing to customers who bought the product on Amazon, eBay, and Etsy. The sales over the past three years have grown substantially from $ 43,000 the first year to $ 232,000 last year. Bill's wife and children run the operations of the business packaging and mailing off over 100 pieces a day via the U.S. Postal Service.

Bill has some advice for folks considering a new business:

1. Surround yourself with as many different opinions as you can. He advises putting your ego aside and actively seeking out advice that counters your own thinking. The direction and success of the business is really dependent upon clear, unbiased thinking.
2. However, with all the advice, be very careful of whom you hire. Early on he hired an attorney that we generally believe is very good advice. In Bill's case he felt that the attorney charged them for a lot of items that they could have done easily themselves but just didn't know. This was compounded by the hiring of a website-design firm that charged them a lot of money for their first site. He advises that simplicity in your legal approach and first website will save you money and allow you to test the business idea.
3. Fail fast. Use early customers and early products to let you test the market. He quickly realized that the initial product would never allow them the type of business they were seeking. In a bold move Bill ended all sales of the initial product and went back to the drawing board for a new design. Today 70 percent of sales is for the AlbumMount product.
4. Sales are about inspiring, not the details of the product. He is solving a problem that collectors of all stripes have. The product is sold through pictures and a community of fans rather than detailed dimensions and product specifications.

Bill and his family hope to grow the business quickly. There has been a resurgence of AlbumMount sales around the world. He has only touched the market thus far.

MiniCase 8

THINKING CRITICALLY

Chris Bisson—Value Connect

Entrepreneurship works best when capability aligns with a known pain point for potential customers. Chris Bisson did just that when he started Value Connect (https://www.valueconnect.ca/) in early 2017.

Chris graduated from McMaster University with a commerce degree in 1993. Over the next few years he worked in customer service for a large financial institution, did a short stint as a penny-stock broker (selling very low cost stocks), and then spent four years working for Levi Strauss & Co. His office at Levi's was located more than an hour from his home in Guelph, Ontario (Canada), and although the work was fulfilling, Chris was looking for something more and closer to home. His wife's cousin (Bob) was a mortgage broker and earning more and more money each year while running his own business.

Chris decided to talk with Bob and shortly thereafter joined his firm that was located 45 minutes away. Chris is talented at math, and he found that all the work involved with being a mortgage broker was right up his alley. A key skill he learned in mortgage underwriting was the valuation of properties that serve as the security for the mortgage.

Chris worked with this firm for several years but really wanted to run his own operation. Chris saw an opportunity for a mortgage brokerage in his own town and reached out to the leading mortgage franchisor in Canada. Ultimately, Chris was able to buy a Mortgage Centre Canada (MCC) franchise in his home town of Guelph for Canadian $16,000 and .03 percent of total bookings. His new business did not compete with Bob's business but did upset a nearby MCC franchisee who felt that he had first right of refusal to open in Guelph if the opportunity was available.

Chris grew the business quickly by developing a solid reputation for the hustle, speed and accuracy of his operation. His wife (also a broker) worked at the business, and it was not long before they were grossing over a Canadian $ 1 million a year. In his dealings with all the parties to real estate transactions, Chris saw an opportunity in the appraisal market due to several factors.

First, after the housing crash of 2008–2010, the Canadian government moved to separate appraisers from loan officers and brokers arranging mortgages. Prior to this time, appraisers effectively worked for mortgage brokers and banks. The broker in this setting had a big incentive to ensure that the value of a property matched the price that had been agreed to by the buyer/seller. This sometimes led to inflated and non-independent valuations and was partly to blame for the housing bubble. Second, Chris saw that the big players in the newly developing industry of Appraisal Management Companies (AMCs) were bidding out work to appraisers in search of the lowest bid. Appraisers were frustrated with procedures that were very paper heavy and poor communication by the AMCs. The appraisers could not do an effective job for what they were being paid. In addition, Chris took note of the fact that none of the competitors was truly integrated since they did not sell the software appraisers use to build reports.

The focus on low cost and poor processes by AMCs resulted in the generation of valuation estimates that the mortgage brokers could not trust. At the same time appraisers were complaining about having to be the lowest bid in order to get any business. Chris saw a perfect opportunity for someone to come into the market with an elegant technology solution that would speed up the process for the appraisers and yet allow prices to be reasonable for the buyers.

In November 2015 Chris hired a marketing research firm to confirm or repudiate his assessment of the market. They confirmed that there was a real opportunity for someone to radically change this industry. Over the next year Chris built the business. He contacted a friend of his who had sold his technology-driven business who joined him as a partner. Chris used stock in the new company as an incentive for the staffing he needed and contracted out the building of the appraisal solution software.

Chris invested Canadian $300,000 of his own money to bring the software from idea, through testing to operationally ready. Chris brought on a partner with a technological background to drive the development process. Along the way the two partners tested each aspect of the software with bankers, appraisers, lawyers, and brokers. They used those tests to craft together a platform that would be desired by all parties. Value Connect owns all the intellectual property related to the operation.

The business went live in February 2017 with a sophisticated website and a lot of legwork-marketing in his town of Guelph. Chris is now looking to raise Canadian $1.5 million from family, friends, acquaintances, and angel investors in order to expand nationwide. He plans to sell capital in 1 percent chunks for Canadian $50,000 each (maximum of 30 percent of the business).

Chris has some advice for potential entrepreneurs:

1. Whatever amount of work you think it is going to take, multiply that by 10;
2. Be mindful of your bank account;
3. Constantly be discussing your idea with potential investors—you don't want to ever "need" the money when you are looking for it. This helps you negotiate from a place of power;
4. Practice before you play. There's nothing worse than not being prepared to pitch your business because you aren't prepared for the opportunity when it lands in your lap;
5. Always have an objective for every interaction or sales call you make;
6. Don't do it alone. Identify the skills you'd need to make your idea reality, and then find people that have those skills and a passion for your idea;
7. Play to win

THINKING CRITICALLY

Ricardo Baldi—Baldi Gardens

Mowing grass for someone can be thought of as a commodity activity—every teenager in the neighborhood is willing to do it for a very small price in most cities. While that low-end yard maintenance is widely available, it is not generally very profitable. Ricardo Baldi has developed a successful strategy of offering a high-quality, contract-based model in this highly competitive market.

Ricado has been in the business for 24 years, having developed a business by doing work he loved for friends. Over the years, he developed a model in which he charges a premium for his work but for a premium product. The core of the model is to do more than simply mow the grass. If that is all he does for a customer, he loses money every time he sends a crew. Instead, the customer signs up for a monthly contract. This contract is at a fixed rate per month, but it covers not only mowing the yard but also maintaining sprinkler system, fertilizing, controlling weed, ranking leaf, and a variety of other activities to ensure the yard is maintained in excellent year-round condition. The monthly fee is the same whether it is the summer or winter, but if the winter is not cold, his crews will be busy in the yard all year. This model of contracts helps in providing more even cash flows throughout the year for the firm. It also ensures maintenance on the yard is done as needed not just when there is a crisis. Such maintenance allows a more rational use of workers since in slower winter months employees can do more substantial activities that may be required on a yard, which in turn allows the firm to maintain their work force through the year.

One of the keys to the success of this model is hiring the right people. The yard maintenance industry is commonly characterized by low wages and low skills. Ricardo focuses on paying a premium for employees to ensure he has the people who can fulfill his strategy. He focuses on hiring people with commitment to a high level of customer service. It is not uncommon for a potential employee to have three interviews with a variety of people in the firm to ensure they are a good match for the firm. The focus is typically not on experience but on the attitude of the person. To ensure that quality is a constant focus, each week the crews receive extra training on a wide range of topics from customer service to specific horticultural activities. These training sessions can be an hour a week in the busy summer period to several hours a week during the slower winter; the workers are paid for this training time. The result is a highly motivated, highly skilled team of individuals. There are three salary employees—Ricardo, his son, and a service manager. Ricardo's wife also works in the firm but draws no salary. The firm has approximately 20 employees with a low turnover relative to the industry. Many of his employees have been with the firm over 10 years.

To ensure that the service is always high quality, four times a year the firm's owner, son, or senior manager call each client to see that all problems are addressed and check on the quality of the work done. The company also addresses any client concerns raised by e-mail the same day. Customers of the firm frequently tell the owner that former lawn care company owners seemed very concerned with them when they signed up for the business but were never seen again. Baldi ensures that the intent and follow through with high-quality service is there every time. The goal being not just to deliver the service to the customer but to build a relationship with the customer. The outcome of this high quality has meant that Baldi is one of the highest rated firms in the area on services such as Angie's List. This high quality is also seen in the fact that he no longer relies on major advertising expenditures but principally word of mouth of satisfied customers and his ratings on Angie's List.

The high level of service provided has resulted in Ricardo also being asked to do many projects at individuals home such as redoing the entire landscaping. To ensure that such activities do not distract from his yard maintenance, he created a separate unit of the business focused strictly on yard projects. The 20 employees of the firm are split approximately equal with half in yard maintenance and half in projects. The firm only focuses on individuals, not commercial properties, since the commercial business is highly price sensitive and generally will not pay for the higher cost/higher quality level of service The strategy has produced long-term success although the firm must constantly adjust as the economy can impact the firm significantly. The strategy not only allows for the maintenance of employment for the 20 employees but also ensures that the extensive capital equipment including the typical lawn mowers and grass edgers plus the six trucks and three cars for service calls are kept busy.

Ricardo's advice for entrepreneurs if they start a firm includes the following:

1. Do not give up. It takes time and effort. At the beginning it is easy to walk away as the start-up will take more time and more money than you expect. He initially loved the horticulture side but to build it into the business it is today took time.
2. Do what you love. If you love your work then even if the money is not as great as you expect, you will be happy, and if you are happy you will do a better job.
3. Good people are key to helping you achieve what you want to achieve. The delivery of quality products is central to charging a premium price. But without good people that quality will never be achieved.
4. Always remember family is important. Baldi Gardens could always be bigger. But the time with his six kids (all of who have worked in the business at different times) is more important. That's one reason that our employees work four days per week, 10 hours per day, so that they have more time with their families. He tries to have company activities every month to have that family feel in the business as well.

MiniCase 10

THINKING CRITICALLY

Kyle Mittendorf—Brilliant Medical Boutique

Kyle Mittendorf was the assistant soccer coach at Vanderbilt University when he and his wife decided to move closer to her family in Texas. His wife had been working in durable medical equipment - DME store; a store in the DME industry could sell a wide range of items including but not limited to wheel chairs and related items for the elderly, mastectomy prosthetics for cancer survivors, and shoes for those with special needs such as diabetics.

The young couple first picked the city they wished to live in—Weatherford, Texas. This suburban city to a large metropolitan area that was experiencing 10 percent growth a year and the average income of the inhabitants was relatively high. Driving around the town they noticed that there were only two DME stores in the city. Visiting each one and talking to the owners just about business and the area they could quickly see that one of the businesses was not healthy and would likely be out of business soon. The second store was doing well, but with 10 percent growth a year in the area, there seemed to be significant potential for a second healthy DME business.

In 2006 Kyle and his wife decided to open their first store in the suburban city. They started the store with a $70,000 loan from the bank. The timing was perfect as the bank in 2006 was very willing to make the loan. Following the 2008 crisis their banker indicated that they would not be able to get a similar loan, not because of their financial status but the new more conservative framework for bank lending. Thus, timing was central to the Mittendorfs ability to start the firm. Kyle and his wife quickly repaid the loan. Since that initial loan they have not taken out any loans for their business other than an operating line of credit, which they keep to a minimum.

The first store the couple opened was in a suburban community they sold a wide range of DME products as the needs varied widely in the community. They made a conscious decision regarding pricing that they could never depend on beating the price of a mass supplier such as Amazon. Instead, they would provide outstanding service and charge a slightly higher price. Some customers do come in, get a price on an item from Kyle, and then look online for the price on Amazon. The customer will find it is cheaper at Amazon, and the store will acknowledge it and wish them well. Fortunately, there are many people focused more on service than price. Individuals cannot wait a day or two to get a product from Amazon if the customer falls and needs a wheel chair or crutches. Other products such as shoes for diabetics and mastectomy prosthetics are custom-fit products, so there is a high level of service in providing them.

The success of the initial store led the young couple to open a second store in the urban area of the metroplex in 2014—in Arlington, Texas. They picked a location next to a major cancer clinic. Kyle knew that patients would want high service with mastectomy prosthetics and related items such as the braziers that go with such prosthetics. Such prosthetics and related items would be the major focus of this store. There was not any other DME company close by. Unfortunately for Kyle and his wife, the industry was undergoing a significant change. Historically, mastectomy surgeries and reconstruction surgeries for women were separate activities. In the last few years, the protocol for treatment has changed such that the mastectomy surgery and reconstruction surgery are combined. This meant that the benefit of locating next to the large cancer clinic never materialized. Instead they found that their mastectomy customers were mostly women who were not buying new products but instead replacing older products that had worn out meaning that sales were much lower than had been anticipated. The sales of other DME products such as wheelchairs and other items were also far lower than desired even if these were not designed to be the major focus of the Arlington store. The area was not as wealthy as their other location, and as a result sales were primarily based upon whether the patient had insurance.

This situation was heightened under affordable care act where coverage became broader with more individuals covered by insurance, but often DME was eliminated from coverage.

Their inability to attract high-quality employees made the need to close the store all the more obvious. Kyle and his wife were very involved in their suburban community, so recruiting employees was not that difficult. However, in the urban area they did not have such relationships and could not find consistently good employees. While in the process of closing the store, Kyle took a wrong turn while driving home and discovered an expanding medical complex in the next largest city to his suburban location—Fort Worth. He knew the medical district was there but did not appreciate how big it had become. The medical footprint of the hospital was also growing significantly, and there was not a DME store in the area. It was also clear that the neighborhoods in the area were relatively well off. Building on these insights, Kyle decided to close the urban store and open in this new area.

The move resulted in a significant increase in business for the store. While Kyle still bills insurance companies, the income of the area is such that he can typically sell products up (selling more expensive versions of the same product) and increase his cash business. For example, following a mastectomy many women have lymph nodes removed meaning they then need to wear a full-arm sleeve that compresses their arm, so it does not swell. The insurance will only pay for a very basic, typically poor quality, $20 sleeve. However, in this area most women will go for the better, more compressing products around $75. Kyle still gets the $20 from the insurance firm, but the other $55 comes in cash from the customer themselves.

The major challenge Kyle now faces is actively managing two stores. The effort required is more than just doubling the responsibility—it is a geometric expansion. The two stores have different customer needs and products. The new store location is close enough to his other suburban location that he has better access to good workers, but it is still a challenge to ensure both business locations are operating as desired. Kyle remains clear that his family remains his key focus and normally does not work beyond nine to five, a five-day workweek. His wife helps with the business books, and together they provide a good living for their family.

Kyle's advice for entrepreneurs includes the following:

1. Be an expert in what you sell. Don't try to compete with everyone. Instead be clear what your business is and why it is successful. He does not try to be Amazon or a more extensive DME that would provide services to rehabilitation facilities. He is a retailer providing high-service levels to his customers.
2. Continue to expand your understanding of the business. There is a twice a year conference for the DME industry. This conference brings retailers and manufacturers together. Kyle tries to attend regularly and gain fresh knowledge.
3. Change is constant, and you have to adapt your firm. One issue for Kyle is insurance—it is in constant flux.

MiniCase 11

THINKING CRITICALLY

Cliff and Jo Ellen Silverman—GaGa Ball Pits

Cliff and Jo Ellen Silverman are serial entrepreneurs who started their latest venture in late 2010 called Coach Cliff's GaGa Ball Pits (http://www.gagaballpits.com/).

So what is GaGa Ball? It is a game that many believe was started in Israel. The game can be played by as few as two or as many people as can fit inside the "Pit." The pit varies in size but is generally octagon or hexagon shaped, with sides that can run any length up to 10 feet long each. Players stand inside the pit with a hand on the wall. The ball (a light-weight inflatable vinyl ball) is tossed up in the air and must bounce twice before a player can touch it. The players all say "Ga" as it bounces twice to start the game (Ga means hit or touch in Hebrew). The goal is to hit another player in the legs below the knees to eliminate them from the game. The last one in the pit wins. A typical game takes about 5 to 10 minutes.

Cliff first discovered GaGa Ball at a daddy/daughter campout in 2010. He was amazed that kids of all ages and their parents could participate in a game that had lots of movement and exercise, while maintaining great competition, fun, and excitement for everyone involved. As a game that's great for any group size and skill level, Cliff saw GaGa Ball as a way to bring parents, kids, and communities together.

Cliff searched the Internet trying to find out where to buy a GaGa Ball Pit or at least the parts to put one together himself. He found very little.

Cliff and Jo Ellen saw a business opportunity. Cliff had extensive knowledge on product design and working with metal from his business venture Karajen Corp. He started designing everything that would be needed to put together a GaGa Ball Pit. He crafted easy to work with brackets and built a pit in his front yard. To build awareness of the product, Cliff and Jo Ellen had their children and friends use the pit while they filmed them playing. They posted the video on YouTube. The Silvermans also built and donated a pit to their daughter's school (a couple of years later the school bought two more). To further promote the product, the Silvermans built a website that allowed individuals who had heard about the product to learn more. Their first sale was for a person's backyard in California, and they were off and running.

The focus of the business is on solid construction with a well-designed, aesthetically looking bracket system that can be customized along with multiple other accessories for the complete game setup. You purchase your lumber locally, which is screwed to the brackets to form the walls. This is to keep the cost down for the customer and saves on shipping. To ensure that the product is easy to build, they provide simple to follow instructions.

Initially, sales were slow but steady. However, to expand more quickly, the Silvermans decided to *brand* Cliff as the Coach and spokesperson for all things "GaGa". They recrafted the website around Coach Cliff, had him speak to groups, and designed videos with Coach Cliff assembling a pit, explaining the rules, and demonstrating good practices.

The Silvermans focus their sales efforts on venues that are looking for activities that everyone would enjoy such as campgrounds, summer camps, religious programs, physical education programs, and the recess areas at schools. They started with a Summer Camp Directors tradeshow that was being held in Texas. They had sold a complete kit to a customer in the area and that same customer volunteered to bring over the whole pit to the show. They set up a booth, and the pit was a hit. They sold kits to more than 50 percent of the people who visited the booth. From this initial success, the Silvermans now attend tradeshows and events for these and adjacent markets. The approach is to set up a GaGa Ball Pit and show attendees how much fun it is and how easy it is to set up.

They now offer brackets in eight colors for their most popular pit system, wall top covers in six colors, quick connect kits for portable units, and other accessories such as GaGa Balls, an ADA compliant doorway, a metal game rules sign, and a laminated rules sheet signed by Coach Cliff. The Silvermans expect to sell 2,000+ full kits in 2017, with kits making up about 63 percent of their total sales and accessories making up the rest. They have also made a deal with a local manufacturer to sell customers structural composite lumber boards (recycled plastic lumber) with pre-drilled holes and have them drop shipped directly to the customer. The firm's success has been so great that Jo Ellen left her full-time job to join the business, and the team has hired a staff of office and assembly employees. Going forward there are more and more competitors entering the market. The knowledge of GaGa is now so great that there are many companies trying to copy the success of the Silvermans. Other competitors have entered the market, but none offer the easy to assemble and customizable system they have. To date, the quality of the products generated and the unique brand of Coach Cliff has ensured the success of the company.

Cliff and Jo Ellen have some advice for folks considering a new business:

1. As cliché as it sounds, make sure you are doing what you love as you will be doing it pretty much all the time. They are fortunate that they work on the business together.
2. If you find yourself constantly coming up with a reason to hold off starting a business, you aren't ready yet. Spend more time researching and planning.
3. Be a creative problem solver when it comes to overcoming obstacles. You will face many, be resilient.
4. Coming up with an idea is such a small part of launching a business. It's more about developing a system and network that is nimble enough to direct and redirect as the market environment, customer, and competition changes.

THINKING CRITICALLY

Jeff Barry—RavioliOli

There are new businesses that do everything correctly, pivot well as the environment changes, have great customer value, and yet still fail to achieve breakeven. Jeff Barry had been serving friends and family his grandmother's ravioli recipes for 20 years. During all that time, he worked in specialized parts of banking, including asset-based financing and equipment leasing. Jeff was essentially a numbers guy who had a passion to start an entrepreneurial venture centered around his specialty approach to ravioli.

Jeff finally decided to get serious about the effort during the recession of 2009. Noticing that the fast casual dining market seemed immune to the recession and was growing like no other part of the market, he felt the time was right for him to start a restaurant based on that ravioli concept. RavioliOli was to be a fast-casual dining restaurant where fresh handmade specialty ravioli were delivered to your table within five minutes of ordering. The location was going to be slightly upscale and the décor was going to be warm, comforting, and comfortable.

Jeff did a complete competitive analysis using himself and his family to learn all they could about competing restaurants. The family would go to various fast-casual concept restaurants and record how many people dined there during lunch and dinner. He tracked average meal ticket prices and looked for locations that had great road access and parking. Building on his understanding of the competition, Jeff then took six months to develop a full business plan that was ready to pitch to investors.

Jeff started his search for investors with a friend who had money to invest. After securing that investment, he was referred to one investor after another, and he was able to quickly raise the capital that he believed he needed to start the company. This included $175,000 of his own money. Securing the location took far longer. He looked at close to a hundred sites with various realtors. Finally, in early 2011, Jeff found the perfect location in Oak Brook, Illinois, just west of Chicago. Jeff really loved the location because of its access to major roads, great parking, visibility, and access to the corporate lunch crowd. Although the real estate market was still reeling, the cost of the lease was substantial (although well within Jeff's business plan projections). After extensive negotiation, Jeff signed a lease for 2,200 square feet and began to generate specific plans for the space. Working with designers and architects, they developed a great space. There is an old adage that says a new business will cost twice as much as you expect and take twice as long. Jeff had heard this and felt like he was prepared when it did happen. However, in the approval process with the landlord and building inspectors, Jeff was surprised to find out that his kitchen was going to require special ductwork that had not been accounted for in the plans. Several other smaller items were also required for unexpected changes, all of which ended up costing an additional $110,000.

As a part of his original business plan Jeff had set aside $220,000 in working capital to take care of contingencies and provide the business with a cash buffer. He decided to have all the small items and the new ductwork installed. RavioliOli opened for business in late February 2012.

Everything was going well at first. There were opening parties, Groupon offers, and lots of press about the new business. However, the working capital fund was rapidly depleting as revenue did not cover expenses. It is not unusual for a new restaurant to take 18 to 24 months to achieve monthly breakeven. In the case of RavioliOli, however, the reserves had been spent early on the ductwork and other items, so Jeff took out an equity line loan on his house for $75,000 and met with the existing investors who pitched in an additional $110,000. Neither Jeff nor the investors took any additional equity with this infusion. As Jeff ran the numbers with the new capital he realized the business needed to have sales of $2,000 every day of the week to achieve breakeven. When you have a

Sunday that brings in only $700, you have to make that up on other days. Jeff thought he could do it but realized it would be hard.

In the meantime, other negative things were happening in the business. Personnel turnover became a critical issue. A key success factor for a restaurant are its cooks. Jeff needed people who could efficiently make the ravioli the desired way. Unfortunately, two cooks left in March and the head chef and store manager left within the first three months. Jeff ended up working at the store 18 plus hours a day trying to ensure it succeeded. As the pressure on the business grew, it increasingly became a family affair as everyone pitched in to serve customers. Sales continued to grow but were not close to breakeven. At the big July 4th festival in Oak Brook, RavioliOli sold 4,000 plus toasted raviolis and then ran out (much to the dismay of the dozens still standing in line). There seemed to be great demand for the company offering.

After nearly driving himself into the ground, Jeff hired an experienced restaurant manager who quickly put procedures in place and relieved Jeff of having to do everything himself at the restaurant. Jeff and the new manager were able to drive costs down some, but the issue remained that they were not hitting $2,000 day ($60,000 month) in revenue. Jeff spent countless hours trying to renegotiate the lease to no avail. He cut back staff as far as he could and still reasonably serve customers.

Jeff met with everyone who would meet with him about the business to get advice on how to turn things around. He learned from experienced restaurateurs that he was right in line with his costs, procedures, and approaches. He was also told it would just take time to develop.

In December 2012, Jeff met with his investors again to secure more funds. The business was out of money and was still losing money each month. The investors had put in all the money they wanted to invest and recommended that Jeff close down the business. Unwilling to take this step just yet, Jeff dipped into his 401(k) retirement fund for $100,000 while not getting any additional share of the business for his new investment. With the ability to keep going with his own investment, Jeff obtained the blessing of his current investors to obtain a new major investor in the business even if their equity was diluted. He was meeting with several potential investors every month seeking fresh capital.

While sales continued at a very slow and yet steady rise, the business was out of money again by February 2013. Jeff met again with his investors. He shared with them that he had an investor who was ready to put in $150,000 and Jeff needed everyone to pitch in another $7,000 to $8,000 ($40,000 total), so the business could stay afloat until April when the new money would come in. All of the investors and Jeff pitched in the money. Unfortunately, however, by April the new investor's circumstances had changed and he decided not to invest in the business.

RavioliOli was simply out of money. The business was now approaching $50,000 in revenue a month. Jeff made the decision to pull the plug on his beloved restaurant 14 months after it had opened.

Jeff has some solid advice for new entrepreneurs:

1. Go with your gut. If it feels right, do your homework and go for it. There are no guarantees in any venture, or even more so, in any job. To the extent that you can, pinch pennies and keep fixed cost as low as possible.
2. Anticipate, Anticipate, Anticipate! Whatever the venture, do things right; you'll know when you break that rule. Start early in your life. . . part of my issue was that I was approaching 50 years old, and had three kids in college, one in high school, and tuition became a huge overhead in the grand scheme of things. I loved running the business, but I hated losing money. Having said that, a very good friend of mine who knows me quite well and saw me sweating out the losses reminded me that money is indeed a renewable commodity and somehow, someway, we always figure out a way to get it back.
3. Although I made many mistakes, I don't regret a single minute. We created memories of a lifetime through our ravioli-making parties, birthday events, family gatherings, catering jobs, special events, and captivating our younger patrons' bright-eyed amazement as we rolled out the ravs. We built something very cool, very different, very original, and something for which I am very proud.

THINKING CRITICALLY

Paul Inserra—American Meltdown

Paul Inserra always loved cooking and the opportunity it provided for experimentation. However, it took quite a while before he realized that this could be his career focus. Eventually Paul and his wife (Alycia) founded American Meltdown (http://www.americanmeltdown.org/) as a food truck.

Paul is a native of the Bronx in New York who went to Fordham University and graduated with a degree in English Literature. When he graduated he did not have any plans for a job, but one of his uncles owned a large marine construction company in Florida and offered him a job there. Paul had a variety of jobs while there including being a cook aboard a rescue tugboat that spent weeks at sea at a time. Paul moved back to New York a year later and spent the next few years as a bartender, a wine distribution salesperson, a freelance writer, and even a food stylist (one who crafts together the food for a photo shoot) for Conde Nast publications. Paul spent his free time and money travelling the world and trying out different foods.

Paul had wanted to live in the Caribbean, and his uncle, who had previously hired him in Miami, offered him another job, learning the marine construction business while living in St. Lucia. It was during this time in St. Lucia that Paul made the decision that what he really loved was food and that he wanted to focus his life there and not in marine-related businesses. After nine months in St. Lucia, Paul moved back to New York and enrolled in the French Culinary Institute (now called the International Culinary Center). During this time he was able to work for the upscale restaurant Quality Meats in midtown as it went through opening and initial operations. While living in New York, Paul realized that he would never be able to afford to open a restaurant there. His parents had moved to a suburb in the Raleigh-Durham, North Carolina, area a decade before, and Paul had been simply amazed at the growth in the area even through the big recession of 2008 to 2010. This led Paul and his then girlfriend (soon to be wife) to move to Raleigh-Durham, North Carolina, in January 2011 and began working on starting a food truck business. The couple had already landed on the idea of a food truck not only to minimize the expense but also for the flexibility it offered.

Paul and his wife investigated what food trucks in the area were serving. The timing was good for several reasons: (1) the recession drove a number of food trucks out of business, so the competition was much lower; (2) that also meant that there were quite a few used food trucks available for purchase; and (3) the regulations for food trucks in Durham were virtually non-existent. The couple wanted to purchase a used truck but ran into a wall with the banks as they tried to get a loan. Eventually they put together funding from themselves, family, and friends to buy and renovate the truck.

In line with lean start-up thinking, Paul and his wife started exploring what type of food truck they should open by hosting tasting parties to determine what would sell best. Given what businesses they did not find in the market, they tested out recipes for a hot dog truck, a Ramen noodle truck, and a grilled cheese truck. They landed on grilled cheese as the best approach based on the tastings they did with friends. Grilled cheese was always the most popular/well received. Using Paul's culinary background, they turned grilled cheese into a gourmet melt concept. It took about three months to get the truck ready, have all the recipes set, arrange the logistics, have the advertising material ready to go, and find some places to start setting up shop.

The couple would tweet out where the truck would be to all their friends and those who signed up to follow them, had the schedule on their website, but mostly worked hard to be visible. Paul worked out getting a spot in front of one of the most popular local breweries on the weekends. Durham is a hotbed for local breweries, and most have no food offering at their locations.

The business is an everyday, all day operation that starts early with preparations and ends late with pulling all the pork off the smoker where they had been all day. The couple's food truck offers many local favorites slathered with cheese (pulled pork, chicken, burgers, figs, bratwurst, and sausage) along with creative offerings that go far beyond an ordinary "melt" like the Matador (manchego cheese and romesco sauce—red peppers, garlic, and almonds—on sourdough bread). The creative nature of the couple's food led to American Meltdown being named one of the "8 Can't Miss Food Trucks in NC" and in 2017 being named by Southern Living as one of the South's Best Food Trucks. The effort to be creative has also paid off with their food being featured in the *New York Times*, *Cosmopolitan*, and *CBS Sunday* morning show along with many local and statewide magazines. In 2015, Paul competed on the popular Food Network Show *Cutthroat Kitchen*. American Meltdown has also been featured in one of the several episodes of *Street Food Diaries* (http://www.americanmeltdown.org/media-horizon/).

Their success (and the truck has been a financial success) led a number of mall operators to approach them about opening in their food courts. Paul and Alycia decided to take a stab at it in late 2015 and opened the first American Meltdown fixed location in the South Point Mall in Durham, North Carolina. Paul says that running a fixed location is a completely different business model and one that has taken some time to get used to doing. It needs to be staffed every hour that the food court is open, and he found that the taste buds of food court customers were different than the people frequenting their food truck. Today Paul runs the food truck on a daily basis, while Alycia runs the food court location.

Paul has some recommendations for anyone considering starting a food truck:

1. Food trucks are a cheaper way to figure out proof of concept. You can open a food truck for $100k or less, even today, while a restaurant will likely run you around $300k or up. It is also an excellent training ground to test your mettle and see if the work load and demands are actually what you want as an entrepreneur.
2. As in any retail business, square footage means a ceiling on how much you can earn. Do not plan on striking it rich in the food truck business or the hospitality industry. There is always the possibility of franchising your concept, but it is a long road to that goal and does not happen quickly, at least from what I have seen in my 20+ years in the industry.
3. Food trucking is as close as it gets to being a modern day pirate; you run a crew, and if you don't score good jobs with good tips, the crew leaves. On the flip side, the new model of food trucking is about moving from one place to another, seeking out the biggest crowds. It is not waiting in one location and hoping for someone to find you.
4. Whether you are a food trucker or a doctor, the ability to adapt on the fly and problem solve is a key to your success. On any given day, you are troubleshooting the gas (typically propane gas on trucks) and electric, mechanical, plumbing, inventory, and cooking systems, and you might not be able to afford to pay or wait around for a professional to fix your issues.

MiniCase 14

THINKING CRITICALLY

Carlo Capua—Z's Café

After graduating from college Carlo Capua went to Japan to teach English for four years and then to Mexico to teach English for another three years. After seven years abroad pursuing his dreams, he returned home where his 63-year-old mother told him she also had a dream. After 40 years of working as a dental hygienist, Carlo's mother wanted to pursue her passion for cooking. For Carlo it was an eye-opening moment when he realized that while his parents had spent their adult lives helping him realize his dreams, they had dreams that had been put on hold. Carlo's next step was to help his mother reach her dream.

He suggested to his mother that they try out working together on a small catering job for a niece who was having a 16th birthday. It was an amazing success, and they agreed to start a small home-based catering business. The business grew sofast that it could no longer be housed in their home. This led Carlo to contact a large number of organizations that he believed might have free kitchen time hoping to lease it during off-peak hours for his fledgling catering business. However, he found that no churches or schools had an interest in leasing their kitchens for several hours a day while they were not in use.

At the same time Carlo and his mom wanted to create a "give-back" component as part of their business model, so they began to research and visit nonprofits working in the community. In one visit to Samaritan House, a charity known for its work with the homeless (many of who have HIV/AIDS), he noticed they had a full kitchen. He started a discussion during that visit and arranged to use their kitchen for two hours a day for the cost of providing their volunteers some boxed lunches. At this stage the catering business was still just Carlo and his mother. As the firm started growing and needed to hire new people, it hired people from the shelter.

In 2009 café space in a public art museum came available. The rent was minimal, and it would allow them to both continue their catering and have a café, called Z's Café (www.zscafe.com); the name is from his grandparents. This also meant he was able to expand the employment of individuals from Samaritan House. These individuals often face challenges that can include being HIV positive, homeless, or having felony convictions on their records. For Carlo, these reentrants to the workforce became his target pool of employees. It was not Carlo's original goal to be a social enterprise, but like many things in life, it happened by chance.

In 2011 the city implemented paid parking at the art museum, which spelled impending doom for Z's Café. Carlo knew he had to move since the cost of parking was almost as much as a meal. It was at that stage that Carlo decided to go back to his original focus of just catering. The reality of the catering business was that it had become large enough that he could specialize. During a typical year he will do approximately 1,000 catering jobs that range from boxed lunches for a small group, to corporate events, and weddings for hundreds. There are three full-time employees and seven part-time staff at Z's Café. Over the years of operation, approximately 120 individuals from Samaritan House have worked for the firm. Today some of his managers who work full time started out, as every employee does, washing dishes.

The employees from Samaritan House are highly motivated, but just as in any restaurant, managing people is one of the most challenging aspects of the business. There are also challenges that a typical business would never address such as when a person has been in prison and they get their first paycheck, how do you help them learn to manage their money. The goal of the Z's Café is not only to be an employer but truly an entity that helps transform the workers lives. The fact that some workers have been there for seven years now not only means these individuals do the training of new workers but also that they understand the transition that occurs.

While Carlo has a social enterprise, he is also clear that it is a for-profit business. He took out a $20,000 loan to start the business, but today the firm is completely debt free. The catering business has approximately $1 million in revenue a year with 50 percent from boxed lunches, 25 percent from corporate functions, and 25 percent from weddings. The pricing of the firm's products is never the lowest but the focus is not to be the highest priced in the market either. Carlos believes that one of the keys to success for Z's Café is its relationships and a high-level of customer service. It is interesting to note that the customer for a wedding is not just the couple but can also be the venue since venue's often suggest to a couple the best companies for catering the complete wedding for them.

Carlo's insights for an entrepreneur include the following:

1. Obtain a mentor for the firm if you can. It took Carlo five years to reach breakeven since he did not have a background in restaurants. Thus, he had lots of trial and error that was expensive. To illustrate the learning, when he started he would typically obtain 20 percent of the bids he put in for catering work. Today it is 70 percent since he knows much better how to operate the business. A mentor to speed up some of this learning would have been helpful to him.
2. A firm does not have to be a charity to have a social impact. Every community has great needs and part of business should be to help solve those needs. But the entrepreneur should recognize that there are also benefits from helping those in the community including community support and free media as individuals and want to help such firms.
3. If you run a business that has a social purpose, the entrepreneur will not only make money but gains from the knowledge of those they work with. It is very easy to take life for granted until you see those whose needs are so great.
4. Finally, it is never too late to follow a dream. At 63 his mother followed hers, and the result was a business that is helping to change the lives of individuals.

Building a Business Plan

Developing a business plan is central to preparing to launch a new business. The key is not the document itself as much as forcing the entrepreneur to think through the multiple dimensions of the business to make sure they line up. Too often new ventures appear to be great ideas but fail because of details that the entrepreneurs did not realize they needed to address. The business plan helps the entrepreneur ensure as few unpleasant surprises occur as possible. It is the discipline and the thought process that occur in writing the business plan that makes the effort so valuable.

There are as many formats for a business plan as there are people to design one. Nevertheless, most business plans have some elements in common. The list below is a comprehensive list of potential elements in a business plan; we would not expect every plan to incorporate all of these elements. The entrepreneur must exercise considerable discretion to determine which elements are important to his or her particular business plan. For example, developing a new restaurant will drive the plan to deal extensively with operational issues since these will be particularly critical to its success. On the other hand, a new bookstore will push the business plan to focus more extensively on marketing as an especially critical factor of success. If the business is an Internet business, then the marketing—particularly how to get through the mass of clutter on the Internet and be one of the top firms that comes up when someone uses a search engine like Google—becomes critical.

We will briefly describe the major areas in a business plan and highlight particularly critical elements that entrepreneurs should include in their plans. Then we will present a plan that was developed by students while they were taking a course using the first edition of this text. It is not an example of a "perfect plan"; rather, it is an example of what might be reasonably accomplished.

Key Parts of the Business Plan

Executive Summary

- Brief Description of the Company
- Mission Statement/Value Proposition
- The Product and/or Services Being Offered
- Competitive Advantages
- Brief Financial Forecast
- Management Team
- Current Advisors
- Financing Requirements and Return Expected

You can conceive of this particularly critical section of the plan as the "hook" that encourages the reader to examine the entire plan. The executive summary is very useful in ensuring that you, the entrepreneur, remain focused in your analysis. If you cannot briefly explain your complete business concept in one to two pages, then you have not thoughtfully and thoroughly analyzed the potential business. You should be clear about how you will provide value to the customers, what the value proposition is for the business, what your competitive advantage is, and how your background has prepared you for this business.

History and Position of the Business to Date

- The Company's Mission
- Company History from Business Conception to This Point
- Management Team and Key Personnel
- Business Structure

This is the section of a business plan, which many entrepreneurs choose not to include. If you have created other businesses and your new business is somehow dependent on those businesses for success, then such information is important. However, for most entrepreneurial businesses, the issues highlighted here simply provide context to potential investors, clients, and/or suppliers.

Market Research

- Target Markets
- Geographic Area Within Which the Business Will Operate
- Competitive Environment and Opportunity Space
- Competitor Analysis
- Position of the Firm
- Market Description
- The Desired Customer
- Market Growth Opportunities

Market research codifies and describes the specific market space that you hope your new business will occupy. The preparation of this section helps assure that there is a group of customers available for your business and that the business will be in a position to acquire these customers.

Business Strategy

- Mission of the Small Business
- Strategy
- Value Proposition
- Evaluation of Competitive Advantage
- Length of Time Before Imitation
- Comparison to Substitutes

You need to specify how the firm will compete in its targeted market. The firm's strategy details not only how you expect it to compete, but it also begins the process of exploring the expected outcomes of that strategy and the potential dangers to the firm from its competitors. The issue of imitation is a continuing one for all organizations as they try to achieve and maintain what is unorthodox about their businesses.

Financial Analysis

- Cash Flow Projections and Analysis
- Ratio Analysis
- Break-Even Analysis
- Expected Gross and Operating Margins

Financial analysis is a major concern for all new businesses. This section in your plan will focus on a discussion of the various financial concerns related to the start-up and running of your business. Tables with your actual data should appear as support for this discussion at the end of your plan. A key part of financial analysis is the funds use. The topics covered here include:

- Funds Required and Timing
- Use of Funds
- Funding Sources
- Valuation
- Distribution of Control

Ultimately you will need money from others and/or will need to be clear about how you will spend the money if you are self-funding the business. Therefore, your business plan needs to specify those numbers. The greater the detail provided, the more help the plan will provide you in establishing benchmarks that can be evaluated to judge your new firm's progress.

Operations

- Location
- Accounting Systems
- Quality Control
- Build Out
- Hours of Operation
- Processes
- Equipment
- Staffing Schedule
- Critical Path Analysis to Start the Business

Operations include the details about how you will operate your business, and these details will differ widely depending on the type of business you are launching. If it is a manufacturing business, then the operations section will be central to your plan. For example, your equipment may be part of the competitive advantage of your manufacturing firm and as such you will want to spend considerable time on that aspect of the business. On the other hand, if your new business is a restaurant, then the equipment is typically generic and not a major factor in the firm's success, so your business plan will minimize its discussion. The location of your restaurant would be an important element of its success, however, so you should elaborate on that aspect of your business.

A particularly important part of the business plan is the marketing. Sometimes it will be a separate section. It addresses issues that include the following:

- Target Customer
- Sales Forecast
- Pricing
- Methods of Promotion
- Promotion Scheduling and Placement

The marketing plan specifies how your firm will reach the target customer. Particularly critical here is the specification of the customers and the details of how you actually will price and promote the product to those customers. One of the most difficult areas for any new business is how to actually reach the customers in a way that they will want to buy your product or service. Getting customers to change to your firm from another is very hard to accomplish.

Risk Analysis

- Discussion of Systems Risks and Controls
- Discussion of Business Risks and Controls

There are risks in every business. You do not need to spend extensive effort detailing the risks, although you want to acknowledge them. For example, we mentioned that young people starting a business may not have extensive prior experience in business. In this section you may wish to acknowledge those risks and illustrate what actions you are taking to ensure the success of the business. For example, if you have obtained a board of advisors consisting of successful business people who will work with you to reduce your risk, then this is an important point to illustrate.

Summary

The next section contains a sample business plan. As you read the plan, remember that we have noted both positives and negatives. As with all plans there are items that need additional research as well as items that are simply not researchable. Entrepreneurs need to gather as much information as they can and present that information as clearly and as concisely as possible. Although there is always other information that they would like to include, ultimately all potential entrepreneurs must make decisions with less than complete information.

Note that many of the sections of this plan do not match the exact order of our key areas list at the start of this appendix. A business plan is not a formula within which the entrepreneur can plug various pieces of information. Instead it is a document that should be read easily and be very understandable. The information should appear where it ultimately makes the most sense as well as where it best supports the entrepreneur's arguments about the new business.

Fraudian Slip

Confidential Business Plan

DRAFT
This is NOT an offering

Table of Contents

AUTHOR NOTE
The Fraudian Slip was a plan created in Dr. Chuck Bamford's Executive MBA elective class in Entrepreneurship at the University of Notre Dame. This course is time-compressed, so it is not possible for the students to continue to refine the plan. Although generally well developed, the plan has flaws (as all do) and is not intended as a perfect example. Instead it is an effective vehicle for discussing the issues developed in this text and demonstrating their application. The format, detail, and approach are expressed quite well. The authors wish to thank the students responsible for this plan: Anthony Baerlocher, Cathy Bush, Mike Frey, Chris Kuhlmann, Nate Lazenga, Natalie Reynolds, Jason Speckman, and Nick Talarico.

Executive Summary

The Fraudian Slip is a dime-sized GPS tracking device intelligently mounted in high-value packages prior to shipping. The disposable device enables continuous, real-time tracking of high-value items, which reduces the number of claims insurance companies must pay out for lost packages or fraudulent claims.

It is estimated that insurance companies pay out over $12 billion annually for fraudulent loss claims (Source: FM Global website). Items sent via shipping companies and couriers can be tracked at various points in time, but the rudimentary scanning and RF trackers most prevalently used can be easily circumvented and fraud is common. Fraudian Slip's device and service provides constant monitoring of packages by providing the location of the package, and it also monitors temperature, humidity, and notifies when a package is opened.

The Fraudian Slip's initial target market is companies that sell shipping insurance (third-party shipping insurers, postal companies, and courier companies). This industry is estimated to be a $4.29 billion industry (Source: IBISWorld 2014).

Ideal customers are insurance companies insuring the shipment of high-value items to reduce claims. Examples include high-value art collections being transferred from a private collection or museum to another museum for an exhibition and expensive prototypes of new products.

Fraudian Slip will train insurance companies to require this value-added service for all customers who ship insurable items that meet a certain value threshold. By requiring the insured party to pay for Fraudian Slip, the insurance company will be able to maintain continuous monitoring of the shipped item(s) at no additional cost. Insurance companies will also be trained to offer the Fraudian Slip as an option for individuals or companies who are shipping

AUTHOR NOTE

Before completing the Executive Summary we would recommend that the plan lists out very specifically who is contributing money, how much they are investing, and what percentage of the company they will receive for this investment. These details are important to potential investors.

Investors are interested in the projected returns of their investment.

Below you will see that the Pro Forma Cash Flows have been presented immediately after the Executive Summary. Without the context of the plan, these are difficult to evaluate at this point. We would recommend that the Pro Forma Cash Flows be placed at the end of the plan.

The business plan is trying to hook an individual's interest. If the investor is interested he or she will go to the appendix.

items that do not have a high enough value to warrant the insurance company to require the Slip. For example, if a company is shipping an artifact from the company's founder that holds little cash value, but much sentimental value, the company could elect to purchase the Slip to maintain a constant awareness of the location and status of the item during the shipping process.

Competitors include the following: (1) Companies that target businesses (Agheera, Spark Nano, Global Tracking Group, Self-Insuring Shipping Cos.) and (2) wholly owned subsidiaries (FedEx's SenseAware).

Insurance companies spend huge amounts of time and money processing and paying claims for items lost or damaged during shipping. Currently there are companies that will customize shipment tracking and monitoring systems for special shipments. However, no company exists that focuses exclusively on catering to the needs of insurance companies. The Fraudian Slip will tailor the delivery of the product and service to the unique demands of insurance companies, offering them a way to reduce fraud payouts and increase customer confidence in the safe passage of their items and the certainty of knowing that their claim will be less likely to be delayed for fraud evaluation.

Current package tracking software focuses on identifying where a package is in the shipping process at given points in time with an aim for providing peace of mind to senders. The Fraudian Slip puts technology in the hands of insurance companies allowing them to continuously monitor an item throughout the shipping process. Insurers can identify where a package has been and what it's been through allowing them to better identify fraud and reduce the cost of reviewing and paying claims.

The Fraudian Slip requests an initial investment of $880,000, which is expected to be adequate to complete the testing phases and initial sales efforts and to fund the company until sales are adequate to produce regular profits, which we anticipate to be 18 months. In exchange for an initial investment of $880,000, Fraudian Slip is offering a 35% equity position with a first right to buy back the equity position.

Cash Flow

THE FRAUDIAN SLIP, LLC CASH FLOW FY2016

	February	March	April	May	June	July	August	September	October	November	December	January
Receipts												
Subscriptions	$ 0.00	$ 0.00	$ 0.00	$ 0.00	$ 0.00	$ 0.00	$ 0.00	$ 0.00	$ 20,000.00	$ 25,000.00	$ 40,000.00	$40,000.00
Policy Receipts	0.00	0.00	0.00	0.00	0.00	0.00	0.00	0.00	0.00	5,000.00	12,000.00	20,000.00
Other	0.00	0.00	0.00	0.00	0.00	0.00	0.00	0.00	0.00	0.00	0.00	0.00
Total	$ 0.00	$ 0.00	$ 0.00	$ 0.00	$ 0.00	$ 0.00	$ 0.00	$ 0.00	$ 20,000.00	$ 30,000.00	$ 52,000.00	$60,000.00
Disbursements												
Maint./Repair	$ 0.00	$ 0.00	$ 0.00	$ 0.00	$ 0.00	$ 0.00	$ 200.00	$ 200.00	$ 200.00	$ 400.00	$ 400.00	$ 400.00
Acquisition	0.00	0.00	0.00	5,000.00	0.00	0.00	0.00	0.00	2,500.00	6,000.00	10,000.00	12,000.00
Lease/Mort.	2,850.00	2,850.00	2,850.00	2,850.00	2,850.00	2,850.00	2,850.00	2,850.00	2,850.00	2,850.00	2,850.00	2,850.00
Utilities	250.00	250.00	250.00	250.00	250.00	250.00	250.00	250.00	250.00	250.00	250.00	250.00
Salaries	23,000.00	23,000.00	23,000.00	35,000.00	35,000.00	35,000.00	35,000.00	35,000.00	35,000.00	35,000.00	35,000.00	35,000.00
Hourly Labor	0.00	0.00	0.00	0.00	0.00	0.00	0.00	3,333.33	5,000.00	8,333.33	8,333.33	10,000.00
Payroll Tax	1,840.00	1,840.00	1,840.00	2,800.00	2,800.00	2,800.00	2,800.00	3,066.67	3,200.00	3,466.67	3,466.67	3,600.00
Sales Tax	0.00	0.00	0.00	0.00	0.00	0.00	0.00	0.00	1,40.00	2,10.00	3,640.00	4,20.00
Insurance	5,500.00	0.00	0.00	0.00	0.00	0.00	0.00	0.00	0.00	0.00	0.00	0.00
General Cleaning	100.00	100.00	100.00	100.00	100.00	100.00	100.00	100.00	100.00	100.00	100.00	100.00
Advertising	0.00	0.00	0.00	0.00	0.00	0.00	0.00	5,000.00	2,000.00	2,000.00	2,000.00	2,000.00
Employee Benefits	7,590.00	7,590.00	7,590.00	11,550.00	11,550.00	11,550.00	11,550.00	11,550.00	11,550.00	11,550.00	11,550.00	11,550.00
Fees/Permits	50.00	0.00	0.00	0.00	0.00	0.00	0.00	0.00	0.00	0.00	0.00	0.00
Credit Card Charges	0.00	0.00	0.00	0.00	0.00	0.00	0.00	0.00	0.00	400.00	960.00	1,600.00
Office Supplies	100.00	100.00	100.00	100.00	100.00	100.00	100.00	100.00	250.00	250.00	250.00	250.00
Accounting/Legal	5,000.00	0.00	0.00	0.00	0.00	0.00	0.00	0.00	0.00	0.00	500.00	0.00
Furniture	3,000.00	0.00	0.00	2,000.00	0.00	0.00	0.00	0.00	0.00	0.00	0.00	0.00
Computers/software	2,500.00	0.00	0.00	2,000.00	0.00	0.00	0.00	0.00	0.00	0.00	0.00	1,200.00
Travel	0.00	4,000.00	2,000.00	0.00	0.00	0.00	2,500.00	2,500.00	4,000.00	4,000.00	4,000.00	4,000.00
Communication	1,500.00	1,250.00	1,250.00	1,250.00	1,250.00	1,250.00	1,250.00	1,250.00	1,250.00	1,250.00	1,250.00	1,250.00
Total	$ 53,280.00	$ 40,980.00	$ 38,980.00	$ 62,900.00	$ 53,900.00	$ 53,900.00	$ 56,600.00	$ 65,200.00	$ 69,550.00	$ 77,950.00	$ 84,550.00	$ 90,250.00
Net Cash Flow	($ 53,280.00)	($ 40,980.00)	($ 38,980.00)	($ 62,900.00)	($ 53,900.00)	($ 53,900.00)	($ 56,600.00)	($ 65,200.00)	($ 49,550.00)	($ 47,950.00)	($ 32,550.00)	($ 30,250.00)
Cash on Hand												
Opening Balance	$ 0.00	$826,720.00	$785,740.00	$ 746,760.00	$683,860.00	$629,960.00	$576,060.00	$ 519,460.00	$454,260.00	$404,710.00	$356,760.00	$ 324,210.00
Investment	880,000.00	0.00	0.00	0.00	0.00	0.00	0.00	0.00	0.00	0.00	0.00	0.00
Receipts	0.00	0.00	0.00	0.00	0.00	0.00	0.00	0.00	20,000.00	30,000.00	52,000.00	60,000.00
Disbursement	53,280.00	40,980.00	38,980.00	62,900.00	53,900.00	53,900.00	56,600.00	65,200.00	69,550.00	77,950.00	84,550.00	90,250.00
Balance	$826,720.00	$785,740.00	$746,760.00	$683,860.00	$629,960.00	$576,060.00	$ 519,460.00	$454,260.00	$ 404,710.00	$356,760.00	$ 324,210.00	$293,960.00

THE FRAUDIAN SLIP, LLC CASH FLOW YEARS 2–5

	Year 2 Q1	Year 2 Q2	Year 2 Q3	Year 2 Q4	Year 3 Q1	Year 3 Q2	Year 3 Q3	Year 3 Q4	Year 4	Year 5
Receipts										
Subscriptions	$ 150,000.00	$ 150,000.00	$ 180,000.00	$ 200,000.00	$ 200,000.00	$ 210,000.00	$ 220,000.00	$ 230,000.00	$ 940,000.00	$ 960,000.00
Policy Receipts	80,000.00	120,000.00	160,000.00	200,000.00	240,000.00	265,000.00	290,000.00	315,000.00	1,340,000.00	1,420,000.00
Other	80,000.00	85,000.00	90,000.00	100,000.00	110,000.00	115,000.00	120,000.00	125,000.00	505,000.00	510,000.00
Total	**$310,000.00**	**$355,000.00**	**$430,000.00**	**$500,000.00**	**$550,000.00**	**$590,000.00**	**$630,000.00**	**$670,000.00**	**$2,785,000.00**	**$2,890,000.00**
Disbursements										
Maint./Repair	$ 1,200.00	$ 1,500.00	$ 1,800.00	$ 2,000.00	$ 2,100.00	$ 2,200.00	$ 2,200.00	$ 2,200.00	$ 8,800.00	$ 8,800.00
Acquisition	36,000.00	30,000.00	30,000.00	30,000.00	30,000.00	30,000.00	30,000.00	30,000.00	120,000.00	120,000.00
Lease/Mort.	8,550.00	8,550.00	8,550.00	8,550.00	8,550.00	8,550.00	8,550.00	8,550.00	34,200.00	34,200.00
Utilities	750.00	750.00	750.00	750.00	750.00	750.00	750.00	750.00	3,000.00	3,000.00
Salaries	105,000.00	150,000.00	150,000.00	150,000.00	200,000.00	200,000.00	200,000.00	200,000.00	800,000.00	800,000.00
Hourly Labor	30,000.00	30,000.00	30,000.00	30,000.00	60,000.00	60,000.00	60,000.00	60,000.00	240,000.00	240,000.00
Payroll Tax	10,800.00	14,400.00	14,400.00	14,400.00	20,800.00	20,800.00	20,800.00	20,800.00	83,200.00	83,200.00
Sales Tax	21,700.00	24,850.00	30,100.00	35,000.00	38,500.00	41,300.00	44,100.00	46,900.00	194,950.00	202,300.00
Insurance	5,500.00	0.00	0.00	0.00	5,500.00	0.00	0.00	0.00	5,500.00	5,500.00
General Cleaning	300.00	300.00	300.00	300.00	300.00	300.00	300.00	300.00	1,200.00	1,200.00
Advertising	6,000.00	6,000.00	6,000.00	6,000.00	4,000.00	4,000.00	4,000.00	4,000.00	16,000.00	16,000.00
Employee Benefits	34,650.00	49,500.00	49,500.00	49,500.00	66,000.00	66,000.00	66,000.00	66,000.00	264,000.00	264,000.00
Fees/Permits	0.00	0.00	0.00	0.00	0.00	0.00	0.00	0.00	0.00	0.00
Credit Card Charges	4,800.00	4,320.00	3,600.00	3,600.00	3,600.00	3,600.00	3,600.00	3,600.00	14,400.00	14,400.00
Office Supplies	750.00	750.00	750.00	750.00	1,000.00	1,000.00	1,000.00	1,000.00	4,000.00	4,000.00
Accounting/Legal	10,000.00	0.00	0.00	0.00	20,000.00	0.00	0.00	0.00	20,000.00	20,000.00
Furniture	3,000.00	0.00	0.00	0.00	3,000.00	0.00	0.00	0.00	3,000.00	3,000.00
Computers/software	3,600.00	2,000.00	0.00	0.00	10,000.00	0.00	0.00	0.00	15,000.00	15,000.00
Travel	12,000.00	12,000.00	12,000.00	12,000.00	20,000.00	20,000.00	20,000.00	20,000.00	80,000.00	80,000.00
Communication	3,750.00	3,000.00	3,000.00	3,000.00	3,000.00	3,000.00	3,000.00	3,000.00	12,000.00	12,000.00
Total	**$298,350.00**	**$ 337,920.00**	**$340,750.00**	**$ 345,850.00**	**$ 497,100.00**	**$ 461,500.00**	**$464,300.00**	**$ 467,100.00**	**$ 1,919,250.00**	**$ 1,926,600.00**
Net Cash Flow	11,650.00	17,080.00	89,250.00	154,150.00	52,900.00	128,500.00	165,700.00	202,900.00	865,750.00	963,400.00
Cash on Hand										
Opening Balance	$ 293,960.00	$ 305,610.00	$ 322,690.00	$ 411,940.00	$ 566,090.00	$ 618,990.00	$ 747,490.00	$ 913,190.00	$ 1,116,090.00	$ 1,981,840.00
Investment	0.00	0.00	0.00	0.00	0.00	0.00	0.00	0.00	0.00	0.00
Receipts	310,000.00	335,000.00	430,000.00	500,000.00	550,000.00	590,000.00	630,000.00	670,000.00	2,785,000.00	2,890,000.00
Disbursement	298,350.00	337,920.00	340,750.00	345,850.00	497,100.00	461,500.00	464,300.00	467,100.00	1,919,250.00	1,926,600.00
Balance	$ 305,610.00	$ 322,690.00	$ 411,940.00	$ 566,090.00	$ 618,990.00	$ 747,490.00	$ 913,190.00	$ 1,116,090.00	$ 1,981,840.00	$ 2,945,240.00

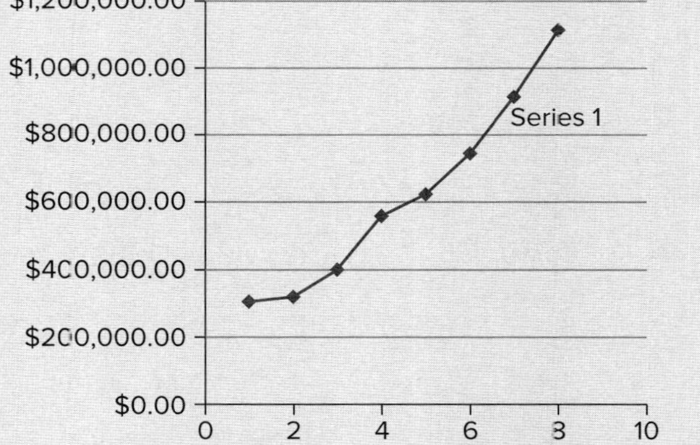

Team

Anthony Baerlocher, MBA
Executive Director of Advanced Game Design, WMS Gaming

Expertise: Intellectual property development and strategy, game design and development, product creation, legal consulting for the gaming industry, math modeling, and development team leader. Entrepreneur.

Cathy Bush, MBA
Bush & Co. Advertising

Expertise: Strategic planning and implementation, marketing, advertising, and public relations. Building teams that increase market share, brand recognition, profitability, and quality performance. Entrepreneur: service firm and manufacturing company.

Mike Frey, MBA
Director of Sales and Marketing, Harlo Corporation

Expertise: Building and leading sales and marketing teams focused to increase market share, brand recognition, profitability, and quality performance. Strategic planning and implementation, product/service development and planning. Entrepreneur: small-business owner.

Chris Kuhlmann, CHFP, MBA
COO and CFO of Lakeland Community Hospital Watervliet

Expertise: Strategic planning, financial operations, and enterprise turnarounds. Revenue cycle streamlining, labor productivity and process improvement, and national wholesale distribution of tools and equipment.

Nate Lazenga, MBA
Design Engineer at Manufacturing Technology, Inc.

Expertise: Design engineer responsible for creating technical execution plans, concepting, designing, detailing, and troubleshooting equipment and tooling. Entrepreneur: founder of a sports organization.

Natalie Reynolds, MBA
Assistant VP, Certus Bank

Expertise: Client operations and management, employee management and motivation, analyzing and achieving operational efficiencies, coordinating multiple departments internally and externally.

Jason Speckman, MBA
Senior VP – Industrial Advisory Services, Cushman & Wakefield

Expertise: Industrial leasing representation and acquisition/disposition services. Underwriting investment real estate, creating and executing extensive marketing campaigns, managing long-term capital transactions.

Nick Talarico, CPA, CIA, MBA
Manager of Internal Audit, Do It Best Corp.

Expertise: Internal auditor with fraud investigation background has audited industries including manufacturing, construction cooperatives, and retail. Creates audit methodology to ensure risks are analyzed during the audit plan process. Audits performed: financial, operational, safety and compliance.

AUTHOR NOTE

Including bios is a crucial part of a business plan. Investors invest in the people who are going to run the business. However, note that the desire for bios can vary widely among investors. Some investors are looking for full-page bios about each founder. Other investors are only interested in the bios if they directly relate to the proposed business. Still other investors want something short about each founder. The plan should be tailored to the specific desires of the investor. In part this is why many business plans put them at the end of the plan.

AUTHOR NOTE
Deciding who the real customer is for a business is crucial. While some believe that the customer is the one who actually pays the business, others believe it is the consumer who must choose the final product/service. There is probably no right answer here; however, the choice made will dramatically affect the organization, operation, and success of the new venture.

Strategy

The real value of the Fraudian Slip is to the insurance company in being able to reduce paid claims for lost, damaged, or stolen shipments that are insured by customers. While it might make sense to employ awareness campaigns to customers, ultimately the path will be a push strategy.

AUTHOR NOTE
The labeling of this device as a GPS device seems simplistic and probably not what the authors intended here. It appears from the description that it is a whole set of capabilities and would suggest that those be listed out very carefully early in the plan.

Fraudian Slip will "push" the value proposition to the insurance companies by offering the GPS device as a means to real-time tracking of insured shipments. This device will be free of charge to the insurance company, as it becomes a pass-through expense to the end customer. In essence, the insurance companies will have to sell this to their customers as a value-enhanced feature. Fraudian Slip will assist its customers in selling this service through three very important steps.

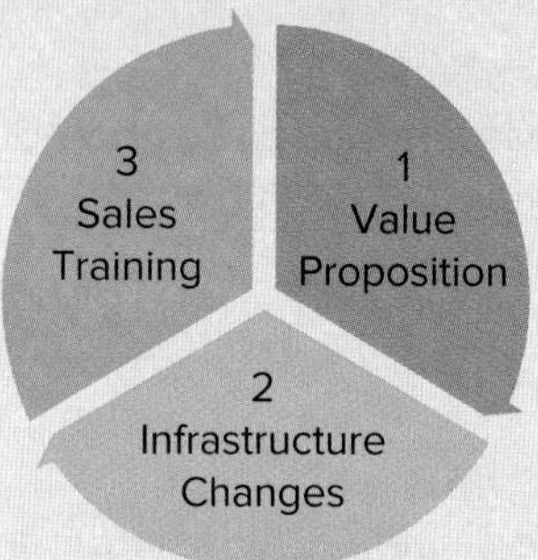

AUTHOR NOTE
Repetition is one of the traditional problems in most plans. The Value Proposition has already been clearly and effectively articulated. There is no value in repeating information in a plan. This would have been cleaned up in the revision process if there had been time to do so. We left this in here as an example of what happens so easily in the development of a plan. Focus on being concise.

2. **Value Proposition** – Fraudian Slip has to do an effective job selling the value proposition to insurance companies. None of the components of the marketing strategy matter if insurance companies are not convinced there are real and tangible savings from lost, damaged, or stolen shipments. Part of this value proposition is to create a marketing strategy so that the insurance company can increase its business with this unique offering.

2. **Infrastructure Changes** – Fraudian Slip will assist the insurance companies in modifying all of their forms, applications, website inquiries, and so on, so that the device/service is an available option to all customers who are insuring their shipments.

3. **Sales Training** – Lastly, Fraudian Slip will train the insurance company personnel on how to effectively promote and sell this option to its customers. This will include information on the device, how it works, and the advantages of real-time tracking. It has been proven that salespeople will more often sell what they know rather than what gives them the biggest commission. Fraudian Slip's job is to make sure they are intimately familiar with all aspects of this service.

Competition

There are several companies who are attempting to provide real-time GPS tracking, but none that focus primarily on the insurance companies who insure worldwide package delivery. In fact, GPS shipment tracking products/systems seem to fall into one of two customer segments: (1) Retail: Products such as the Spark Nano are sold on eBay.com, Amazon.com, and other retail sites meant for use by the end user and (2) Wholesale/Industry: A common target is either shipping companies that move products globally or companies that have large fleets where logistics are essential for efficient deployment of trucks. Below are some examples.

	FRAUDIAN	AGHEERA	SPARK NANO	GLOBAL TRACKING GROUP	SUBSIDIARY CORPS. I.E. FEDEX "SENSEAWARE"
True Real-Time GPS Tracking	√	√	√	√	×
Monitors Speed	√	×	×	√	√
Monitors Temperature	√	×	×	×	√
Monitors Humidity	√	×	×	×	√
Notifies Upon Opening	√	×	×	×	×
Primary Customer	Insurance Cos	Shipping Cos	Retail/Industry	Retail/Industry	Shipping Cos
Retail Availability	√	√	√	√	×
Fee Structure	Per Use	Per Use	Per Unit	Per Unit/Rental	Per Use

Business Model Design

Currently the shipping industry experiences exposure to risk when a parcel owner ships high-value items. Figure 1 shows the current setup of the shipping industry. If the package does not reach the intended user either because the product is lost or because the package is fraudulently rerouted, the insurance company must pay out claims. Paying out claims is a real concern for any insurance company. If the insurance company can track packages and review the route of the package from start to finish, it can reduce the number of claims it must pay by finding lost packages and more successfully identifying instances of fraud.

Figure 1

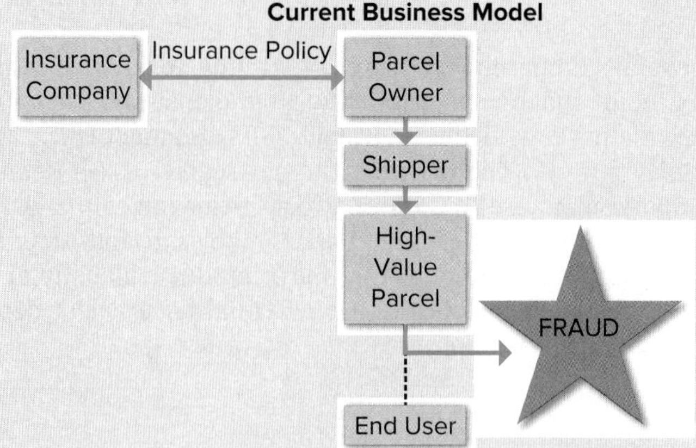

AUTHOR NOTE
An effective diagram like this one makes the whole process visual and takes the place of hundreds of words. We recommend the use of pictures, diagrams, and charts as much as possible.

AUTHOR NOTE
Here is a prime example of where a picture or drawing is absolutely needed. The reader has no ability to visualize the actual look of the product. As the plan is discussing the product, a whole group of questions now become relevant:

1. How does this one small device do all these amazing things?
2. How will this small, inexpensive device have sufficient battery power?
3. It appears that the device must transmit. How will it accomplish this in a steel container aboard a ship?

Putting yourself in the chair of the reader allows you to effectively address questions as they would logically arise in the reading of the plan.

There may be very effective answers to these questions.

The Fraudian Slip is a total solution that helps insurance companies reduce their exposure to claims by reducing their risk through tracking via the Fraudian Slip device. This device is an extremely small and portable electronic transmitter for real-time tracking of insurable items that easily slips into parcels. Fraudian Slip manages the entire process for the insurance companies. When a policy is sold, Fraudian Slip is notified, which sends a device to the shipper, monitors its progress, and reports back to the insurance underwriter when the package is delivered or tampered with. Figure 2 shows the new business model after the Fraudian Slip enters the marketplace.

Figure 2

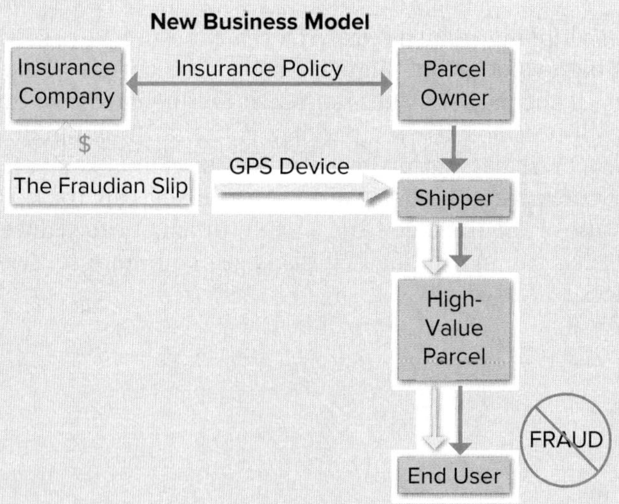

New Business Model

Insurance Company
Insurance Policy
Parcel Owner
$
The Fraudian Slip
GPS Device
Shipper
High-Value Parcel
FRAUD
End User

Revenue Generation

The Fraudian Slip's value to insurance companies allows four different forms of revenue generation.

1. Every parcel that is considered "high replacement value" must have the device in order to be shipped. Every one of these shipments will yield $100 per policy to the company. High replacement value is anything over $20,000.
2. Parcels that are considered with high sentimental value, regardless of replacement value, may have the device included in their shipping. These will also yield $100 per policy.
3. In addition to the policy, the company will charge a 1% premium based on the value of the product being shipped.
4. Client account subscription fees will generate $5,000 per year.

AUTHOR NOTE
This picks up on one of the most important elements of a plan. That is the BUSINESS MODEL. There are millions of great ideas out there; it is those that can be turned into a profitable model that will be funded and developed. Here the authors need to develop how the full business model will work.

Example:
$20,000 Rolex shipped within the United States.
Common insurance premium for jewelry: $3.00 per $100* in value + $100 Fraudian Slip coverage
$20,000/100 = $200
$200* 3 = $600
$600 + $100 = $700
Fraudian Slip Premium:
$20,000 *.01 = $200
Total premium insure charges $900
*(P.A.F. Insurance posted rates)

AUTHOR NOTE
This is an excellent section that is too wordy. This needs to be turned into a graph/chart/picture that achieves the same result.

Marketing

Sales Cycle/Customer Acquisition: Cargo-related crime is estimated to cost the United States economy more than $12 billion annually in merchandise losses (Source: FM Global website).

The target market is the 15 largest underwriters of freight insurance. These underwriters provide insurance to FedEx, UPS, as well as International Intermodal cargo carriers. This is a relatively concentrated industry, which means very few companies share a very large risk.

A partial list of target customers includes the following:

- Parcel Insurance Plan: UPS and FedEx
- Catlin Group: Capacity is up to US $30 million on any one shipment
- FM Global
- P.A.F. Insurance

Our sales force will research and target certain people within the insurance providers, including but not limited to, policy makers, risk analysts, and risk mitigation officers. Decision makers, once identified, will be contacted. Our service will be compelling, and we will acquire customers because:

- Fraudian Slip will reduce the dollar amount underwriters will pay out, thus increasing their profitability and lowering their risk exposure.

- Tiered packages will offer varying levels of service, and offerings can be tailored to the needs of the individual customer.

A graphic representation of this process is below:

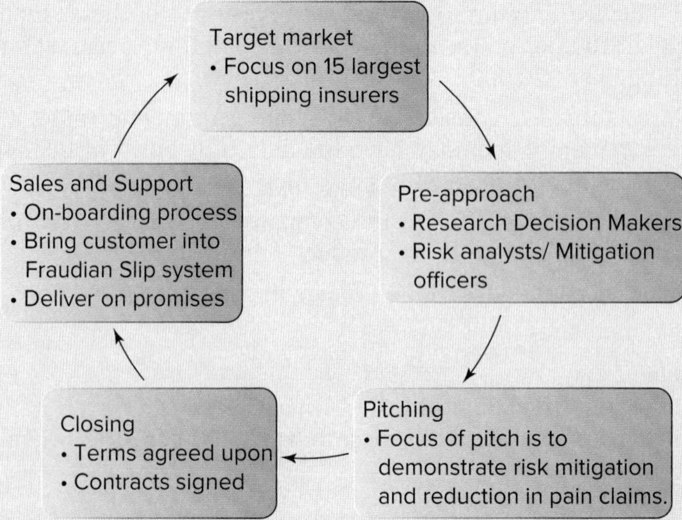

Milestones

Fraudian Slip, currently in the pre-seed stage, is looking to partner with a venture capital firm to launch the start-up phase of the risk reduction technology company.

The funding will allow us to:

- Develop a viable technology device.
- Build the products and online service for initial beta testing with customers.
- Develop a marketing and sales plan for the launch.

Initial development will take nine months, followed by product testing with customers for approximately five months, then a full launch. This short time is due to sourcing the devices and not fully developing them. Many of the foundations for this technology, such as multisensor and real-time GPS devices, are already available and are used in global supply chains. We will license the current technology and incorporate it into our design while developing the online application. The online application will allow users to view real-time data such as location, temperature, and light exposure to determine if a package has been opened while in transit. The following is a high-level schedule of some significant milestones for this initiative:

AUTHOR NOTE

There is a rule of thumb we have already discussed in the text. That is, all plans take twice as long as you expect and cost twice as much. The authors need to detail out the steps with a timeline and cost column for each of the bigger elements they list below in their Milestone chart.

MILESTONE	MILESTONE GOAL
Complete Design Specifications—Tracking Device	The architectural design satisfies all product requirements, is FAA, DOT, UL, and FCC approved, and is suitable for input into the detailed design process.
Complete Prototype	Design implemented, approved, and is suitable for device development.

(continued)

MILESTONE	MILESTONE GOAL
Complete Online Application	Design implemented, approved, and is suitable for input into the development of code.
Sales and Marketing to Acquire Customers	Approved sales and marketing plan implemented.
Testable Version of Device and Online Application—Beta	Preidentified initial customers will conduct beta testing.
Ship Final Version to Customers	With testing completed, final version ready for shipping to customers.

Upon investment of capital for Fraudian Slip, a detailed schedule will be created by the assigned project team to include all tasks and deliverables.

Exit Strategy

Exit Timing

- Anticipate an exit in approximately five years of receiving funding. However, the optimal time to harvest will be assessed on an ongoing basis by monitoring current EBITDA and the median EV/EBITDA multiple within the Commercial and Professional Services industry.

Mode of Exit

- Mode of exit will likely be a disposition to an established investment firm or a firm that is attracted to the relationship with shipping and/or the insurance industries—two industries that will never disappear.
- No intention to merge with another company based on existing goals of ownership individuals. However, ownership will consider a merger if it is determined to be in the best interest of the shareholders.
- Do not anticipate that an IPO will be the optimal exit strategy because of the requirement to disclose certain information that competitors can access and to avoid difficulties with vendors.

Estimated Reversionary Value Range

- Anticipated median EV/EBITDA multiple range for Commercial and Professional Services industry in year 5 is 9.0–10.0 times EBITDA.
- Projected EBITDA in year 5 is $963,400.

AUTHOR NOTE

This is a crucial section for an investor. This needs to be fully developed.

1. Who might be interested in acquiring this company?
2. What is the company worth? Need to do a valuation analysis.
3. Need to reference the Pro Forma Cash Flow chart (another reason to put it at the end) and explain how these numbers work.
4. Where did the EBITA number come from for the industry? How did the authors calculate it for the Fraudian Slip?

Harvest is a tough issue. Some investors don't like to see anything about harvesting because they want the founders committed to success. Most investors want to look at this potential in great detail before they consider investing and would require far greater financial information.

This plan is a great foundation for that effort and could easily be extended.

A

activity ratios Ratios that measure the efficiency with which you are handling the resources of the business.

ADA Americans with Disabilities Act.

agency theory A managerial theory that argues that individuals act to maximize their own benefit. Thus, in settings where there is a split between ownership and control (most publicly traded corporations), the agents (managers) must be monitored, or they will act to maximize their own benefit, not necessarily that of those who own the firm (the shareholders).

anchor stores Major retail stores, such as department stores in a mall. They serve as the anchor for the retail establishment.

asset-based lending A loan provided for the purchase of a necessary asset for the business.

asset lease A form of lease tied to a particular asset used by a business to conserve cash and maintain the latest versions of whatever equipment is available.

asset valuation A method of business valuation that simply totals all of the hard assets of the organization and adds in a goodwill value.

B

balance sheet Summary of the assets and liabilities of the small business.

benchmarking Working with and learning from a company outside of your industry that has a particular skill that is potentially critical to your operation.

board of advisors Individuals outside the small business that advise the firm; formed at the discretion of the founders (regardless of the legal form chosen).

bonus A reward offered to the employees based on their performance; similar to profit sharing. Typically, bonus systems are not as well defined as profit sharing; instead, the level of reward is left more to the discretion of the small business owner.

bootstrap marketing Marketing efforts that require little capital.

bounded rationality Rational decision making that is constrained by the background and history of the person making the decision.

brainstorming A creative process whereby a group of individuals are brought together and asked to generate ideas with little or no effort made to evaluate the potential for each idea.

break-even analysis Tool for the analysis of when the firm will reach breakeven.

break-even point The level where revenue coming into the firm is sufficient to cover expenses. When starting a business, it will take time for the business to reach this level.

budget Projection of all the costs that will be incurred by the organization over, say, the next year, and allocation of that expense evenly over the relevant time period.

business angels High-net-worth individuals that invest in businesses; a business angel does so not as a business but as an individual.

business brokers Businesses that specialize in selling businesses.

C

capabilities Resources that combine to allow the firm to perform functions.

capitalization of earnings valuation A method of valuation achieved by taking the earnings (net profit) of the organization, subtracting out or adding back to it any unusual items that the lender or investor feels are not customary, normal, or usual items, and dividing that figure by a capitalization rate.

cash flow Total dollar inflow minus total dollar outflow of the business.

commission Some percentage of sales, paid by the small business owner and typically associated with the compensation of sales representatives.

competitive advantage Those things that your business does better than anyone else in your industry.

competitive map An analytical tool used to organize information about direct competitors on all points of competition.

contract An agreement between two parties to perform certain activities for some consideration.

contract sales force Independent salespeople with a wide variety of experiences and contacts, provided by companies on a contract basis.

copyright Ownership of creative materials the copyright holder has generated, such as books, magazines, advertising copy, music, artwork, or virtually any other creative product, whether published or unpublished.

cost-plus pricing The price of a product or service, obtained by the small-business person's initial determination of the cost structure, followed by the owner's determination of the desired profit margin, and finally, the addition of that profit to the cost.

credit card Card entitling the owner to use of revolving credit that is not tied to any particular asset, does not have a set repayment schedule, and is usually tied to a much higher relative interest rate.

critical path chart Chart that demonstrates how the activities necessary to start the firm fit together and build on each other. This chart allows you to understand which activities can occur concurrently and which must already be in place before the next activity can occur.

crowdfunding Funds received by a business by soliciting a large number of very small investors usually via the Internet.

current assets Assets such as cash or those assets that can easily be converted to cash, such as accounts receivable and notes receivable.

current liabilities Liabilities or debts that the small business has to pay within one year. These include accounts payable, notes payable (such as bank notes), and accrued payroll.

D

debt A generic term to describe any type of non-equity funding tied to the business.

deviation analysis Analysis of the differences between the predicted and the actual performance.

discrimination Hiring, dismissal, level of pay, or promotions based on the basis of race, color, gender, religious beliefs, or national origin of the employee. Such actions are prohibited by federal and state laws.

draws A distribution of funds from the business. It is usually in the form of a cash dispersion in advance of salary, a bonus, an expected year-end distribution, and the like.

E

economic rents Financial gains garnered from an asset or capability that are in excess of the ordinary returns in that particular industry.

economies of scale A condition that allows the long-run average cost to continue downward as production increases. It leads (in its most extreme case) to a condition where a single firm producing 100 percent of the production is the most efficient. In reality this condition is moderated by the ability of management to control the size.

elasticity of demand Consumers' response to price changes. For example, as the price of luxury items increase, the demand usually declines as these goods are not essential and their purchase can be delayed. This would be called elastic demand. However, items such as cancer drugs typically have inelastic demand as you will not stop using them as price increases.

entrepreneurial breakeven When a new venture's net cash flows exceed the initial investment plus the time value of the money invested.

equity Investment in the small business by the owners of the firm.

equity investment Funds received by the business in exchange for a percentage ownership of the business.

equity theory The theory that we all judge how we are treated relative to how we see others being treated.

exit barrier Barriers, such as investment in capital assets, that keep a firm from leaving that industry.

F

factoring The practice of selling accounts receivable at a discount to another company in order to receive immediate cash.

Fair Labor Standards Act (FSLA) The act that established a minimum wage for workers.

family business A business that is run by and for a particular family.

first-mover advantage The phenomenon whereby the first firm to a market obtains the loyalty of the customers.

fixed assets Assets that have a physical presence; they include land, buildings, office equipment, machinery, and vehicles.

fixed costs Costs that must be paid no matter how many goods are sold, such as rent for the building.

float The difference between when the money goes out and when it comes in. For example, if you deposit a check today in payment for some good, typically you do not receive cash when you deposit it. Instead, there is a period of float before it is credited to your account.

followers Firms that enter a market after the first mover.

Fortune 500 The list published annually by *Fortune* magazine listing the 500 largest corporations (by sales) in the United States.

fragmented markets Markets in which no one competitor has a substantial share of the market and the means of competition varies widely within the same market space.

franchise agreement The basic contract generated by the franchisor for all franchisees; it usually contains clauses requiring the purchase of supplies, the displaying of marketing material, and the payment of fees that are based upon the sales of the branch operation.

franchisee The entrepreneur that buys the franchise from the franchisor.

franchisor The firm that originates the idea for the business and develops the operational methods, all of which are then sold to franchisees.

G

gap analysis A relatively simple process of systematically examining the difference between what was expected and what occurred. Thus, there is an examination as part of opportunity analysis of opportunities in the marketplace and the individual firm's ability to address those gaps with its accumulated skills, history, and so on.

general partner In an LLP, the individual considered the manager of the firm, who, as such, has unlimited liability for any debts or judgments against the firm.

grants Special funds, neither equity or debt, designed to aid businesses in specific areas.

H

harvest plan A plan to exit the small business. This typically means sell the business to another firm or take it to an IPO.

hourly wage The amount paid per hour for work performed.

human resources Defined in economics as the quantity and quality of human effort directed toward producing goods and services.

hybrid compensation system A system employed by a small business where there is a salary along with the commission.

I

income statement Revenue of the firm minus expenses.

incubator Facilities that house new businesses, providing many critical services for these new businesses.

independent representatives Representative for a variety of products for a number of companies in that given domain who tries to sell those products.

industry Those direct competitors selling similar products/services within a specified geographic radius that is consistent with a customer's willingness to travel to purchase the product/service.

initial public offering (IPO) The initial listing of a firm as a public entity in the public equities market.

intangible assets Resources and capabilities in a business that are not physical but are just as critical to success, such as relationships with a key supplier.

J

job description Description of the duties involved in a job that is to be filled.

L

legitimacy The acceptance by key stakeholders, such as customers and suppliers, that you are a genuine business that will still be in operation next year.

leverage ratios Financial calculations used to examine the relative level of indebtedness of the small business.

liquidity ratios Financial calculations that measure the short-term ability of the firm to meet its obligations.

LLC A limited liability corporation.

LLP A limited liability partnership.

loan A contractual agreement whereby the firm receives some amount of money that must be repaid over a specified period of time at a specified interest rate.

long-term liabilities Liabilities that are owed by the business and are ultimately due more than a year from the current date. These include mortgages payable, owners' equity, and stockholders' equity, which is the investment by these individuals in the business.

loss leader A product sold by a business at a nonoperating loss (i.e., the price accounts for only the actual cost of the product) to simply get customers in the store.

M

market estimation A method of business valuation that involves taking the earnings of the small business and multiplying that figure by the market premium of companies in its industry.

marketing plan The plan developed by the small business to specify who the customers are and how they will be attracted to the company.

metric A measure to evaluate whether a person or firm is meeting its goals.

mission statement A brief statement that summarizes how and where the firm will compete.

mixed-model promotions Promotions that have a cost but also have an element of community support.

N

normal or ordinary competitive factor Describing those areas of a business that are simply standard practice in the industry and are necessary for the business to be a player.

O

organizational slack Excess resources in an organization; typically found in large organizations rather than small businesses.

OSHA The Occupational Safety and Health Administration, which is charged with protecting the health of workers.

P

partnership A category of business formation that includes both general and limited types.

patent A claim of intellectual property that covers a specific innovation.

performance review A review by the small business owner of an employee's goals and the outcomes on those goals over some given time period.

perquisites Benefits paid for by the company. Examples include vacations, vehicles, loans, gifts, and financial contributions to retirement plans.

price/earnings (P/E) ratio A value derived from public companies that divides the current earnings per share into the price per share.

pricing floor The break-even point, or the lowest amount that can be charged.

production chart A chart that provides a detailed understanding of a firm's production process.

profit and loss statement (P&L statement) A financial statement that summarizes the revenues, costs, and expenses incurred during a specific period of time.

profit sharing A firm's offer to share a percentage of the profits at the end of the year or some other period of time with the employees. This is used, for example, in a hybrid system, in which the firm may set some relatively low level for salary.

profitability ratios Financial calculations that evaluate the performance of the firm and its ability to make economic rents over and above its costs.

pro forma Method by which a business owner estimates what the balance sheets and income statements will look like at some point in the future.

promotion The means by which a small business advances its product or service.

pure promotions Promotions that are strictly a financial arrangement in which you pay for some output, such as a radio advertisement.

R

ratio analysis A series of ratios along four areas of company performance (liquidity, activity, leverage, and profitability) that provides a picture of the health of the company.

resource-based analysis A methodology and theoretical approach that examines the functioning of the business in terms of whether a product or service simultaneously meets the criteria of being rare, durable, nonsubstitutable and valuable.

S

SaaS (software as a service) This business model is based on providing all or most of the business value electronically and remotely.

salary A set amount of compensation for a given time period.

sales management The method, means, and individuals that produce the relationship with the customer.

Search Engine Optimization (SEO) A term for all the efforts made to increase the visibility and placement of business information.

sensitivity analysis An examination of the best- and worst-case cash flow scenarios.

shrinkage The difference between what is sold and what was brought into the business.

Small Business Assistance Centers Centers funded by the Small Business Administration that advise individuals wishing to start new businesses.

sole proprietorship The simplest form of business organization, characterized by the fact that the person who owns the business and the business itself are treated as the same entity.

stakeholders Individuals or other organizations that impact the success of the business.

strategic alliances Firms joined together to form long-term, mutually complementary relationships.

strategy The broad approaches the small business will use to accomplish its mission.

strip shopping center A small retail center located typically along a major road. The center has only small businesses, and the center itself occupies only a small strip of land along the major street.

Subchapter C Corporation An organizational form that treats the firm as a unique entity responsible for its own taxes. There are no limitations to shareholder participation and the "owners" are protected beyond their equity investment.

Subchapter S Corporation An organizational form that treats the firm as an entity separate from the individuals. This allows the owner(s) to treat the income as they would if the firm were a sole proprietorship or a partnership. It has limitations in the number and type of shareholders.

substitute A product that performs a similar function or achieves the same result, but is not a precise imitation.

supplier credit Another form of nonequity funding that is available. Suppliers often will provide credit on both physical assets (refrigerators, molding equipment, etc.) and the actual supplies provided.

sustainable competitive advantage An advantage that others cannot immediately copy.

synergy The connection between the entrepreneur's skills, understanding of an industry, and the ability to create a competitive advantage such that the sum of the parts of the new business is greater than the individual parts alone.

T

tangible assets Hard assets, such as equipment or a location.

threats to operational financing Specific threats to the new venture in financing its growth, including high development costs, rapid expansion plans, high inventory needs, and/or an entrepreneurial team with a low asset base.

threats to profit margin The threats created to the success of a new venture related to its ability to establish and maintain a high-margin product or service.

threats to sales generation schemes Threats created to a new venture regarding its opportunity to sell to many customers and to obtain repeat business.

time value of money The calculation of the value of your investment in time and money if you did not do the proposed venture, based on the realization that there are other uses of your investment dollars and your raw time.

trademark Claim of intellectual property that is associated with a specific business. This may be the name of the firm, a symbol representing the firm, or its products.

turnaround The effort to reverse the decline of a business.

U

unemployment compensation The provision of financial assistance for some period of time to those people who lose their jobs through no fault of their own; every state has a law providing such assistance.

Uniform Franchise Offering Circular (UFOC) The principal governing mechanism of the franchisor/franchisee relationship.

United States Small Business Administration (SBA; www.sba.gov) The agency officially organized in 1953 as a part of the Small Business Act of July 30, 1953, to "aid, counsel, assist and protect, insofar as is possible, the interests of small business concerns." It is a wealth of information and assistance at all levels of organizational development and management.

unusual or unique competitive factor Describing those areas of a business that are unique or unusual when compared to the standard practices of the industry, and that provide the opportunity for the business to gain value over and above the ordinary returns in the industry.

V

variable costs Expenses that vary according to how many goods are sold or produced.

venture capital fund A fund that is organized to make significant equity investments in high-growth new ventures.

virtually free promotions Promotions that have a very limited financial cost but have a time-commitment requirement from someone in the firm.

W

workers' compensation The provision by law of some type of compensation to employees who are disabled or injured while on the job.

case index

subject index